"It will be a tragedy of inestimable proportions for the American people if that great nation eats its own legendary commitment to freedom from within. Equally, to lose the leadership of the world's most powerful champion of liberty would be truly dangerous for non-Americans everywhere in these increasingly unsettled times. Os Guinness has gifted us magnificently with the insights and understanding of a lifetime in this book, which really needs to be read—urgently—across the length and breadth of the world."

John Anderson, deputy prime minister of Australia 1999–2005

"Os Guinness has stood as a beacon of eloquence and insight. In a host of important books, he has chronicled the struggle of those who resist the modern world's descent into carnival culture. *Last Call for Liberty* is his masterwork— an urgent guide that leads out of the maze America has wandered into. For those who seek to understand the best of freedom's vital gifts, Guinness is the master class leader."

Shelby Coffey III, vice chairman of the Newseum and former editor of the *Los Angeles Times*

"A timely and important book from one of the most insightful observers of American society and politics. Guinness argues that America's future depends on learning the right lessons from America's past. Provocative without being incendiary. Sobering without being gloomy. Inspiring without being glib."

Peter Feaver, professor of political science at Duke University

"With moral clarity and a deep sense of history, Os Guinness discerns the taproot of America's republican achievement as well as the forces that threaten to tear it asunder. In this penetrating critique of American democracy, Guinness emerges as the English voice of Alexis de Tocqueville— and not a moment too soon. Perhaps only an Englishman could deliver such a powerful reminder to Americans about why their revolution in human liberty has succeeded where others have failed. Against the prophets of gloom, *Last Call for Liberty* charts a pathway toward American renewal rooted in a bracing vision of human freedom."

Joseph Loconte, associate professor of history at The King's College in New York City, author of *God, Locke, and Liberty: The Struggle for Religious Freedom in the West*

"If you care about the future of America—no matter where you are on the political spectrum—then do yourself a favor and read this book. I believe you will be encouraged to look at America in a new light, and hopefully all who love her will find a new energy to make her healthy again and keep her strong. Freedom-loving people everywhere will be grateful you did."

John Brandon, former vice president, Apple Inc.

LAST CALL

for

LIBERTY

HOW AMERICA'S GENIUS FOR
FREEDOM HAS BECOME ITS
GREATEST THREAT

OS GUINNESS

IVP Books

An imprint of InterVarsity Press
Downers Grove, Illinois

InterVarsity Press
P.O. Box 1400, Downers Grove, IL 60515-1426
ivpress.com
email@ivpress.com

InterVarsity Press® is the book-publishing division of InterVarsity Christian Fellowship/USA®, a movement of students and faculty active on campus at hundreds of universities, colleges, and schools of nursing in the United States of America, and a member movement of the International Fellowship of Evangelical Students. For information about local and regional activities, visit intervarsity.org.

All Scripture quotations, unless otherwise indicated, are taken from the New American Standard Bible®, copyright 1960, 1962, 1963, 1968, 1971, 1972, 1973, 1975, 1977, 1995 by The Lockman Foundation. Used by permission.

Some content in chapter five first appeared in Os Guinness, A Free People's Suicide: Sustainable Freedom and the American Future (Downers Grove, IL: InterVarsity Press, 2012). Used with permission.

Some content in chapter six first appeared in Os Guinness, The Global Public Square: Religious Freedom and the Making of a World Safe for Diversity (Downers Grove, IL: InterVarsity Press, 2013). Used with permission.

While any stories in this book are true, some names and identifying information may have been changed to protect the privacy of individuals.

Published in association with the literary agency of Wolgemuth & Associates. Author photo courtesy of Lancia E. Smith Photography on behalf of the C.S. Lewis Foundation.

Cover design: David Fassett
Interior design: Daniel van Loon
Cover images: tattered American flag: © JamesBrey / E+ /Getty Images
old yellowed paper: © ke77kz / iStock / Getty Images Plus
blue sky: © czekma13 / iStock / Getty Images Plus

ISBN 978-0-8308-4559-0 (print)
ISBN 978-0-8308-7337-1 (digital)

Printed in the United States of America ♾

InterVarsity Press is committed to ecological stewardship and to the conservation of natural resources in all our operations. This book was printed using sustainably sourced paper.

Library of Congress Cataloging-in-Publication Data
A catalog record for this book is available from the Library of Congress.

P	23	22	21	20	19	18	17	16	15	14	13	12	11	10	9	8	7	6	5	4	3	2	1
Y	37	36	35	34	33	32	31	30	29	28	27	26	25	24	23	22	21	20	19	18			

DOM

And with gratitude to Daniel Elazar,

Abraham Joshua Heschel, Leon Kass,

Jonathan Sacks, and Michael Walzer,

great Jewish thinkers whose work illuminates freedom's past

as it inspires and instructs freedom's future

Let my people go!

MOSES, TO THE PHARAOH OF EGYPT, EXODUS

This day I call heaven and earth as witnesses today against
you, that I have set before you life and death, blessings and
curses. Now choose life, that you and your children may live.

MOSES, TO THE PEOPLE OF ISRAEL, DEUTERONOMY

Remember the earliest of days; grasp the years of generations
that have been. Ask your father—he will tell you all;
ask the elders of your kind, and they will say.

MOSES, DEUTERONOMY

The citizens chafe impatiently at the least touch of authority, and at
length . . . they cease to care even for the laws, written or unwritten. And
this is the fair and glorious beginning out of which springs dictatorship.
. . . The excess of liberty, whether in States or individuals, seems only
to pass into excess of slavery. And so tyranny naturally arises out of
democracy, and the most aggravated form of tyranny and slavery out
of the most extreme form of liberty.

PLATO, THE REPUBLIC

We can endure neither our vices nor their cures.

LIVY, THE HISTORY OF ROME

A man in a boat began to bore a hole under his seat. His fellow
passengers protested. "What concern is it of yours?" he responded. "I
am making a hole under my seat, not yours." They replied, "That is
so, but when the water enters and the boat sinks, we too will drown."

RABBI SHIMON BAR YOHAI

Should any one of our nation be asked about our laws, he will repeat them as readily as his own name. The result of our thorough education in our laws from the very dawn of intelligence is that they are, as it were, engraved on our souls.

JOSEPHUS, CONTRA APIONEM

Pray for the welfare of the government, for if not for the fear of it, each man would swallow his neighbor alive.

RABBI HANINA

When words lose their meaning, people lose their liberty.

CONFUCIUS

Thus a good man, though a slave, is free; but a wicked man, though a king, is a slave. For he serves, not one man alone, but, what is worse, as many masters as he has vices.

ST. AUGUSTINE, CITY OF GOD

For so long as one hundred men remain alive, we shall never under any condition submit to the domination of the English. It is not for glory or riches or honors that we fight, but only for liberty, which no good man will consent to lose but with his life.

THE DECLARATION OF ARBROATH, SCOTLAND, 1320

The best instituted governments, like the best constituted animal bodies, carry in them the seeds of their destruction: and though they grow and improve for a time, they will soon tend to their dissolution. Every hour they live is an hour the less that they have to live.

HENRY ST. JOHN, VISCOUNT BOLINGBROKE, 1738

Free peoples, remember this maxim: liberty can be gained, but never regained.

JEAN-JACQUES ROUSSEAU, *THE SOCIAL CONTRACT*, 1762

*There is not a more difficult subject for the understanding of
men than to govern a large Empire upon a plan of liberty.*

EDMUND BURKE, SPEECH, 1776

The cause of America is, in a great measure, the cause of all mankind.

THOMAS PAINE, *COMMON SENSE*, 1776

*Posterity! You will never know how much it cost the present generation
to preserve your freedom. I hope you will make good use of it. If you do
not, I shall repent in heaven that I ever took half the pains to preserve it.*

JOHN ADAMS, APRIL 1777

*Society cannot exist unless a controlling power upon the will and appetite
be placed somewhere; and the less of it there is within, the more there must
be without. It is ordained in the eternal constitution of things, that men
of intemperate minds cannot be free. Their passions forge their fetters.*

EDMUND BURKE, *LETTER TO A MEMBER OF THE
NATIONAL ASSEMBLY OF FRANCE*, 1791

*All projects of government formed of a supposition of continual
vigilance, sagacity, virtue, and firmness of the people, when possessed
of the exercise of supreme power, are cheats and delusions.*

JOHN ADAMS, DEFENSE OF THE UNITED STATES CONSTITUTION, 1794

It is seldom that liberty of any kind is lost all at once.

DAVID HUME

The preservation of the sacred fire of liberty, and the destiny of the republican model of government, are justly considered as deeply, perhaps as finally staked, on the experiment entrusted to the hands of the American people.

GEORGE WASHINGTON, FIRST INAUGURAL ADDRESS, 1789

Let us with caution indulge the supposition that morality can be maintained without religion. Whatever may be conceded to the influence of refined education on minds of peculiar structure, reason and experience both forbid us to expect that national morality can prevail in exclusion of religious principle.

GEORGE WASHINGTON, FAREWELL ADDRESS, 1796

I should have loved freedom, I believe, at all times, but in the times in which we live I am ready to worship it.

ALEXIS DE TOCQUEVILLE, DEMOCRACY IN AMERICA

I have already said enough to put Anglo-American civilization in its true light. It is the product (and one should continually bear in mind this point of departure) of two perfectly distinct elements which elsewhere have often been at war with one another but which in America it was somehow possible to incorporate into each other, forming a marvelous combination. I mean the spirit of religion and the spirit of freedom. The rest of democracy in America essentially plays out these themes and their successes, their failures, their weaknesses, their promises, and their threats.

ALEXIS DE TOCQUEVILLE, DEMOCRACY IN AMERICA

There is nothing more arduous than the apprenticeship of liberty.

ALEXIS DE TOCQUEVILLE, DEMOCRACY IN AMERICA

Our political problem now is "Can we, as a nation, continue together permanently—forever—half slave and half free?" The problem is too mighty for me. May God, in his mercy, superintend the solution.

ABRAHAM LINCOLN, LETTER TO GEORGE ROBERTSON, 1855

I have long been convinced that institutions purely democratic must, sooner or later, destroy liberty, or civilization, or both.

LORD MACAULAY, LETTER TO A FRIEND, 1857

I am filled with deep emotion at finding myself standing here in the place where were collected together the wisdom, the patriotism, the devotion to principle, from which sprang the institutions under which we live. . . . I have never asked anything that does not breathe from those walls. All my political warfare has been in favor of the teachings coming forth from that sacred hall. May my right hand forget its cunning and my tongue cleave to the roof of my mouth, if ever I prove false to those teachings.

ABRAHAM LINCOLN, AT INDEPENDENCE HALL, PHILADELPHIA,
EN ROUTE TO HIS INAUGURATION, 1861

May we not justly fear that the awful calamity of Civil War, which now desolates the land, may be but a punishment, inflicted on us, for our presumptuous sins, to the needful end of our national reformation as a whole People? We have been the recipients of the choicest bounties of Heaven. We have been preserved, these many years, in peace and prosperity. We have grown in numbers, wealth and power, as no other nation has grown. But we have forgotten God.

ABRAHAM LINCOLN, NATIONAL FAST DAY PROCLAMATION,
MARCH 1863

Responsibility: A detachable burden easily shifted to the shoulders of God, Fate, Fortune, Luck, or one's neighbor. In the days of astrology it was customary to unload it upon a star.

AMBROSE BIERCE, *THE DEVIL'S DICTIONARY*

In the strictest sense the history of liberty dates from 1776, for "never till then had men sought liberty knowing what they sought."

LORD ACTON

The instructions of a secular morality that is not based on religious doctrines are exactly what a person ignorant of music might do, if he were made a conductor and started to wave his hands in front of musicians well rehearsed in what they were performing. By virtue of its own momentum, and from what previous conductors had taught the musicians, the music might continue for a while, but obviously the gesticulations made with the stick by a person who knows nothing about music would be useless and eventually confuse the musicians and throw the orchestra off course.

LEO TOLSTOY, *A CONFESSION AND OTHER RELIGIOUS WRITING*

Starting with unlimited freedom, I arrive at unlimited despotism.

FYODOR DOSTOEVSKY, *THE POSSESSED*

The American Government and the Constitution are based on the theology of Calvin and the philosophy of Hobbes.

JAMES BRYCE, *THE AMERICAN COMMONWEALTH*

Ideas are dangerous, but the man to whom they are least dangerous is the man of ideas. He is acquainted with ideas and moves among them like a lion-tamer. Ideas are dangerous, but the man to whom they are most dangerous is the man of no ideas. The man of no ideas will find the first idea will fly to his head like wine to the head of a teetotaler.

G. K. Chesterton, Heretics

If there is one fact we really can prove from the history that we really do know, it is that despotism can be a development, often a late development and very often indeed the end of societies that have been highly democratic. A despotism may almost be defined as a tired democracy. As fatigue falls on a community, the citizens are less inclined for that eternal vigilance which has truly been called the price of liberty; and they prefer to arm only one single sentinel to watch the city while they sleep.

G. K. Chesterton, The Everlasting Man

I believe that each of us today has been instilled with a new consciousness and is more aware of the necessity and fundamentally sacred character of intellectual freedom than in former times. For it's always that way with the sacred value of life. We forget it as long as it belongs to us, and give it as little attention during the unconcerned hours of our life as we do the stars in the light of day. Darkness must fall before we are aware of the majesty of the stars above our heads. It was necessary for this dark hour to fall, perhaps the darkest in history, to make us realize that freedom is as vital to our soul as breathing to our body.

Stefan Zweig, "In This Dark Hour," 1941

Do not rejoice in his defeat, you men. For though the world has stood up and stopped the bastard, the bitch that bore him is in heat again.

Berthold Brecht, The Resistible Rise of Arturo Ui, 1941

I often wonder whether we do not rest our hopes too much upon constitutions, upon laws and upon courts. These are false hopes; believe me; these are false hopes. Liberty lies in the hearts of men and women; when it dies there, no constitution, no law, no court can save it; no constitution, no law, no court can even do much to help it. And what is this liberty which must lie in the hearts of men and women? It is not the ruthless, the unbridled will; it is not freedom to do as one likes. That is the denial of liberty, and leads straight to its overthrow. A society in which men recognize no check upon their freedom soon becomes a society where freedom is the possession of a savage few; as we have learned to our sorrow.

JUDGE LEARNED HAND, NEW YORK, 1944

What had happened in the great age of Greece happened again in Renaissance Italy: traditional moral restraints disappeared, because they were seen to be associated with superstition; the liberation from fetters made individuals energetic and creative, producing a rare fluorescence of genius; but the anarchy and treachery which inevitably resulted from the decay of morals made Italians collectively impotent, and they fell, like the Greeks, under the domination of nations less civilized than themselves but not so destitute of social cohesion.

BERTRAND RUSSELL, HISTORY OF WESTERN PHILOSOPHY

Freedom is the freedom to say that two plus two makes four. If that is granted, all else follows.

GEORGE ORWELL, *1984*

The first condition of freedom is its limitation; make it absolute and it dies in chaos.

WILL AND ARIEL DURANT, THE LESSONS OF HISTORY

*It is indeed a truth, which all the great apostles of freedom
. . . have never tired of explaining, that freedom has never worked
without deeply ingrained moral beliefs and that coercion can be
reduced to a minimum only where individuals can be expected
as a rule to conform voluntarily to certain principles.*

FRIEDRICH HAYEK, *The Constitution of Liberty*

*What is to the one the road to freedom, seems to the other the reverse. In
the name of liberty the road into serfdom is trod. To renounce liberty in
a free decision counts for many as the highest freedom. Liberty arouses
enthusiasm, but liberty also arouses anxiety. It may look as if men do
not want liberty at all, indeed as though they would like to avoid the
possibility of liberty.*

KARL JASPERS, *The Origin and Goal of History*

*Having lived in Poland and later in Germany, I know what America
really means. For generations America was the great promise, the great
joy, the last hope of humanity. Ten years ago if I had said to students
that America is a great blessing and an example to the world, they would
have laughed at me. Why speak such banalities? Today one of the saddest
experiences of my life is to observe what is happening to America morally.
The world once had a great hope, a model: America. What is going to
happen to America?*

RABBI ABRAHAM HESCHEL, *Moral Grandeur,
Spiritual Audacity*

*No one has changed a great nation without appealing to
its soul, without stimulating a national idealism.*

ROBERT BELLAH, *The Broken Covenant*

Yet if the gross national product measures all of this, there is much that it does not include. It measures neither the health of our children, the quality of their education, nor the joy of their play. It measures neither the beauty of our poetry, nor the strength of our marriages. It pays no heed to the intelligence of our public debate, nor the integrity of our public officials. It measures neither our wisdom nor our learning, neither our wit nor our courage, neither our compassion nor our devotion to our country. It measures everything, in short, except that which makes life worth living, and it can tell us everything about our country except those things that make us proud to be a part of it.

ROBERT F. KENNEDY, KANSAS CITY, 1968

If all values are relative, then, for example it is ultimately impossible to say anything good or bad about slavery or Adolf Hitler. It is only possible to say that one likes or dislikes Hitler in the same way that one likes or dislikes corn flakes for breakfast. To the founders, this view would have cut against the grain of reason and common sense. The choice between democracy and Nazism is not a choice between Cheerios or Rice Krispies, but a choice between justice or injustice, indeed life or death.

DANIEL ELAZAR, COVENANT AND CONSTITUTIONALISM

Standard works on the history of the politics of freedom trace it back through Marx, Rousseau and Hobbes to Plato's Republic, Aristotle's Politics, and the Greek city states (Athens in particular) of the fifth century BCE. To be sure, words like "democracy" (rule by the people) are Greek in origin. The Greeks were gifted at abstract nouns and systematic thought. However if we look at the "birth of the modern"—at figures like Milton, Hobbes and Locke in England, and the founding fathers of America—the book with which they were in dialogue was not Plato or Aristotle but the Hebrew Bible. Hobbes quoted it 657 times in The Leviathan *alone. Long before the Greek philosophers, and far more profoundly, at Mount Sinai the concept of a free society was born.*

RABBI JONATHAN SACKS, COVENANT AND CONVERSATION: EXODUS

Freedom is more than revolution. The pages of history are littered with people who won their freedom only to lose it again. The "constitution of liberty" is one of the most vulnerable of all human achievements. Individual freedom is simple. Collective freedom—a society that honors the equal dignity of all—depends on constant vigilance, a sustained effort of education. If we forget where we came from, the battle our ancestors fought and the long journey they had to take, then in the end we lose it again.

RABBI JONATHAN SACKS, *THE JONATHAN SACKS HAGGADAH*

The problem isn't that Johnny can't read. The problem isn't even that Johnny can't think. The problem is that Johnny doesn't know what thinking is. He confuses it with feeling.

THOMAS SOWELL, THE HOOVER INSTITUTION

Democracy only gives people the kind of government they deserve.

DAVID GOLDMAN, *HOW CIVILIZATIONS DIE*

Civilization hangs suspended from generation to generation, by the gossamer strand of memory. If only one cohort of mothers and fathers fails to convey to its children what it has learned from its parents, then the great chain of learning and wisdom snaps. If the guardians of human knowledge stumble only one time, in their fall collapses the whole edifice of knowledge and understanding.

JACOB NEUSNER, *CONSERVATIVE, AMERICAN AND JEWISH*

Can the West overcome the forgetfulness that is the nemesis of every successful civilization?

LEE HARRIS, *CIVILIZATION AND ITS ENEMIES*

CONTENTS

INTRODUCTION

A NEW, NEW BIRTH
of FREEDOM?

*W*ith America bitterly divided and American public life sinking into chaos and conflict, may a visiting foreigner be permitted a word? For admirers of America today, sleep has become fitful. The great American republic is in the throes of its gravest crisis since the Civil War, a crisis that threatens its greatness, its freedom, and its character. As with that earlier time of terrible, self-inflicted judgment, the deepest threat is not the foreign invader but the American insider. The problem is not America against the world, or the world against America, but America against itself, citizens against citizens, government against citizens, one president against another president, and one view of America in radical opposition to another. Americans have become their own most bitter enemies, and even the enemies of their centuries-old republic.

The stock market may soar for the moment, the big-box stores may be packed during sales, and the sports and entertainment machines may hum with their daily headlines. But no one should be deceived. Radical, violent, and antidemocratic movements are being fomented and funded on both the Left and the Right. The Left sees only the danger of the Right, and the Right the danger of the Left, so extremism confirms and compounds extremism.

Political debate has degenerated into degrading and barbaric incivility, and wild talk of spying, leaking, impeachment, governability, the Twenty-fifth Amendment, and even assassination and secession is in the air. American leaders and opinion leaders are at each other's throats, intent on tearing each other apart. Careless with their insults and their incitements, many Americans are seething with rage over other Americans. America is locked in a mortal struggle for what each side believes is the soul of the republic. Heedless of the consequences, each side thinks the worst of the other, the once-visionary leadership of the free world has ground to an inglorious halt, and the suddenness of America's decline is shocking as well as tragic to its admirers.

One index of a healthy, free, and democratic society is its ability to deal constructively with differences and disagreements. How then are we to understand America's much-touted political shift from "loyal opposition" to "resistance," as one political party opposing the other presents itself in a term used by the French patriots resisting the Nazi occupation, while it fights back in the style of Saul Alinsky's *Rules for Radicals*? What we are seeing is not politics as usual but political warfare in a dangerously radical style and led by leaders who should know better. For when words break down, conflict and violence are never far away, and even careless talk of assassination is a diabolical form of violence.

The world is witnessing the aggressive spread of a cancer in the constitutional republic that America was designed to be and has been for nearly two and a half centuries. But this deterioration into an extreme political warfare is simply one measure of the crisis of American democracy. Americans from the highest levels of leadership and mainstream press down are transforming George Orwell's daily exercise of "Two Minutes of Hate" into a twenty-four-hour barrage of negative headlines, ad hominem attacks, insults, abuse, threats, unsupported allegations, and wild conspiracy theories—all of which amounts to a political and cultural hysteria that, for a free society, verges on madness and self-destruction.

The full measure of the crisis can be gauged by the vacuum of leadership at the highest level, for as yet there are many partisans and few statesmen. No Abraham Lincoln has stepped forward to speak on behalf of the better angels of the American republic. If anyone did, their task would be gargantuan, for the present generation has rejected both the vision and the manner of the sixteenth president as decisively as many have rejected that of the founders. There is too little statesmanship to match the gravity of the hour, and too little analysis that goes beyond supporting one side or the other, or that delves down to the real roots of the problem. For the deepest crisis touches on an issue more profound than almost all the present discussion, and as deep to America as the evil of slavery—a fundamental clash over the freedom and the nature of the American experiment that lies at the heart of the republic.

If nations are to be understood by what they love supremely, then freedom is and always has been the key to America. But the question facing America is, what is the key to freedom? The present clash is not simply between Republicans and Democrats, conservatives and liberals, rich and poor, urban and rural, heartlanders and coastals, or even globalists and nationalists, important though these differences are. The deepest division crosscuts these other differences at several points. At the core, the deepest division is rooted in the differences between two world-changing and opposing revolutions, the American Revolution of 1776 and the French Revolution of 1789, and their rival views of freedom and the nature of the American experiment.

It could be argued that the clash is simply between the old, classical American liberalism and the new Left/liberalism that emerged from the 1960s. But it is deeper than that. The fundamental clash is between the spirit, the heirs, and the allies of 1776 and the ideas that made the American Revolution versus the spirit, the heirs, and the allies of 1789 and the different ideas that made the French Revolution and seeded the progressive liberalism of the Left (with the later help of thinkers such as Friedrich Nietzsche, Antonio Gramsci, the Frankfurt School, and Michel Foucault).

The pressing clash is therefore a life-and-death conflict between two Americas, two revolutions, and two futures. Following the seismic sixties, when the chasm opened in its current form, a massive floodtide of philosophical, religious, cultural, and political disagreements has swollen into public disputes that now engulf the nation in a second civil war, though along very different lines and for the moment a cold civil war. The outcome is crucial for both America and the world. It calls into question the American republic as it was founded, and it calls into question the United States as the world's lead society and the champion and exemplar of human freedom for the world. As history underscores, the way of 1789 (aided and abetted by the heirs of 1917, the Russian revolution, and 1949, the Chinese revolution) has led and will always lead to catastrophe for the cause of freedom and a liberal political order, whereas the way of 1776—for all its shortcomings—has led to some of freedom's greatest successes, however much maligned today.

Restore or repeal and replace?[1] That is the question for the American republic as it was founded. There is no escaping the coming showdown, for Americans are fast approaching their Rubicon. Is 1776 to be restored (with its flaws acknowledged and remedied) or is it to be replaced by 1789 (and its current progressive heirs)? The outcome will favor one view of freedom or the other, or perhaps the abolition of freedom altogether. For the two main rival views are far more contradictory than many realize, and with their scorched-earth attitudes and policies, they cannot live with each other forever. The middle ground is disappearing. A clean sweep of the cultural landscape is what each wants, and neither will talk of compromise nor allow anything to stand in its way. Either the classical liberalism of the republic will prevail and 1776 will defeat 1789, or the Left/liberalism of 1789 will defeat 1776, and the republic will fail and become a republic in name only. The American republic divided in this way cannot stand. The United States can no more continue half committed to one view of freedom and half committed to the other than it could live half slave and half free in the 1860s.

This crisis is an American crisis. For those on one side, the classical liberals and the present-day conservatives, the American Revolution launched history's noblest experiment in freedom, justice, and a liberal political order. The American experiment was undergirded by the Jewish and Christian faiths, and while never perfect and at times far from perfect, it represents an achievement of the human spirit worthy of celebration and emulation. For those on the other side, the Left/liberals, the progressives and the cultural Marxists, that vision of America should be castigated, not celebrated. America has shown itself to be hegemonic, inherently flawed and hypocritical, and at times racist, sexist, imperialist, militarist, and genocidal. These criticisms have been delivered along with an implacable animosity to religion as the enduring source of repression and the greatest remaining obstacle to full freedom, and delivered as part of the war cry of a very different revolution with very different assumptions and ideals.

The present crisis is an American crisis for the obvious reason that it touches the heart of America. It is so in another sense too—there is a long tradition that when Americans are disillusioned with America, they look to European ideas that are fatefully different from the ideas and ideals of the American Revolution. Examples would include Thomas Jefferson's fascination with the French Revolution in its early stages, John Reed's attraction to the Russian Revolution, Ezra Pound's falling for Mussolini and the rise of Italian fascism, and after the 1960s, the many on both the left and the right who have become enamored with ideas such as those of Friedrich Nietzsche, Antonio Gramsci, Herbert Marcuse, and Michel Foucault.

Needless to say, the issues between the different sides are for Americans to debate and resolve. But such are the stakes for all humanity, particularly when the debate turns to the future, that perhaps an outsider may raise some questions. What is freedom, and what are the terms of the American experiment? Which of the two rival views of freedom best serves the interests of human flourishing? Which of the two grounds the vision of a free and just society for all citizens, based on the dignity of every human person and allowing for disagreement and opposition? Which view allows a free people to sustain their freedom under the challenging conditions of the advanced modern world and the global era? How will the American experiment survive in the world of posthumanism? Statements about freedom are often deceptively simple, though profoundly consequential, yet they are the issues at the crux of the American crisis. The outcome of the struggle will determine the future of the American republic. It may also determine the future of humanity itself.

But let one thing be clear from the start, or we will be sidetracked at once as a thousand discussions are now. The present obsession with President Trump, whether supporting or opposing him, is a massively distorting factor for a simple reason: *Donald Trump is the consequence of the crisis and not the cause.* The "Never Trumpers," both Democrats and his fellow Republicans, and politicians, journalists, academics, as well as celebrities, have developed such a manic obsession about the president that they cannot see straight or talk of much else. Above all, they miss a crucial fact. The president did not create America's present crisis. The crisis created the president, and the crisis is older, deeper, and more consequential than any president. Regardless of this administration, its opposition, and its outcome, what matters in the long run is understanding and resolving the American crisis itself.

It is true that character always counts in the presidency and unquestionably it will count in this one. Yet President Trump is not the real issue. He is not the cause of the crisis, as his critics assert. Nor will he be the solution, as his defenders hope. Donald Trump's election was like a giant wrecking ball that stopped America in its tracks, and it allows space for Americans on all sides to consider where they see the republic now, and where they think it should go. For Americans who are willing to pause and understand, the present moment is an opportunity as well as a necessity. The most crucial issues have little or nothing to do with the president, and they will still be there after he has gone. It is these deepest issues that need to be faced and addressed while there is still time.

Another Time That Tries the Soul

Once again we find ourselves in times that try men's souls and test the mettle of all convictions—and this time on the grandest scale of global affairs. The facts of our times are there for anyone to see. What matters are their meaning, the issues that they spawn, and the stakes that humanity is playing for as this generation makes its decisions and demonstrates them in its actions. Americans are debating on behalf of their own future, but Americans must never forget that today's debate about America is also a debate about the future of the world.

The twenty-first century now summons the world's two leading nations to their greatest hour—the United States and China. How and where will they lead the world in the first century of the truly global era? How will they relate to each other, and how will they avoid the "Thucydides Trap" (the disastrous clash between a ruling power and a rising power)? They are the world's two greatest superpowers, both have been nations that are empires by any other name, but they now stand in a curious relationship to each other. By far the older nation, China is now the younger in terms of its entry onto the stage of the modern world, whereas the younger, America, now appears the older as its people and their society show signs of extreme fatigue and irresponsibility after leading the world for little more than a hundred years. In their significance for humanity and the world at large, America claims to stand for freedom and therefore carries the hopes of the world's desired future, whereas China still stands for authoritarianism and the sort of past that much of today's world desires to leave behind.

Yet does America still really stand for freedom? And if so, what sort of freedom, and how is America standing for it? That is the issue. Freedom is one of the deepest and almost universal desires of humanity. Lord Acton, the great historian of freedom, claimed that "the development of liberty is the soul of history."[2] But there are profound disagreements over how to pursue it. Philosophically, freedom raises the deepest questions about humanity, about our human differences from the animals and the rest of creation, and our responsibility for our fellow humans and for the rest of the universe. And practically, freedom raises the immense challenges of building and sustaining societies that respect human dignity and create freedom for all human beings, whatever their race, religion, ideology, language, gender, culture, or political philosophy—one of the rarest and most challenging achievements of history.

The task before America is therefore plain. America must make clear what it now means by *freedom*, and which of the two visions it now chooses: 1776 and the classical liberal freedom of its founding, or 1789 and the Left/liberal freedom of today. Along with the gravity of its own internal crises, America also faces a world on fire, the decline of Western civilization, a faltering search for a new world order, a slate of global problems that are unprecedented, and the uncharted waters of the human future troubled by such challenges as artificial superintelligence, singularity, and posthumanism. With such monumental items on the agenda, is America still prepared to shoulder its historic task on behalf of freedom, or is that a luxury it can no longer afford? Will the torch of freedom be handed to someone else or extinguished altogether?

There is no question that for all their shortcomings, Americans have written glorious earlier chapters in the story of freedom. This was supremely so in the generation of George Washington and his fellow founders, who dared to fight for and build such a free republic; in the life and work of Abraham Lincoln that was spent to preserve the republic from tearing itself apart over the evils of slavery that contradicted the founders' freedom; in the achievements of such leaders as Franklin Roosevelt and Ronald Reagan, who staved off the menace of totalitarianism in the twentieth century; and in the countless voices of preachers and prophets, such as Martin Luther King Jr., who over the generations have kept on calling America back to its high ideals and noble mission whenever they were slipping or betrayed.

Yet lofty as these accomplishments were, they all fade into the past as the present challenge looms. This challenge does not come from outside America but from within. It represents a threat that may even surpass the menace to freedom of twentieth-century Soviet communism or Hitler's National Socialism, and a domestic radicalization as dangerous to the republic as the radicalization of Islamic extremists. Hitler was defeated in World War II, but the spirit of Nietzsche still lives on in the American Right. Stalin's successors capitulated at the end of the Cold War, but the spirit of Marx still lives on in the American Left.

Does America still have the will and the strength to rise to the demands of the present hour, or has its success made it complacent and its power made it corrupt, and have America's exertions left it tired and unable to carry the torch of freedom as today's challenges require? Have Americans divested themselves of their historic mission on behalf of freedom, and are they now merely content to live out their brief chapter in history and guarantee their mention in the grand annals of freedom's past? Do enough Americans even care today, and do they understand what freedom is and what freedom requires? Have they faced up to the deadly double threat posed to America from outside—the post-truth climate of contemporary ideas, and the post-human rights conditions of brutal conflict on the ground in many parts of the world? And do Americans so take freedom for granted that it is already halfway to being lost?

Such questions abound, for the emotions and attitudes that have flickered across America's face recently have left even its admirers in dismay. America needs a second *Mayflower*, it is said, to sail for tomorrow's new world, but where is this new world to be found? The nation needs another Paul Revere to raise the alarm about today's clear and present dangers, but how would such a voice be distinguished from the surrounding cacophony of fear and alarmism? It is time for a twenty-first-century Publius to pick up the mantle of Alexander Hamilton, James Madison, and John Jay, and set out where their great endeavors have brought us, but how is such seasoned reflection to be heard in the age of the sound bite and the angry blog? America needs an Abraham Lincoln in our day to review how the republic is faring nearly two and a half centuries after its founding, and what it requires to heal its divisions and lead the nation forward, so that its best days truly lie ahead. But is there a Washington, an Adams, a Madison, a Jefferson, a Lincoln, a Roosevelt, a King, or a Reagan in the land?

Questions like these explode in a thousand forms. But anyone pursuing the logic of their thrust will confront a stunning surprise: America's deepest crisis lies at the point of what has always been America's greatest strength—freedom. What has long been America's most stirring ideal, its earliest passion, its noblest and most widely shared value, and today perhaps America's only nearly universal point of appeal is also the ideal that is at the heart of the American crisis. *America's genius for freedom has become its Achilles' heel and a leading source of America's divisions and potential destruction.*

Much of the way Americans now think of freedom is unrealistic and unsustainable. And worse, certain movements launched in the name of freedom represent a political and cultural counterrevolution that openly breaks with freedom as the American republic has known it. They claim they are righting wrongs and expanding freedom to ever-new levels, but in the eyes of their critics their "total" or "absolute freedom" is nothing less than "the destruction of freedom in the name of freedom."[3] Which side is right, and which should Americans follow? Those are America's decisions, but the significance of the question is plain. The chaos of American politics is the outworking of the real conflict of our times—America's profound clash over fundamental differences about what constitutes freedom and, therefore what constitutes humanity, justice, social change, and the human future.

President Wilson called for "a world safe for democracy." President Kennedy called for "a world safe for diversity." Such are the confusions and contradictions surrounding freedom in America today, and its damage to the cause of freedom throughout the world, that it is time to consider what it would mean to call for "a world safe for liberty," and whether there is an American leader with the courage and wisdom to sound that call and set out that vision.

Same Word, Different Meanings

America means freedom, and Americans are sure of that, but what does freedom mean? Americans are not so sure about that, and many of their fights are over different ideas of freedom. So the world has to listen to America boasting about its freedom while also fighting over it and undercutting it without realizing it. What Americans need, to echo Lincoln, is a *new, new* birth of freedom.[4]

That terse comment by a United Nations diplomat sums up a surprising and mostly overlooked challenge facing America today: the crisis of freedom. In a dangerously divided America, freedom is just about the last thing that both sides still appeal to. But do they stop to ask what they actually mean by *freedom*? Do they recognize they have entirely different views in mind? Are their views of freedom sustainable, or are they unrealistic and fated to wither and die? What might a "new, new birth of freedom" actually mean, and what would it take to bring it to birth? Is it possible that American freedom has degenerated beyond recall?

As so often, Lincoln saw the crux of the problem clearly in his day and addressed it resolutely. Speaking at a fair in Baltimore in April 1864, he referred to rumors then swirling about a massacre of three hundred black troops in Tennessee. Behind the incident, he said, lay a bitter clash, but not just of arms. The North and the South were both fighting for freedom, but with two entirely different conceptions of freedom.

> The world has never had a good definition of liberty, and the American people, just now, are much in need of one. We all declare for liberty: but in using the same word we do not all mean the same thing. With some the word liberty may mean for each man to do as he pleases with himself, and the product of his labor; while with others the same word may mean for some men to do as they please with other men, and the product of other men's labors.

"The shepherd drives the wolf from the sheep's throat," Lincoln continued, "for which the sheep thanks the shepherd as a liberator, while the wolf denounces him for the same act as the destroyer of liberty, especially as the sheep was a black one."[5]

We all declare for liberty: but in using the same word we do not all mean the same thing. Lincoln's comment is even more true today, when once again American differences over freedom have become pronounced and damaging. Most twenty-first-century Americans never stop to ask if they have a good definition of *freedom*, whether they are in need of one, and whether their notions of freedom are solid and sustainable.

The clash of competing freedoms may be viewed in historical terms, as in the differences between the North and the South. It may be viewed in international terms, as in *freedom fighter* against *terrorist*. It may be viewed in moral terms, as in *prolife* against *prochoice*. It may be viewed in sexual terms, as in those who believe in a *natural* or *created order* (male and female) and those who believe in an order that is only *socially constructed*. It may be viewed in the differences between liberals who would tighten government control of economics but loosen government control of social issues, and conservatives who would do the reverse. Or, as we shall see, it may be viewed in civilizational and ideological terms as in the difference between the 1776 view of freedom, which has long animated America, and the radical 1789 views of freedom that are now part and parcel of postmodernism and being promoted all around the world.

In these and countless other conflicts in which freedom is viewed quite differently, *the differences make a difference*, including differences in the way in which the differences are fought out. It is therefore vital for freedom's sake to disentangle the various differences, to see that the differences are handled openly and deliberately, and to see how the different choices have dramatically different consequences. If Americans fail to do this, the differences, whether open or submerged, will increasingly divide and weaken America, and freedom itself will be the loser.

Throughout his lifetime, Lincoln reflected long and deeply on freedom. Most famously, his Gettysburg Address called for a "new birth of freedom" for a nation that had been "conceived in liberty" but had almost destroyed itself in the Civil War. He delved into its most profound issues, such as the ultimate question of how a nation that has won freedom can sustain it, when the fact is that never before in history has freedom lasted. ("As a nation of free men," he warned in a speech at the Lyceum in Springfield, Illinois, in 1838 when he was only twenty-eight, "either we shall live free for all time, or die by suicide."[6]) But Lincoln's thinking was also unafraid to begin at the beginning, starting with the elementary question of defining freedom clearly, so that freedom is not confused, fought over, and lost. These three kinds of issues are America's challenge today: the elementary issue of what *freedom* means, the ultimate issue of how it is to be sustained, and the practical issue of how it can be restored when it has been nearly lost. All three issues are raised by the confusion and clash over the definition of freedom that underlies many of today's conflicts in American public life.

There is no question that urgent and controversial problems are now bristling on America's national agenda and debated fiercely in countless elections and across a thousand forums. At the end of the Bush and Obama administrations, for different reasons, the United States stood with its international leadership called into question. Having squandered the historic opportunity of its unipolar moment following the collapse of the Soviet Union, the United States is weaker now than it has been since before the beginning of World War II. But more importantly, the United States is facing a heaving sea of problems at home: hollowed-out beliefs and weakened ethics; declining trust in institutions and leaders; self-enriching elites; cancerous racism; pay-for-play and dirtbag politics; politicized criminal justice; crony capitalism; blinkered higher education; collapsed civic education;

biased mainstream press; journalistic collusion with political interests; politicized corporations; decaying infrastructures; crippling national debt; a surveillance state spying on its own citizens; porous borders; a demographic time bomb; failing inner cities that are the equivalent of failing states elsewhere; fractious culture warring; a toxic madness of gossip, suspicion, cynicism, and conspiracy theories; open talk of states' secession; an epidemic of opioid addiction; a swollen prison population; widespread symptoms of social stress, anxiety, and loneliness; a rise in suicides; and now a deadly attempt by both Left and Right to undermine each other's legitimacy as American and democratic.

All that, and American society is more divided—politically, economically, racially, ideologically, culturally, and religiously—than at any time since its house was divided and nearly fell in the Civil War.[7] Distinguished America scholars, such as Robert Putnam and Charles Murray, have written trenchantly on the different crises that call into question the "American dream" and "what makes America America." Yet few Americans have focused on how these crises are rooted in conflicting views of freedom, and how these conflicts affect the daily experience of freedom for Americans themselves.

Uncle Sam's Tutorial

The grand significance of freedom in history, and for America, is plain. "Let my people go!" From the ringing cry of Moses to Pharaoh; to the heroic stands of the Greek warriors at Thermopylae, Marathon, and Salamis; to the shouts of "Libertas! Libertas!" by the assassins of Julius Caesar with their blood-soaked daggers still in their hands; to Magna Carta wrung from King John in 1215; to the great Revolutions of 1688, 1776, 1789, 1917, and 1949; and right down to the courageous and sustained victories over Hitler's "master race" and Lenin and Stalin's "master class," freedom has been a prominent and irrepressible feature of world history and certainly of Western civilization in a thousand ways. Freedom is an idea and an ideal that lights the human mind and far outweighs the might of the chariot, the tank, the missile, and the jackboot. Millions of people, some well known and many more unknown, would second the great Scottish cry in the Declaration of Arbroath in 1320, the Scots' own declaration of independence and their first national covenant: "It is not for glory or riches or honors that we fight, but only for liberty, which no good man will consent to lose but with his life."[8]

Such an affirmation must be balanced. Freedom may be the glory of humanity and a bedrock essential if human beings are to express their significance and be themselves, but there is another side to the story. The history of freedom also includes the story of missed targets, tarnished hopes, broken promises, shabby failures, and dark and despicable contradictions. If the entire history of human civilizations were to be squeezed into a single hour, freedom and free societies would enter only in the last few minutes. And all too often many of the noblest stands for freedom had to be fought against the terrible denials of freedom inflicted by freedom-loving people on other peoples and even on their fellow citizens.

France's "Liberté, Egalité, Fraternité" ended in the Reign of Terror, the massacre of the Vendée, and dictatorship, while Marx's "triumph of the proletariat" led to Stalin's terror famines in Ukraine, the mass slaughter of Mao Zedong's Cultural Revolution, and Pol Pot's killing fields in Cambodia. Most recently, the world has watched appalled as the heady hopes of the Arab Spring spiraled down to the savage cataclysm of jihadi barbarism and brutality across the Middle East. And of course, many of the American founders owned their own chattel slaves even as they penned their stirring declarations about freedom. Once again Lincoln was both penetrating and more consistent: "He who would be no slave must consent to have no slave. Those who deny freedom to others, deserve it not for themselves."[9]

Nothing except love and justice fires the human heart like freedom. But the glorious and seemingly irresistible blaze of freedom has left in its wake a trail of burnt-out ideals. Liberty, hypocrisy, and cynicism have never been too far apart. The gap between desiring liberty and delivering liberty can grow wide and deep. America itself, historians say, is shot through with paradox: an "empire of liberty" built by anti-imperialists and the "land of the free" built on the backs of slaves.

Does that mean that *might* outweighs *right* on the great scales of history, that lasting freedom is a will-o'-the-wisp, and that free societies are always fated to be rare, fleeting, and corrupted? If even the glory of Athens, with its brief, bright blaze of liberty degenerated so miserably and so fast, what hope is there for other cities and other nations? Why is it so hard for any people to sustain freedom? Why have certain nations been able to achieve freedom for their citizens but have found it difficult to perpetuate freedom from one generation to the next?

Plainly, freedom poses questions that get harder as they go farther, and the nations that have attempted to answer them become fewer in the rarified atmosphere of the high-altitude challenges of history. The simple fact is that stable societies that respect human dignity for everyone are rare, challenging, and a remarkable accomplishment. So the elements of history that come together in a grand crescendo to trumpet what America has achieved are unique. The United States is the world's first nation that has attempted to make freedom its supreme love, and place it at the center of its political order and its entire way of life. When it comes to the core of American national character, America stands and falls on its record of freedom. All of which is why America's choice over freedom will be so decisive and consequential today—America's identity, character, and future are at stake.

Nothing less than the ultimacy of freedom has been the bold, proud case that America has presented before the bar of history. On behalf of freedom, America has shouldered a destiny that goes far beyond the bounds of its own shores and own times. And today, when freedom has become almost universally prized but still rare and not easily attained, America stands confidently and defines itself and its mission by freedom alone. More than any other nation on earth, past or present, America celebrates itself as the "land of the free," the "noble experiment" in freedom (George Washington), the "fairest Field of Liberty that ever appeared on Earth" (John Adams), an "empire of liberty" (Thomas Jefferson) "conceived in Liberty" (Abraham Lincoln), with citizens called to be bearers of "the ark of the liberties of the world" (Herman Melville) and destined to be "watchmen on the walls of world freedom" (John F. Kennedy).[10] The motto of the state of New Hampshire might well be America's motto too: "Live Free or Die." America, Secretary of State Henry Kissinger wrote, is "the modern world's decisive articulation of the human quest for freedom."[11] For all America's evils and hypocrisies, Shelby Steele writes, "Freedom is still our mother tongue."[12]

The truth is that many Americans need to be woken up from their slumbers and self-congratulation, and many need to be called back from the chaos of their infighting. They need to recognize the rarity, audacity—and fragility—of what they have achieved, and to see how their present behavior is threatening to squander their great heritage. Above all, Americans must recognize that two competing views of freedom are locked in a mortal struggle. The question is which of the two, 1776 or 1789, is the surest guide to full and lasting personal and political freedom.

For those who are not American, the same point can be expressed more prosaically and in a way that even many critics of America would agree with. It is a simple matter of fact that at the very moment when more and more of the world's peoples are crying out for freedom, America stands, and can be studied, warts and all, as history's longest-running experiment in freedom. America is the world's most public tutorial in the demanding discipline of the politics of freedom. For better or worse, it is not China, India, Germany, Brazil, Canada, Britain or France, Italy or Spain, the European Union, and certainly not Russia or Iran, but America that represents freedom for the world. Like the Greek giant Atlas with the world on his shoulders, Uncle Sam still carries the double responsibility of claiming to be the world's lead society as well as the pioneer, the precedent, and the pattern for freedom itself.

Do Americans still believe they can succeed where all other attempts at lasting freedom have failed so far? Do they wish to? How is freedom faring in the "land of the free"? What is the real "state of the union" concerning freedom? What does the rising generation, those supposed to be America's latest apprentices in freedom, show us of the prospects for America's championing of freedom in the future? Do twenty-first-century Americans measure up to their ancestors' and history's best understanding of freedom, and do they match their ancestors' realism as to why all earlier bids for freedom were short-lived? Will some future generation of Americans know how to respond when the day comes, as come it surely will, when America's rivalry with other nations grows intense and American freedom begins to decline, as all other nations and their freedoms have in their turn?

Checklist for a Healthy Freedom

My approach here is straightforward. It is time to face the present crisis and use it to concentrate the American mind and to reexamine the character and condition of freedom. What America needs is a virtual "national town hall meeting," a nationwide conversation to discuss the state of America's freedom, to debate and vote on the important differences between different views of freedom, and to address the points in which freedom needs to be restored. Extremists on both the left and the right are trying to shut down public debate and prevent such a discussion from ever happening. Equally, the mainstream press and media only cover and review opinions that fit with their own perspective. Yet Americans must not be intimidated and the debate must not be silenced. This national conversation must take place, and it must engage the younger generation. It must take seriously the comprehensive challenges of history, and it must do justice to the astonishing contribution of the founding generation, despite their obvious failings.

What follows is a straightforward call to Americans to consider why this is an urgent moment for the renewal of America's freedom and what it would require. My approach is simple and straightforward: to set out a citizens' checklist of ten questions that are essential for assessing the character and health of freedom, and the requirements for its restoration and renewal. Americans must decide where they are, choose which of the two great revolutions best fosters freedom, and commit themselves to what needs to be done to restore a vital and sustainable freedom. The task is great and the hour is late.

In the harsh light of fifty years of fruitless culture warring and the bitter current divisions, the challenge is daunting. Can the present generation of Americans repeat Hamilton's twin tasks of "reflection and choice," and do so with an understanding and appreciation for what freedom means and what it requires, especially in the world of today? Contrary to ancient pagan fatalism, as well as to modern forms of scientific determinism, the same beliefs that once grounded and guaranteed the high view of freedom also mean that history is not fate, and the rise and fall of nations is never inevitable. It is time for Americans to remind themselves what gave rise to their freedom, to assess where they stand today, to refuse the seductions of false freedoms, and to decide what they need to do to restore the health of freedom while they can.

Some will say that this focus on freedom is a luxury item in a world burdened by the threat of war, disease, terror, human trafficking, environmental degradation, and nuclear proliferation. That will not be the case for those who understand the place and importance of freedom in America. Freedom is no luxury to America. Freedom is America's supreme love—and America's identity, America's genius, America's promise, and America's grand purpose in the world. America stands or falls according to its beliefs and behavior over freedom. Without freedom, or with a changed view of freedom, America would no longer be America. So if America is not to follow Athens and Rome and suffer a fall beyond belief, the unthinkable demands careful thought and resolute decision and action today.

As we have said, America's genius has become its Achilles' heel, and America's supreme love has become its idol. The first words of the writing on the wall are there for those with eyes to see. Before the moving finger writes more, it is time for America to pay attention to the urgency of renewing its commitment to freedom. If Americans fail to do this, history's stern sentence will be spelled out to the end. Like many a great nation and superpower before, America's experiment in freedom will have been weighed in the balances and found wanting.

America's present carelessness about freedom betrays a lack of respect for freedom that is born of arrogance and a hubris that is bred by the illusion of invulnerability. The present moment therefore represents a *kairos* moment for America. It carries a blend of crisis, opportunity, and judgment, both for America and for America's significance for the world. There is an urgent need for a national conversation about freedom, a restoration of what has been forgotten, and a political, civic, and spiritual renewal of America's covenant of freedom.

America will always and only be as great as the ideals by which Americans actually live. The outcome need not be dire if America returns to its right mind, with a true American homecoming and rededication to freedom. The hour is late, the challenge is daunting, and the outcome is there for history and the world to watch, even though the response is for Americans alone to make. Are there enough Americans who care enough to wrestle with freedom and what it requires? To discern the decisive differences between 1776 and 1789? To count the cost of choosing wisely between true freedom and the allure of false freedom?

The first question on the checklist is basic and beguilingly simple, but the fact that so many Americans have no answer, or the wrong answer, speaks volumes for the crisis of freedom. The question is, do you realize where your freedom came from?

DO YOU KNOW WHERE
YOUR FREEDOM
CAME FROM?

*T*he story is told of the time when Winston Churchill was being shown around Colonial Williamsburg, and the guide began to wax eloquent about the town that was the cradle of "the revolution against the English."

"Revolution against the English!" the future prime minister snorted. "Nay, it was a reaffirmation of English rights. Englishmen battling a Hun king and his Hessian hirelings to protect their English birthright." Or as he said on a more formal occasion, "The Declaration of Independence is not only an American document. It follows on the Magna Carta and the Bill of Rights as the third great title-deed in which the liberties of the English-speaking people are founded."[1]

Churchill well knew that King George III was English-born and spoke English, unlike his German father and grandfather. But he was referring to what the colonists called "the ancient liberties of the English," or what have more recently been called the distinctive benefits of the English-speaking world or "Anglosphere."[2] The revolutionaries certainly portrayed themselves as oppressed and aggrieved (the "slaves of King George"), but they were actually fighting for freedom, from freedom, and as some of the freest people in the world of their times, and they believed that freedom was their birthright as Englishmen. As John Adams put it, "The patriots of this province desire nothing new; they wish only to keep their old privileges."[3]

What was Adams referring to? Even before the Magna Carta, there had been a robust tradition in common law that set out the liberties of Englishmen that no king or noble could transgress. These ancient liberties included the common law, the right of habeas corpus, trial by a jury of one's peers, elected parliaments, taxation by consent, safeguards for property, and above all the notion of government by consent (King Edward I: "What touches all should be approved by all"). And they expressly stood against the statist trends in their day, and especially the Renaissance restoration of the Roman principle of *lex regia*, the idea that the will and pleasure of the king was law—which James I had given a Christian twist in his notion of the divine right of kings.

Not long before the sailing of the *Mayflower*, Sir Edward Coke had been foremost in championing these ancient liberties, as in his ringing declaration on behalf of Parliament against James's son, Charles I. The sovereign power, or the power claimed by the sovereign, weakened the Magna Carta, he trumpeted. "Take heed what we yield unto; Magna Carta is such a fellow that he will have no sovereign."[4]

The "ancient liberties of the English" have been traced back to their origins in German forests and open-air clan meetings, their crossing the English Channel with the Saxons, their repression under the Norman Conquest after 1066, and their reemergence under the barons who faced down King John at Runnymede. The line between the ancient Witan (council of the "wise men") and modern Westminster is not always clear and straight, but it never disappears and it grew stronger all the time. Following the English Revolution and the rise of the Whigs, these ancient liberties became a well-known feature of the English in Europe. (In Mozart's opera *The Abduction from the Seraglio*, one of the characters says with pride, "I am English, born of freedom.")

This strong and ancient notion of personal freedom crossed the Atlantic with the American colonists, along with many cherished symbols of freedom, such as the liberty tree and liberty poles. In William Penn's words, "Every Free-born subject of England is heir by Birth-right unto that unparalleled privilege of Liberty and Property, beyond all the Nations in the world beside."[5] There is no question that, viewed together, these "ancient liberties" were crucial to the spirit and the demands that led to the Revolution, but by that name they have little appeal today. They would be familiar to historians, lawyers, and devotees of Winston Churchill and his vision of the English-speaking peoples. But in the wider American culture they have been eclipsed for many reasons—the decline of the special relationship under Barack Obama's postcolonialism, the diminishing influence of New England, the repudiation of the founders, the disdain for all things WASP, and the rising antiwhite movement across America. ("The white race is the cancer of human history," Susan Sontag wrote in 1967.[6] The "key to solving the social problems of our age is to abolish the white race," an American historian claimed.[7]) Plainly, it would take a Lincoln or a Churchill to revive the notion of the ancient liberties of the English and give it any positive resonance in the national conversation today.

Where then is the source of American freedom, and why does the story of freedom matter? *The first question therefore asks, do Americans realize where their freedom came from?* The story of freedom is essential and foundational to the sustaining of freedom. Scholars have recently explored the contribution to freedom of the eleventh-century "Paleo-Indians" in the American Northwest, but their direct contributions to American freedom and to 1776 are vague at best. Far more people assume quickly that "American democracy" must obviously come from democratic Athens or perhaps from Roman civic virtue, but that too would be wrong. For much as the founders tried to learn from classical models of Greek and Roman governance, and to build Capitol Hill in honor of their style, they were extremely wary of direct democracy because of its short-lived history and its turbulent record. A different, surprising, and far more important past deserves to be remembered and brought into the discussion today: the forgotten contribution of the Jews and Mount Sinai, and the way in which it both built on and decisively advanced the "ancient liberties of the English."

The Great Gift of the Jews

"What makes this night unlike all other nights?" This famous two-thousand-year-old question from Second Temple times has always been asked by the youngest Jewish child at a Seder. It was designed to provoke an annual commemoration and retelling of the defining moment of Jewish history—the Passover night more than three thousand years ago that launched the exodus from Egypt, which formed the birth of the Jewish nation. Like all traditions, it has doubtless been reduced at times to rite words in rote order, but it is one of the world's oldest surviving rituals. It is also history's most successful retelling of history and an indispensable key to the miraculous survival of the Jewish people across the centuries and across the world, despite their persecution and their scattering. No other people can lay claim to any similar long-enduring celebration, but the exodus stands as much more than a Jewish parallel to the celebration of July Fourth. As the oldest political vision in the West, it is the direct ancestor of the Fourth of July, and it holds the missing key to America's independence, to America's freedom, to America's history, and therefore to the renewal of America's freedom today—but in ways that few Americans now appear to understand.

Daniel Elazar, Michael Walzer, Rabbi Jonathan Sacks, and others have all argued that the book of Exodus is the master story of Western freedom and the ultimate regime change in history. Savonarola, the reforming monk, cited it in his celebrated "bonfire of the vanities" in Florence. John Calvin expounded it in Geneva, and Zwingli in Zurich. John Knox thundered its lessons in Edinburgh. Oliver Cromwell declared that it was "the only parallel of God's dealing with us that I know" as he and his fellow Puritans led the English Revolution. William Bradford sailed the *Mayflower* under its inspiration, John Winthrop cited it in his famous sermon "A Modell of Christian Charity" onboard the *Arbella*, both Benjamin Franklin and Thomas Jefferson proposed to use its themes in the Great Seal of the United States, the African American slaves use it to express their longings for freedom in their immortal spirituals ("Go down, Moses"), and Martin Luther King Jr. preached from the story in his last sermon the night before he was assassinated in April 1968. To anyone who knows the story and the lessons of Exodus, there is no situation so bad that need stay as it is. There is always the possibility of another way and a better situation. There is always the possibility of liberation. There is always the hope of freedom.

In a Thanksgiving sermon in 1799, Abiel Abbot spoke for many Americans of his generation when he said, "It has often been remarked that the people of the United States come nearer to a parallel with ancient Israel, than any other nation upon the globe."[8] Years later, the poet Heinrich Heine widened the same point: "Since the Exodus, freedom has always spoken with a Hebrew accent."[9]

To be sure, 1776 was soon countered by 1789. Later, Friedrich Nietzsche attacked the exodus as the event that subverted the freedom that he advocated. In his first essay in *The Genealogy of Morals*, he argued that Israel's liberation from Pharaoh was simply the beginning of a two-thousand-year "slave revolt in morals," the tragic moment when resentment won and the elevation of the herd overturned the rightful place of the hero.[10] Unable to fight the strong with strength, Jews and Christians gained their revenge by a reversal of values, making the strong bad and the weak good. Thus the strength of the strong was turned into weakness, and the weakness of the weak into strength. This ignominy, Nietzsche held, was started by the Jews and continued by Christians, and it needed to be redressed by the rise of the Superman. For the same reason, it is plain that the exodus theme does not resonate through the revolutions of 1789, 1917, and 1949. Exodus for the leaders of those revolutions was a step backward, and their revolutions had no time for the Bible, its ideals, and its ways of promoting change. Clearly, the Russian and Chinese revolutions were all for 1789 and not 1776.

Sinai Before Athens

Exodus was clearly central to the American Revolution and American revolutionaries. It was important as far more than a one-off precedent, far more than a template for personal salvation, and far more than merely a matter of heart-stirring rhetoric ("Let My people go"; "Proclaim liberty throughout the land" [Ex 5:1; Lev 25:10]). For at the heart of the exodus story is a template for society, for human personhood, for freedom, for justice, and for social change that shaped the American Revolution in highly practical ways. So much so that it has been truly said that Exodus and its influence on freedom long preceded Athens, has far outlasted Athens, and has strongly surpassed Athens in shaping some of the most important features of modern freedom in the eighteenth century and today. As Rabbi Sacks claims, "Ancient Israel was where the idea of freedom was born, and in many respects it remains a surer guide to liberty than the short-lived democracy of Athens."[11]

Liberty as more than liberation, the rule of law, the consent of the governed, the responsibility of rights, the separation of powers, the notion of prophetic critique and social criticism, transformative servant leadership, the ethics of responsibility, the primacy of the personal over the political—all of these ideals and more are the legacy of Exodus, and their effect was to provide a massive boost for the ancient liberties of the English. Most importantly, the Sinai covenant at the heart of the exodus story came to America with the English and put its stamp on American history through its decisive contribution to the US Constitution and the notion of constitutionalism. For as Elazar, Walzer, and other scholars have demonstrated, the classical categories of monarchy, aristocracy, and democracy are not the only way to classify societies. A different and helpful perspective emerges if societies are classified according to their founding rather than their types of government.

When classified according to their founding, four major types of society are prominent. First, there are *organic societies*, societies that are linked by blood, kinship, ancestral ties, and intimate acquaintance, often appearing to go back into the mists of time—for example, Scottish clans and African tribes. In such societies the individual tends to be regarded merely as part of the whole. Second, there are *hierarchical societies*, societies that are linked by force and conquest, such as kingdoms and empires—for example, the Roman Empire, the Prussian monarchy, and Chinese communism today (Voltaire described Prussia as "an army transformed into a state"). Divisions, classes, and castes are usually a feature of such societies. Third, there are *contractual* societies, societies based on a series of legal contracts that serve the interests of the citizens and allow for a politics that promotes the pursuit of self-interest. And fourth, there are *covenantal societies*, societies that are linked by choice and binding agreement, such as ancient Israel after the Sinai covenant, Switzerland after the birth of the Helvetic Confederation in 1291, and the United States after rejecting the Articles of Confederacy and passing the US Constitution in 1787.

The Reformation's application of covenantalism to politics, and its impact on the rise of constitutionalism, long preceded the work of Thomas Hobbes, John Locke, and the notion of social contract, let alone the Enlightenment. And its rediscovery in the 1950s has been hailed as "a truly seminal concept in Western civilization" and "the jewel in the crown of the new science of politics of the modern epoch."[12] If Lincoln, Elazar, and Walzer are right, Americans are not simply an "almost chosen people." They live in an "almost covenanted polity" and they were the heirs of the Jewish "almost democracy."[13]

Unique and Influential

To be sure, there were covenants outside the Bible, such as the Hittite suzerainty treaties, the Celtic oath societies, and Alexander the Great's Corinthian League, by which he tried to provide bonding for his vast Hellenic empire. ("We have declared in our treaty that all Greeks shall bind themselves by oath to the mutual defense of their freedom and autonomy.")[14] There were also earlier covenants in the Bible: with Noah on behalf of humanity after the great flood, and with Abraham as father of his family. But Israel's covenant at Mount Sinai was unique.

First, God himself was a partner to the covenant, even though he was the sovereign king in relation to the subordinate king, the people of Israel.

Second, the covenant included all the people of Israel—men, women, children, and both the born and the yet to be born. ("Speak to the entire assembly of Israel and say to them . . ." [Lev 19:1-2 NIV].) In Michael Walzer's words, "The agreement is wholesale; all the people accept all the laws," and the result is an "almost democracy."[15] This principle, as I said, stands in strong contrast to most of the other suzerainty treaties, which are usually agreements between two individuals, a sovereign king and a subordinate king. It is also in complete contrast to the hierarchical and top-down governments of the rulers of Babylon and Egypt, and in strong contrast to Athenian government too, whether by aristocrats or democrats.

Even Athenian democracy was strikingly different from the covenant at Mount Sinai. While it differed from the earlier Greek oligarchy, it still included only men, and then only some men—those with the proper pedigree who had undergone military training, who were never more than 20 percent of the population. It excluded other men, such as farmers, laborers, mechanics, and resident aliens, and it excluded women, children, and slaves. Behind this democratic view was the Greek notion of hierarchy that was the equivalent of the Hindu caste system. As Plato expressed it, some people were golden, some silver, and some merely bronze and baser metals.[16] Or more simply, in Aristotle's terms, some are born to be rulers and others to be ruled—these people are slaves by nature. Through the notion of the born and the unborn, the Sinai covenant also stands in marked contrast to America's exaggerated generationalism. Far from marking off each generation as absolutely unique and radically different from the generation before and the generation after, it builds the Jewish people into an intergenerational community. It thus binds together the past, the present, and the future to form a live tradition that links the generations. No individual life, Rabbi Heschel writes, is a purely private concern. Each "is a movement in the symphony of ages."[17]

Third, the articles of the Sinai covenant covered the whole of life, so that freedom was not just a moment of liberation but a people's way of life for generations. It included what they wore, how they worked and rested, how they farmed, how they ran their businesses, how they treated the poor and the stranger, and how they understood time and history, and it was all aimed

at creating a just, free, and good society that was decisively different from
the pagan empires the Jews had been freed from.

In sum, all the people and all of life were included in the terms of the
covenant, so that it has been said that Israel was quietly democratized long
before fifth-century Athens, and quietly made egalitarian long before the
American and French revolutions. But what mattered supremely, and what
shaped the later course of covenants, constitutionalism, and republican
freedom, were the three central features of the covenant at Mount Sinai.

The Great Precedent and Pattern

First, the covenant was a matter of *freely chosen consent*. Three separate times
the Jewish people were asked for their response, and they answered, "All that
the LORD has spoken we will do," and they answered "with one voice" (Ex
19:8; 24:3, 7). In other words, they ratified the covenant voluntarily. Jonathan
Sacks underscores the profundity of this fact. "A far-reaching principle is
here articulated for the first time: *There is no legitimate government without
the consent of the governed, even if the governor is creator of heaven and earth.*
. . . God is not a transcendental equivalent of a Pharaoh. The commonwealth
he invites the Israelites to join him in creating is not one where power rules,
even the power of heaven itself."[18]

Jewish commentators also point out that, though the Torah contains 613
specific commands, there is no Hebrew word for *obey*. The nearest is *shema*
the word for *listen* best translated in the old English terms *hearken*, *heed*, or
pay attention, which put the emphasis on the freedom and responsibility to
listen, to deliberate, to decide for oneself, and then to act accordingly. There
is no sense of blind obedience in the Muslim sense of Islam as "submission."
The Jews were indeed bound by the covenant, but as Walzer underscores, they
were "freely bound."[19] Their assent to the covenant was not simply a matter
of power and obedience, as the Hittite vassal treaties were. Their assent and
adherence was a threefold blend of obedience, gratitude for their liberation,
and admiration—the recognition of the wisdom of the laws they were ac-
cepting. ("What great nation is there that has statutes and judgments as
righteous as this whole law which I am setting before you today?" [Deut 4:8].)

Importantly, the result is a *nomocracy*, the freely chosen rule of law, rather
than a *theocracy*, the direct rule of God. The latter term was chosen fatefully
by the Jewish writer Josephus but ignored the key place of the people's

consent. Importantly too, this incident is the earliest and weightiest example of the notion that is vital to free societies—"the consent of the governed."

Second, the covenant was a matter of a *morally binding pledge*. It is this moral dimension that makes a covenant different from a contract, a political covenant stronger than a social contract, and a covenant of marriage before God deeper and more lasting than a civil marriage. (The Old English term *wedlock* was far from what it sounds like—a relationship that is a form of locked-up captivity and the butt of countless wedding jokes. *Wedlock* is a compound of the word *wed*, or pledge, and the word *lac,* or gift, so that marriage was the freely given pledge of love.)

A covenant is based on the foundational moral act of one person making a solemn promise to another person or to many others. This promise is both an expression of freedom and an assumption of responsibility. The freedom that is the heart of consent to the covenant carries within it the responsibility that is the heart of the obligation to the covenant. Thus people who covenant, whether in marriage or in nation building, make a morally informed and morally binding mutual pledge to each other that creates trust. The trust created by this mutual pledge is all-important because it replaces the need for force and regulation in relationships. It acts as the glue that binds as well as the oil that smooths.

Here is the significance of the Pledge of Allegiance and of standing during the national anthem that America needs to recapture, and that those who "take a knee" need to remember. Both are a solemn commitment to the American republic's obligation on behalf of "liberty and justice for all." At least two considerations are at stake. First, the freedom of conscience includes the right to the freedom of dissent, but dissent from the pledge and disrespect for the anthem are far more than dissent over party or political policy. They are a tacit rejection of the covenant/constitution itself. Second, dissent from them in the name of justice is contradictory and self-defeating, for it undermines the very standard and the obligation through which justice in America is to be achieved.

Needless to say, both these points carry weight only if 1776 and the American republic are to continue as they have always been understood. For Americans who still believe in the American republic, the better way is to take the Pledge of Allegiance and the national anthem out of the realm of the platitudinous, and expand its obligations to any who are currently excluded—

Dr. Martin Luther King's "promissory note" once again. But of course, this point is null and void if taking a knee is in fact a stand on behalf of 1789 and a different concept of freedom and revolution from that of 1776.

Those who make a covenantal/constitutional pledge voluntarily shoulder a responsibility and become partners in an ongoing project that none of them could undertake alone. They freely mortgage themselves and put themselves under an obligation to their fellow-citizen covenanters and to the future. They are promise makers and covenant partners, so they are promise keepers who have pledged to keep their word. The trust-creating reliability of the covenant partners over time is a key to the strength of the promise and therefore the success of the covenant.

Covenantal (and constitutional) societies therefore require a serious responsibility from their members (and citizens), which neither kings nor dictators require. Indeed, the personal and interpersonal takes priority over the political, responsibilities precede rights, and rights only grow out of responsibilities and have no meaning by themselves. The history of covenantal (or constitutional) societies can therefore be read as a commentary on the durability of the love and loyalty of the people and their leaders to the covenant partnership. This is surely a provocative reminder to America today. It is the antithesis of contemporary American relationships demonstrated in, say, the hookup culture of the sexual revolution, but the point is becoming ever clearer: Freedoms that frustrate the deepest longings of the human heart will always disappoint and prove to be a betrayal.

A covenant is broader and a contract is narrower, the one being emphatically moral and the other being purely legal. When the covenant is also "with God," or a constitution is "under God," the binding pledge is given the force of the ultimate standard of accountability (and in that sense the final "check and balance"). Both covenant and contract are completely different, of course, from modern "freedom of choice." We live in a day when consumer choice has become more noncommittal and nonbinding. Indeed, it has to be so if there is to be a constant turnover of sales. Which modern person in their right mind would make a choice that mortgages their future and rules out a thousand new possibilities of the latest and greatest (and cheaper, faster, fresher, and more powerful) that will soon be on offer, whether a new smartphone, a new car, a new house, or a new husband, wife, or partner? Hence the growing preference for renting over owning, cohabitation over marriage, and the rise of such fast-growing businesses as Uber, Lyft, and Airbnb. And hence the underlying contradiction between the attitudes of market-based consumer societies and the ethos of spiritual, moral, and political faithfulness. To be sure, advertising works to build brand loyalty, even though the essence of consumerism undercuts it, but brand loyalty is a pale shadow of covenantal-love loyalty.

All for One and One for All

Third, the covenant was a matter of *reciprocal responsibility of all for all.* Long before the celebrated maxim of the Three Musketeers, "All for one and one for all," the Jewish covenant embedded the pledge of responsibility to God and all other Jews. It included the profound new ethic, "You shall love your neighbor as yourself," and it reached out in care for the widow, the orphan, and even the stranger. ("Love the stranger, for you were strangers in the land of Egypt" [Deut 10:19 NKJV].) Indeed, as the rabbis pointed out, the celebrated command to love of the neighbor comes only once in the Torah, whereas the far more unlikely command to the love of the stranger, and so to resist tribalism, ethnocentrism, and xenophobia, comes no fewer than thirty-six times. In Walzer's words, "We are responsible for our fellows—all of us for all of us."[20]

Remarkably, the reciprocal responsibility even included the rights of the future, for its terms covered not only the born but the unborn and yet to be born. ("The LORD did not make this covenant with our fathers, but with us, *with* all those of us alive here today" [Deut 5:3].) There was equality of dignity for each individual before the covenant, and there was also equality of responsibility for all for all others who were within the covenant. By definition, the "stranger," the "foreigner," the "outsider," and "the other" are not "people like us," to use Aristotle's term. But while none of them are in our image and "people like us," they are all in God's image, and as such they must be treated with dignity and compassion.

This ethic of responsibility later became the Jewish principle that "All Israelites are responsible for one another." It meant, one rabbi said, that there was not one covenant at Sinai but 600,000 covenants, as all the Israelite men signed onto the covenant's pledge. No, said another rabbi, there were really 600,000 times 600,000 covenants as everyone made a covenant not only with God but with all their fellow Israelites.[21] When the celebrated Rabbi

Hillel was asked if he could explain the essence of Judaism while standing on one leg, he replied that nothing could be simpler: "Do unto others as you will have others do unto you. The rest is commentary."

In our own day, Rabbi Sacks underscores the simple but profound result: "A covenant is a pledge between two or more partners, each of whom respects the freedom and integrity of the other, to be loyal to one another and to do together what neither can do alone."[22] Excessive dependency is a problem in any society, and so also is excessive autonomy. But such is the covenantal responsibility of each person, and the responsibility of each for each other, and all for all, that a covenantal community becomes a community with a partnership and a project at its core. Our concern here is the decisive influence of covenantalism on politics, but it has major implications for other areas of life too. In a later chapter we will look at the notion of the civil public square as a form of covenantal pluralism, and its resolution of the problem of living with our deepest differences. Covenantalism has been applied to business too, as in the new economics of mutuality, pioneered by Bruno Roche and Jay Jakub, and set out in their *Complementing Capitalism*, and by Michael Schluter and David John Lee in *Relational Manager*.

The Tragedy of the Commons

Can it be said today that all Americans are responsible for all Americans? Or has American individualism shattered the bonds of solidarity and mutual responsibility beyond repair? The covenantal basis for both individuality and solidarity is quite clear, captured in the famous rabbinic saying "If I am not for myself, who will be? And if I am only for myself, what am I?" In the same vein, Elazar suggested that, just as the French saluted each other as "citizen" and the Russians and Chinese as "comrade" in the heyday of their respective revolutions, Americans should salute each other as "partner." For every American should look at all other Americans and know that together they are partners in the American experiment, the American freedom project, and the American way of life. "We the people" have come together to form a partnership nation on behalf of freedom that creates a just and peaceful community of free people.

This means that the measure of the reciprocal responsibility of all Americans for all Americans is the yardstick of the health of the republic. The Pledge of Allegiance is therefore no idle recitation. It should be unthinkable that any American leader should regard other Americans as "deplorables" or as anything other than fellow Americans and partners in the great cause of human freedom and justice for all. It is a mark of great leaders, not just that their followers have faith in them but that they have faith in their followers and can inspire them to live up to their ideals.

Today, America shows signs of two clear contrasts to this solidarity of covenantal partnership. The first is *politicization*, the idolatry of politics that trusts politics to do more than politics can do, and therefore turns all issues into political issues. The result is to prioritize the political at the expense of the personal. This priority grows from the Greek view that the polis, or city, is the highest form of allegiance, so that politics as service to the polis is the highest calling. From the covenantal perspective, by contrast, politics is important but is limited and kept in its place ("How small, of all that human hearts endure, / that part which laws or kings can cure"). Also, because power is the currency of politics, politics is especially prone to corruption and the abuse of power ("All power tends to corrupt"). Wisely understood, politics is downstream from the more creative and culture-shaping spheres of society, and it is always vital to remember the old maxim "The first thing to say about politics is that politics is not the first thing."

The second contrast to covenantal solidarity is what is now known as the *tragedy of the commons*. In a highly individualistic society, each person takes back a little of their public commitment, thinking that their part is so small that no one will notice. Rabbi Sacks tells an old Hasidic story that captures the problem of such tiny acts of selfishness. There was a European village where it was decided that each villager should donate an amount of wine to fill a vat to present to the king on the occasion of his visit to the village. Secretly at night over the next few weeks, however, each villager took some of the wine, rationalizing the theft with the thought that such a small amount would not be missed. Each one then added water to the vat, so that the vat remained full to the top. When the king arrived, the villagers presented the vat to him, and he drank from it, but was disgusted. "It is just plain water!"[23]

The point is clear. The responsibility for a covenantal (or constitutional) society lies with each citizen, and it begins and ends with each one doing their part—in solidarity with other covenant partners. In Elazar's words, "In all its forms, the key focus of covenant is on relationships. A covenant is the constitution of relationships."[24] Such a covenantal (constitutional) republic can die, not just because of bad government but death through a million tiny acts of selfishness. Americans should stop to ponder this point. Under the impact of radical individualism, America has become the land of the autonomous and unencumbered self, and the tragedy of the commons is far advanced in America.

George Bernard Shaw summed up the nihilism and irresponsibility of the European way of life in his own time when he said, "The golden rule today is that there is no golden rule." Oswald Spengler blamed such selfish attitudes for the "failure of nerve" of the West at large, and such practical results as demographic childlessness that followed it: "It is all the same whether the case against children is the American lady who would not miss a season for anything, the Parisienne who fears that her lover would leave her, or the Ibsen heroine who belongs to herself—*they all belong to themselves and they are all unfruitful.*"[25] With the exception of Switzerland, Europe is not committed to covenantal arrangements, whereas America ostensibly still is. Yet the reality is now hard to see in America. The irresponsible society and the irresponsible generation think only of themselves. They take no thought for others, including the wider world and those as yet unborn.

There is an elemental lesson here that Americans must not miss. The term *republic* was coined by Cicero in the first century BC, but its meaning "public things" or "the property of the public" was anchored by the Sinai covenant centuries earlier. *Democracy as a notion has next to no moral content and absolutely no social content whatsoever, whereas covenantal (or constitutional) republicanism is moral at its heart and creates a society before it creates a state. It therefore puts responsible relationships and the common good at the heart of life and society.* Covenantal (or constitutional) republicanism rises and falls on the moral integrity and the social responsibility of the relationships of the citizens and on the condition of the common good. The implications for America could not be plainer and more challenging. Vital though presidents and governments are, relationships matter more to freedom than regimes. The personal and the interpersonal precede the political. Both the American family and the American republic were once rooted in covenants, so there is an iron link between the health of marriage, the health of families, the health of schools, the health of the common good, and the health of America, and to loosen one is to loosen the others. Improved gun laws may or may not help to curb the destructive ugliness of America's social violence, but there is no question that good relationships will always do more than the best of gun laws. It is no accident that the gunmen in America's tragic massacres are the "loners and disconnected"—those with no true relationships.

Thus the importance of the condition of American society, its marriages, its families, its schools, its voluntary associations, its civic education, and its handing down from generation to generation—all these things will always determine the state of the union more than the character of the president, the nature of the state, the size of the military, or the condition of America's roads, railways, bridges, and tunnels. America's obsession with presidents and presidential elections is expensive, diverting, and foolish.

The notion of democracy is designed to answer the question, Who rules? (Though as we shall see, even its answer to that question is weaker and less clear than many people think.) But covenantal republicanism answers a far deeper question, How are the democratic citizens who rule to relate to each other in ways that ensure a just, free, open, and caring society? Americans today celebrate democracy and downplay republicanism, when for those who prize freedom the priority should be the other way around.

Rediscovery at the Reformation

The impact of the covenant and the notion of covenantalism can be seen in three periods in history. First, and most obviously, the Sinai covenant constituted the Jewish people and formed the Jewish nation. It is notable that the covenant constituted the Jewish way of life and the Jewish political arrangements centuries before Israel chose a Jewish king hundreds of years later. And the covenant continued to be the decisive factor in the way they lived long after the catastrophic disasters of AD 70 and AD 133. The Jews had lost their temple, their monarchy, their capital city, their priests, their prophets, their homeland, their independence, and almost their will to survive. (At the climax of the persecution under the Emperor Hadrian, there were rabbis who said that "by rights we should issue a decree that Jews should not marry and have children, so that the seed of Abraham comes to an end of its own accord.")[26] In other words, in the blackest night of Jewish experience the covenant was the key to Jewish survival. It was not only a framework for life but an anchor and a lifeline in the storms of evil that the Jewish people suffered.

The basic lesson of Jewish covenantalism is unmistakable. Relationships matter more than regimes, the character of society preceded the character of the state, and the law came into being before the entry into the land. This central concern for the quality of a community means that the character of the state follows the quality of the relationships of the people who comprise it. As the community and the society goes, starting with the family and the school, so goes the state, and not the other way around.

Second, the precedent and pattern of the Sinai covenant was rediscovered and developed by the Reformation. Along with the truths of calling and conscience, it became one of the three most decisive gifts of the Reformation that shaped the rise of the modern world. Switzerland, the Netherlands, Scotland, England, and the United States—each was powerfully shaped by the Reformation and in its turn helped to shape the modern world, the last two in particular because of their influence in secular history. The Sinai covenant was especially important to the Reformed wing of the Reformation and the thinking that spread out from Calvin's Geneva and Zwingli's Zurich. The Jews had famously said, "Our people is a people only in virtue of its Torah," and an old Calvinist adage made the same point: "Where the Reformed are, there will be the covenant." The Jews were constituted by the Torah, and the Reformers were constituted by the covenant, and without them neither would have been anything. In the words of William Perkins, the great Cambridge teacher of countless Puritans, "We are by nature covenant creatures, bound together by covenants innumerable and together bound by covenant to our God. . . . Blessed be the ties that bind us."[27]

Sadly, Roman Catholic thought in Europe was emphatically not covenantal. From the fourth century through to the Renaissance in the late fifteenth century, the government of the Roman Catholic Church had been hierarchical, not covenantal. In its triumph over the other religions in the Roman Empire, the Catholic Church took over more of the existing Greek ideas and more of the existing Roman institutions than it thought through critically—so that the papacy, for instance, too often reflected the ways of the Caesars, not the biblical view of leadership. It was therefore no accident that the Church perpetrated the most egregious evils of Christendom as a direct result of the corruption of the hierarchical power of church leaders.

Lord Acton's famous maxim that "absolute power corrupts absolutely" was written to counter an uncritical defense of the Borgia popes. Both that and his fierce opposition to papal infallibility in 1870 (as a devout Catholic himself) were formulated in light of the corruptions of hierarchical power. More recently

Pope John Paul II confessed the sins of the church more than sixty times, but there is no question that they were sins and they were evil, and that they stemmed from the corruptions of the Church's hierarchical power. (For example, the evils of the Spanish Inquisition, the Index, the forced baptism of the Jews, and the horrendous notion that "error has no rights.")

It may seem graceless to mention this point after Vatican II and the great sea change in the Catholic Church over freedom and religious freedom. And the problem is not simply Catholic. German Protestants and American secularists must acknowledge their own part in suppressing the significance of the Jewish and biblical roots of freedom—German Protestants through their cowardly attempts to de-Judaize the Christian faith in the 1930s, and American secularists today through their adamant refusal to take the Jewish and Christian faiths seriously in public discussion. It is important to acknowledge the Jewish roots of the Revolution for two reasons. For one thing, it took American Catholics, shaped by America's principles and experience, to change the Church's mind at Vatican II. For another, the traditional Catholic position was both obvious and crucial to the generation of the American Revolution. They expressly fought for freedom of religion and conscience through the disestablishment of religion because of their bad experiences of established churches in Europe.

John Jay, for example, knew firsthand accounts of the persecution of his Huguenot family in France. John Leland was a Baptist pastor and friend of James Madison, who put the point bluntly:

> The church of Rome was first constituted according to the gospel, and at that time her faith was spoken of through the whole world. Being espoused to Christ, as a chaste virgin, she kept her bed pure for her husband, almost three hundred years; but afterwards she played the whore with the kings and princes of this world, who with their gold and wealth came in unto her, and she became a strumpet: as she was the first Christian church that ever forsook the laws of Christ for her conduct and received the laws of his rivals, i.e., was established by human law, and governed by the legalized edicts of councils, and received large sums of money to support her preachers and her worship by the force of civil power.[28]

In short, the church went badly wrong, first the Catholics and later some of the Protestants, when it was corrupted by the power of establishment. In

Tocqueville's more gentle comment: "Whenever a religion joins forces with political powers, the alliance is bound to be onerous for religion."[29]

Sadly, too, the tragic fact is that reactions to Europe's corrupt and oppressive state churches, mainly Roman Catholic and supremely in France, are the single most important factor behind the intensity of European secularism and secularity today. French attitudes in particular hardened after the St. Bartholomew's Day massacre and the later expulsion of the (covenantal) Huguenots, and France became the epitome of a centralized, authoritarian, bureaucratic, and oppressive state, typified equally by Louis XIV, the Jacobins, and Napoleon (and in many people's minds today by Brussels and the European Union). The net effect was that for much of European history, religion and freedom were at loggerheads. Slowly, under the impact of the Reformation thinking and its restoration of the covenant, this alignment was reversed. Rediscovering the Bible and its relevance, the Reformers restored the significance of the Sinai covenant and applied it to their political arrangements—in Switzerland, the Netherlands, Scotland (the Covenanters, Whiggamores, and later Whigs), and in England, where it became a blueprint for "the revolution of the Saints" under Cromwell and the Puritans. With the failure of the Puritan Commonwealth and the restoration of Charles II to the throne in 1660, covenant politics became "the lost cause" in England—but only for it to migrate to New England, where it was to become the winning cause on a far bigger stage and with far greater significance.

From the *Mayflower* to the *Arbella,* and from Plymouth Rock to the Massachusetts Bay and beyond, the notion of covenant was applied to churches and marriages, and then to townships and commonwealths. It became the characteristic and unmistakable form of governance in seventeenth- and eighteenth-century New England. The Massachusetts Constitution of 1780, for example, is the oldest surviving written constitution in the modern world, and John Adams drafted it expressly in covenantal terms. ("It is a social compact, by which the whole people covenants with the each citizen, and each citizen with the whole people, that all shall be governed by certain laws for the common good.")[30] As if to doff his cap to what he knew was the wellspring of constitutionalism, John Adams wrote, "I will insist that the Hebrews have done more to civilize men than any other nation."[31]

The third period of influence is the most recent. In the eighteenth century, the covenant tradition merged with the new science of politics and flowered into the notion of constitutionalism, and in that form it has influenced many countries across the world ever since. Yet many Americans today still fail to appreciate the fundamental point. The US Constitution, which has been the pacesetter document for so many other countries and constitutions, is in essence a form of national and somewhat secularized covenant—and a notion that goes back to Mount Sinai. As such, it has all the strengths and weaknesses of the covenantal form of government, but it represents a direct and comprehensive contrast to the alternative of organic, hierarchical, and purely contractual forms of government. In Lord Acton's estimate, covenantal federalism in America (the term *federal* comes *foedus*, the Latin for covenant) "has produced a community more powerful, more prosperous, more intelligent, and more free than any other which the world has seen."[32]

Faith and Freedom Hand in Hand

It is essential to understand both the strengths and the weaknesses of the covenantal and constitutional form of government, and for the purposes of assessing American freedom today one strength is paramount: covenantal politics restored the vital link between faith, freedom, and equality. The ideal of free and equal citizens is an extremely challenging ideal. No society has attained it for long. But in our own day, in spite of the constant obsession with equality, current inequalities and mistaken policies are driving us further away from the ideal than ever. We must therefore be prepared to consider what the notion of covenant promises. In Rabbi Sacks's words, it holds out the vision of "a republic of free and equal citizens held together not by hierarchy or power but by the moral bond of covenant."[33]

Daniel Elazar makes the same point applied to early American history.

> Perhaps the greatest achievement of the new covenantalism was to restore the alliance between religion and liberty that had been sundered when Christianity became the established church of the Roman Empire 1200 years earlier. . . . It is a historical fact that those groups that accepted the covenant theology and made it the cornerstone of their faith were also the groups that became committed earliest to human liberty and contributed most to its advancement.[34]

Both Christians and secularists alike need to ponder these two claims, for the significance of covenant is as misunderstood by many Christians as it is by atheists. Alexis de Tocqueville captured the link between faith and freedom pointedly. He opened his introduction to *Democracy in America* with his well-known contrast between what he found in America and what he knew from his own country, Catholic France. This contrast was also the general experience of many European countries with their established churches. In the old world, "Religious men do battle against liberty, and friends of liberty attack religion," he noted.[35] For an illustration he might have quoted the popular saying of the encyclopédist Denis Diderot, which was picked up by the Jacobins in the French Revolution. There would never be real freedom, he argued, until "the last king was strangled with the guts of the last priest." In ever-hierarchical and always-centralized Catholic France, Church and state, throne and altar had long been in collusion, and both were oppressive, so the revolution set its sights on both and overthrew them both.

America was quite different, Tocqueville observed. Religion in America was disestablished, yet through its indirect influence it had become "the first of the political institutions."[36] "In France, I knew, the spirit of religion and the spirit of liberty almost always pulled in opposite directions. In the United States I found them intimately intertwined."[37] The reason lay in the covenantal understanding of freedom. Faith, once disestablished and voluntary, was the guarantee and guardian of freedom. "Puritanism," Tocqueville noted, "was not just a religious doctrine; in many respects it shared the most absolute and democratic and republican theories"—in other words, covenantalism.[38] Sovereignty rested with the people and not the state. Edmund Burke made the same point in his defense of the American colonists before the Parliament. Their passionate love of freedom was natural and should have been expected. After all, the New Englanders were the "Protestants of Protestantism and the dissenters of dissent." Citizens under the covenantal form of governance held faith and freedom together.

The Weak Links in the Chain

The weaknesses of covenantalism also need to be understood. Covenant thinking and covenant politics are as vital today as in the heyday of their rediscovery in the sixteenth century. For as many have noted, covenantal thinking cultivates the political equivalent of Martin Buber's I–Thou relationships, and while always stressing the overall bonds of community, covenantal citizenship thrives on the We–Thou conversation between citizens. No one is a citizen alone, any more than anyone can think entirely alone, or come to know their own identity entirely alone. As Rabbi Sacks underscores, gifts such as human love and human friendship are covenantal goods, in the sense that the more you give them away, the more you enjoy them as you receive them in return. Financial goods, such as money and property, are different, and a matter of zero-sum dealing. If you give away a million dollars, you are a million dollars poorer, but if you give out love and friendship, you almost always receive more in return, and multiplied.

Five hundred years ago, as the influence of the Reformation spread, the notion of covenant appealed especially to countries that were fluid, less settled, and at the frontiers of mainstream Europe—Switzerland and Scotland, for example, rather than France and Spain. Today, covenantalism holds out a similar political promise. It reinforces such notions as freedom, equality, responsibility, and community, while avoiding the advanced modern tendency to swing between the extremes of atomized individualism and centralized authoritarianism—or between the extremes of the Left and the Right, and the political bookends of anarchy and despotism.

It goes without saying that not all relationships should be covenantal. The marriage bond is covenantal at its beginning, but families are largely organic in character, just as an army or an orchestra should properly be hierarchical. A truly democratic orchestra or army would quickly be a disaster. But communities and political orders such as a republic flourish within covenantal agreements. It is obvious too that there are certain requirements for covenantal politics if it is to work well—supremely the maintenance of a living transmission through storytelling, education, and even song. Rabbi Sacks notes,

> *To defend a land, you need an army, but to defend freedom, you need education.* You need parents, families, and homes and a constant conversation between the generations to see that your ideas are passed on to the next generation and never lost. . . . You achieve immortality not by building pyramids or statues— but by *engraving your values on the hearts of your children, and they on theirs, so that our ancestors live on in us, and we in our children, and so on until the end of time.*[39]

When public as well as private life is shaped by covenantalism, Sacks writes, "Politics has never been more radical, more ethical, and more humane."[40]

Promise Makers, Promise Breakers

It is important to say that there are weaknesses in covenantal politics, as in all forms of human politics, and these should be understood clearly—two above all. The first weakness is that covenantalism requires promise keeping, but we humans do not keep promises well. We make and break promises, both as individuals and as groups and nations. Making promises is the natural expression of human freedom. The Pledge of Allegiance is therefore a key part of the American republic's two-way promise: the pledge of the citizen to the republic, and the promise of the republic to the citizen. For Americans to make the pledge is to give their word of honor to stand by their promise, which is why standing rather than kneeling is the perfect expression of the pledge. Kneeling, by contrast, is a posture that expresses either worship or subservience, both of which are appropriate in other settings, but neither expresses what is being spoken and performed in the act of standing during the national anthem.

The taking-a-knee controversy in the National Football League in 2017 is misguided for another reason. It disrespects the authority and standard it must appeal to in fighting injustice—if the American republic is to fulfill its promise to its citizens, overcome its shortcomings, and achieve an ongoing and "more perfect union." By disrespecting the anthem and the flag, the activists are disdaining the promissory note. Which means that either they are cutting off the branch they are sitting on or, more radically, that they are appealing to a revolution other than 1776. Martin Luther King Jr. hated racism and injustice no less passionately than today's activists. But he believed in the American Revolution, so he appealed to the Declaration of Independence as America's "promissory note." As the promissory note, the Declaration (and its symbols: the flag and the anthem) deserved and required respect as the American standard by which the evils of racism could be judged and fought. The kneeling controversy is therefore self-defeating when appeals to freedom of speech are used to undermine the promissory note altogether. One suspects that some of the activists do indeed have a different revolution in mind.

Regardless of the controversies surrounding the pledge, making promises and keeping promises are two different things, and the Bible itself candidly exposes this weakness in promise keeping. The problem is writ large in the cycle of degeneration and renewal in the book of Judges, which comes not long after Exodus, and later in the checkered story of the Jewish kings. There is a cycle of nature (spring, summer, autumn, and winter), and there is a cycle of human failure (corruption, oppression, capitulation, redemption, and corruption again). They each require festivals to address the significance of their differences, but the first cycle is inevitable, whereas the second is preventable. Strikingly, the greatest, wisest, and richest of all the Hebrew kings, Solomon, demonstrates the corruption the most clearly. He so glorifies himself and his building ventures that he turns his entire people back into a slave labor force and turns himself into "another Pharaoh" and Israel into a "second Egypt."

This candidly acknowledged failure creates the impetus for the characteristically Jewish notion of the Messiah and messianism. Whether the longed-for Messiah is true or false, religious (as in the desired Son of David) or secular (as in the nineteenth-century visions of Rabbi Marx), the messianic longing is for a second liberation to fulfill the first. It is a radical and visionary response that springs from the assumption that the exodus of the first liberation has proved crucially incomplete or has failed. The messianic hope is pregnant with meaning for the Jewish and Christian sense of history. But it is also crucial for the revolutionary secular Left, because secular messianism is essentially an expression of the failure of secular liberationism. With no divine Messiah in view, secular messianism becomes a dream politics of the Left. It is called on whenever history's progressives have not progressed as promised, when the "long march" has gone through the institutions and got nowhere, and when the Babel project has foundered yet again.

To counter the dynamics of this spiritual and moral entropy, the Bible constantly warns against the danger of idolatry and self-glorification. It demonstrates the crucial importance of the prophetic corrective and teaches the requirement of faithful transmission of covenantal commitments—from leaders to their people, from parents to children, and from generation to generation, and it underscores the necessity of renewing the covenant when it is forgotten or broken. Yet in spite of all this, the record of covenant keeping will never be perfect. It will often be broken, and the messianic hope will burn brightly in contrast. Moses, the first liberator, and the coming Messiah, the second liberator, are the Bible's two bookends for holding together freedom and hope. Thus the free person's task in any age is to live responsibly in the roller-coaster interim, always looking to the past with gratitude and humility, but always working toward the future with hope and energy. Life lived this way calls for engagement with hope and humility. Where we are going gives strength to what we are doing, and what we are doing becomes a sign of where we are going.

Many people have recognized this core problem of promise keeping and responded to it in different ways. One response was to see the flaw and exploit it cynically. In the Renaissance, for instance, Machiavelli turned the weakness into a virtue when he openly called for the prince to break his word whenever he needed to as a matter of statecraft. "The promise given was a necessity of the past: the word broken is a necessity of the present." Since politics has no relation to ethics, "a wise ruler ought never to keep faith when by doing so it would be against his interests."[41] Power, not trust, is the coin of the realm for Machiavelli's prince—a philosophy and an attitude that is common again under the terms of postmodernism.

Another response was to rue the flaw and then use it to reject the notion of covenantalism itself. Philosopher David Hume, for example, writing from covenanting Scotland, raised the simple question, "Why are we bound to keep our promises?" He argued that promise making is "the most mysterious and incomprehensible operation that can possibly be imagined."[42] Famously, he demonstrated in his own life that he had no intention of upholding what he considered impossible and unnecessary. Once, after he had fallen into a bog near Edinburgh, he called for help and said he was willing to recite the Lord's Prayer to induce a rescuer to help him, only to mock the woman once he was back on terra firma. If Paris was worth a mass for Henry IV, reciting the Lord's Prayer was an easy price for Hume to pay for his rescue. What was one more false and fickle oath if all oaths were false and fickle?

Yet another response was to face the flaw realistically and then attempt to strengthen promise keeping by safeguarding the place of truth, trust, oaths, vows, and loyalty. ("So help me, God.") That concern was the reason why John Locke advised against respecting freedom of conscience for atheists. The problem was not that he was prejudiced, that his much-vaunted "tolerance" stopped short of tolerating atheists, or that he was inconsistent and hypocritical, as he is often accused of being. It was rather that since atheists did not believe in God, Locke did not think they had a standard by which to make oaths that were needed if the bonds of social trust were to be maintained.

Accountable? Who Says?

The second major weakness of covenantalism is closely related to the first. Any rejection of the standard, before which the covenantal pledge was made, means an automatic relaxing of accountability, and without accountability, covenantalism and constitutionalism weaken and fall apart. For the Jews at Sinai, the covenant was "with God"; for most of American history, the covenant was genuinely "under God"; but now it has become a constitution "without God." The recent determination to remove both the term and the truth of "One nation under God" raises the question of accountability again. Kingdoms, empires, dictatorships, totalitarian governments, and authoritarian religions require no consent other than submission—blind, grudging, and sullen if necessary. But covenantal faiths and constitutional societies are nothing without the free and uncoerced promise making and promise keeping of their adherents and their citizens. Tether-free societies simply do not last. Hence the importance of the Pledge of Allegiance and civic education again, not as a formality but a reality.

Needless to say, the alternative to promise keeping is a resort to force, and therefore to the state as the only agent strong enough to hold citizens accountable and to provide the common superstandard of accountability. Statism and the creation of Leviathan was Thomas Hobbes alternative to covenantalism. Despite his formal nod to God and his multiple references to the Bible (far more than to the Greeks and the Romans), Hobbes had no real place for God in his "new science of politics." It was to be a secularized form of contractual, not covenantal, governance. But he was candid enough to spell out the price that people would have to pay—and that Americans will have to pay today—if they reject God as the final standard of accountability. If the government was to do what Hobbes needed the government to do, and to help people escape the brutal state of nature, the state that would replace God would have to become god—or in Hobbes's own words, Leviathan would have to be a "mortal god."

The new government, Hobbes wrote, would be "made by covenant of every man with every man," as everyone would say to everyone else, I give up my right to govern myself, and I authorize the ruler, on the condition that you too give over your right to the ruler, and support all his actions. When this happens, he argued, the united people are "called a COMMONWEALTH. . . .

This is the generation of that great LEVIATHAN, or rather to speak more reverently, of that mortal god, to which we owe under the immortal God, our peace and defense."[43] You can escape the brutal state of nature, Hobbes promises. Peace, order, and stability can all be yours, but the price is steep. You may escape the "war of all against all" on one side, and you may step away from your dislike of any binding agreement with God on the other side. But your only option is to surrender to the "mortal god" of the all-powerful state, which as it grows will claim absolute arbitrary power over everyone and everything.

Make no mistake: the logical outcome of those who reject covenantalism (or constitutionalism) today is state control. There is undoubtedly a danger in what Leo Strauss called *reductio ad Hitlerum*—making Hitler the essence of all evil, and using him as the final argument to win arguments. But there have been too many political religions and too many semidivine states on both the left and the right to ignore the problem of statism, or what used to be called statolatry. "Man . . . must venerate the state as a secular deity," Hegel said.[44] "To be a nation . . . is the religion of our time," declared the German nationalist Ernst Arndt.[45] Abolish God, Chesterton commented on such claims, "and the Government becomes God. That fact is written all across human history."[46] Supporters of 1789 and Left/liberalism should take careful note. The invasion of the private sphere, Christopher Dawson wrote, is "the original sin of every totalitarian system."[47] For all the fancy Left/liberal blather about diversity, unity without God soon becomes enforced unity, which is another name for coercion and uniformity and the totalitarian suppression of real diversity. Thanks to political correctness, the process is well under way in America, and there is no greater need than the need to defend and expand the remaining spheres of freedom.

The Real Breaking of the Covenant

Far more than fussiness over history is at stake in these issues. If the notions of covenant and constitution are central to the founding of the American republic, then the health or sickness of their condition must be central to any assessment of the state of the union, for quite literally they constitute America. A founding creates a nation's DNA and establishes the lines along which it will develop until and unless it is defeated or taken in a completely different direction. No one can hope to make America great again in any direction without understanding what made America great in the first place.

America can neither be understood right nor led well unless the covenantal and constitutional character of American freedom is taken into account. Covenantalism and the essential responsibility it requires of citizens provide the missing key to restoring American freedom today—unless it is taken a quite different direction.

When Abraham Lincoln traveled to Washington to begin his presidency in February 1861, the storm clouds of war were darkening. He stopped in Philadelphia to pay his respects to Independence Hall and the two great documents that had been debated and framed there, the first being nothing less than America's "birth certificate." Citing Psalm 137, he solemnly made his own covenantal pledge: "I have never asked anything that does not breathe from those walls. All my political warfare has been in favor of the teachings coming forth from that sacred hall. May my right hand forget its cunning and my tongue cleave to the roof of my mouth if I ever prove false to those teachings."[48] Lincoln's parallel with the Hebrew psalm and its undying devotion to Jerusalem is stunning, and it shows up the chasm between him and many American leaders today. No people in all history have had a love for their city like the Jews for Jerusalem, even when they were separated from it for nearly two thousand years, yet Lincoln takes that supreme attachment as the standard for his love for the principles enshrined in America's founding documents.

Few American leaders today have such an understanding of where the greatness of America came from. Such an inaugural trip to Philadelphia now would be little more than "optics" or tourism at best and hypocrisy at worst, for both the founders and their ideas are now under a cloud. There are four main ways Americans dismiss their covenantal past and weaken the role of the founders and the Constitution today. Indeed, it was the fateful convergence of these dismissals in the 1960s that created the cultural chasm between 1776 and 1789 that divides America now.

First and foremost, many Americans have rejected the founders because of their failure to address "America's original sin"—the evil of slavery and their treatment of women and Native Americans, and the rank hypocrisy that was the result. Many people outside the United States had pointed to this hypocrisy—most famously the English writer Samuel Johnson: "How is it that we hear the loudest yelps for liberty among the drivers of negroes?"[49] Unquestionably, then, the founders' silence over slavery was not unwitting.

It was the Faustian bargain made by the supporters of the US Constitution in 1787. Many of them personally opposed slavery, but they remained silent at the convention because if they had insisted on tackling the problem, as Samuel Hopkins and others urged, the Southern states would never have signed the Constitution. This devilish agreement carried over an egregious evil and created a blatant hypocrisy—the gap between the American genius for freedom and the reality of slavery, and thus between America's ideals and self-image as the "land of the free" and the sordid realities of the long degradation of the African slaves and then of African Americans. Plastering over this blatant hypocrisy left the evil unaddressed, and the contradiction festered like an open wound until the stench could be disguised no longer. The hypocrisy was then ripped open by the civil rights movement to expose the ugly gangrene of racism for what it was.

The same was true of other inconsistencies and distortions from the founders' America—supremely the treatment of women, of Native Americans, and the treatment of other nations through America's sense of manifest destiny and exceptionalism. One after another, different sixties movements such as the women's movement, the sexual revolution, and the antiwar movement echoed the civil rights movement, called the status quo into question, and sent shockwaves through the complacency and triumphalism of postwar America. What happened next is what matters today and what shaped the present polarizations: *American liberalism lurched sharply to the Left in the sixties and became the Left/liberalism of today.* Since then, Left/liberalism has been characterized by liberal shame, a discomfort with the founders, a decisive distancing from the American past, an unease with white dominance, an open animosity toward religion, a tendency to view ethics in public rather than personal terms, a proneness to disrespect the flag, and—fatefully—an openness to ideas and trends that owe more to 1789 than to 1776.

With hindsight, it is now clear that this lurch leftward was the real broken covenant. The critical shift led in its turn to the celebrated Rudi Dutschke–style, Left/liberal "long march through the institutions" in the decades after the sixties. The outcome was that Left/liberalism has captured the three main centers of American ideas and educated opinion that shape American culture: the universities, the press and media, and the world of entertainment. In the process, the triumph of Left/liberalism has turned American history into a museum of evils, inflamed the culture wars, and bred the disagreements that have created the present bitter divisions between ordinary Americans and the educated American elites—and called into question the great experiment itself. Theodore Roszak wrote famously of "the making of the counter-culture" in the 1960s. It took much longer than he thought, but fifty years later its success is close even though many of the original revolutionaries did not live to see their triumph.

Among the many consequences of the great lurch left, the change in America's way of addressing evil is titanic. Despite their tragic blind spots, the founders were generally realistic about the potential for corruption and the abuse of power. Equally, both the Jewish and Christian faiths, though frank about evil and injustice, emphasize the necessity for repentance and the possibility of forgiveness when addressing wrongs. Only through a separation of powers can abuse be prevented, and only through repentance and forgiveness can wrongs be addressed as wrongs, the past be left behind as the past, and the future be opened as the arena of the genuine second chance. From Samuel Hopkins to Abraham Lincoln to Frederick Douglass to Martin Luther King Jr., those who addressed the evils and hypocrisies of their times did so within the double framework of the biblical faiths and America's founding declarations (Lincoln's "new birth" of freedom, for example, and King's "promissory note" of the Declaration).

No excoriation of slavery is more searing than Frederick Douglass's 1852 speech, "What to the Slave Is the Fourth of July?" Even today it brings tears to the eyes, anger to the heart, and a stunned sense of wonder that such awful things could ever be countenanced in the "land of the free." Distancing himself from the founders, he repeatedly calls them "your fathers," and he then passionately attacks both the barbarism of slavery and the multiple hypocrisies of the "nation's inconsistences" over slavery. Yet Douglass still finishes his magisterial speech with unshaken confidence in the Constitution—"interpreted as it ought to be interpreted, the Constitution is a GLORIOUS LIBERTY DOCUMENT. Read its preamble, consider its purposes. Is slavery among them? Is it at the gateway? It is neither."[50]

Many sixties radicals, and Left/liberals later, part company with Frederick Douglass, Booker T. Washington, and Martin Luther King Jr. at that point. They reject that recourse emphatically, and in doing so they wittingly or unwittingly break with the American covenant decisively. Such was the depth of the evils exposed that they rejected the Bible, the founders, and the American founding altogether. Traditional America, they charged, had been shown up as inherently, foundationally, and chronically "racist," "sexist," "militarist," and the like. And in the process of this dire shift in diagnosis, two fateful things happened. First, much of American liberalism itself lurched left and changed—from the classical and "capital L" liberalism of the founders and their heirs to the Left/liberalism of the radical movements that from then on have viewed America in a harsh and less flattering light. There could be no turning back to the America of the founders or to any serious talk of a "promissory note."

Also, in rejecting both the founders and the Jewish and Christian perspective that underlie them, the radicals also turned from the biblical vision of justice to a secular view of justice as all-out, power-based confrontation. Whereas the former requires repentance, which requires an acknowledgment of both wrongs and responsibility, and then works for reconciliation and restoration, the latter aims only for redress and reparation that can be little more than revenge. The result of this shift is turning America into the land of vengeance. Victims seeking vengeance for a lengthening list of past sins produce more victims, who in turn seek fiercer vengeance that produces even more victims. And so it goes, eye for eye, tooth for tooth, murder for murder, and massacre for massacre.

Where will it end? Oddly, these brave new radicals do not realize how they are prone to violence because they are Rousseau's children and utopians rather than heirs of the realism of Madison and the Bible. Yet it is actually their utopianism that drives them to violence. With utopian visions dancing before their eyes, they believe that only a clean sweep of the past can usher in a world of justice and freedom. Thus baby, bathwater, Bible—and now statuary, memorials, and all—have to be flung out of the window if there is to be a fresh start. As always, the utopians' fresh start has to begin with a clean slate, and as always it takes violence to wipe the slate completely clean. Once again the violent echoes of 1789 are drowning out the cautionary realism of 1776.

Second, there are Americans, such as historian Charles Beard and his progressive school, and many recent thinkers and historians, such as Howard Zinn, who claim that they have "seen through" the founders' real agenda and exposed them for the economic interests that lay behind their thinking and their policies. Later historians have dismissed this charge as "quasi-Marxist nonsense," but such charges gained their appeal because they debunked the mythical view of the founders, and they fit the postmodern analysis that everything can be reduced to its power equations.[51] Far from disinterested statesmen and heroes, the founders had rigged the system to thwart true democracy, Beard and the postmodernists argue. They were "hard-fisted conservatives" out to "protect their own interests and those of their class."[52]

Third, there are other Americans, such as progressive leaders from Woodrow Wilson and John Dewey to Barack Obama, who have praised the founders for their contribution in their day, but insist that their work, however brilliant in their time, is now outdated and needs to be revised for the changing needs of today's generation. There are in fact inherent problems in such progressivism and its dismissal of the past. Above all, it stands or falls by the Enlightenment belief in continuous advance, whether through the state (for those on the left), the market (for those on the right), or science and technology (for everyone, but the elites above all). The Enlightenment's continuous advance has simply stalled, at least for the moment, and it did nothing to prevent the horrors of the Holocaust, the world wars, and the genocides in the twentieth century. Whether the progress hoped for was for human advance in general or the American dream of economic betterment in particular, the evident frustration and cynicism in the younger generation stems from its bitter conclusion: For most Americans, the promised future may not be better than the past.

Behind this practical weakness there were always theoretical flaws in progressivism. For a start, it was a parasite on the biblical view of time and hope, and it provided no standard by which to judge the progress that it claimed. Aside from the positive connotations of the word *progress*, the term *progressivism* could as easily be *regressivism*, for some of its "achievements," such as the expanded state, are a step backward for personal freedom, not forward. G. K. Chesterton noted this inherent problem when he remarked, "Progress is simply a comparative of which we have not settled the superlative."[53] T. S. Eliot remarked similarly on "an age which advances progressively backwards."[54]

More importantly, progressivism requires certain assumptions for it to succeed. Many of its advocates do not hold these assumptions, and their philosophies have no right to them. Progressives often quote Martin Luther

King Jr., who was quoting Theodore Parker from the nineteenth century: "The arc of the moral universe is long, but it bends towards justice." But in the very speech when King used this phrase, in his sermon from the Torah at Temple Israel of Hollywood in February 1965, he pointed out that many people do not have either the assumptions or the ideology to be able to undergird such a confident view of progress. Their idea of progress was no better than the notion King attacked, citing Thoreau, as "improved means to an unimproved end."[55] When progressives breezily claim to be on the "right side of history" and consign their opponents to "the dustbin of history," they simply cannot justify their claims. Indeed, they have no more credibility than Nikita Khrushchev when he angrily pounded the podium at the United Nations with his shoe and shouted, "Whether you like it or not, history is on our side. We will bury you!"

Such is the power of hope, of course, that in good times the appeal of the progressive attitude will always be stronger than its rationale. And what affects politics is the progressive attitude, and in particular the over-spill from its disdain for the past, in this case the past of the founders. Just before he retired as Secretary of State, Dean Acheson was speaking to a prominent European. "Looking back," he said, "the gravest problem I had to deal with was how to steer, in this atomic age, the foreign policy of a world power saddled with the constitution of a small, eighteenth-century farmers' republic."[56]

Fourth, there are still others, perhaps now the majority of Americans, who have simply forgotten the founders. They have grown hazier and hazier in their understanding of the founders and the genius of their contribution—beyond some scant references on July Fourth. For all practical purposes, many Americans have simply forgotten the founders, and in the process have also lost touch with the founders' view of covenant and the Constitution and its requirements. For John Winthrop, in 1630, covenant was at the heart of their purpose in coming to America. ("We are entered into Covenant with him for this work, we have taken out a Commission.")[57] But by the time of Lyndon Johnson's inauguration in 1965, the terms of the covenant had changed in a marked way, and the covenant was with the land and not with each other, let alone God. ("They came here—the exile and the stranger, brave but frightened—to find a place where a man could be his own man. They made a covenant with this land.")[58] More recently, apart from a brief and ineffectual mention by President Clinton in his early days, the notion of covenant has disappeared almost completely.

These four dismissals are different, but their combined effect has been to sever America's covenantal roots, banish the founders, distance the past, and stretch the elasticity of the Constitution to the breaking point. Now, under the fig leaf of the mantra "constitutional" and "unconstitutional," the declining prestige of the Constitution can be pressed into the service of any person or group that can grasp the levers of government power and press their own agenda. The irony is that in its assault on the past, contemporary America is becoming all the more captive to the past. Imagining itself free, it shows itself bound more than ever and unable to make real progress.

This is not the place for a comprehensive description of Left/liberalism and its links to 1789. My concern is the difference between 1776 and 1789 and its implications for freedom, which will unfold as we proceed. I am certainly not arguing that everyone on the American Left mimics the Jacobins and the sans-culottes, works for a full-blown Marxist revival, or subscribes to what Roger Scruton calls the "stunning 'nonsense machine'" of the foggy thought and impenetrable language of many postmodern European writers.[59] But the undeniable links and clear resemblances between 1789 and the American Left are what matters. The former struggled for *liberté* and *egalité*, the latter for "liberation" and "social justice." The former won through violent revolution, whereas the latter seeks to win through a cultural revolution, after which the elite imposes its will through administrative and bureaucratic procedures (regulative bodies and the law courts). And both are characterized by their reliance on the state, their open hostility toward religion, their radical separation of religion and public life, their attempt to control language in order to control reality (French and Soviet "Newspeak," "doublespeak," and American "political correctness"), their unashamed espousal of power, their egalitarian appeal to envy rather than liberty, and their naive utopianism that the removal of repression will mean the fulfillment of freedom.

No one should fail to see how these resemblances between Left/liberalism and 1789 add up to a triple tragedy after America's triumph over the Soviet Union in 1989. America has not only rejected its covenantal/constitutional heritage of freedom but wasted the rare and historic opportunity of its "unipolar moment," and is now in danger of surrendering to the way of thinking that led to the collapse of its former enemy.

For the purposes of this chapter, however, the question is: Has the Left/liberal exposure of hypocrisy in the sixties helped America move beyond the evils and hypocrisies of the past? On the contrary. Within the worldview of Left/liberal secularism there was no repentance required and no forgiveness to be offered, in contrast to Lincoln and King. So the effect of the harping on the evils of America's racism, sexism, and militarism has been to make America's evils irredeemable. Pounding on the "sins of the fathers," and assaulting the "structures of domination," a brigade of angry activists has forged a culture of grievance, resentment, anger, and *victim playing* turned *power mongering*. But they have stoked the problems, not solved them. Instead of remedying the evils and reconciling the parties, the Left/liberal activists have refought the battles of the past, widening the wounds to the present generation and spreading the devastation far beyond their original victims. And they have done so in a way that poisons American life and American politics from top to bottom.

The result is an American past that can never be atoned, an American debt that can never be repaid, an American apology that will never be accepted, an American hope that will forever be dashed, and an American credibility that is increasingly threadbare to America's own youth, let alone to the watching world. If this Left/liberal view prevails finally, the American project of freedom is tainted forever and finished.

From a covenantal perspective, the ultimate challenge is to see what happens to America when Americans finally render the Constitution ineffectual—what happens when Americans lose the sense of purposeful history that came with covenant and close down their horizons to the endless currents, eddies, swings, counterswings, graphs, statistics, pie charts, and punditry of modern political science, what happens when the "parchment barriers" prove too flimsy and even the "flexible constitution" becomes too elastic and there is effectively no constitutional framework at all. What happens when freely chosen consent is only a charade, and there is no morally binding pledge, no reciprocal responsibility of all for all, no checks and balances, no insistence that no one is above the law, and every American and American movement does what is right in their own eyes? Will Yeats's celebrated "center" still hold? Will the American falcon, "turning and turning in the widening gyre," be able to hear the falconer? The overwhelming evidence of history would suggest that if such a day were to come, there would be only one possible outcome for the republic when "mere anarchy is loosed upon the world."

Richard Niebuhr captured the gravity of the earlier American view of covenant, and in a way that makes contemporary citizenship appear lightweight and casual by contrast.

> Covenant was the binding together in one body politic of persons who assumed through unlimited promise responsibility to and for each other, and for the common laws, under God. It was government of the people, for the people, by the people, but always under God, and it was not natural birth into natural society that made one a complete member of the people, but always the moral act of taking upon oneself, through promise, the responsibility of a citizenship that bound itself in the very act of exercising its freedom. For in the covenant conception the essence of freedom does not lie in the liberty of choice among goods, but in the ability to commit oneself for the future to a cause and in the terrible liberty of being able to become a breaker of the promise, a traitor to the cause.[60]

Will it be said that freedom was too hard a challenge for Americans to overcome? Here, then, is the first question on the checklist that Americans must answer constructively: Do you remember where your freedom came from?

Does the difference between republicanism and democracy still matter? What is the significance of the clash between supporters of the original constitution and supporters of an ever-changing living constitution? What is the state of the ethics of responsibility today? And if the notion of covenant is in the DNA of America, what happens if it is abandoned, deliberately or unwittingly? The challenge for Americans today, while they are still powerful and prosperous, is to remember the long road to freedom they have traveled, and to pay attention to its lessons while there is time for renewal.

ARE THERE ENOUGH
AMERICANS WHO
CARE ABOUT FREEDOM?

*T*hings are so bad in America that the only solution is to burn the whole system down, and start all over again." That radical-sounding statement came from a student at Cal Berkeley, but a young woman who in fact was far from radical or revolutionary, and quite different from the stereotype of the Berkeley student. Did she know she was echoing Saul Alinsky's words, "Burn the system down!" from the opening page of his *Rules for Radicals*?[1] Most probably it was her own student summary of the multiple crises in America today, and she said it with a tone of weary cynicism. All the political answers she had been taught had been weighed and found wanting. Each one was forlorn or a sham, and none of the ideals that she and her friends had grown up with could be counted on to do better.

Her generation, some of her fellow students argued, knows it has nothing constructive to offer and feels it is all the wiser for not having to pretend otherwise. All the grand political visions from Plato to Machiavelli to Madison to Marx had argued their case to the world and had been riddled with bullet-hole objections in their turn, so there was no point in presenting yet another vision to be instantly struck down. No belief can hope to carry the day. Beliefs are simply fated to be piñatas for scholars and radicals to smash, and the faster each one falls to the ground the better. The safer course is to realize that you cannot defeat the system with any belief that can hope to carry the day, so to join in the fun and treat all ideas with irony and detachment and watch to see their fate exposed in their turn. How else can anyone maintain their sanity in a world gone mad? Idealists are foolish to expose their hearts. Realists are wise to shield themselves. Cynicism and jaded irony are the ultimate shield against vulnerability. The canny way is to play life like a game of poker and cover your cards with a wink, a quip, or a put-down.

I have encountered several varieties of such cynicism among young Americans. Sadly, they tend to prize their suspicion as the fruit of their hard-won wisdom, when in fact they are merely captives to the spirit of their age, for postmodern thinking and advertising reinforce their suspicion and cynicism at every turn. The post-truth world was hailed by Nietzsche in the 1880s, championed by Michel Foucault in the 1960s and 1970s, and trumpeted by *The Economist* in 2016, as if its first pioneer and worst villain was Donald Trump. Needless to say, the post-truth problem is far older and goes far wider than any current controversies, and Americans have yet to address some of the worst damage it has caused—including the widespread American proneness to what Rabbi Heschel warned of as "the escape to suspicion."[2]

The problem of power is only the most obvious of the problems of post-truth thinking. Thanks to Nietzsche and to later depth psychology, post-truth thinking breeds suspicion and cynicism because it calls into question all motivation. Neither truth nor goodness nor any other ideal are ever pursued wholeheartedly and for their own sake alone. Humans always have mixed motives. We do things for ourselves and for our own self-interest.

That point is clearly part of the Bible's realism too, but without the principles that accompany it in the Bible, it causes irreparable damage. The result, Heschel notes, is that "suspicion is the shortest way to the understanding of human nature. This it seems is the modern version of the Golden Rule: *Suspect thy neighbor as thyself.*"[3] Suspicion breeds suspicion, just as conspiracy theories breed conspiracy theories. Foster them both in the incubator of the social media, and it sets off a massive chain reaction and destroys the honesty and trust that are essential to freedom.

Such post-truth suspicion hits America particularly hard because the American republic is expressly a nation "by intention and by ideas." Suspicion by default poisons all integrity and compromises all idealism. No one, it argues, is ever simply and straightforwardly honest, patriotic, and a lover of freedom. Advanced education delivers us from such naivety. Everyone has their price, and for everything there is always another reason. We know too much now to be fooled, and only a simpleton or a child can still believe innocently in nursery tales about "the land of the free." Rabbi Heschel continues:

The hysteria of suspicion holds many of us in its spell. It has not only affected our understanding of others but also made us unreliable to ourselves, making it impossible to trust either our aspirations or convictions.

The self-suspicious man shrinks from the light. He is often afraid to think as he feels, afraid to admit what he believes, afraid to love what he admires. Going astray he blames others for his failure and becomes more evasive, smooth-tongued and deceitful. Living in fear, he thinks that ambush is the normal dwelling-place of all men.[4]

More than half a century after Heschel wrote those words, American public life has degenerated even further, led by ambush journalism, feet-of-clay tabloids, and the weaponizing of suspicion through psychiatry. Most appallingly of all, in post-truth America, power allied with suspicion has led to the politicizing of psychiatry or the psychiatrizing of politics. Groundless accusations of mental instability and senility were once the diabolical tools of repression wielded by Soviet and Chinese tyrants. Now they are the shameless, run-of-the-mill accusations of American liberals and journalists who do not realize what they are doing.

Fortunately, there is still a world of difference between such post-truth powermongering and the attitude of the radicals who would truly like to burn America down. The latter are a Taliban-like attempt to sandblast history and remove all traces of America's original sin of racism and its impurities. As I write, the immediate targets of the extreme Left are Confederate statues and memorials, but some of America's new Jacobins are baying for more aristocratic blood. Thomas Jefferson and George Washington are among those currently in their sights, and among non-Americans whose statues have been already vandalized are Father Serra, founder of the Californian missions; Christopher Columbus; and even the French heroine Joan of Arc. To be consistent, of course, they should blacklist the Democratic Party itself, for its role in the defense of slavery, and even in the rise of the Ku Klux Klan, is undeniable. But then, if anyone and anything at all is to be left standing, there must be a better way to deal with the crooked timber of humanity and the sins and evils of the past.

Fortunately again, however, both of these "burn America down" attitudes are a long way from the majority of Americans. But the many current crises show that American shame and negativity have gone far deeper than many suspected, and they have swept up some surprising recruits at a surprisingly high level. Robert E. Lee fought for Virginia rather than for slavery, but it was a Virginia senator who called for Lee's statue to be removed from the US Capitol and replaced by that of Pocahontas. Clearly, mainstream America has been pushed onto its back foot, and many of its responses are confused and uncertain as it waits for a Lincoln-like champion to stand up for its best while acknowledging and remedying its worst. But together, all such responses raise the second question on the checklist: *Do enough Americans care enough about freedom to think through its significance in the present turbulent crisis?* From a visitor's perspective, it is increasingly hard to be sanguine, but the question must be raised because it is the citizens' response that counts.

Open-Endedness Is Inescapable

Doubtless many Americans would simply prefer to keep their heads down, avoid all controversial questions, and hope that they and the country will survive the storm. Others, maybe, are raising and (without realizing it) answering the question: Are the arduous requirements of responsible freedom worth the price? Without realizing it, they are all opting for happiness rather than freedom as they try to lessen the demands of freedom and avoid (a.k.a. "appease") the ugliness of the extremes of those already rejecting it. But there is a simple reason why no type of denial will work. Freedom is inescapably central to America, and so long as freedom lasts, the struggle for freedom and the adventuring on behalf of freedom are unending. Like the future, freedom is open-ended and conditional, and its challenge is posed freshly every day to every generation and with ever-new questions raised. The "errand into the wilderness" does not stop, even if the terrain of the wilderness changes. The "frontier spirit" cannot rest, though today's frontiers are quite different from those facing the pioneers. Open-endedness and conditionality are a constant challenge for freedom, and no generation can claim immunity.

This means that there are always two moments of special danger for freedom. The first is when any generation is tempted to think it unfair that their ancestors committed them to the arduous task of sustaining freedom. Why should they bear the price? Aren't they entitled to enjoy the fruits? The second and obvious danger is when freedom grows complacent, when a free people settle down and are tempted to believe that freedom has arrived and is now assured. Their victories and their monuments in stone are the proof of their lasting success. When this happens, a free people shifts mentally from the challenge of open-endedness to the presumption of certainty and lulls itself to sleep with the assurance that they know why their success is guaranteed and permanent.

That happened to ancient Israel, Michael Walzer observed, when the "conditionality," the "if-then mutualism," or the "if" and "if not, not" of the original Sinai covenant was transformed into the surefire guarantee that God was behind King David's royal house, regardless of how the Israelites behaved.[5] The most common way Americans make an equivalent shift is through a false reliance on "American exceptionalism," as if that claim were a guarantee from history that America is decisively and permanently different from other nations, and its freedom would last forever.

Open-endedness means there is no ducking the questions that Americans must continue to face. The American story is neither a fairy tale (the American revolutionaries defeated their colonial oppressors and lived happily ever after) nor does it have to be a classical Greek tragedy (in its soaring triumph, the United States inevitably came to suffer from hubris and brought on its own nemesis). Open-endedness is intrinsic to freedom, and America's freedom has to be shouldered constantly in two senses: America has a foundational commitment to both the "American project" and the "American experiment."

In the case of the American project, the challenge to freedom stems from the fact that America is a nation by intention and by ideas, and freedom is America's central idea. The project therefore poses its question directly to American citizens and addresses their ongoing will and ability to create and sustain a free society. Freedom is a project because it is never a given but an ongoing task, so the question posed by the American project today is, Are you up to the task in your time, and are you still committed to the mission? No other nation can answer that question for America, and each generation of Americans must shoulder their responsibility for the task in their turn.

In the case of the American experiment, the question posed is slightly different and raised before a far larger gallery of spectators in light of the grand record of history. America has made grand claims about freedom to the world, both at its founding and throughout its story. It must therefore answer for those claims and do so honestly. Is the great American experiment in freedom thriving, and on what grounds does it still hope to succeed when all previous experiments in freedom have so far failed?

Either way, the truth stands. American freedom is open-ended by definition, and its challenge is unending. This open-endedness will continue for as long as the project and the experiment thrive, and it will end only by their failing. Freedom can succeed by triumphing over one enemy after another, expanding into one area after another, or including one new oppressed minority or group after another. Each advance would signal a genuine triumph, but America can never pronounce that freedom has succeeded once and for all, only that it has thrived *so far*. There can be no announcement of "Mission Accomplished" on the deck of any warship. It was George Washington himself who called America "the great experiment," but the awareness of the open-endedness goes back far earlier than the founders—to the New England Puritans and their "errand into the wilderness," and behind them to the Jewish Torah and Israel's exodus from Egypt and journey to the Promised Land. Seeing themselves as living before God and bound in their different ways by their freely chosen covenants, both the Jews and the Puritans understood the ongoing responsibility of freedom and the significance of the choices they were making. Freedom was an ongoing task and a continuing mission.

Separated by many centuries, the Jews and the Puritans in their turn each believed that they were created by a free God and called and covenanted to be a free people, so they were capable of choice and were responsible to choose between right and wrong, truth and falsehood, justice and injustice, and responsibility and irresponsibility. And because their choices were open-ended, they could always choose to bring down on themselves a curse as easily as a blessing, and disaster as well as success. In the Torah, this was the choice Moses presented to his people in his last great speech before his death. "I call heaven and earth to witness against you today, that I have set before you life and death, the blessing and the curse. So choose life in order that you may live, your and your descendants" (Deut 30:19).

This solemn commitment to the covenant and its choice was originally enacted for the Jews between the lush and fertile Mount Ebal and the barren and desolate Mount Gerizim. One was the dramatic symbol of the blessing they could choose and the other the symbol of the curse they might bring on themselves. Would they live up to their calling and define themselves according to their national distinctiveness and thrive? Or would they follow the natural course of the nations around them, many of them far greater and more glorious, and decline and die? The choice was theirs and the choice was consequential. So also is America's choice today.

We talk today of *cutting* a deal, but the term comes from "cutting a covenant." Those who bound themselves through the covenant passed between the two halves of sacrificial animals laid on the ground. That act symbolized how the cutting in two of things normally united spoke of the binding together of parties previously divided. It also symbolized what the parties solemnly chose to be their own fate if they violated the agreement. They understood that the covenant was conditional, consequential, and costly. Centuries later, John Winthrop spelled out the same elemental terms, the same basic alternatives, and the same essential responsibility of freedom as he preached on the rolling deck of the *Arbella* in the Atlantic in 1630. He and his Puritan colleagues, he reminded them, were free to obey the terms of their new covenant with God and each other and so be "a City upon a Hill," or to break their covenant and become "a story and a byword through the world."[6]

The current parties to the American covenant have multiplied by many millions, but the same conditions, the same open-endedness of the project, and the same challenge of the experiment confront Americans today as they did the Jews and the Puritans earlier. Choose freedom and live in the light of all that freedom requires, and Americans and their freedom can hope to thrive and endure—potentially, forever. But live another way, neglecting what freedom means and what freedom requires, and Americans and their freedom will decline as surely as the sun sets in the sky and nations decline and fall in time.

In sum, two truths confront Americans in every generation: The great experiment is conditional, and the citizens of the American republic are responsible. There can be no end to the open-endedness of the challenge of American freedom, short of its breakdown. Each generation of Americans must therefore bear their responsibility for freedom in their own time, though none can know how the experiment will end after them. Needless to say, the conditionality is easier of the two because it only needs to be remembered, whereas the responsibility has to be shouldered. Responsibility, or the lack of it, is the fly in the ointment today. Modern America, driven by consumerism, entertainment, and an ever-expanding state, is a society for the servicing of needs of every sort. Rights and rights talk therefore far outweigh responsibility, yet rights without responsibilities are simply politicized self-interests, and they sound the death knell of republican freedom.

We certainly know how other experiments have ended. All history is our teacher—for example, about the failed Athenian experiment in democracy. But in America's case we simply do not, and cannot, know what will happen until it happens. Hence the wisdom and force of the long-running maxim "Eternal vigilance is the price of freedom." Hence the importance of diagnosing the state of the union with relentless honesty. And hence the need to work to renew the covenant of freedom when it has broken down or shows clear signs of disrepair.

No one knows the outcome for America. I make no predictions, though in calling for a decisive choice and for a renewal of freedom, this book is an expression of hope and not a jeremiad. It is written with the same conviction that Winston Churchill expressed in his famous Iron Curtain speech in 1946, after World War II. There had never been a war in all history that was easier to prevent without the firing of a single shot if people had only listened. In the same way, no national decline would be easier to prevent than the decline of the American republic today—if only American leaders and citizens were to pay attention to the wisdom of the ages regarding the character of freedom and what lasting freedom requires.

Will Americans pay attention to the wisdom of history? Statues may be toppled and memorials defaced, but can the enduring problems of the human heart and society be sandblasted so easily? In the hysteria of the present crisis, no one should hold their breath. What is beyond question is that history's longest-running experiment in freedom and the world's most public freedom tutorial have both reached a critical stage today. Unless this crisis is addressed resolutely, the American republic will be facing a major time of trial to match such previous times of trial as the Civil War, the Depression, World War II, and the Cold War. That is what I mean when I echo Tom Paine and say that these are the times that try men's souls and that America's genius for freedom is becoming America's Achilles' heel.

Still Torchbearers for the World?

Freedom talk is cheap in America today. It often has the tones of complacency, self-congratulation, and (with marketers marketing and politicians running for office) self-promotion. This is not unexpected in an age drunk with its own heady cocktail of individualism, libertarianism, consumerism, and narcissism, when "It's all about us" and "I, my selfie, and me." Today, Sherry Turkle writes, we are all "personal brand managers," and many are suffering from "presentation anxiety."[7] It was not always so. The founders' generation was braced by their awareness that when they picked up the torch of freedom, it was not just for themselves but in the light of history and on behalf of humanity. The delegates to the Constitutional Convention, James Madison declared, were "digesting a plan which in its operation wd. decide forever the fate of Republican Govt."[8] If the convention were to fail, Benjamin Franklin declared, "mankind may hereafter from this unfortunate instance, despair of establishing Governments by Human Wisdom and leave it to chance, war and conquest."[9]

Later, following the success of the convention, Washington set out America's titanic challenge with an equal sense of moment in his first inaugural address—"the sacred fire of liberty and the destiny of the republican model of government" were staked on "the experiment entrusted to the hands of the American people."[10] Walt Whitman stated the same conviction in the nineteenth century: "America is really the great test or trial case for all the problems and promises and speculations of humanity and of the past and the present."[11]

The word *intentional* is overused today, as if life were ours for each of us to control and steer with ease. Yet it is true that, unlike almost all other countries at the time of the Revolution, the United States was a nation by intention and by ideas. It was a "designer nation," "the first new nation," at least in the modern world, for the same was true earlier of the Jewish people as they were forged and constituted by their covenant at Mount Sinai. America was nothing less than a freedom project and a liberty movement— which meant two things: First, America was founded by certain people at a certain time, with certain ideas and a certain purpose. And second, freedom was not seen as a given but as an accomplishment that needed to be sustained with resolution and courage.

It was this awareness that set America off from most other nations at the time. With the distinguished exception of John Jay, who was a French Huguenot, most of the founders were British, and most of them were English. But England itself was anything but a nation by intention and ideas. Philosopher

Roger Scruton captured the difference succinctly. "England was not a nation or a creed or a language or a state but a home. Things at home don't need an explanation. They are there because they are there."[12] Or as G. K. Chesterton remarked, "We admire things with reasons, but love them without reasons."[13]

America's revolutionary character comes with its own considerable cost. Since America is a nation by intention and by ideas, it will always rise and fall, flourish or falter, according to the strength of those ideas and according to the way it sustains and improves them, or fails to sustain and improve that founding and those beginnings. The United States is different from most families, tribes, and nations on the earth, whose origins recede into the impenetrable mists of time and are defined only by such factors as language and geography. Like the Jewish people, America is a nation created at a specific moment in history and in the full light of day, and expressly shaped by certain specific ideals and ideas, and not others. It therefore has a mission and a task, and so long as freedom remains central to this purpose, American freedom requires freedom's schools as much as freedom's armies.

In the famous words of Alexander Hamilton's first essay in *The Federalist Papers*,

> It has been frequently remarked that it seems to have been reserved for the people of this country, by their conduct and example, to decide the important question, whether societies of men are really capable or not of establishing good government from reflection and choice, or whether they are forever destined to depend for their political constitutions on accident or force.[14]

Historians have observed that in the two decades prior to the Constitutional Convention, "American political discourse was an ongoing public forum on the meaning of liberty."[15] Would that the same compliment could be paid to the rising generation of today's young Americans, so that they might repeat that achievement in our time. For what is needed today is a rousing national debate about freedom and its requirements, which might lead in to a national reaffirmation and restoration of American freedom, and even to the rejuvenation of freedom for the wider world. No less than that is at stake in our day.

Natural forces such as gravity will always operate in the universe, whether we believe in them or not, and we cannot defy them for long. But a created political order like the American republic is different. It depends on a constant and determined effort to maintain the beliefs that made it what it is, and therefore on constant storytelling from generation to generation. If the day ever comes when the American people cease to tell the stories or divest those beliefs, or the beliefs themselves lose their compelling power, the republic will be in trouble, and sooner or later it will experience inevitable decline and collapse. America's freedom project would have failed, its great experiment in freedom would be over, and its mission and task would have been aborted. And with that failure would come a wider eclipse of freedom in the world and a return to the age-old human politics of power and the twin scourges of tyranny and war.

Will it be said that freedom was too hard a challenge for Americans to overcome? This, then, is the second question on the checklist that Americans must answer constructively: *Do enough Americans care enough about freedom to take stock of where America is today, to think through the significance of freedom in the present crisis, and to debate the choices with the gravity and civility that such grand stakes require?*

For a long time, Americans and others have argued that the American way of constitutional governance is the answer to the supposed inadequacy of more traditional nations in responding to the conditions of modernity. The modern world's "first new nation" was ideally placed to answer the challenges of modernity, it was held. In contrast, societies linked by organic ties, such as African tribes, and nations built on hierarchical power, such as the Chinese, were considered less viable in the open and fluid conditions of advanced modernity. But this claim assumed that America's constitutional way of governance has navigated the rapids of advanced modernity with assured success. America's present problems show that is not so. Thus, unless the United States renews its way of governance, surmounts the present crisis of freedom, and once again shoulders its historic mission on behalf of freedom, the world could be facing an unwelcome fact: Advanced modernity has put severe strains on all the major forms of human governance, including the American, so that stable and lasting freedom for all the world's peoples is as far away as ever.

QUESTION THREE

WHAT DO YOU
MEAN *by* FREEDOM?

A rose is a rose is a rose," Gertrude Stein said famously. In other words, some things are what they are, self-evidently so, and easily described. But that is not true of everything. We cannot simply say that "freedom is freedom is freedom" and hope to capture what freedom is. In America today, as throughout history, there are profound disagreements over what freedom is and how it is to be won. Like the road to hell, many a road to serfdom is paved with good intentions. They are shining shortcuts thought to be easy steps to liberty until they aren't.

There is a subtlety and complexity to freedom. If we are not to be seduced by its slogans, stay content with clichés, or be deceived by propaganda, we must explore its riddles. Only experience and history will demonstrate which view of freedom is realistic and genuinely delivers. Freedom talk is not enough, and freedom protests may lead in the wrong direction. We live in an entitlement society, but no one can claim a right to be free without effort or responsibility. Freedom needs to be won, worked at, and sustained, and for that to happen, it needs to be understood. We always need to ask questions of freedom, to see whether it has become ungrounded or whether it has been subtly distorted so that it is leading to slavery, not freedom. Question Three therefore raises a foundational question: *What do Americans now mean by freedom?*

The essence of human freedom can be stated simply: *Freedom is the capacity to exercise the will without interference or restraint as the genuine expression of who you are.* Or more simply, *freedom is the ability to decide what you want to choose and do what you want to do.* Or more simply still, *freedom is the absence of coercion.* Lord Acton, the great historian of freedom, defined freedom as "the assurance that every man shall be protected in doing what he believes is his duty against the influence of authority and majorities, custom and opinion."[1] Friedrich Hayek, the British-Austrian economist, wrote similarly that freedom describes "the absence of a particular obstacle— coercion by other men."[2] Rabbi Jonathan Sacks defines freedom as "the ability to choose between alternatives and to act in accordance with one's choices."[3]

"Self-determination," "the power to do the duty that you yourself determine," "acting in accordance with one's choices," "the absence of coercion." Such definitions sound straightforward. And at least they help to identify certain foundational assumptions that underlie freedom. Most people, though not all, can agree on them. But in fact they raise a host of questions that we will need to explore.

First, freedom is a matter of the human will. Free people, we say, are those who act "of their own volition." They "vouch for themselves" in their choices and determine what they will say and do with no coercion, external manipulation, or undue outside influence to sway what they choose. Needless to say, this assertion of freedom stands squarely against all ancient and modern forms of determinism, whether we humans are said to be determined by the stars, as the Babylonians calculated; by fate, as the Greeks held; by social and economic forces, as Karl Marx believed; by psychological forces, as Sigmund Freud claimed; by our instincts and our genes, as many philosophers and scientists now say; or by algorithms, as many futurists now claim. At some later point we must also answer how we can justify the claim that genuine freedom exists, because there are major thinkers today, such as the new atheists, who deny that human freedom is real, and there are others who have given up on the task of justifying it. But for the moment it is enough to state that the human will is essential to freedom. If the will is not decisively free, regardless of the influences that may bear on it, it makes no sense to talk of human freedom and free societies. Human freedom requires some genuine freedom of the will.

Second, freedom entails the idea of commitment making and keeping a promise. The free person acts into time, and therefore into the future, and thus into history. When any of us makes a simple statement such as "I'll be there," or "See you tomorrow," we are not only expressing our will and stating an intention, but making a promise to the future. If we then go on to keep the promise, and we say or do whatever we have said we would say or do, we have kept the promise to ourselves and to the future. In that sense we have been predictable and proved trustworthy. Such promise making not only expresses the free person's freedom but establishes a chosen obligation and helps to build social order. By acting true to our stated intentions, we live true to ourselves, fulfill our obligations, become predictable to others, and therefore prove trustworthy. Our behavior is not random, but in line with what we determined and what we said. It is predictable, in the sense that other people can calculate the outcome from our stated intentions. They can count on what we said.

Just so, trust in any society is built as free people make promises and keep their promises—whether in small and insignificant actions or in all-important commitments, such as marriage and public office. That is a key part of the trust that comprises social capital and makes a good society. Through our words, we make and keep promises to each other. And through making and keeping promises to each other, we build the trust that acts like a social glue and makes our communities peaceful, orderly, and gracious. Or conversely, we don't keep our promises or are taught that promises don't matter—and trust breaks down. Promise keeping is therefore vital because suspicion, rumors, deceptions ("fake news"), and behavior such as promiscuousness all undermine trust. And when trust is betrayed, it removes the insulation against feelings of insecurity and injustice, which in turn leads to grievance, anger, and social conflict.

Writing as an atheist, Friedrich Nietzsche underscored the point that human freedom is a matter of promise making. In his essay *On the Genealogy of Morals* in 1887, he argues that the "free man" or the "sovereign man" is the person with an enduring and indestructible will who is entitled to make promises because he has the power to keep them. At the heart of nature itself is the task of "breeding of an animal which is *entitled to make promises.*" Such a promise is "an ongoing willing of what was once willed."[4] He quickly added that this task is "paradoxical," because humans make promises, but do not go on to keep them. Instead, they are prone to deliberate, intentional, and "active forgetfulness," by which they can excuse their failure to be true to their word.[5]

This human inability to keep promises and be true to our word is the chronic problem that dogs the politics of freedom as well as the course of love, marriage, relationships, and free societies in general, including

America. The highest form of promise making is a covenant, and even covenants are routinely broken. But the central point stands and becomes clearer still: Freedom entails promise making and promise keeping as the key to good and lasting human relationships and healthy societies. When we say that trust has broken down in America, we are saying that Americans at many levels are no longer keeping the promises that they make as free people. Post-truth America has become a land strewn with broken and betrayed promises. Indeed, post-truth Americans, from their leaders down, are becoming the personification of the unbound and unaccountable. Increasingly, there are no binding ties, only egos, interests, and hookups, and along with trust, freedom is the loser.

Third, freedom includes the notion of human responsibility. Freedom means deciding between choices and acting on our choices. Each choice could have been otherwise if we had not chosen as we did. Freedom therefore means shouldering responsibility for the choices we have made. No child, slave, or robot is free in this way. Citizenship is an adult task. A free people who will to choose freely are answerable for themselves, for their actions, and for the consequences of their actions. Indeed, the person who makes a promise becomes a debtor in relationship to other people, and those to whom the promise is made become the creditor. Only when the promise is kept is the debt discharged. Responsibility therefore means ensuring fulfillment, and through such responsibility trust is maintained and social capital built.

The responsibility that is at the heart of freedom has two companion responsibilities that are also crucial: the self-restraint that in exercising its own freedom respects the equal freedom of others, and the self-governance that in living rightly makes external compulsion unnecessary. In Lord Moulton's magnificent description, responsible freedom is "obedience to the unenforceable." Naturally, such responsible freedom does not come easily, and to be realistic the self-restraint freedom requires usually restrains only those who choose to be conscientious and desire to be free. And even then it requires effort, practice, and discipline: Nietzsche's "long obedience in the same direction" and Tocqueville's "habits of the heart."

Such freedom is challenging and always consequential. It is a matter of gritty realism rather than idealism. Freedom does not mean that because we are free, we can elect to be responsible if we choose to be—as if responsibility were a higher level add-on for the virtuous. Responsibility, rather, is the soul of freedom. Freedom means that precisely because we are free *we are responsible whether we like it or not.* Conversely, we would cease to be free if we were not responsible. When we exercise our will to make our own choices and make our promises to the future, we are responsible for the consequences that follow. Some will be intended and some unintended, but freedom means that free people shoulder that responsibility as part and parcel of what it means to be free. Their word is their bond until they have fulfilled what they said.

In an age obsessed with entitlement and rights, the responsibility and duties at the heart of freedom often gets selective attention. Take the difference in attitudes toward responsibility in smoking or sex. The former touches on the issue of responsibility for death, and the latter on responsibility for life. With smoking, responsibility has now been widened to cover "thirdhand smoking"—the residual tobacco smoke that remains after a cigarette has been extinguished and the smoker has gone, a cocktail of toxins that can be as deadly as the original smoke itself. But with sex, it is held that initial "consent" is all that matters, and there is no further responsibility. Consensual sex is considered consequence free, so that, in contrast to smoking, all "third-party outcomes" are irrelevant—whether a sexually transmitted disease, an abortion, an unwanted child, a fatherless family, a family condemned to poverty, a young person with a future crisis of identity, or a community saddled with a social crisis. As I write, a star athlete is known for having more than a dozen children by nearly as many women. Does such behavior demonstrate America's enhanced degree of liberty and virility, or does it represent America's serious deficit in personal and social responsibility for life?

In sum, freedom and responsibility are inseparable and at the heart of growing into adult life and citizenship. Thus, where there is no desire to lead a responsible life, as with an endlessly delayed adolescence, or where there is no ability to do so, as with an excessive external control, there is no freedom. Free societies are responsible societies with citizens who are ready, willing, and able to assume personal responsibility. True freedom means that free people make choices, consequential choices, and whatever the unforeseen consequences or unexpected aftermaths, there is no shrugging off the fact that they acted freely and are responsible for the outcomes.

Fourth, freedom is a matter of power. In that sense it can be said that freedom empowers, just as power frees. If power is defined as the capacity to exert the will *despite resistance*, then power is essential to freedom. When people forget the place of power in freedom, they obscure the fact that many of the problems and pitfalls surrounding freedom grow from the confusion of freedom with power. But when power itself is mistaken for freedom, as if freedom were no more than power, as in postmodern philosophies that are the heirs of 1789, the result can be deadly. Freedom assumes and requires power, but to become free and to stay free requires much more than power.

That is where the poisonous seeds of Nietzsche's view of freedom lie. He insists that our human "instinct of freedom" is nothing more than the "will to power." "Why stroke the hypersensitive ears of our modern weaklings?"[6] Alinsky concurs with Nietzsche, "Power is the right word."[7] In their view, freedom and power are one. But as we watch the endgame unfold, one thing will become ever clearer: freedom that is only power will always be corrupted, for power not only oppresses the weak, it corrupts the powerful themselves. Power without principle is a toxic corrosive. Unprincipled power inequalities, whether they play out in harassment issues, financial manipulation, or political corruption, are always lethal for freedom.

Today's talk of a post-truth world should sound an alarm, for it is a world of power alone. A post-truth American republic will prove to be a contradiction in terms. It cannot long endure, for a free society without truth is a society that is literally out of its mind. Post-truth thinking and speaking destroy human freedom, article by article, press release by press release, op-ed piece by op-ed piece, attacking it sentence by sentence and tearing the meaning out of the words themselves. Deprived of truth, the American faculty for freedom will be bred out of the American character. Full-blown, the post-truth world creates the conditions for what Augustine of Hippo called the "lust to dominate," which itself becomes "dominated by its passion for domination." Poisoned in this way, post-truth "freedom" will always end in bullying and bondage, enslaving others and in the process enslaving itself and hastening its own self-destruction.[8] No one should be deceived by the silken rhetoric that conceals the iron fist. Saul Alinsky praised Lenin for his pragmatism: "He said that the Bolsheviks stood for getting power through the ballot, but would reconsider after they got the guns!"[9]

Genuine liberal debate is a win-win proposition that relies on truth and not simply power. It is a quintessential expression of true liberalism. Freedom-loving liberal argument respects the dignity of the opponent, strives for truth as the outcome, and relies always on rational persuasion, not coercion. When a true liberal debater honors these principles, and then prevails in argument and establishes the truth, everyone is a winner. Even a person shown that they were wrong now knows what is right and has been led to understand it with respect. In that sense, they are freer too, even if defeated in argument.

Post-truth discourse, in contrast, is a lose-lose proposition because its sole consideration is power. With its insults, abuse, venomous ad hominem attacks, its refusal to compromise, and its fight to the death for victory at all costs, post-truth argument is not about truth at all. It is about power and winning, and as such it comes from the same post-truth stable and has the same goal as fake news. Even when power-based arguments win, their victories are pyrrhic because everyone loses. The attackers may degrade their opponents, but in the process they degrade themselves and diminish the republic and the cause of true liberalism. Nothing could be closer to the logic of 1789 and its notions of power, and nothing further from the "better angels" of the freedom of 1776 and its roots in the dignity of the person, the priority of truth, and the importance of persuasion.

Fifth, freedom is not only a matter of choice but of having genuine options from which to choose. The highwayman's classic cry, "Your money or your life!" represents a definite choice, stark though it is. But it is not exactly the choice that freedom-loving travelers would like to choose from—above all they desire to keep both their money *and* their lives. The advance of radical Islamism at the point of the sword is similar ("Submission to Allah or death!"). Not far off are the dictatorial demands of the new "antidiscrimination" regulators ("Endorse the sexual revolution's values or lose your livelihood!"—violations of conscience that a judge in New Mexico appallingly described as "the price of citizenship").[10] The choices offered by a consumer society are similarly deceptive. They may appear to be freedom's cornucopia of plenty. But when all that consumerism offers us is too much to live with and too little to live for, it actually steals from us the choice of a good life that is anything more than a life with goods.

On the other hand, there are phantom freedoms dangled before our eyes that are deceptive because they are neither realistic nor feasible. As with the judgment of Tantalus, their promised delights are always just beyond reach. Various offers of freedom today defy reality. For the announcement has gone out that through the advances of science, technology, marketing, politics, and surgery, we are assured that infinite openness, boundless opportunity, and innovation without end are now possible for all, especially for the wealthy and the famous for whom such products are the perks of their purchasing power. "So be whoever and whatever you wish to be." Everything, including your identity, can now be self-chosen, subjective and shifting according to your age, the size of your wallet, and your preferences—and here to help you are the goods, the life experiences, and the identity fashion kits to make your dreams possible.

The plain truth is that freedom is always limited by reality, but properly understood, that limitation is in fact what supports freedom and separates it from chaos. As the French philosopher Helvetius commented, "It is not lack of freedom not to fly like an eagle or to swim like a whale." Humans are not eagles or whales, so the path to freedom requires an understanding of reality and truth. Freedom requires a designed end and purpose (or telos), freedom requires a framework, and freedom requires a way of life that fits genuine human freedom. Without these essentials, the lure of phantom freedom will turn out to be a mirage and a prelude to disaster, as Icarus discovered.

Sixth, freedom itself is not an end but a means to a goal. To achieve freedom may be a passionate goal, as when a prisoner plans to escape his bars, an alcoholic works to recover from his addiction, or a nation conspires to throw off an oppressor. But the freedom won is still only a means to an end. As we shall see, *freedom from* has to lead to *freedom for.* As such, *freedom from* provides the power that can be directed toward some goal other than freedom itself. The released prisoner, the recovered alcoholic, and the newly liberated people are now free to use their new freedom on behalf of any goals in life they desire. But freedom is only the means, and each individual and each nation must answer for themselves as to what they are using freedom for, and whether they are using it well.

Seventh, freedom has a social and collective dimension. It is not purely individual. Any community or country requires at least three essentials if it is to achieve freedom for everyone, not just the few. It requires foundations, in the sense of the philosophical and ethical underpinnings that can ground freedom as genuine and secure. Only solid foundations can help freedom avoid the charge that freedom is really a fiction and that the human will is in fact subject to fate or determining forces. Next, freedom requires personal self-restraint, in the sense that unrestrained individual freedom tends to undermine itself by running to excess. And, last, freedom requires that individuals know how to respect the equal freedom of all others. Only if each individual respects the equal freedom of all the others can wider society become free, peaceful, orderly, and stable, and so reach the goal that the Jewish and Christian Scriptures call the well-being of shalom and the Enlightenment called "human flourishing."

Ponder Wisely, Choose Well

It is precisely because freedom is so human—and so desirable, so consequential, and so easily squandered—that we must always clarify what we mean by freedom. There will always be unintended and unforeseen consequences from even our best choices. We are human and we are finite, so we will never know exactly how our decisions will turn out. But for those foolish enough not to reflect on the meaning of freedom, the ratio of bad choices and consequences to good choices and consequences will demonstrate the measure of their folly.

Many people would agree with most of the seven points outlined previously. Postmodernists, however, see freedom very differently. They reject truth and equate freedom with power. But a far greater range of differences emerge when we raise some of the basic questions surrounding freedom and what we mean by freedom in practice. Consider some of the most common confusions surrounding freedom. Everyone who loves freedom must be clear where they stand on such issues, and they must be realistic about the consequences that are foreseeable.

The point is not that if we think about freedom, we will all end in agreement. We won't—however noble and well intentioned we may be. Nor is the point that if we think clearly, we will come to a common mind. It is rather that we all need to make our decisions about freedom in light of where those different choices are likely to lead—and likely to lead us not just as individuals but as families, as communities, as societies, as nations, and now even as we lead our world and decide our human future. Living with our deepest differences means that we must acknowledge and negotiate different ways of seeing freedom.

This book sets out ten major questions to consider in exploring freedom. The list is not exhaustive, and not all the questions are of equal importance. But they demonstrate what needs to be thought through if Americans are to attain a realistic view of freedom, and to know what choices they must make today and what responsibilities they must shoulder if freedom is to flourish. Some of the issues can be expressed briefly, and some will take longer, just as some answers will be simple, some more complicated, and some highly controversial. In almost all cases the differences between 1776 and 1789 will become significant and consequential.

Readers of some of my earlier books, such as *A Free People's Suicide* and *The Global Public Square*, will hear some themes and arguments repeated, but with a different thrust and new material. The first of those two books discussed the importance of sustainable freedom to the American experiment. But that issue is abstract for many Americans. This book goes deeper and raises the foundational question that is being raised by current controversies: What *is* freedom? And which of today's two rival views, 1776 or 1789, has the better answer to that question, and one that will allow the American republic to survive and flourish?

Our discussion will highlight the inadequacies of a purely linear argument, for freedom and the tasks of living a good life and creating a free society are best understood as America's living story rather than an abstract system of thought. Thinking through the choices surrounding American freedom today is rather like a game of chutes and ladders. Some choices represent ladders that lead to great leaps forward, others to setbacks and falls, but there is no standing still.

The difference, of course, is that the game depends on chance and the roll of the dice, which is the antithesis of freedom. America's great experiment, in contrast, depends on the human will or, rather, on more than three hundred million human wills and their combined choices and the combined consequences of all those choices in the present generation. Only so is the great experiment handed down from generation to generation for each generation of Americans to engage and to play their part in their turn.

National or Political Freedom?

In clarifying what we mean by *freedom*, Americans must first be clear as to whether they are speaking of *national* freedom or *political* freedom. National freedom refers to the capacity a nation has to exert its will in relation to other nations and to the rest of the world, whereas political freedom refers to the degree of freedom that citizens enjoy within the nation. The difference is important. In the fifth century BC, for example, the democratic citizens of Athens proudly considered themselves to be "the school of Hellas" and the paragons of political freedom. And by contrast with the rest of the world and with most humans who had gone before them, they were. Their freedom was remarkable, and they prized it in a manner that preceded the ideals of John Milton, John Stuart Mill, and nineteenth-century liberalism by more than two thousand years. In the famous words of Pericles's "Funeral Oration" at the outset of the Peloponnesian War,

> The freedom which we enjoy in our government extends also to our ordinary life. There, far from exercising a jealous surveillance over each other, we do not feel called up to be angry with our neighbor for doing what he likes, or even to indulge in those injurious looks which cannot fail to be offensive, even though they inflict no positive penalty.[11]

Live as you please and do what you like, so long as you do no harm to others. Few libertarians could say it better today. Liberal freedom was personal freedom.

Yet that was political freedom, and remarkable as it was for its time, it was limited and in that sense inconsistent. In sharp contrast to the Jewish covenant at Sinai that included everybody, even the unborn, Athenian democracy included the small percentage of free men who made up the Athenian Assembly. But it did not include the rest of the men, and it certainly did not include the women of Athens, the children, the foreign visitors, and the slaves, and it had nothing to do with the way Athens ran its international affairs. Athens did not behave abroad as it claimed to behave at home—as the tiny island of Melos discovered to its cost when it tried to stay neutral in the Peloponnesian War. Facing the Athenian ultimatum of slavery or death in 415 BC, the Melians appealed to Athenian honor and to their status as neutrals between Athens and Sparta. But they were brushed aside with brutal cynicism. Athens would not bother to justify its invasion by making specious claims that both sides knew were hollow. The blunt fact was that "you know as well as we do that the right, as the world goes, is only in question between equals in power, while the strong do what they can and the weak suffer what they must."[12]

Were the Athenians innovators in this brutal expression of unblushing realpolitik? Far from it.

> Of the gods we believe, and of men we know, that by a necessary law of their nature they rule wherever they can. And it is not as if we were the first to make this law, or to act upon it when made; we found it existing before us, and we shall leave it to exist forever after us; all we do is make use of it. Knowing that you and everybody else, having the same power as we have, would do the same as we do.[13]

But freedom for the Athenians went hand in hand with slaughter for the islanders when they stood in the way of the Athenian war machine. Empires and freedom sit together uncomfortably, and nowhere more than when the assertion of freedom becomes another name for the reckless exercise of power.

Like many earlier and later empires, such as the European empires or the de facto empire of superpower America, the very people who congratulate themselves on their freedom at home, and for fighting for freedom abroad, can easily become oppressors overseas or be perceived as such by their victims. The Portuguese, Spanish, Dutch, French, British, and other European nations need only think of their colonialism and its multiple stains. Americans must face not only such horrific incidents as My Lai in Vietnam and Abu Ghraib in Iraq, but the strategic folly, the historic aftermath, and the appalling death toll of the bungled invasion of Iraq and the meddling in Libya. When the well-intentioned goal of exporting democracy is based on military might and not on a realistic understanding of freedom, it becomes a sure road to disaster and a vulnerability to the charge of hypocrisy. Sadly, America no longer means freedom to much of the world. Such a lack of realism and consistency will always breed immense cultural and political problems, as today's Middle East illustrates clearly. But the same weakness commonly recurs in many views of freedom, when two things are lacking.

For a start, such an inconsistent view of freedom hurts others because it lacks the principle of reciprocity that genuine freedom requires if freedom is to walk hand in hand with justice. The Golden Rule applies to freedom. There is no claim to freedom for anyone anywhere that is not at once a claim to freedom for everyone everywhere. Such consistency is of course easier said than done. The hardest thing is to be free in such a way that one person's freedom does not restrict another person's freedom and vice versa—which is where the practical challenges start and things get complicated.

Winston Churchill, for example, was often criticized for his passionate and simultaneous defense of both liberty and empire, as if they were entirely contradictory. Yet part of his defense of empire was on behalf of liberty. He gave a stout defense of India's sixty million "untouchables," and could not stand the hypocrisy of the upper-caste Brahmins of his time. At one and the same time, he declared, they took part in elevated Oxbridge discussions of John Stuart Mill, the great philosopher of freedom, and then showed complete indifference to the suffering and even the existence of their fellow Indians, the Dalits, or "untouchables."

Churchill's inconsistency pales into insignificance beside the inconsistency of the American founders. They trumpeted freedom before the world and declared freedom for themselves, only to deny it to their slaves. It was the inconsistency of this very evil that grew into the rank hypocrisy that triggered the sixties' revulsion against 1776 and the swing to 1789. Consistency over freedom can be difficult, but debates about it should be candid, and both the charges and the responses should be humble. If Americans must never forget the fatal contradiction over slavery that betrayed the promise of the American founding, Christians must never forget the evils of the church's blatant denials of freedom down the centuries.

Such American and Christian hypocrisies have had a profound impact on history, and neither will be lived down easily. But there are many other examples of blind spots today. For example, why do many Muslims welcome the right to convert to Islam but justify killing a person for apostasy—in other words, deny someone the reversible and reciprocal right to convert *from* Islam? Or again, why do many advocates for the sexual revolution emphasize freedom of choice and demand full legal protection for those who freely choose an alternative lifestyle, but insist that counseling for those who freely choose to change from the alternative lifestyle should be made illegal? Or again, why did the determinedly liberal and anticolonial Obama administration forcibly impose its sexual agendas on cultures around the world in a manner that was experienced by many countries as a new "cultural colonialism"?

Such inconsistencies are impossible to miss, and they are unacceptable to anyone who cares for a consistent freedom that also serves justice for all.

Those who insist on their own freedom at the expense of the freedom of others may be powerful enough to press their demands regardless of the freedom of others, but they should be under no illusions: Their insistence is an abuse of the power that is implicit in their freedom. In overriding the freedom of others they are contradicting the genuine freedom they claim to promote. As George Orwell wrote, "When the white man turns tyrant, it is his own freedom that he destroys."[14]

The Parable of the Tribes

There is also a further problem. Inconsistent views of freedom not only oppress others, they eventually corrupt the free themselves. By ignoring the power factor in freedom, the powerful create a fatal blind spot that distorts and damages the possibility of achieving lasting freedom for themselves. By definition, power is essential to freedom, for without power freedom could not exert its will. But unbridled freedom, or freedom that is stripped down to power alone, is dangerous because it is no longer restrained by justice, mercy, and a consideration for others—in a word, by principle. Under the guise of freedom, such power may oppress the powerless, but the less obvious, though equally great danger is that such power will corrupt the powerful themselves—the chronic curse of empires, whether political, religious, or commercial, and the chronic curse of ideologies in the post-truth age when power is the only consideration.

Lord Acton's maxim is famous. "Power tends to corrupt; and absolute power corrupts absolutely. Great men are almost always bad men."[15] It was written in response to someone who had defended the Borgia popes as being above the judgment of other humans. The unrestrained power of the free is one of the greatest enemies of freedom. This stark truth forms half of one of the most precious truths offered by Jews to the world: "Freedom abused sours life, whereas suffering shared sweetens hardship."

Andrew Schmookler has captured the enduring dilemma of unprincipled power in his "parable of the tribes." What will happen if a group of tribes live close to each other, and all but one are committed to peaceful coexistence? One is willing to use force and violence to pursue its ends. There are only so many options for the peaceful tribes facing the violent tribe—destruction, submission, flight, or imitation—a peace-loving tribe takes to powermongering too to defend itself. The last option enables the peaceful tribe to survive, but at a price. It survives only by becoming more like the violent enemy it seeks to resist. Schmookler's lesson is one that should be branded indelibly on the hearts and minds of Americans now espousing a post-truth postmodernism that glories in realpolitik and power. "In every one of these outcomes the ways of power are spread throughout the system."[16]

The reason why this happens underscores Lord Acton's maxim perfectly. Schmookler argues it's because "power is like a contaminant, a disease, which once introduced will gradually but inexorably become universal in the system of competing societies."[17] To be sure, most ordinary Americans do not knowingly subscribe to the truth-free philosophy of postmodernism advocated by Friedrich Nietzsche and Michel Foucault. But having been careless about truth and relativism for several generations, Americans have welcomed the post-truth world without realizing it, and are now beginning to experience what it means—the will to power working its way out as powermongering in politics, fake news in journalism, domestic abuse in families, conspiracy theories in the social media, and a general bullying in social and sexual relationships. Truth-free power has contaminated the American republic, and American freedom is being rendered powerless.

Internal or External Freedom?

Second, Americans must be clear whether they are concerned with *internal* freedom or *external* freedom, or both. Individualism is highly pronounced in our advanced modern societies, and libertarianism is the default philosophy of millions. The current ruler in America is the unencumbered American self, and the reigning ethic is radical autonomy. The right to privacy is presumed to be sacrosanct (though in fact increasingly threatened by surveillance and bureaucratic regulations). "Don't tread on me," "the right to be let alone," and "Not in my backyard you don't" (NIMBY) are not only slogans and bumper stickers but the core attitudes of the modern heart. In such a world all that matters is external freedom. What you do with your internal freedom is considered your own business and nobody else's.

We forget that for most of human history it was not this way, and there was a good reason why. It was certainly not this way for the early Americans whose visions of freedom inspired them and paved the way to the revolution that built that freedom into a political system. Their natural talk was communal. It was all about "covenant," "community," "civil life," the "common good," "the good of all," and the "commonwealth," just as ours is all about autonomous individualism. They spoke as freely of responsibilities and duties as we speak freely of rights and entitlements. Indeed, they thought that excessive autonomy was a form of license that was just as much of a problem as excessive dependency. They would have considered our present attitudes unrealistic and foolish, and there were good reasons why. For one thing, they lived in and depended on community in direct ways that we do not need to. For another, to almost all the world's great religions and most of history's respected philosophies, internal freedom mattered more than external freedom, and without internal freedom external freedom counted for little.

Jews, Stoics, Hindus, Buddhists, and Christians, for example, all had very different views of what they considered freedom and therefore salvation, and what they aspired to as the good life. They differed strongly over what freedom meant, why it mattered, and how it could be achieved. But they all agreed in stressing that internal freedom was prior in time and higher in importance than external freedom.

For Confucians, and for Stoics such as Seneca and Epictetus, the poor man in his hut with internal freedom was freer than the rich man in his palace with all his wealth and luxuries. For Siddhartha Gautama, the Buddha, it was only when he had left his princely kingdom and attained a state of "right-mindfulness" beyond the extremes of self-indulgence on one side and asceticism on the other that he could achieve the enlightenment of the "not-self" and could exult, "It [not I] is liberated." For both of them, external freedom was a matter of almost complete indifference.

Like the Buddha, Jesus of Nazareth called his followers to his way, though it was radically different from the way of the Buddha. As a Jew, Jesus called his followers to a way of life that reflects the Jewish view of the essential goodness of creation and the importance of life within law. So the way of Jesus, like Judaism itself, is world affirming, whereas the way of Buddha reflects the Eastern view of reality as illusion (*maya*) and is therefore world denying. But Jesus stands with Buddha, the Stoics, and the Torah in stressing that the inner is more important than the outer—though their respective notions of the inner are quite different. His revolution did not begin in the streets, as did that of the Zealots of his day and the French and Russian revolutionaries later. For Jesus, both the problem and the solution began in the heart. "Above all else," King Solomon had written earlier, "guard your heart, for everything you do flows from it" (Prov 4:23 NIV).

Jesus taught the same. Many of the religious leaders of the day were obsessed with a myriad of rules and regulations covering what people put into their mouths, but that for Jesus was irrelevant. The root of the human problem lay in the heart, and it was from the heart that its poison spread. "For out of the heart come evil thoughts, murders, adulteries, fornications, thefts, false witness, slanders. These are the things which defile the man; but to eat with unwashed hands does not defile the man" (Mt 15:19-20). The same point is true for America today: Freedom's most critical battlefield, where the wars are lost and won, is always the human heart. Enviers, slanderers, and haters, for example, can never be free. Freedom, as Tocqueville emphasized centuries later, is always a matter of the "habits of the heart."

The Hebrew Torah teaches plainly that whereas God creates order, humans create chaos, and the root of the human problem lies in the heart. As Rabbi Heschel writes, "Evil in the heart is the source of evil in deeds."[18] Or in the words of Rabbi Sacks, "The human drama can be summed up as follows: *God is free, God creates order. God gives man freedom. Man then creates chaos.*"[19] Not long after Genesis describes the fall of humanity, God himself delivered the blunt assessment that "every inclination of the thoughts of the human heart was only evil all the time" (Gen 6:5 NIV). The Bible's underscoring of *every*, *only*, and *all the time* are unmistakable, and this Jewish understanding carries a vital implication. Evil has an internal as well as an external face. Rabbi Sacks again: "Evil has two faces. The first—turned to the outside world—is what it does to its victim. The second—turned within—is what it does to its perpetrator. Evil traps the evildoer in its mesh. Slowly but surely he or she loses freedom and becomes not evil's master but its slave."[20]

Great African American leaders such as Frederick Douglass and Booker T. Washington understood both the primacy of internal freedom and the fallacy of those who stop short with external freedom alone. Booker T. Washington was freed by Lincoln from slavery in Franklin County, Virginia. His memoir, *Up from Slavery*, is remarkable for its complete absence of any bitterness. "I resolved," he wrote, "that I would permit no man, no matter what his color might be, to narrow and degrade my soul by making me hate him. . . . I pity from the bottom of my heart any individual who is so unfortunate as to get into the habit of holding race prejudice."[21] In strong contrast, he wrote, there were those then (and those today) who make it their business to keep stoking racial wrongs in the public square. "Some of these people do not want the Negro to lose his grievances because they do not want to lose their jobs."[22] Born in slavery and later facing the evils of the Ku Klux Klan, Booker T. Washington knew the degradation of slavery all too well and hated it as an institution, but he was a man without bitterness. The stark contrast between the spirit of such great African American champions and that of many of today's activists is stunning. These opponents of slavery knew that freedom that begins in the heart cannot issue in hate, whereas activism that is not free in the heart only compounds hate even as it claims to fight hate.

Along with notions such as the presence of sin and the passing of time, the primacy of the heart is central to the realism of the biblical view of humanity, freedom, and change. From the master story of the exodus to the manifesto of Jesus' announcement of the kingdom of God, it is clear that the biblical view of freedom is radically different from Eastern freedom (such as the Hindu notion of *moksha*). It does not withdraw from the world. It engages the world in ever-widening circles of justice and compassion that are fired by a passion for external freedom. But it begins in the heart, and it never reaches farther and lasts longer than when it stays consistent with the internal freedom of the heart. According to this view, individual lives and the general conditions of wider society will never be free unless there is freedom in the hearts of the liberators as well as those they set out to free.

Needless to say, this recognition of the primacy of the heart does not mean that either governments or laws should attempt to regulate the inner world of the mind and the heart. That was the horrible mistake of the medieval world and of twentieth-century totalitarianism in both its left-wing and right-wing forms. And as we shall see, it is increasingly the mistake of the American Left. In both the medieval and the modern case it flows from a form of government that is based on power and is willing to invade even the private sphere. *For freedom-loving people, the private sphere is the inner sanctum of freedom, just as freedom of religion and conscience is the inner sanctum of the mind and spirit.* No one has the competence to invade the private sphere, and above all to invade the heart and mind of the individual person, and it is emphatically not the business of the government.

Yet when it comes to our hearts and our minds, governments are both incompetent and incontinent. They cannot judge, but they will not stop, so down that way lie the dire evils of increased surveillance, coerced consciences, empires of the mind, political correctness, thought police, torture, and the vile notion that "error has no rights"—and the death of true liberalism and a free society. But for those who take inner freedom seriously, and therefore see freedom of religion and conscience as inviolable, it means that no free societies can ever turn a blind eye to schooling and to the cultivation of virtues and the "habits of the heart." Far from civic luxuries, they are essential to freedom, and outer freedom by itself will never be enough. A key part of true freedom, the highest part in fact, will always be the self-restraint that is "obedience to the unenforceable." A high and widely respected view of human dignity is the final barrier against the all-seeing and all-intrusive state that knows no limit to its appetite.

Freedom From and Freedom For

Third, Americans must be clear whether they are speaking of *negative* freedom or *positive* freedom. Always a vital distinction, the difference between the two aspects of freedom was underscored by the life and work of the Oxford philosopher Isaiah Berlin. I well remember dinners at All Souls College, Oxford, when the rich, deep eloquence of his voice warmed to the importance of the subject. Put simply, negative freedom is *freedom from*, whereas positive freedom is *freedom for* and *freedom to be*. In English, one word, *freedom*, covers both meanings, but in Hebrew there are two different words—*hofesh*, meaning "freedom from," and *herut*, meaning "freedom for." Both aspects of freedom are absolutely necessary. Negative freedom, or freedom from, is foundational and essential, and all views of freedom require it. No one who is subject to the will of another or under the power of an external force can claim to be free. This person is either a child or a slave. It does not matter whether that power is political, as with an unjustly jailed dissident; chemical, as with a heroin addict or alcoholic; psychological, as with the victim of a playground bully or domestic violence; or spiritual and intellectual. All freedom, however understood, must begin with freedom *from*.

Importantly, within the biblical view that shaped the early Americans, negative freedom was not simply preliminary in time, it was *prophetic* in terms of truth. Slavery in Egypt was to be replaced by social justice in Israel, and remembering the former was to be a spur to the Jews maintaining the latter. The same was true of Christian conversion and its relationship to Christian living, as exemplified in the abiding popularity of John Newton's song "Amazing Grace," as a slave trader turned Christian convert. And the same should be true for American freedom: precisely as Americans remember what they were freed from, and remember the thousand and one oppressions from which others need to be freed as they were once freed, American freedom can maintain an animating gratitude that keeps it from the complacency that is the beginning of the end of freedom. In short, telling and retelling American history is as important to American freedom as American law schools.

Yet negative freedom is still only half the story. By itself, negative freedom leads only to license and would end in either chaos or tyranny. No one achieves full and genuine freedom unless they go on to experience positive freedom—the freedom to be and the freedom for whatever vision they believe is their purpose and fulfillment in life. This point is the watershed truth for understanding freedom, and it entails two vital dimensions. First, *freedom is not the permission to do what you want, but the power to do what you ought.* And second, such freedom is not individual only. *Each person's freedom is free only to the extent that each one respects the equal freedom of all others too.* Universal freedom therefore means freedom for everyone in a double sense— *freedom for each person* and *freedom for all in the service of the good of all.*

Therein, of course, lies the rub. There are three distinct sides to freedom, and they each save us from another side that by itself can easily go wrong. Negative freedom sets us free by saving us from despotism, legalism, and overregulation, which are the fruit of positive freedom gone wrong. Positive freedom makes us truly free by saving us from anarchy, lawlessness, and anomie, which are the fruit of negative freedom gone wrong. And collective freedom means that no individuals are fully free unless their freedom respects the freedom of all others, without which individual freedoms have gone badly wrong, favoring the rich, the powerful, and the talented at the expense of others.

Negative freedom assumes little except the desire to be free, and does not pause to ponder the impulse behind that desire. In the form of libertarianism, it is unquestionably the going desire of many if not most young Americans today. They simply desire freedom from all restraints, and who can blame them? But there are two potential flaws at the heart of this desire. As Abraham Heschel notes, negative freedom "not only overlooks the compulsions which often lie behind our desires; it reveals the tragic truth that freedom may develop within itself the seed of its own destruction."[23]

To be sure, almost everyone can agree on the importance of negative freedom because it means only freedom from constraint and coercion. Indeed, it is essential to saving us from the extreme of authoritarianism. But positive freedom is where the debates and disagreements begin, because it assumes and requires more. *Positive freedom requires a vision of truth, character, ethics, and the common good—for unless we know the truth of who we are and how we are supposed to live and to live with others, we cannot hope to attain the freedom of being ourselves and offering the same freedom to others.* How we view the truth of who we are will be decisive for determining our ability to attain the freedom of what we desire to be and for deciding whether claims for freedom are true or false. As G. K. Chesterton observed, "You can free things from alien or accidental laws, but not from the laws of their own nature. You may, if you like, free a tiger from his bars; but do not free him from his stripes. Do not free a camel from the burden of his hump: You may be freeing him from being a camel."[24]

Once again, a major flaw in American freedom today stems from carelessness about the so-called post-truth world—in other words, the world of postmodernism that Nietzsche ushered in during the 1880s. Freedom without truth is completely and utterly impossible. Without truth there is no freedom, and it is no accident that all the celebration of the post-truth era has led to a corresponding rise in fact-checking, because life with no truth is impossible. It is also a common mistake to reduce the positive-negative distinction to an argument between conservatives and liberals, as if conservatives advocate the former and liberals the latter. Both are essential to a healthy view of human freedom, and the counterbalancing emphasis on positive freedom was once a clear liberal theme too. Henry David Thoreau wrote in his *Journal*, "Do we call this the land of the free? What is it to be free from King George the Fourth and continue slaves to prejudice? What is it to be born free and equal and not to live? What is the value of any political freedom, but as a means to moral freedom?"[25] After all, as he wrote later in *Walden*, "It is hard to have a southern overseer, it is worse to have a northern one; but worst of all if you are the slave driver of yourself."[26]

The fact is that there is simply no substitute for positive freedom, and no amount of negative freedom alone will ever make up for its absence. But that point raises several difficulties for a free society such as America.

Most people today do not take the time to explore the notion of an examined life and the good life, so they rarely consider the truth of who they are.

Following the ravages of postmodern philosophy and the current vogue for a post-truth world, the notion of truth has itself been called into question today.

Truth implies falsehood, and together they both imply certain things that should be avoided as wrong, which flies in the face of the modern talk of total freedom, complete relativism, and absolute nonjudgmentalism, with no limits at all. All too often, Dostoevsky's "If God is dead, everything is permitted" becomes the unspoken attitude that *any denial of total freedom is a total denial of freedom*—which in turn flouts reality and ends in folly.

Ours is a world of exploding pluralism in which "everyone is now everywhere," so modern diversity raises the specter of competing, if not clashing, visions of positive freedom. Whose view is to be encouraged, and how are we to live with the clash of differences, so that each person's freedom respects the freedom of others (the subject of question six)?

Before moving to All Souls College, Oxford, Berlin had lived much of his life in Russia, where he witnessed the evils of the Soviet idea of positive freedom, and he knew the terrible experiences of his people, the Jews, under the claims of medieval Catholic dogma. He was therefore notoriously chary of all claims to positive freedom. Yet in private conversations Berlin always insisted that both aspects of freedom were equally essential to the understanding of freedom as well as to the achievement of full human freedom. For freedom faces not one danger but two equal though opposite dangers: from one side, the danger of despotic control, from which we are saved by negative freedom; and from the other side, the danger of chaotic lawlessness, from which we are saved by positive freedom. Negative freedom is therefore vital, but by itself it is only a half-truth and, pursued for its own sake, it turns out to be a fool's gold. It is urgent for Americans today to consider the fateful difference between "do as you please" freedom and "do as you ought" freedom. The only question is whether that recognition will come in time for the American republic to survive.

Does It Really Matter?

National or political freedom? Internal or external? Negative or positive? Are such distinctions important, or are they only a matter of semantic fussiness? Many people today would dismiss such questions as a waste of time.

Let those worry about them who care. All that matters, such people say, is that freedom is real in practice, which for most of them means that freedom is defined as external and negative freedom. Americans should be free to do whatever they like, so long as they do no harm to anyone else. Nothing else is anybody else's business, so outer freedom is sufficient, and if outer freedom is in place, society can afford to ignore inner freedom. Or at least, they say, it is for each individual American to decide whether inner freedom is their concern. It is no business of anyone else, and it is certainly not the business of the government.

Such attitudes are widespread, not only in America but throughout the modern world. Philosopher John Gray highlights the appeal of negative freedom as the indispensable beginning of freedom: "Negative freedom is 'true' freedom because it best captures what makes freedom valuable, which is the opportunity it secures to live as you choose."[27] That is true and understandable, but negative freedom is only the beginning of freedom, and there are major reasons why the distinctions matter and why the present generation needs to think more deeply about the nature of full freedom.

The first two reasons lie at the heart of the fundamental contrast between the American Revolution and the French Revolution and its heirs. They each have radically different views of freedom. The first concerns the reason why 1776 emphasized positive freedom and 1789 emphasized negative freedom. For those who are heirs of 1789, freedom is essentially negative and external, liberation from whatever is considered externally repressive—variations on the famous theme set out by Jean-Jacques Rousseau at the beginning of his *Social Contract*: "Man is born free, but he is everywhere in chains."[28] Get rid of whatever are reckoned to be the chains, 1789 claims, and humanity will then be free. But for those who are heirs of 1776 and the Jewish and Christian understanding, freedom certainly begins with the negative and the external, but that is only the beginning. Freedom has to grow to be internal and positive freedom too. Liberty is more than liberation. It starts with liberation, but it requires truth, character, and an ethical way of life in order to flourish.

In the Jewish and Christian understanding, freedom is more than a question of simply being free or not free, for as Rabbi Sacks points out, true freedom is like art, literature, music and poetry, and other achievements of the human spirit. It "needs training, discipline, apprenticeship, the most demanding routines and the most painstaking attention to detail.

No one composed a great novel or symphony without years of prepa-
ration."[29] Liberty in this view begins with liberation, but it does not end
there. It is a process and a matter of growth, discipline, and hard work. It
is a person-by-person and a generation-by-generation achievement, and
not a once-for-all, hand-me-down legacy. In a word, it takes positive
freedom to fulfill negative freedom.

Once again, negative freedom by itself is deceptive. It carries a siren
lure that needs to be clearly recognized and firmly resisted if it is not to
shipwreck more American views of freedom. Rabbi Heschel captures the
point with precision:

> For freedom is not an empty concept. Man is free to be free; he is not free in
> choosing to be a slave: he is free in doing good; he is not free in doing evil. To
> choose evil is to fail to be free. In choosing evil, he is not free but determined
> by forces which are extraneous to the spirit. Free is he who has decided to act
> in agreement with the spirit that goes beyond all necessities.[30]

The second reason Americans need to think more deeply about the distinctions stems from another aspect of the contrast between 1776 and 1789,
and it explains why so many libertarian views of freedom are shortsighted.
As freedom *from*, negative freedom is empty freedom. It says nothing about
what freedom is *for*. Only positive freedom has content and therefore has a
hope of being solid and lasting. Thus freedom-loving people cannot afford
to put their confidence in what is only negative and limited from the start.
The contrast between the revolutions is all too clear here. For 1776 and its
heirs the focus was on truth, whereas for 1789 and its heirs the focus was on
power. The former stresses inner freedom as well as outer freedom, and both
negative and positive freedom, whereas 1789 stresses outer freedom over
inner freedom, and negative freedom at the expense of positive freedom. For
1776, freedom is viewed as *personal* freedom *from* government control,
whereas 1789 views freedom as *progressive* freedom *through* government
control. The former is realistic about human nature and the potential for the
abuse of power, and therefore takes "under God" seriously, whereas 1789 is
utopian about human nature, and has no final accountability.

These differences work their way out in numerous different ways—for
example, in their different attitudes to how they pursue change and transform
societies. Central to 1789 and the eighteenth-century Enlightenment was a

new view of revolution that placed its confidence in the power of reason and attempted to transform societies by working from the outside in—in other words, by starting with political institutions, and above all by changing the structures of the state and using them to transform citizens coercively.

The spirit of 1776 was quite different. The "lost cause" of the English Revolution of 1640 and the successful American Revolution of 1776 are often described as conservative, and they were. But in fact they were also profoundly radical in their realism. They took their cue from the Hebrew Scriptures, held up Israel's exodus from Egypt as their pattern for liberation, and took seriously the biblical view that change and transformation must always include inner freedom, which will take time. They were revolutions in the hearts and minds of the people before they were revolutions in the streets, and the streets (and the ardors of the revolutionary war) never overwhelmed the hearts and minds of the people and their leaders. In 1818, John Adams wrote famously that America's "real revolution" was the revolution before the Revolution: "The Revolution was effected before the War commenced. The revolution was in the hearts and minds of the people; a change in their religious sentiments of their duties and obligations. This radical change in the principles, opinions, sentiments and affections of the people, was the real American Revolution."[31]

In stark contrast, the French (1789), Russian (1917), and Chinese (1949) revolutions were radical but utopian, and destructive because they were utopian in the sense that they believed in human perfectibility. They rejected the Bible and took no interest in the exodus as a pattern for liberation but instead took their cue from the philosophies of Jean-Jacques Rousseau, Karl Marx, and Mao Zedong, respectively. They started as revolutions in the streets and were led by elites rather than being in the hearts and minds of the many. In each case these three revolutions attempted a total transformation of human behavior through manipulating the levers of state power. But they utterly failed to transform human nature; they each produced forms of revolutionary government that were even more tyrannical than the ancien régimes they replaced, and they each created killing fields that are an indelible stain on their memory.

A key feature of the difference between these two types of revolution was the biblical insistence that change takes time, that transformation requires patience and can afford to be incremental, and that it will always fail if it does not take seriously the primacy of the human heart and its freedom. To be sure, there is a potential danger in the 1776, Jewish and Christian approach to social transformation. It may be realistic about the importance of inner change to the point where it degenerates into quietism and ends in supporting the status quo and changing nothing. But the clear and certain danger in the approach taken by 1789 and its heirs on the left today is unmistakable. It is utopian, and it must therefore close the gap between the ideal and the real by using coercive means to transform society into its image of the ideal society. That coercion may sometimes be crude, through state violence as in totalitarian societies, or it may be subtle, through the systematic imposition of overburdening regulations and laws, as in the efforts of socialism and the sexual revolution in modern democratic societies. But because it is utopian, it will always have to be coercive in the end.

No one should fool themselves into thinking that the choice between these visions of freedom is merely theoretical, for the practical differences are as stark as night and day. In the same way, Americans must size up today's claims for change and revolution, and examine their underlying philosophies. Do they come closer to the ideals and ways of the American Revolution or to the ideas and practices of the French, Russian, and Chinese revolutions? Here, as ever, differences make a difference. And there is always a final factor. If the four revolutions are assessed in terms of their contributions to human freedom, only one conclusion is possible: The French, Russian, and Chinese revolutions were each a failure. Only the American Revolution, even with its shortcomings, was an overall success in terms of freedom. Unless there is a decisive restoration of 1776, and this time an expansion of its promise to everyone, every movement toward 1789 will sentence America to recurring bouts of the abuse of power that betray a fatal disease in the health of the republic.

Americans must debate these differences and decide these definitions with care. They are not rolling the dice, as in a game of chutes and ladders. Each decision they make means that they land on certain squares and not others. There are choices and there are consequences, and Americans therefore have to be clear what their choices are, why they are making them, and what their consequences may be. Those who emphasize the primacy of outer transformation proceed one way and must do so as a matter of their principle and its logic, whereas those who emphasize inner transformation proceed another way and must also do so as a matter of principle and logic.

For the utopian, the revolutionary is the poet who works with the dream of a clean slate and the blueprint of a more perfect society—as Mao Zedong set out to do for China. For the conservative the revolutionary is the realist who understands the necessity of inner transformation and the free choice that it requires.

The Land of the Free and the Indebted

The third and fourth reasons to take inner freedom and positive freedom seriously are that they are vital to shaping society constructively, and without them American society is prone to a serious malaise. Devotees of negative freedom constantly tell us that we are "free to do whatever we like, so long as we do no harm to others." Negative freedom is all that matters. California, for example, is often hailed as the state for freedom par excellence—"Think what you like, say what you feel, go where you want, do what you choose, and dream what you wish."[32] From the free-speech movement, the hippie, and the surfboard to the laptop, the iPhone, and the driverless car, California's freedom is always boundless and infinite, and we haven't seen anything yet, we are told.

Such claims overlook the fact that negative freedom, by itself, is negative in another sense too. *Negative freedom is a freedom to which no one has ever said no, and by definition no one can ever say no.* As a freedom from any and every no, negative freedom is totally unbounded, which is both its appeal and the seeds of its own self-destruction. The resulting irony is striking to outsiders, though rarely addressed by Americans. The proud boast that America is the "land of the free" obscures two equally obvious facts. At the personal level, the land of the free is also the land of a thousand compulsions, addictions, and recovery groups. (In 2015, deaths through drug overdoses were more than those by gun homicides and car crashes combined.) And at the public level, the land of the free is the land of growing surveillance (the so-called Gaze of the Guardians),[33] deep financial indebtedness, and constant eruptions of rage, resentment, and accusations of hate from one group or another. Hegel's argument that slavery gives rise to a culture of resentment can be turned around: a culture boiling with resentment, as America is today, is a sure sign that the people are not as free as they think they are.

Love means always caring enough to say no. Every responsible parent knows that. Yet Americans are becoming unbounded, unbridled, unbuttoned, and unblushing in both their language and their behavior. Almost anything now goes in America, and most Americans love to have it so. Yet Americans are far from being as free as they boast. The reason for the contradiction is simple, and it would have been plain to the ancients. External freedom without internal freedom is hollow, and negative freedom without positive freedom is dangerous. They may even provide a mask that obscures dire forms of bondage. Whatever people may claim, no one addicted, no one caught in debt, and no one driven by rage, resentment, hate, cruelty, or rank bad manners is free. Addiction, debt, rudeness, resentment, rage, and hate are chains as heavy as those holding down any convict or slave, and more and more of American public life is held by these addictions or fueled by these emotions—on both the right and the left, and among the "elites" as much as the average Joe. With no repentance now required of perpetrators, and only rare forgiveness now offered by victims, it becomes impossible to draw a line between the American present and the past. So the past remains present, and the anger, grievances, and resentments from slavery and the other evils of three hundred years of America's past accumulate steadily and now have the American present in a stranglehold. Twenty-first-century America is anything but the land of the free.

There are many needed responses to this situation, but the underlying principle is the same. We humans are free to choose, yes. We all have willpower. But freedom always carries an open-ended either-or potential. So while we are free, we are also responsible, in that we are never free from the consequences of our choices. We can make a perfectly free choice to do either right or wrong, or tell the truth or tell a lie (and obviously our views of those things may differ too). But if we choose to do what by our own lights is wrong, and we do not check and reverse that choice, it will lead from wrong choice to repeated wrong choice, to habit, to compulsion, and finally to addiction. In short, there are habits of the heart when we deal with the good, the true, and the beautiful, and there are habits of the heart when we deal with the bad, the false, and the ugly. With pornography, as with lying, alcohol, drugs, and countless other choices, there is a point at which willpower becomes powerless and freedom ends up as addiction. In short, there is a point at which we simply cannot stop. As Alcoholics Anonymous is famous for emphasizing, an important moment comes when the only element of control we have left is to admit that we are out of control. We are no longer free. We are addicts. We are powerless. And we need help from a power higher than ourselves.

The Bible and the Jewish sages have taught this all along. At first, the evil impulse is "as thin as a spider's gossamer, but in the end it is as thick as a cart rope." It starts as a "wayfarer," then becomes a "guest" and finally turns into a "master."[34] In his *Confessions,* St. Augustine described the outcome of the process in his own life with a candor that was remarkable for a Christian bishop in the fifth century, let alone the wider standards of his day. And he speaks directly to our own day when the excesses of advanced modern freedom have led to numerous addictions. "Because my will was perverse, it changed to lust, and lust yielded—to become habit, and habit not resisted became necessity. These were like links hanging one on another—which is why I have called it a chain—and their hard bondage held me hand and foot."[35] According to the realism of this view, sin is the fruit, the judgment, and the punishment of sin.

Sir Walter Scott famously made the same point in the nineteenth century in connection with lies, rather than lust, and President Clinton illustrated it equally famously in the twentieth—both of them in terms of a free choice to tell a lie rather than tell the truth. "Oh! what a tangled web we weave, / When first we practise to deceive!"[36] Choose to do wrong or choose to lie, and what starts in freedom ends in bondage. Just so, too many American companies now believe their own PR and do not realize how they have descended into mediocrity, and too many American celebrities have fallen captive to their own conceits and prisoners to their own pride. The plain lesson is that full freedom requires truth and inner freedom, and not just outer freedom. Outer freedom exercised without the guidance of truth and inner freedom may lead directly to forms of inner bondage that require rescue and recovery from outside.

Again, the question arises as to whether current American views of freedom take this truth into account—for example, the total freedom and the complete nonjudgmental relativism advocated by the sexual revolution. There are many views of freedom that flatter to deceive, and we must assess them with a realism born of history and tough-minded thinking.

America's Catch-22

The fourth major reason why it is foolish to be satisfied with negative freedom (freedom from) is that this mistake exacerbates a serious condition

in American society—the *frustration gap* between the promise and the fulfillment of American individualism. Individualism and its promise of indi-
vidualization ("You are free to be whoever you wish to be") are both strong
in America, and here to stay. But while the stress on negative freedom promotes the promise, the absence of widely available positive freedom pre-
vents the fulfillment. The result is that individuals are caught in a bind. They
are officially and, as it were, de jure free. The right to the pursuit of happiness
is inalienable. So says the Declaration of Independence, and so says the
American dream and the allure of its ever-changing and ever-new do-it-
yourself consumer identities and lifestyles. So say radical new philosophies
such as social constructionism. Never has the day of self-assertion and self-
discovered happiness seemed brighter, yet individuals are still not de facto
free or free in reality. And without positive freedom (freedom for) they can
never hope to close that gap and become truly free.

Just as the Israelite slaves were ordered by their Egyptian taskmasters to
make bricks without straw, and under the same deadline, so today's
American individuals have the allure of a thousand freedoms dangled before
them but are not given the positive freedoms to make them possible. Rarely
have humans ever been freer than middle- and upper-class Americans today.
They can become almost whomever they like, do almost anything they wish,
go almost anywhere they desire, and see and know almost whatever they
want to discover. Yet as with the Hebrew slaves, the outcome can be insufferable. Making bricks without straw was unreasonable and impossible. Just
so, Americans set out daily to make millions of individual self-assertions at
the invitation of negative freedom, but without the complement of positive
freedom they prove a recipe for massive frustration. They are chasing a will-
o'-the wisp that dances ahead of them but can never be caught.

Little wonder so many Americans fail in their pursuit of happiness. For
all their touted freedoms, they are restless and dissatisfied, and sometimes
confused and angry. They were told they were free and given a thousand
recipes for happiness. Why then do they feel so frustrated and anything but
free or happy? Why are the magazines and marketers able to sell them a
whole new range of options the next week or month? The truth is that many
of the promised consumer freedoms turn out to be insignificant, and the
promised life transformations turn out to be impossible. The outcome is a
further twist in the corruption of public life through life politics. Citizens of

the American republic degenerate into individual Americans, each with their own hurts and prejudices. Society then becomes another word for *peg communities*, communities on which hurting and angry individuals can hang their grievances. Thus the search is mounted for scapegoats and strangers to blame, and politics and the public square become the arena in which squabbling egos can air their resentments and fight for their interests. And a crucial reason for this catch-22 is simply the lack of a wise understanding of positive freedom.

Again, will it be said that freedom was too hard a challenge for Americans to overcome? Here, then, is the third question on the checklist that Americans must answer constructively: *How do you define* freedom *today?* What is your own working definition? How do your friends and colleagues understand freedom? What will happen if most Americans continue to focus on external freedom rather than internal freedom and on negative freedom rather than positive freedom? Have you chosen carefully between the different conceptions of freedom that come from 1776 and 1789? What place do you give to the role of the heart and to the importance of the habits of the heart?

The recurring theme in this third question on the checklist is inescapable: choices have consequences. As Americans choose their freedom and make their beds, so they will lie in them. And there will of course be consequences, whether they are conscious of their choices or not. How much better to make the choices with the full clarity that we ought to bring to our choices. The politics of freedom is strenuous enough for those who understand its demands, but for those too careless to understand it, the consequences and the unforeseen consequences are likely to be unpleasant. The choices are for Americans to make and for Americans to reap. It is time for Americans, from each successive president to the youngest school child, to explore what they mean by *freedom*, and to know whether they have thought through the outcome of the kinds of freedom they are pursuing.

QUESTION FOUR

HAVE YOU FACED UP *to* *the* CENTRAL PARADOX *of* FREEDOM?

*F*reedom is not free." Those four simple words are prominent on the wall of the Korean War memorial in Washington, DC. They play on each other to form a stirring reminder of the sacrifice that Lincoln called the "last full measure of devotion" in the defense of freedom.[1] But that gentle paradox pales beside the dark conundrum that lies at the heart of freedom itself: *The greatest enemy of freedom is freedom.* If the first sentence is as inspiring as it is short, the second is sober and arresting. Bluntly nonheroic and quite unsuitable for carving on any memorial wall, this paradox is etched indelibly into history itself, and it stands menacing and mocking across the path of all who are naive enough to think the course of freedom is smooth. Far from easy, both freedom and the politics of freedom are not only demanding but in a sense doomed—unless the paradox is faced squarely and overcome. For all who love freedom, there is no way around this paradox except to confront it and pick up the gauntlet thrown at our feet with such a sardonic challenge. The fourth question on the checklist therefore asks: *Have Americans faced up to the central paradox of freedom, that freedom is the greatest enemy of freedom—including American freedom?*

History by itself should be sufficient to cure us of naivety about freedom. Freedom may be glorious, but free societies are few, far between, and fleeting. If the hundred-centuries clock of civilization were to be compressed into a single hour, today's interest in freedom and democracy would appear only in the last few minutes before midnight. Freedom requires a certain view of human dignity and independence, and until quite recently only two societies with world influence have attained those ideals. The first was the Jews, with their view of the human person as made in the image of God, and the second was the Greeks, with their view of the *logos*, or reason within each person. The Romans owed much to the Greeks, just as the later Europeans and the West at large owed much to the Greeks and Romans, but even more to the many gifts of the Jews and the Bible when mediated through the Christian faith (which Benjamin Disraeli described as "Judaism for the multitudes").

As a young poet, William Wordsworth hurried to Paris at the beginning of the French Revolution in 1789 and heralded it with a breathless naivety that later turned into bitter disappointment. ("Bliss was it in that dawn to be alive / But to be young was very heaven!")[2] The great Whig statesman Charles James Fox gushed similarly in calling it "the greatest event it is that ever happened in the world."[3] In 2010, many Westerners responded to the Arab Spring in the same giddy way. They were intoxicated with the dream of freedom and democracy breaking out all over the world. Their instant celebrations of claims to freedom and their facile ideas of the easy export of democracy showed they had not digested Edmund Burke on the French Revolution, and their naivety was shown up yet again. People who prize freedom and know the grand paradox of freedom should never be naive, and they should never put their trust in freedom itself, for freedom alone can never bear the weight of freedom without the foundation and framework it requires. Freedom unsupported and unbounded has a chronic habit of undermining and destroying itself. Again and again history teaches an unforgiving truth: With freedom, more may mean less, and too much of a good thing becomes a bad thing as freedom falters and fails in one of three routine ways.

First, freedom commonly fails when it runs to excess and breeds permissiveness and license. This is behind the iron link between anarchy and tyranny.

Second, freedom fails when people who love freedom so long to be safe and secure that their love of security undermines their freedom. ("The dangers of life are infinite," Goethe is known for saying, "and among them is safety.") This danger surfaces in today's tensions between security and privacy ("One nation under surveillance" again).

Third, freedom fails when free societies become so caught up in the glory of freedom that they justify anything and everything done in its name, even things that quite clearly contradict freedom. In particular, freedom always sours when it is used to mistreat or oppress others. Which is why so much of the world finds recent American discussions of torture so troubling and the American lack of any serious discussion of "collateral damage" in war equally troubling.

It hardly needs to be said that recent decades have offered numerous examples of each of these corruptions of freedom writ large in both American society and foreign policy. But the added seriousness of the choices comes from the fact that the differences between the different views of American freedom now on offer are as great as the differences that led to the Civil War. Under the leadership of Abraham Lincoln, victory in the Civil War confirmed the overall direction of America's founding and reinforced its commitment to freedom by correcting the major contradiction the founders had left unsolved. Restore or replace? Following the 1960s, many versions of freedom have repudiated both the founders and the past, and the question is whether this shift will succeed in winning the day, and if it does, will it advance freedom or set freedom back?

The Spirit and the Structures

There are three major reasons why freedom has proved to be the greatest enemy of freedom, and history is the principal witness to the way each of them works its way out in reality and how they combine to form a deadly trio. The first reason is political. Baron de Montesquieu noted in his eighteenth-century classic *The Spirit of the Laws* that free societies require a combination of the *structures* of freedom and the *spirit* of freedom. But these two things rarely travel in tandem for long. The structures of freedom supply the outer framework of freedom and include such things as a wise constitution, good laws, and such foundational notions as the rule of law and the right to personal property. But they are not the heart of freedom, as some who focus on them alone seem to think. They are only the external framework. When carefully designed and laid down well, these structures of freedom provide an indispensable setting for freedom, and they can be counted on to last for a considerable time. But by themselves they are not enough.

The heart of freedom is what Montesquieu calls "the spirit of freedom." His great disciple Alexis de Tocqueville famously called it the "habits of the heart." The spirit of freedom concerns the attitudes and convictions that grow from the foundations of human freedom itself. First, there must be the foundational faith that grounds and guarantees that we are indeed free. Second, there must be the respect that is prepared to grant similar freedom for others. And third, there must be the responsible self-restraint that issues from self-rule or mastery of the self, which issues in turn to the "obedience to the unenforceable" that true freedom requires. When such a spirit of freedom flourishes, it makes policing and extra levels of law and regulations redundant.

The trouble is that while this spirit of freedom is essential, it is neither easy nor durable. Such a spirit, or such habits of the heart must be cultivated afresh in every citizen and in every generation. An open fire needs a hearth and a grate, but a hearth and a grate provide no warmth unless the wood in it is lit, logs are added and kept burning, and the fire is constantly stoked. Like such a fire, the spirit of freedom is not self-fueling. It has to be inspired and passed on from leaders to followers, from parents to children, from teachers to students, and from generation to generation, and it has to be constantly kept alive though a myriad of symbols, celebrations, and reminders. Unless this spirit of freedom is transmitted successfully, including civic education, the structures of freedom simply cannot keep freedom healthy by themselves. Americans, take note: It is naive to think that freedom will survive through relying on the US Constitution alone. Unless the spirit of freedom is kept burning brightly in every generation, American freedom will die.

This means simply that a free society is always one generation away from losing freedom, and it must pay constant attention to what freedom requires if it is to thrive. We humans require food and water, fire requires fuel, and freedom requires the cultivation of the habits of the heart and the self-control that they empower. Any nation may keep its constitution in place for a long time, may keep its armies in a state of constant readiness, and may multiply laws endlessly in a well-meaning attempt to hedge freedom around in countless ways. But all that will amount to nothing if freedom's triple foundation wears thin, the self-mastery of the citizens slackens and frays, and the habits of their hearts cool off and die. A huge part of America's present troubles can be illuminated by that single principle alone. The ancient maxim runs "Who is mighty?" Not one who can conquer his enemies but the "one who can conquer himself." Obedience to the unenforceable and the self-mastery of emotions, thought, and speech are not exactly America's strongest suit today.

Needless to say, there are many factors in America today that have made such habits difficult and such a healthy transmission rare—broken families, the focus on negative freedom, the foolish rejection of civic education, the triumph of feelings in an expressive culture, and the disparaging of the past for a start. The result is that the habits of the heart that are essential for sustaining American freedom are seriously malnourished or dying. The current cynicism of the millennial generation is telling. The lunacy of generationalism and the deliberate aggravation of the divisions between the generations ("It's a generational thing. You wouldn't understand.") means a disastrous dropping of the baton in the great relay race of the American story. The pulse beat of American continuity is suffering from a serious arrhythmia.

When Freedom Flourishes

The second reason for the paradox is ethical, and it poses an even stiffer test. Freedom requires order and therefore restraint, yet the restraint that is most appropriate to freedom is self-restraint—the famous "obedience to the unenforceable"—but self-restraint is the very thing that freedom undermines when it flourishes. Thus the heart of the problem of freedom is the problem of the heart, because free societies are restless at their core and always anxious to throw off restraint.

Why so? Talk of restless hearts sounds psychological at best and pious at worst, but it was argued strenuously by thinkers who were highly political and anything but pious. Machiavelli, for example, understood that political restlessness is rooted in the fact that human appetites are by nature insatiable because our reach is greater than our grasp. We "desire everything" but we are unable "to secure everything." The result is that human "desire is always greater than the power of acquisition."[4] Montesquieu argued the same point. Freedom-loving people have an "uneasy spirit," he wrote, that leaves them "always inflamed."[5] Needless to say, he made these observations long before the rise of modern American consumerism that gains its life from stoking human desire and restlessness to higher and higher levels.

Another way of stating the same point is that the consent of the governed is at the heart of democracy and is crucial to both freedom and its legitimacy, but it is beguiling because it masks a challenge. In a democratic republic such as the United States, "We the people" are simultaneously both the rulers and the subjects, so freedom depends constantly not only on the character of the nation's leaders but also on the character of is citizenry.

The flaw in that reliance is plain. Such are human passions and the political restlessness they create that the self-renunciation needed for the self-restraint to sustain freedom is quite unnatural. It goes against the grain of humanness—especially in peaceful and prosperous periods, when it seems that no one is required to rise above private interests and remember the common good, and especially in bitterly anxious times such as the present, when so many citizens contradict rather than consent to the government that is them. In recent years, the United States has reached the absurd point that is the bane of presidents and the Congress alike: No sooner do Americans send their representatives to Washington than they turn on Washington and claim that Washington no longer represents them.

The core problem can be expressed simply like this: Such is the human propensity for self-love—or thinking and acting with the self as center—that the virtue it takes for citizens to remain free is quite simply unnatural. America today is a republic in which the private trumps the public and consumerism whispers to Americans in a thousand ways, "It's all about you." Citizens then tell the government to "get off our backs" even though the government is their own just-chosen representatives, and it supposedly governs them with their free consent and backing.

The result, in Montesquieu's words, is that the self-rule and the self-renunciation needed for freedom are "always a painful thing." The natural bent of self-love is toward domination and not self-restraint, so the will to power at its heart will relentlessly seek to expand unless it meets resistance. Freedom therefore naturally thrives on freedom, and mistaking power for freedom expands naturally to create the abuse of power that throttles freedom—that is, unless freedom is checked and balanced strongly, wisely, and constantly. If freedom is not checked in this way, or worse still, freedom is defined only negatively (as freedom from constraint, as it is in much of America today), then once again freedom undermines itself.

Anyone in search of evidence need look no farther than the twentieth century. Reject authority, deny truth, dismiss virtue, ignore restraint, and glorify power and as sure as eggs are eggs, liberty will become license, equality will become leveling, and justice will become the power moves of the powerful. Authoritarianism will be on its way, whatever the sugarcoating of democratic wording. And logically, how could it be otherwise? The need for restraint under authority is at the heart of the paradox, and it explains how the rich and the powerful so easily lose their freedom. Being powerful and mistaking power for freedom, the upper classes and the elites rule everybody—*except themselves*—and so become slaves. Failing to rule themselves, they either become slaves to their own unchallenged ideas, which become an obsession, or slaves to their own unbounded behavior, which becomes an addiction. Long ago, Plato warned that this is how an "excess of liberty" becomes an "excess of slavery."[6]

This aspect of the paradox carries a warning for the supporters of 1789. They criticize 1776 for the oppression of its "cultural hegemony" over American life and seek to assault it through their own sustained cultural subversion. But do they show signs of encouraging greater freedom in the spheres where they have "won hegemony" themselves? The university world with its political correctness and intolerance would suggest otherwise. As the paradox demonstrates, power can undermine oppression, but by itself it cannot establish freedom.

Who then is truly free? The free person is not the person who controls others, for that is merely a matter of power. Truly free persons are those who control themselves, which again circles us back to inner freedom and positive freedom. True freedom comes from victory over the passions, and therefore from the character that is built on habits of the heart that in turn are built on obedience to the unenforceable—a rare pattern among Americans of power and wealth today.

The Tyranny of Freedom and the Freedom of Tyranny

The third reason for the paradox is spiritual and psychological. For freedom to be exercised well—that is, in a manner that is appropriate to freedom—freedom assumes and requires responsibility. The self-restraint of freedom and the self-reliance of responsibility go hand in hand. But self-reliance and responsibility are anything but simple and straightforward, and the deepest source of the paradox can be tracked down in the dark corners of the twisted paths by which we humans often try to evade responsibility. There is at times what appears to be a tyranny in freedom, just as there appears to be a freedom in tyranny. *The result is a fear of freedom that ends in the desire for freedom from freedom.*

No faith in history has put a higher emphasis on the ethics of responsibility than the Jewish people, yet it did not come easily. At the heart of the Torah's view of sin is the notion of the evasion of responsibility (for example, Cain's infamous question, "Am I my brother's keeper?" [Gen 4:9]). Michael Walzer reflected on the paradox in commenting on the Israelites' grumbling against Moses in the desert after they were liberated from the Egyptian Pharaoh. What the complainers did was transform Egypt in their minds from being the "house of slavery" into a "house of freedom." Most remarkably, when Korah rebelled against the leadership of Moses, he went so far as to describe Egypt as "a land flowing with milk and honey," the cherished term for the Promised Land (Num 16:13). "Indeed," Walzer concludes, "there is a kind of freedom in bondage. . . . The childish or irresponsible slave or subject is free in ways the republican citizen or Protestant saint can never be. And there is a kind of bondage in freedom: the bondage of law, obligation, and responsibility."[7]

Dig deep into this paradox and you can understand the disastrous endings to which freedom so often leads—it explains why freedom is less straightforward and free societies are always harder than people think, why so many people submit willingly to real tyranny, why human beings are so easily swayed by group-think and mass movements, why it becomes so easy to "go along to get along," and why democracy can so easily end in dictatorship. In 1935, as Western democracies were obsessed with the rise of fascism and communism, Christopher Dawson warned of the coming danger of democratic societies making the same universal claims on the life of the individual as totalitarian societies did. He called it "democratic totalitarianism."[8] This problem grew from a double error: confusing freedom with democracy, and regarding democracy and dictatorship as opposites. "The truth is, unpalatable though it may be to modern 'progressive' thought, that democracy and dictatorship are not opposites or mortal enemies, but twin children of the Great Revolution [in France, in 1789]."[9]

Erich Fromm's *Escape from Freedom* is a classic analysis of the paradox of freedom. Writing as the world recoiled in horror at what totalitarianism had wrought in the Second World War, he argued that modern people had been freed from the bonds of traditional society, but had not gained a new freedom in the positive sense, so they were left in a modern no-man's-land—isolated, anxious, and powerless. "This isolation is unbearable" to a modern person, and the solution is "to escape from the burden of his freedom into new dependencies and submissions." Fromm described the result as the "totalitarian flight from freedom."[10] The grand paradox of freedom therefore grows out of the ambiguity at the heart of freedom. Freedom is a call to responsibility that can be frightening. For some people, freedom is a "cherished goal," whereas for others it presents a threat and "a burden too heavy for man to bear."[11] Earlier, he had arrived in America as a refugee from Nazi Germany. From his experience he concluded that "millions in Germany were as eager to surrender their freedom as their fathers were to fight for it; that instead of wanting freedom, they sought for ways of escape from it."[12]

The same temptation and dynamic can also be seen at the early stages of liberation, and not just at the end. It illustrates again that freedom is never simply a matter of either-or (bondage or freedom) but of more-or-less freedom. There is an obvious sense in which we can be described accurately as "free" or "not free." People who are imprisoned are obviously not free, so that when they are released and out of the prison gates, they are free. Yet that simple term *free* masks the deeper sense in which they may be externally free but far from fully free. In the case of many prisoners, that lack of full and real freedom is the reason for the high rate of recidivism and the fact that, unless they experience a deeper change in life, so many soon find themselves back behind bars again.

The classic example of this ambivalence toward freedom was the Israelite exodus from Egypt. Once the waters of the Red Sea had closed over the horses and chariots of their pursuers, they were genuinely free. God had rescued them from Egypt, and the "house of bondage" lay behind them. But were they fully free? Plainly they were free and they were not free, as they themselves betrayed in their infamous "3 Gs"—their *grumblings* (and the ten incidents of complaints that mirror the ten plagues), their *going back* (or their repeated threats to do so), and the other *gods* they lapsed into worshiping (and in particular the golden calf of the Egyptian bull-god Apis).

Walzer calls this effect the "attraction/revulsion" principle of freedom and slavery. The Israelites may have groaned under the harsh conditions of slavery, but they were also more attracted to the world of their taskmasters than they may have admitted to themselves. After years in the Egypt of the great pharaohs, a society that was the most advanced and prosperous of its day, the Israelites must have become somewhat naturalized and Egyptianized despite themselves. They may have been slaves in Egypt, but they had grown accustomed to a slave's-eye view of the lifestyle and comforts of Egypt. They had been at the bottom of the social order of Egypt, but the bottom rung in Egypt was still higher than the top rung in other parts of the world, and their hankering after "fleshpots," "leeks," and "cucumbers" showed how they had grown accustomed to the benefits of the good life in Egypt.

To underscore the point, their freedom had not brought them to the Promised Land of milk and honey, but only out into the howling wilderness, which by contrast with Egypt was harsh and barren, so even their newfound freedom faced them with a daily reminder of all they had lost and were missing. The people of Israel, Savonarola thundered in his diatribes at the "bonfire of the vanities" in sixteenth-century Florence, had become "half-Egyptian." More graphically still, their own Hebrew prophets later charged them with having "committed whoredoms in Egypt" (Ezek 23:3 KJV).

In sum, the ambiguity of freedom looms large again and has to be faced. It was one thing for God to free the Israelites externally and quite another for them to grow fully free, and to confuse negative freedom with full positive freedom was to court disillusionment. Liberty is deeper and more difficult than liberation. Personal and social transformation takes longer than revolution. Self-reliant responsibility is far harder than easygoing entitlement. With their characteristic candor, the Jewish sages noted wryly that it took one day to take the Israelites out of Egypt, but forty years and counting to take Egypt out of the Israelites.

Put differently, there are situations that can make freedom appear deceptive and far too costly. Freedom trumpets its irresistible offer, but then it appears dishonest because the cost is hidden in the small print. Who in their right mind would not wish to be free? But have we all read and agreed to the hefty price tag that it charges—whether to live with freedom, to defend freedom, or to sustain freedom? For there are situations where the challenge of rising to the responsibility of freedom seems like a challenge too many, and there is a moment when it is tempting to duck the responsibility and sink into a nonresponsible passivity and then submission. At such a moment, it is easy to fall for the deceptive idea that there is tyranny in freedom, and then to fall for the equally deceptive but even more disastrous idea that there is freedom in tyranny. How else can it be explained that so many Russians still long for a restoration of the Soviet Union, so many Haitians continue to hanker after the days of the Duvaliers, and so many Iraqis regret the overthrow of Saddam Hussein? How else can we understand how so many Americans drank the Kool-Aid at Jonestown or surrendered themselves and their children to David Koresh in Waco? How else is it that America today is all about rights and entitlements, and so little about responsibility?

Real freedom is difficult, demanding, and disciplined. Freedom is a task that takes time, that takes training, and that takes transmission. Freedom is hard work and a long-term project, and nothing is more inviting than abdicating from the weighty burden of freedom. Abdications from royal thrones are rare and often surrounded with shame, as in the case of Edward VIII stepping down from the throne to marry his mistress, Wallace Simpson. But the abdication of citizen-kings and queens is routine and easy. The responsibility of freedom may be arduous, but there is always a strong man willing to take over the burden. There is always a utopian ideology offering to submerge the loneliness of individual responsibility in the warm embrace of a cause, the offer of free stuff, bread-and-circuses diversions, entitlement programs, and in the end a welfare mentality that will end in a general dependency. Far too often a large part of the citizenry will be ready and willing to surrender its freedom and to serve a leader or a movement that beckons with the best offer of an easier life.

Nietzsche scorned the enervating effects of freedom and democracy for this reason: It was a breeding ground for the "last men" he despised, those little people who were obsessed with health and happiness, who took no time to think about life, and who had little courage to live. "The democratic idea favors the nurturing of a human type prepared for slavery in the most subtle sense of the term. Every democracy is at one and the same time an involuntary establishment for the breeding of tyrants, taking the word in all its connotations, including those of a spiritual nature."[13]

At a lower level still, the paradox of freedom can descend to a truly diabolical state, and each of the great secular revolutions has demonstrated its own horrifying violations of freedom perpetrated in the name of freedom. In 1794, Robespierre captured the paradox at its vilest in his rationale for France's reign of terror: "The government of the Revolution is the despotism of liberty against tyranny."[14] The "despotism of liberty"? What an extraordinary and revealing phrase. When the great Austrian statesman Metternich watched what happened in the French Revolution, he remarked tartly, "When

I saw what people did in the name of fraternity, I resolved, if I had a brother, to call him cousin."[15]

The paradox of freedom is no respecter of individuals or of religions and ideologies, but there are religions and there are generations that are more vulnerable than others. President George W. Bush generously challenged the idea that Arabs desired freedom and democracy any less than Americans, but the Iraqi people and its leaders did not prove worthy of his trust. Other Arabs have argued openly that Muslims tend to glorify authoritarian leaders because of the centrality of the notion of submission (the root meaning of *Islam*). When the Syrian poet Adonis was asked why Arabs were so prone to submit to dictators, he answered, "Some human beings are afraid of freedom." Was it, he was asked, because Muslims identified freedom with anarchy? "No, because being free is a great burden. It is by no means easy. . . . When you are free, you have to face reality, the world in its entirety. You have to deal with the world's problems. On the other hand, if we are slaves, we can be content and not have to deal with anything. Just as Allah will solve all our problems, the dictator will solve all our problems."[16]

Many Muslims would dispute this claim, but they must counter it in life rather than words. So too must Americans, for the rhetoric of freedom will no longer do. Responsibility and self-reliance were once powerful features of the American character and way of life, and Americans have inherited powerful political brakes to stop the advance of extreme authoritarianism on their side of the Atlantic.

But the best brake pads wear thin, and responsibility is not a prominent feature of the easygoing leisure-and-entertainment society that America has become. There have long been repugnant extremists on the right, such as the white supremacists and the Ku Klux Klan, but those who monitor the left-wing extremism now marching out of the shadows of American political life should remember Governor Huey Long's pronouncement: "When fascism comes to America it will be called 'anti-Fascism.'" The press and many Americans tend to use "alt" (alternative) only of right-wing extremism, but one of its original meanings was "anarchists, lunatics, and terrorists." Witness the expressly fascist style of "antifa," or the self-proclaimed antifascist movement, with its violent anarchist and Marxist roots, and the ugly violence of its masked and hooded assaults on defenders of freedom of speech.

Tocqueville, after all, commented long ago on the contradictions at the heart of democracy. The people are

> excited by two conflicting passions: they want to be led and they wish to remain free. As they cannot destroy either the one or the other of these contrary propensities, they strive to satisfy them both at once. They devise a sole, tutelary, and all-powerful form of government, but elected by the people. They combine the principle of centralization and that of popular sovereignty; this gives them a respite: they console themselves for being in tutelage by the reflection that they have chosen their own guardians. . . . By this system the people shake off their state of dependence just long enough to select their master and then relapse into it again.[17]

Again, will it be said that freedom was too hard a challenge for Americans to overcome? Here, then, is the fourth question on the checklist to be answered constructively: *Have you faced up to the central paradox of freedom?*

Why is it so difficult to be free and self-restrained? What are some of the factors today that undermine a strong sense of personal responsibility? What is the state of civic education in the circles in which you grew up and now live? No American who loves freedom can afford to ignore the paradox of freedom. The thrust of this fourth question is plain. Freedom is the greatest enemy of freedom, and only those who understand freedom realistically can hope to escape the toils of the paradox. Are Americans facing the paradox realistically, or has the entitlement society greased the skids toward its return? Are young Americans trained in a robust, responsible, and self-reliant freedom that can resist the siren seductions of the paradox, or has political correctness dulled the independence of their minds? Only by facing up to the paradox of freedom can Americans survive and thrive as a free people in true freedom.

HOW DO YOU PLAN *to* SUSTAIN FREEDOM?

*I*n 1916, General John Pershing was sent to lead an expedition against Mexico in retaliation for Pancho Villa's attacks on American border towns that year. One of his close aides was Captain Hugh Johnson, renowned for his intellectual prowess, and Pershing asked him to lead a study of a background issue that puzzled him. The Mexicans had taken the US Constitution as their model when they drafted their own, but it had not given them any of the strength and stability that the American Constitution had conferred. Mexican democracy was marked by turbulence and volatility, and could hardly be judged a success, and it was this that made the prospects of a lasting solution difficult.

Earlier, the great Latin liberator Simón Bolívar had been forced to admit the failure of Gran Colombia, his dream of a pan-Hispanic empire. All who supported his revolution had only "plowed the sea," he declared. "There is no faith, no trust in [Spanish] America, neither in individuals nor in nations. The constitutions are books, the treaties are scraps of paper, the elections battles, liberty is anarchy, and life a torture."[1]

After making a comparative study of the two constitutions and the two societies, Captain Johnson concluded that what the Americans could count on and the Mexicans lacked was simple: trust—trust between citizens, trust in leaders, and trust in institutions. When it came to the two governments, American citizens trusted their leaders and their institutions, whereas Mexicans had a residual mistrust of politicians and all who held political power. The two constitutions may have been similar, but the two societies were quite different. To express the reason for the difference in terms that Montesquieu and Tocqueville would have used, both the United States and Mexico had roughly the same structures of freedom in terms of the constitutions and the laws, but Mexico lacked what Montesquieu called the "spirit" of freedom, what Tocqueville called the "habits of the heart," and what was the direct legacy of covenantalism to American freedom and trust.

A century later, it is clear that America has grown more like Mexico than Mexico had grown like America. Covenantalism, reciprocal responsibility, loyalty, and trust have all eroded across American life—in marriages, families, communities, businesses, and public life. Political scandals such as Watergate have triggered steadily declining trust across many American institutions, most notably trust in the Congress and the political class, and the 2016 US presidential campaign was distinguished not only for its relentless nastiness but for the record levels of distrust and the deeply negative attitudes to both candidates, Hillary Clinton and Donald Trump. And the aftermath of the election was even worse.

Yet individual Americans, even presidents, are not the only problem.[2] They are significant only insofar as they demonstrate the condition of the American society and the political system itself. One undisputed exception in history was George Washington himself, as his character outweighed both his ideas and his actions, and created trust. Washington was truly "the indispensable man" of the American Revolution, as historian James Flexner described him, and he was so by force of his character rather than his ideas or his eloquence. In this and other similar examples he was a "one man check and balance" on the abuse of power, and decisively so, well before the Constitution framed the principle in law.

Earlier, Montesquieu had underscored the rarity and importance of such character-bred moderation in leaders. "Great men who are moderate are rare: & it is always easier to follow one's impulse than to arrest it . . . it is a thousand times easier to do good than to do it well."[3] Jefferson wrote in the same vein, "The moderation and virtue of a single character probably prevented this Revolution from being closed, as most others have been, by a subversion of that Liberty it was meant to establish."[4] Similarly, Abraham Lincoln wrote later, "Nearly all men can stand adversity, but if you want to test a man, give him power."[5]

Even Washington's adversary George III was impressed. When his royal portrait painter, Jonathan Trumbull, told the king that Washington intended to retire to his farm after the Revolutionary War was over, he was surprised. "If he does that," the king remarked—and Washington went on to do it not once but twice—"he will be the greatest man in the world."[6]

Such heroic character shone brighter still when Washington became the first president. Then when he retired and died soon after, the tributes soared higher and higher until he was first elevated into the Moses who had led his people out of bondage and then—in "the apotheosis of Washington"— divinized as the creator, savior, and father of his people. In the more straightforward words of Congressman Henry Lee at his memorial service, he was "First in war, first in peace, first in the hearts of his countrymen."[7] Far more, John Adams added, "For his fellow citizens, if their prayers could have been answered, he would have been immortal."[8]

Excessive adulation of this sort, and the impulses toward a powerful civil religion that lay behind it, are naturally suspect today. But those who are zealous in debunking them often go to the other extreme and miss their real significance. For the founders, Washington's exemplary character was not just the happy fluke of an exceptional individual at an opportune moment, or even the social product of a young nation's subconscious search for a center of national unity to replace an overthrown king. Its significance was at once simpler and more profound: character, virtue, and trust were a vital part of the founders' notion of ordered liberty and sustainable freedom, and in a way that is sharply different from today.

Which raises the fifth question on the checklist: *Are Americans prepared for the challenge of sustaining freedom?*

The Gorilla in the Room

In my years living in America, I have consistently noted two things to my surprise: The sole American answer to how freedom can be sustained is the Constitution and its separation of powers, and the rest of the founders' solution is now almost completely ignored.

It was not always so. Historians point out that the modern elevation of the Constitution as the sole foundation and bulwark of American freedom reached its present height only in the 1930s. That was no accident. Significantly, it came right on the heels of a general secularization of American law that has led in turn to a general legislation of American life. The preceding decades were the time when legal contracts were strengthened and sharpened to replace the weakening moral considerations such as character and trust (the "My word is my bond" of an earlier time).

Significantly too, the elevation of the Constitution came after long periods of surprising earlier neglect. Michael Kammen has even written of the recent "cult of the Constitution" and of "the discovery of the Bill of Rights." The motto of the American Liberty League in 1936 stated this elevated view beyond doubt—"The Constitution, Fortress of Liberty." The timing and context of that tribute are revealing. The US Constitution and all legal contracts were elevated at the very moment when faith, character, virtue, and trust began to be denigrated and relegated to the private sphere. The framers' famous separation of powers between the executive, the legislature, and the judiciary is unquestionably distinctive and fundamental to the American vision of enduring freedom. But as an answer to how freedom must be sustained, it is neither an original solution nor was it the founders' complete solution.

For one thing, even the separation of powers was once far stronger than it is today. It originally included a robust view of the rights and powers of local government to balance the power of the states, and of the rights and powers of the states to balance the rights and powers of the federal government— Tocqueville saw the first of these as the seedbed of American freedom, and Alexander Hamilton praised the second as "a double security to the people."[9] Needless to say, this entire dimension has been emasculated, starting with responses to the Civil War and accelerating through the deliberate centralization of government under the progressives and the Depression-era leaders—and climaxing in the last decade.

All in all, this radical loss of local self-government and the unchecked growth of centralized federal government has been the result of three things: old evils such as slavery and new dangers such as terrorism that made it necessary, new technologies and procedures such as computerized bureaucracy that made it possible, and new ideologies such as progressivism that made it desirable. The Fourteenth Amendment and its nationalizing consequences, for example, were the steep but understandable price of rectifying the Constitution's greatest flaw—the blind eye turned toward slavery. To be sure, the federalizing trend was therefore necessary and inevitable, but what is inexcusable is the lack of a careful, compensating devolution to restore the balance of individual self-reliance and local self-government. Face the facts:

the full system of checks and balances that the founders designed has gone, and the shift to the centralized, the elitist, and the bureaucratic has only been reinforced by globalization.

For another thing, as I have repeated so often because it is even more often ignored, the great European commentators stressed that freedom in modern societies must be maintained and assessed at two levels, not just one: at the level of the Constitution and the structures of liberty, and also at the level of the citizens and the spirit of liberty. Focusing solely on the separation of powers at the level of the Constitution is sobering enough, but it misses an equally important slippage at the level of citizens.

For yet another thing, the framers held that, though the Constitution's barriers against the abuse of power are indispensable, they were only "parchment barriers" and therefore could never be more than a part of the answer. And in some ways they were the secondary part at that. The US Constitution was never meant to be the sole bulwark of freedom, let alone a self-perpetuating "machine that would go by itself." The American founders were not, in Joseph de Maistre's words, "poor men who imagine that nations can be constituted with ink."[10] Without strong ethics to support them, the best laws and the strongest institutions would only be ropes of sand.

Jefferson even argued to Madison, who strongly disagreed with him, that because the earth belongs to the living, "no society can make a perpetual constitution. . . . Every constitution then, and every law, naturally expires at the end of 19 years. If it be enforced longer, it is an act of force, and not of right."[11]

More importantly, as Judge Learned Hand declared to new American citizens in Central Park, New York City, in 1944: "The Spirit of Liberty" is not to be found in courts, laws, and constitutions alone. "Liberty lies in the hearts of men and women; when it dies there, no constitution, no law, no court can even do much to save it. While it lies there, it needs no constitution, no law, no court to save it."[12] The nation's structures of liberty must always be balanced by the spirit of liberty, and the laws of the land by the habits of the heart.

All of which means there is a deep irony in play today. Many educated people who scorn religious fundamentalism are hard at work creating a constitutional fundamentalism, though with lawyers and judges instead of rabbis, priests, and pastors. *Constitutional* and *unconstitutional* have replaced the old language of orthodoxy and heresy. But unlike the better angels of religious fundamentalism, constitutional fundamentalism has no recourse to any divine spirit to rescue it from power games, casuistry, legalism, litigiousness—and eventually calcification and death.

So reliance on the Constitution alone, and on structures and laws alone, is foolish. But worse, the forgotten part of the framers' answer is so central, clear, and powerful that to ignore it is either willful or negligent. What the framers believed should complement and reinforce the Constitution and its separation of powers is the distinctive moral ecology that is at the heart of ordered liberty. Tocqueville called it "the habits of the heart," and I call it *the golden triangle of liberty*—the cultivation and transmission of the conviction that *freedom requires virtue, which requires faith, which requires freedom, which in turn requires virtue, which requires faith, which requires freedom,* and so on, like the recycling triangle, ad infinitum.

In short, sustainable freedom depends on the character of the rulers and the ruled alike, and on the vital trust between them—both of which are far more than a matter of law. The Constitution that is the foundational law of the land should be supported and sustained by the faith, character, and virtue of the entire citizenry, which comprises its moral constitution or habits of the heart. Together with the Constitution, these habits of the heart are the real, complete, and essential bulwark of American liberty. A contractual society grounded only in a consensus forged of calculation and competing self-interests can never last. It is as foolish for America to debase its moral currency as it is to debase the American dollar. Freedom requires limited government, but limited government requires unlimited character in the citizens, the habits of the heart.

No Straw Men, Please

Before we go a sentence farther, let me be absolutely plain. It would be a cardinal error not to recognize the originality of the modern liberal republicanism of the majority of the American founders and its crucial difference from two other positions: the classical republicanism of Greece and Rome, and the republicanism of the so-called devils party led by Machiavelli, Francis Bacon, Thomas Hobbes, and others.

The founders' position was a significant advance on the earlier conception of the relationship between freedom and virtue. In the opening sentence of his *Discourses on Livy*, Machiavelli professed himself to be a revolutionary innovator, like Christopher Columbus and Amerigo Vespucci, who had discovered new orders in the world. But it was the founders' generation that gave the world the real "new order of the ages" (novus ordo seclorum), and their vision was in direct and deliberate contrast not only to the classical republicans of Greece and Rome but to Machiavelli and his disciples.

Ironically, the great Florentine used to harp on the purported realism of his insistence that he had found the effectual truth of the matter, in contrast with the utopianism of the republics of Plato and others. But in the name of realism, he was highly unrealistic, as are many contemporary American advocates of realpolitik who ignore the place of human fallibility and the limited but essential place of virtue.

Between the old orders of Athens, Sparta, and Rome, and the "new order of the ages" wrought in Philadelphia lay not only two millennia in time but a chasm in thinking led by such revolutionaries as Machiavelli, Montaigne, Bacon, and Hobbes. Among many differences, one is striking above all. Whereas liberty for the Greeks and the Romans was supremely a matter of political reason, virtue, and what they did in public life, for modern people it is also and even more a matter of what is done in private life too, while there is less place for public reason and the common good, and none at all for virtue.

To be sure, Jefferson argued strongly for classical republicanism. He believed, along with many classical, Renaissance, and some Enlightenment republicans, that the newborn American republic could and should be sustained by virtue alone, especially the virtue that was bred by farming and stewardship of the land. (Montesquieu: "The Greek political writers, who lived under popular government, acknowledged no other force able to sustain them except that of virtue.")[13]

In strong contrast, the authors of *The Federalist*, along with other liberal republicans, were insistent that in a commercial, as opposed to a classical republic, virtue alone could never sustain freedom, and that commerce was as important as farming for cultivating virtue. There could be no simple-minded mimicking of the Greeks and Romans, Hamilton declared. "We may preach till we are tired of the theme, the necessity of disinterestedness in republics, without making a single proselyte . . . it is as ridiculous to seek for models in the simple ages of Greece and Rome, as it would be to go in quest of them among the Hottentots and Laplanders."[14]

Yet many Americans today have gone to the opposite extreme from Jefferson's, and one that the founders disapproved of equally. *If reliance on "virtue alone" is an unrealistic way to sustain freedom, so also is reliance on a "constitutional separation of powers" alone.* If liberty is to endure, the twin bulwarks of the Constitution and the golden triangle of liberty must both play their part. To replace "virtue alone" with "no virtue at all" is madness, and what the Wall Street crisis of 2008 showed about unfettered capitalism could soon be America's crisis played out on an even more gigantic screen. Leadership without character, business without ethics, and science without human values—in short, freedom without virtue—will bring the republic to its knees.

To put the point more broadly, in human affairs there will always be a limit to "the plannable, the legislatable, and regulatable," and only the fool or a utopian will try to leap over this built-in boundary. Or as T. S. Eliot wrote famously in *The Rock*, it is folly to dream of "systems so perfect that no one will need to be good."[15] Down that way, and at the point where our brave new realists are foolishly unrealistic, lies disaster for America.

Nothing Less Than the Real Thing

There is still more to be said about the proper place of virtue in guarding freedom. First, *some* virtue (rather than virtue *alone*), along with checks and balances, will always be needed because humans play what Aristotle called a "double game." According to the Bible, we humans are "flawed." We represent Kant's "crooked timber of humanity" ("Out of the crooked timber of humanity, no straight thing was ever made," which itself comes from the Bible: "That which is crooked cannot be made straight" [Eccles 1:15 KJV]). We humans act politically, inspired not only by faith, virtue, courage, honor, excellence, justice, prudence, generosity, and compassion, but also by self-interest, self-preservation, power, greed, vanity, revenge, and convenience—and wise governance must take both sides into account.

In Rome, there was a divided consulship to keep power from falling into the hands of a single dictator, though the clearer Jewish and American separation of powers is required to offset the foolish idealism of trusting in virtue alone. But substantive virtue—and not only a separation of powers—is required to offset the dangerous realities of the negative side of the human double game. Checks and balances by themselves will never be enough.

Second, this urgent and practical need for substantive virtue calls into question two strategies that some Americans count on to fill in for the loss of the founders' virtue. Both have worked in the past, but neither will work today if there is no place given to virtue at all.

One strategy is to rely on the faux virtue that in a democracy can parallel the faux honor that Montesquieu described in a monarchy. ("In well-regulated monarchies, everyone will be something like a good citizen while one will rarely find someone who is a good man.")[16] Where there is at least lip service paid to virtue, as Rochefoucauld observed famously, "hypocrisy is an homage that vice pays to virtue," so that hypocrisy may sustain a semblance of virtue even where there is no real virtue. People "proud of hiding their pride" can parade their faux virtue of humility, and so on. Bernard Mandeville made the same point in *The Fable of the Bees*: "The nearer we search into human Nature, the more we shall be convinced that the Moral Virtues are the Political Offspring which Flattery begot upon Pride."[17]

Unquestionably, that possibility worked well in the past when a broad Christian consensus was in place. There were publicly accepted standards people were supposed to live by and were supposedly living by. Machiavelli's originality was simply to turn the age-old practice of hypocrites into the newfangled philosophy of statesmen, and so to make "the appearance of virtue" operational rather than virtue itself. This, of course, was a pretend virtue that had no link to genuine virtue at all. Needless to say, this had always been played on skillfully by hypocrites, demagogues, and cynics alike.

But the pretense of virtue requires an essential condition: faux virtue, or hypocrisy, works when real virtue is honored, and there is enough of it to imitate in flattery. For that reason, it will not work as well today because of a double handicap. On the one hand, much of the United States has reached the point where virtue is hardly esteemed at all, or at least not welcomed in the public square, and where vice is often flaunted—"Greed is good," and the like. Where this is the case, there is no need for hypocrisy to flatter anything but itself, and faux virtue is redundant. On the other hand, under postmodern conditions where knowledge really is power and everything is other than it appears, there is no point even to appearing virtuous, for any true and straight-forward virtue is impossible and not worth the imitating.

The second possible form of substitute virtue is the sturdier pragmatic virtue that is driven solely by the requirements of commerce, a functional virtue parallel to the real virtues that Max Weber described as "the Protestant ethic." Such a virtue, or more properly virtues, was once real and powerful in America, and it provided the thrust that propelled America toward the heights of its economic prosperity. But they too have lost their strength in the contemporary world.

The empire of consumerism has undermined the Protestant ethic, and virtues such as "delayed gratification" have been shouldered aside by the clamor for "instant gratification." And a prominent and almost comic feature of the American business world are the recurring spasms of concern about "corporate ethics," though when the spasms have passed, what seems to have been remedied is ever-tightening legal and regulatory compliance rather than character.

Hackles Raised

But who today acknowledges the gorilla in the room? Read the speeches and the writings of the American founders on freedom, virtue, and faith, and it is impossible not to notice a body of teaching that is clear, strong, and central—themes that, as historian Bernard Bailyn observes, are "discussed endlessly, almost obsessively, in their political writings."[18] Yet somehow these themes are ignored today in the terms in which they were written. For needless to say, the framers' position raises hackles in many circles, as will the present argument unless considered without prejudice.

For a start, the golden triangle links freedom directly to virtue. In a society as diverse as today's, that raises the question, Whose virtue? and in an age that prizes toleration it raises the specter of "virtuecrats" itching to impose their values on others. Worse still, the golden triangle links freedom indirectly to faith. I would soften that to a "faith of some sort" and broaden it to include naturalistic faiths too, but it still prompts a barrage of instant dismissals that blows dust in the eyes of anyone trying to take freedom and the founders seriously.

One common line of dismissal is to say that the founders need not be taken seriously. They were only indulging in civic rhetoric for occasions such as July 4. Another approach is to say that the founders referred to religion and republicanism so often because they were children of their times, and their times were much more religious than today's. Yet another is to argue that while the founders counted on faith to help sustain freedom, two hundred years on Americans have other points of reliance, so that freedom today no longer requires virtue, or virtue faith. Yet another line of dismissal is to say that, as over the contradiction between freedom and slavery, the founders were quite simply hypocrites.

Men Rather Than Angels

All such objections are important and must be answered, but they are moot if Americans today do not understand the framers' golden triangle and its importance to sustainable liberty. Unquestionably the framers knew from history and their own experience that the wrong relationship of faith and virtue to freedom had been and would always be disastrous for both freedom and faith.

In addition, political philosophers earlier and elsewhere—most vociferously in France—had linked republicanism strongly with irreligion, along the lines we see today in France, Turkey, and secularist totalitarian countries. An oppressive monarchy and a corrupt state church were seen as one and the same, and republicans longed to be rid of both.

Thus, beyond any question, the way the American founders consistently linked faith and freedom, republicanism and religion, was not only deliberate and thoughtful, it was surprising and anything but routine. In this view, the self-government of a free republic had to rest on the self-government of free citizens, for only those who can govern themselves as individuals can govern themselves as a people. As for an athlete or a dancer, freedom for a citizen is the gift of self-control, training, and discipline, not self-indulgence.

The laws of the land may provide external restraints on behavior, but the secret of freedom is Lord Moulton's "obedience to the unenforceable," which is a matter of virtue, which in turn is a matter of faith. Faith and virtue are therefore indispensable to freedom—both to liberty itself and to the civic vitality and social harmony that go hand in hand with freedom.

Burke wrote in full agreement, "Manners [or moral standards] are of more importance than laws."[19] Rousseau had written similarly that mores, customs, and traditions, which are "engraved neither in marble nor in bronze but in the hearts of the citizens" form "the true Constitution of the State" and the "Keystone" of a republic.[20]

Tocqueville emphatically agreed. His objective in writing *Democracy in America* was not to turn the French into Americans, for liberty should take many forms. "My purpose has rather been to demonstrate, using the American example, that their laws and, above all, their manners can permit a democratic people to remain free."[21]

People today who tout the superiority of their "realism," who espouse the Machiavellian view, and who reject any place for virtue in favor of self-interest and self-preservation should ponder the logic and lesson of the Civil War. As John Quincy Adams lamented before the war, high ideals and cool judgment were on the side of freedom in the North, whereas passion and eloquence were on the side of oppression in the South. Why? The contrast demonstrated "how much more keen and powerful the impulse is of personal interest than is that of any general consideration of benevolence or humanity."[22] Neither the Civil War nor the civil rights movement could have been won on the basis of the philosophy of Machiavelli, Hobbes, and Locke—or of today's postmodern thinkers.

But that said, the golden triangle of liberty must be stated with great care. For a start, the word *requires* in "freedom requires virtue, which requires faith" does not mean a legal or constitutional requirement. The First Amendment flatly and finally prohibits the federal government from requiring faith in any established way. But a proper and positive understanding of disestablishment leads directly to the heart of the framers' audacity: *The American republic simultaneously rests on ultimate beliefs, for otherwise Americans have no right to the rights by which they thrive, yet rejects any official, orthodox formulation of what those beliefs should be.* The republic will always remain an undecided experiment that stands or falls by the dynamism of its entirely voluntary, nonestablished faiths.

Also the framers did not believe that the golden triangle was sufficient by itself to sustain freedom without the complementary safeguard of the constitutional separation of powers. That fallacy dogged many classical republics—they trusted too naively in virtue. As Madison warned, faith, character, and virtue were necessary but not sufficient in themselves to restrain a majority from overriding the rights of a minority.

> What motives are to restrain them? A prudent regard to the maxim, that honesty is the best policy, is found by experience to be as little regarded by bodies of men as by individuals. Respect for character is always diminished in proportion to the number among whom the blame or praise is to be

divided. Conscience, the only remaining tie, is known to be inadequate in individuals; in large numbers little is to be expected of it.[23]

Faith, character, and virtue were necessary and decisive, but never sufficient by themselves. They must be balanced by the immovable bulwark of constitutional rights, especially for those in the minority.

Above all, the point must be guarded from a simple misunderstanding. The framers' near unanimity about the golden triangle of liberty did not mean they were all people of faith or they all agreed about the best way to relate religion and public life, or they were individually paragons of whatever faith and virtue they did espouse. In the language of Madison's *Federalist* 51, they were "men rather than angels."

For a start, the framers demonstrated a wide spectrum of personal beliefs. Most were regular churchgoers, for whatever motive, but they ranged from orthodox Christians, such as John Jay and George Mason, to deists, such as John Adams and Thomas Jefferson, to free thinkers, such as Benjamin Franklin. In addition, the framers argued for different views of religion and public life, ranging from Patrick Henry's bill to support all churches to Jefferson's restatement of Roger Williams's "wall of separation." And as I stressed earlier, it is beyond question that several of them were distinguished for their vices and hypocrisies as well as for their virtues.

Freedom Requires Virtue

Yet for all these differences, inconsistencies, and hypocrisies, the framers consistently taught the importance of virtue for sustaining freedom, which is the first leg of the golden triangle: *freedom requires virtue*. As Benjamin Franklin tersely stated, "Only a virtuous people are capable of freedom."[24] Or as he stated it negatively in his famous maxims: "No longer virtuous, no longer free; is a maxim as true with regard to a private person as a Commonwealth."[25]

"Statesmen, my dear Sir, may plan and speculate for liberty," John Adams wrote to his cousin Zabdiel in 1776. "The only foundation of a free Constitution is pure Virtue, and if this cannot be inspired into our People, in a greater Measure than they have it now, they may exchange their Rulers, and the forms of Government, but they will not obtain a lasting Liberty."[26] Or as he wrote to Mercy Otis Warren the same year, "Public virtue cannot exist without private, and Public Virtue is the only foundation of Republics." If the success of the Revolution were to be called into question, it was "not for Want of Power or of Wisdom, but of Virtue."[27]

A key article in the influential Virginia Declaration of Rights in 1776 explicitly denies that "free government, or the blessings of liberty, can be preserved to any people but by a firm adherence to justice, moderation, temperance, frugality, and virtue." New Hampshire went further, substituting for "virtue" "all the social virtues."[28]

As these quotations show, evidence for the first leg of the golden triangle is profuse—so much so that it is tempting to reach for one of the multitude of "quote books" that form part of the arsenals on either side of the culture wars. In contrast, works such as Edwin Gaustad's *Faith of the Founders* or James Hutson's *The Founders on Religion* establish the claim beyond argument, but with the solid reliability of distinguished historians.[29]

Let me underscore four points that deserve deeper thought because they stand out so sharply from much opinion today.

First, the reason for the need for virtue is simple and incontrovertible. Only virtue can supply the self-restraint that is the indispensable requirement for liberty. Unrestrained freedom undermines freedom, but any other form of restraint on freedom eventually becomes a contradiction of freedom. For Burke, this was the dangerous irresponsibility of the French freethinkers: "They explode or render odious or contemptible that class of virtues which restrain the appetites."[30]

Second, the founders went beyond broad general statements on the importance of virtue to quite specific applications, such as the need to integrate virtue in both private and public life. "The foundations of our National policy," George Washington wrote in 1783, "will be laid in the pure and immutable principles of private morality" (a phrase repeated word for word in his First Inaugural Address in 1789).[31] "The foundation of national morality," John Adams wrote similarly, "must be laid in private families."[32]

Character Counts

This tirelessly repeated conviction lay behind the framers' insistence on the importance of character in leadership. The golden triangle challenges the rulers as much as the ruled. In his "Dissertation on the Canon and Feudal Law," John Adams directly addressed the issue of preserving liberty. He concluded that the people "have a right, an indisputable, unalienable, indefeasible, divine right to that most dreaded and envied kind of knowledge—I mean of the characters and conduct of their leaders."[33] Note the astonishing string of words that today would be naturally associated with terms such as *freedom* and *rights*, but which Adams applies to the citizens' right to know the *character* of their leaders.

Were the framers correct that character counts in leadership? Many in today's debate would dismiss their concern summarily. In a day when followers are obsessed with rights and leaders with powers and privileges, mention of virtues is irksome. And with religion widely privatized and the public square increasingly considered the realm of processes and procedures rather than principles, character and virtue are often dismissed as private issues. In the run-up to President Clinton's impeachment, for example, educated opinion was vociferous that the character of the president was irrelevant as a public issue. For all that many scholars cared, the president might have had the morals of an alley cat, but however shameless he was, his character was a purely private issue. What mattered in public was competence, not character.

But there is another party in the debate, one taught by history and experience to prize the place of character in leadership. Montesquieu even claimed that "Bad examples can be worse than crimes," for "more states have perished because of a violation of their mores than because of a violation of the Laws."[34]

The story of the American presidency, and more recently of presidential candidates, could teach this lesson by itself. "The destruction of a city comes from great men," Solon warned the Greeks. "It's not easy for one who flies too high to control himself."[35] "The passions of princes are restrained only by exhaustion," Frederick the Great remarked cynically about absolute monarchs. "Integrity has no need of rules," Albert Camus wrote more positively, and its converse is that no amount of laws and regulations can make up for lack of integrity in a leader.[36]

George Reedy, press secretary to Lyndon Johnson, looked back on his experience close to the Oval Office: "In the White House, character and personality are extremely important because there are no other limitations. . . . Restraint must come from within the presidential soul and prudence from within the presidential mind. The adversary forces which temper the actions of others do not come into play until it is too late to change course."[37]

One of the strongest but strangest endorsements of the importance of character comes from Richard Nixon himself. "C.Q." (character quotient), he claimed, was just as important as IQ in political leadership and in choosing personnel.[38] Ironically, no one need look further than his own administration for graphic illustrations of his point. Led by Henry Kissinger and Alexander Haig, not to mention the president himself, the towering egos, prickly vanities, bitter jealousies, chronic insecurities, and poisonous backbiting of his White House virtuosi were a major factor in the tragedy of his own undoing.

According to this party in the debate, character is far from a cliché or a matter of hollow civic piety. Nor is it a purely private matter, as many claimed in the scandal over Clinton's affair with a White House intern. History shows that character in leaders is crucially important. Externally, character is the bridge that provides the point of trust that links leaders with followers. Internally, character is the part gyroscope, part brake that provides the leader's deepest source of bearings and strongest source of restraint when the dizzy heights of leadership mean that there are no other limitations. Watching and emulating the character of leaders is a vital classroom in the schooling of citizens. "In the long run," James Q. Wilson concluded, "the public interest depends on private virtue."[39]

Whatever position one takes on the issue, it would be rash to dismiss the framers' position as empty rhetoric—not least because the framers expressly denied that it was. "This is not Cant," John Adams wrote to the same cousin, commending his teaching of virtue, "but the real sentiment of my heart."[40] That freedom required virtue, they believed, was a matter of political realism and a serious part of the new science of politics.

The Great Conversation

Third, the framers' conviction about freedom's need for virtue is part of their engagement with the great conversation that runs down the centuries from the Bible and the classical writers of Greece and Rome. To dismiss their point without realizing why and how they entered the conversation would be presumptuous, and to pretend today that we have no need for the wisdom of the great conversation would be foolish. For example, in May 1776 when John Witherspoon, president of Princeton and the "great teacher of the revolution," preached his landmark sermon on the eve of the Revolution, he openly addresses the classical concern about the corruption of customs and the passing of time—both of which for him are the product of sin and the corruption of human nature.

In his support of the coming revolution Witherspoon was bold and un-equivocal—"I willingly embrace the opportunity of declaring my opinion without any hesitation, that the cause in which America is now in arms, is the cause of justice, of liberty, and of human nature."[41]

But as the only minister who was to sign the Declaration of Independence, Witherspoon was no jingoistic cleric indiscriminately sprinkling holy water on the muskets on the eve of battle. Instead, he looked ahead to the moment after the euphoria of victory when citizens should appreciate the need for "national character and manners." Nothing is more certain, he warned, than that a corruption of manners would make a people ripe for destruction, and laws alone would not hold things together for long. "A good form of government may hold the rotten materials together for some time, but beyond a certain pitch, even the best constitution will be ineffectual, and slavery will ensue."[42] The golden triangle was not sufficient, but it was necessary.

George Washington's Farewell Address in 1796 engages the same conversation. Whether original to him or the work of Alexander Hamilton, his point is unmistakable: "Of all the dispositions and habits which lead to political prosperity, Religion and morality are indispensable supports. In vain would that man claim the tribute of Patriotism, who should labor to subvert these great pillars of human happiness, these firmest props of the duties of Men and citizens."[43]

Supports, pillars, props, foundations, wellsprings—Washington's choice of words tells the story by itself of how freedom requires virtue. But he too was aware of the classical understanding of decline and fall, and he addressed it directly even at that dawn-fresh moment in the new republic. "Can it be that Providence has not connected the permanent felicity of a nation with its virtue?" he asked rhetorically. To achieve such "permanent felicity," or Adams's "lasting liberty," he counseled them as "an old and affectionate friend" that they would need virtue to "control the usual current of the passions, or prevent our Nation from running the course which has hitherto marked the Destiny of Nations."[44]

If being a "nation of nations" means that Americans should have a wiser perspective on the wider world, then being the latest in the grand succession of superpowers means that Americans should also have a "history of his-tories" to offer a wiser perspective on the long reaches of time.

When Tocqueville came to write about America, he knew it would be difficult to rally his fellow Frenchmen to such an idea, but he would try nonetheless. As he wrote to Eugene Stoffels, a friend, "To persuade men that respect for the laws of God and man is the best means of remaining free . . . you say, cannot be done. I too am tempted to think so. But the thing is true all the same, and I will try to say so at all costs."[45]

By design or by neglect, Americans continue that great conversation today, and it would be the height of folly to pretend otherwise—which is precisely why it is easy for a visitor to enter these debates today, for they are not unique to Americans.

Emphatically Positive Freedom

Fourth, the framers' insistence on the importance of virtue for freedom puts them squarely against much modern thinking in the debate between neg-ative freedom, or freedom from interference, and positive freedom, or freedom for excellence. The American Revolution was unashamedly in favor of negative freedom. Quite simply, the Declaration of Independence is the grandest and most influential statement of freedom from interference in history. But unlike many modern citizens, the founders did not stop there. They were equally committed to the complementary importance of freedom for excellence. Their aim, as we saw, was liberty and not just liberation and independence.

In other words, the founders held that not just individuals but the re-public itself had an ongoing interest in the virtue of the citizenry. Private virtue was a public interest not only for the character of leaders but for ev-eryone, and this was a prime motive in the rise of the common schools and the place of public education. Article three of the Northwest Ordinance, passed by the Confederation Congress and affirmed by the First Congress under the Constitution, stated plainly at the outset: "Religion, morality, and knowledge being necessary to good government and the happiness of mankind, schools and the means of education shall for ever be encouraged."

Does this mean, as some charge, that the framers were smuggling an ar-istocracy of virtue back into the republic and were therefore undemocratic and fall foul of Tocqueville's accusation that Athens was an "aristocracy of masters"?[46] In a sense the answer is yes. The republic clearly required leaders and citizens who took virtue seriously, especially at the level of the highest national affairs. In the picture that Cicero used before the Roman Senate, citizens whose character and virtue can be "weighed" are worth more to the republic than citizens who could only be "counted."

But the accusation of an American aristocracy of virtue is miscast. In a democratic republic the size of the United States, the choice is not between an aristocracy and no aristocracy, or between aristocracy and pure democracy. Representative democracy is inevitably aristocratic in one sense, for it chooses the few to represent the many.

Thus as soon as the choice is made for *representative* rather than the *direct* or *complete* democracy of Athens, there will have to be explicit or implicit criteria for the way citizens choose who will represent them. Rule out virtue as a criterion and something else will take its place—most probably money or fame. Benjamin Rush lamented long ago that America was becoming a "bedollared nation."[47] As contemporary American politics illustrates all too clearly, the founders' aristocracy of virtue has been well and truly replaced by what the English writer William Cobbett called the worst of all aristocracies—"moneyed aristocracy."[48] Money rather than monarchy and plutocracy rather than theocracy are the chief threats to republicanism today.

Some Americans, such as Ross Perot, Mitt Romney, Michael Bloomberg, and Donald Trump, can use their wealth to pursue the presidency. Others, such as Bill Clinton and Barack Obama, use the presidency to pursue wealth. But either way the rule of money in American public life expands in leaps and bounds, so that like Athens, the United States is becoming an "aristocratic commonwealth," and even worse, a full-blooded plutocracy that is increasingly shut off to the moderately wealthy and the poor.

Without virtue, there would be no freedom. Indeed, without virtue there would be no citizens at all, for it takes a certain virtue to transform the private concerns of individuals into the public concerns of citizens willing and able to participate in the common discussion of the common good. In the language of the Athenian democrats, it takes virtue to transform the "idiot" (the purely private person) and the "tribesperson" (the member of a group) into the "citizen." For all these reasons, the framers were as committed to positive freedom as to negative freedom. They were convinced that personal virtue was a public matter for the republic, whatever the private concern for virtue that the individual, the family, and the faith community might also have. That freedom requires virtue, then, is the first leg of the golden triangle.

Virtue Requires Faith

If the framers' position on virtue is suspect today and needs to pass through stringent intellectual security checks, how much more so their views on religion. Indeed, they are an open battleground, and all the earlier qualifications about virtue need to be underscored once again, and others added. (The founders were not all people of faith, and had different views of the relationship of religion and public life, and so on.) Yet the overall evidence for what they argued is again massive and unambiguous, even from some of the more unlikely sources such as Jefferson and Paine: the founders believed that if freedom requires virtue, *virtue in turn requires faith* (of some sort).

"If Men are so wicked as we now see them with Religion," Benjamin Franklin said, "what would they be without it?"[49]

"It is impossible to account for the creation of the universe without the agency of a Supreme Being," George Washington wrote, "and it is impossible to govern the universe without the aid of a Supreme Being."[50]

"We have no government armed with powers capable of contending with human passions unbridled by morality and religion," John Adams wrote. "Avarice, ambition, revenge or gallantry would break the strongest cords of our Constitution as a whale goes through a net. Our Constitution was made only for a moral and religious people. It is wholly inadequate to the government of any other."[51]

"Should our Republic ever forget this fundamental precept of governance," John Jay wrote about the importance of faith for virtue, "men are certain to shed their responsibilities for licentiousness and this great experiment will surely be doomed."[52]

"The only surety for a permanent foundation of virtue is religion," Abigail Adams wrote. "Let this important truth be engraved upon your heart."[53]

"Can the liberties of a nation be thought secure," Thomas Jefferson wrote, "when we have removed their only firm basis, a conviction in the minds of the people, that these liberties are the gift of God? That they are violated but with his wrath? I tremble for my country when I reflect that God is just, and that His justice cannot sleep for ever."[54]

"Is there no virtue among us?" James Madison asked. "If there be not, we are in a wretched situation. No theoretical checks—no form of government can render us secure. To suppose that any form of government can secure liberty or happiness without virtue in the people is a chimerical idea."[55]

"The wise politician," Alexander Hamilton wrote, "knows that morality overthrown (and morality must fall with religion), the terrors of despotism can alone cure the impetuous passions of man, and confine him within the bounds of social duty."[56]

Did this emphasis on religion mean that the framers were arguing for an official "Christian America"? Not at all. Unquestionably most Americans at the time of the Revolution were either Christians or from a Christian background, and most American ideas were directly or indirectly rooted in the Jewish and Christian faiths. Thus even Franklin as a free thinker, writing to Ezra Stiles in 1790, made clear that he would never become a Christian, yet stated as his opinion: "As to Jesus of Nazareth, my Opinion of whom you particularly desire, I think the System of Morals and his Religion, as he left them to us, the best the World ever saw or is likely to see."[57]

But the historical and statistical importance of the Christian faith in 1776 did not for a moment translate into any official position for the Christian faith or for any formal notion of a Christian nation. Joel Barlow, who negotiated the Treaty of Tripoli with the Pasha in 1796, may have been a deist with little sympathy for the Christian faith, but his famous clause to the treaty caused little stir at the time: "As the government of the United States of America is not in any sense founded on the Christian religion . . ."[58]

Beyond that untypically bald statement, the First Amendment, on the one hand, barred any official national establishment of religion, and over the next decades the states came slowly into line until the last establishment had gone. On the other hand, many of the framers, and later President Eisenhower in the 1950s, spoke of religion in generic rather than specific terms, and they advocated religion only for secular or utilitarian reasons that the Romans understood well and on which Edward Gibbon commented famously. Religion, at the very least, was the sole force capable of fostering the virtue and restraining the vice necessary for the health of the republic.

Significantly, Franklin, for example, went on from the earlier quotation to underscore that he was interested in "the fundamental Principles of all sound Religion," which he found in many sects and faiths. And what concerned

Washington in his Farewell Address was not religious orthodoxy itself but the eminently practical point that "true religion and good morals are the only solid foundations of public liberty and happiness."[59] For his part, Jefferson greatly preferred Unitarianism to the Christian faith, and eagerly looked forward to its expected triumph over traditional faith, but his interest was not in polemical issues. "Both religions," he wrote, "make honest men, and that is the only point society has any authority to look to."[60]

What About Atheists?

Did this emphasis on religion mean that the framers did not grant freedom of conscience to atheists, or that they thought atheists would not be good citizens? Again, emphatically not. In addition to the First Amendment, the Constitution itself required that there be no religious test for office in the United States. Properly speaking, atheism (or secularism as a practical form of atheism) is itself a worldview or form of faith, though expressly naturalistic and nonsupernatural. But regardless of philosophical niceties, the framers were emphatic that the right of freedom of conscience, or religious liberty, was absolute, unconditional, and a matter of equality for all.

As early as 1644, Roger Williams had staked out the radical position in *The Bloudy Tenent of Persecution* that freedom of conscience or "soul freedom" meant "a permission of the most paganish, Jewish, Turkish, or anti-Christian consciences and worships, be granted to all men in all nations and countries."[61] A century and a half later the same note of universality and equality rings out clearly in 1785 in Madison's "Memorial and Remonstrance": "Above all are they to be considered as retaining an 'equal to the free exercise of Religion according to the dictates of conscience.'"[62] John Adams wrote unequivocally to his son, "Government has no Right to hurt a hair of the head of an Atheist for his Opinions."[63]

It must be added, however, that like Voltaire and other Enlightenment philosophers who disdained religion, the founders were less sanguine about the consequences of a government of atheists or a society of atheists—"It would be better far," John Adams wrote, "to turn back to the gods of the Greeks than to endure a government of atheists."[64]

Secularists, of course, are free to counter the founders' misgivings by demonstrating their capacity to build an enduring nationwide foundation for the virtues needed for the American republic on entirely secular grounds,

grounds that need no place at all for religious beliefs. Thoughtful atheists, such as Christopher Hitchens, stated this claim boldly in theory, but its challenge remains to be picked up in practice. The plain fact is that no free and lasting civilization anywhere in history has so far been built on atheist foundations. At the very least, it would be a welcome change for secularists to shift from their strident attacks on religiously based virtues to building their own replacements and attempting to persuade a majority of their fellow citizens of their merits.

What are we to make of the founders' misgivings about a society of atheists? Is it an inconsistency, or a form of hypocrisy, perhaps even an egregious contradiction like their views of slavery? Were they simply reacting to the excesses of the French Revolution? There was certainly an element of the latter. Washington referred delicately in his Farewell Address to the malign influence of "refined education on minds of peculiar structure," and Hamilton blasted the French radicals more openly. "The attempt by the rulers of a nation to destroy all religious opinion, and pervert a whole people to Atheism," he wrote, "is a phenomenon of profligacy reserved to consummate the infamy of the unbridled reformers of France!"[65]

But the founders' position was far more thoughtful than just a reaction. They were convinced that only faiths that (in modern parlance) were *thick* rather than *thin* would have the power to promote and protect virtue. After all, raise such questions as, Why be virtuous? What is virtue? and What happens if someone is not virtuous? and anyone can see the faiths have more to say about the inspiration, content, and sanctions for virtue than any other form of human thought—and certainly so for the overwhelming majority of people outside university circles.

Needless to say, individual atheists and secularists can be virtuous too, far more so in some cases than many religious believers. But the political question is whether atheism and secularism can provide a sufficient foundation to foster the needed virtues of the wider citizenry over the course of the running generations. This task waits to be demonstrated.

Cynical or Utilitarian?

The founders' stress on the need for faith can be expressed cynically, and Gibbon is often quoted for his famous comment on the Roman attitude toward religion. Voltaire scornfully dismissed religion for "respectable people" like himself and his friends, though he advocated it for the rest: "I want my lawyer, my tailor, my servants, even my wife to believe in God, because it means that I shall be cheated and robbed and cuckolded less often."[66] But the evidence from the American founders suggests that they were utilitarian rather than cynical. They sincerely believed that, even if they themselves did not share the faith, it would take faith to do the job of shaping the virtue needed to promote and protect republican freedom.

For some of the framers, though, such a view was unquestionably utilitarian *and* somewhat cynical. But it was not necessarily hypocritical. And it was this functional appreciation of faith that lay behind several incidents for which the framers have been charged with hypocrisy—for instance, the story Ethan Allen told of a friend meeting President Jefferson on his way to church one Sunday "with his large red prayer book under his arm," and exchanging greetings.

> "Which way are you walking, Mr Jefferson?" the friend asked.
>
> "To church, Sir," the president replied.
>
> "You going to church, Mr J. You do not believe a word in it."
>
> "Sir," said Mr Jefferson, "No nation has ever yet existed or been governed without religion. Nor can be. The Christian religion is the best religion that has ever been given to man and I as chief Magistrate of this nation am bound to give it the sanction of my example. Good morning, Sir."[67]

Jefferson's example is instructive. In two important areas there was a striking gap between his private and public views—over slavery, and over religion in public life. In the case of slavery, it is hard not to conclude that the writer of the Declaration of the Independence was hypocritical. He owned more than three hundred slaves in his lifetime, he had more when he died than when he wrote the Declaration, and he imported slaves into France, where he knew slavery was illegal and not customary, as it was in Virginia. But beyond his vested interest in his own slaves, there was always his anguish over the unavoidable dilemma he saw: the slaves' freedom would endanger America's freedom. In his own words, he was caught as he admitted between "Justice in one scale, and self-preservation in the other."[68]

In the case of religion in public life, Jefferson was probably not so much hypocritical or anguished as utilitarian and savvy. He was a deist who undoubtedly loathed organized religion and serious theology of all kinds—Protestant, Catholic, and Jewish. He believed the Christian faith had been seriously corrupted and would soon be replaced by Unitarianism, and he was a church-state separationist who fiercely defended his "wall of separation." Yet as the conversation with Ethan Allen shows, whether Jefferson was two-faced or simply utilitarian, there is no question that he also believed that freedom requires virtue, and virtue faith, and that he as chief magistrate must support certain public expressions of faith.

Faith Requires Freedom

Needless to say, the third leg of the golden triangle is the most radical, and if the first two legs challenge the unexamined assumptions of many liberals today, the third does the same for many conservatives: *faith requires freedom*.

Nothing, absolutely nothing in the American experiment is more revolutionary, unique, and decisive than the first sixteen words of the First Amendment that are the religious liberty clauses. At one stroke, what Marx called "the flowers on the chains" and Lord Acton the "gilded crutch of absolutism" was stripped away.[69] The persecution that Roger Williams called "spiritual rape" and a "soul yoke," and Lord Acton called "spiritual murder," was prohibited.[70] The burden of centuries of oppression was lifted, what Williams lamented as "the rivers of civil blood" spilled by faulty relations between religion and government were stanched, and faith was put on its free and fundamental human footing as "soul freedom," Williams's term for what was a matter of individual conscience and uncoerced freedom. The Williamsburg Charter, a celebration of the genius of the First Amendment on the occasion of its two hundredth anniversary, summarized the public aspect of this stunning achievement:

> No longer can sword, purse, and sacred mantle be equated. Now, the government is barred from using religion's mantle to become a confessional State, and from allowing religion to use the government's sword and purse to become a coercing Church. In this new order, the freedom of the government from religious control and the freedom of religion from government control are a double guarantee of the protection of rights. No faith is preferred or prohibited, for where there is no state-definable orthodoxy, there can be no state-definable heresy.[71]

The First Amendment was of course no bolt out of the blue. It was the crowning achievement of the long, slow, tortuous path to religious liberty that grew out of the horrors of the Wars of Religion and the daring bravery of thinkers such as Roger Williams, William Penn, John Leland, Isaac Backus, George Mason, Thomas Jefferson, James Madison, the Culpeper Baptists, and many others.

Many of the great peaks of this story and many of the greatest protagonists of religious liberty lie in the terrain of American history. In the "argument between friends," for example, the maverick dissenter Roger Williams clashed with the orthodox John Cotton of Boston in challenging the notion of the uniformity of religion in a civil state and the doctrine of persecution that inevitably accompanied it. This pernicious doctrine, he said, "is proved guilty of all the blood of the souls crying for vengeance under the altar." In its place, he asserted, "it is the will and command of God that . . . a permission of the most paganish, Jewish, Turkish, or anti-Christian consciences and worships, be granted to all men in all countries: and that they are only to be fought against with that sword which is only (in soul matters) able to conquer, to wit, the sword of God's spirit, the Word of God."[72]

Almost like an echo, Madison rang out the same themes in his "Memorial and Remonstrance" protesting against Patrick Henry's proposal to levy a religion tax that everybody could earmark for the church of their choice. No, the little man with the quiet voice protested, hammering home point after point with precision as well as force, this was absolutely wrong, and there was a better way. All Madison's principles are as fresh today as when he wrote them. Freedom of conscience, for example, is the single best antidote to the radical extremism of the Islamists, as it is to the state-favored secularism of the European Union, and as it is to the illiberalism of American legal secularism. Coercion and compulsion, from one side, and exclusion from the public square, from the other, all contradict conscience, and therefore freedom, at its core.

Without coming to grips with freedom of conscience in every generation, Islam cannot modernize peacefully, Europe cannot advance freely, and America will never fulfill the promise of its great experiment in freedom. The present liberal reliance on such purely negative notions as hate speech and hate crimes is both inadequate and foolish, and can even be dangerous. Without acknowledging the cornerstone place of religious liberty, Europe will not be able to accommodate both liberty and cultural diversity, Muslims will not be able to maintain the integrity of their own faith under the conditions of modernity—let alone learn to live peacefully with others—and America will never create the truly civil and cosmopolitan public square that the world requires today.

In 1792, Madison captured the originality of what they had attempted in creating the Constitution. "In Europe, charters of liberty have been granted by power. America has set the example and France has followed it, of charters of power granted by liberty."[73] His point remains, along with its challenge. The liberty of the American republic is not self-sustaining, and it needs a safeguard beyond that of the Constitution and its separation of powers. But what does it take to turn parchment barriers into living bulwarks? What is the catalyst that can bond together the external laws of the Constitution with the internal commitments and duties of citizens—rulers no less than ruled? The framers' answer was to understand, cultivate, and transmit the golden triangle of liberty, and thus the habits of the heart that sustained the citizens and the republic alike.

The founders' solution was an attempt at true liberal education or *paideia*. There is simply no schooling and no apprenticeship that is more challenging yet more fruitful than that of the politics of freedom. Freedom requires virtue, which in turn requires faith of some sort, which in turn requires freedom. Only so can a free people hope to remain "free always." Once again, it is imperative to appreciate how this indispensable cultivation and passing on the "spirit of freedom" and the "habits of the heart" goes all the way back not simply to Tocqueville, Montesquieu, and Burke, but to Judaism and the Sinai covenant. This fundamental Jewish difference from the superpowers of the ancient world is stunning, and no one has expressed the point better than Rabbi Sacks:

> What endures and what wanes? What survives and what is eclipsed? Ancient Egypt and ancient Israel were two nations that posed the great question of time: how in a world of flux and change, do we create something that defeats mortality? The Egyptians gave one answer, a response that has long appealed to emperors and kings. We defeat time by creating monuments that will outlive the winds and sands of time. Ancient Israel gave a different and altogether counter-intuitive reply. . . . You achieve immortality not by building pyramids or statues—but by *engraving your values on the hearts of your children, and they on theirs, so that our ancestors live on in us, and we in our children, and so on until the end of time.*[74]

Again, will it be said that freedom was too hard a challenge for Americans to overcome? Here, then, is the fifth question on the checklist that Americans must answer constructively: *Are you prepared for the challenge of sustaining freedom?*

What is the link between freedom and virtue? What would be the objection to restoring the golden triangle of freedom today? What do those who reject the founders' system for sustaining freedom propose to put in its place? Is American civic education what it should be? The fact is that freedom is the greatest enemy of freedom, and it never lasts forever, so the task of sustaining freedom is the greatest challenge that faces a free society. The founders' answer is unquestionably the most ingenious solution ever proposed in history of freedom, but for various reasons most Americans now reject it or have largely forgotten what it is. But that raises a further question: If Americans do not agree with the founders' solution, do they have in mind a better way to sustain freedom? Or are they courting the inevitable outcome of failing to do so? Only history will tell, and history's options for the outcome are strictly limited.

HOW WILL YOU
MAKE *the* WORLD
SAFE *for* DIVERSITY?

*Congress shall make no law respecting an establishment
of religion, or prohibiting the free exercise thereof.*

FIRST AMENDMENT OF THE US CONSTITUTION

*T*o be honest, I am somewhat embarrassed. We have been promised
millions of dollars to celebrate freedom of speech and freedom of the
press, but virtually no one has come forward to celebrate religious freedom.
What would you propose that would be worthy?" It was August 1986, and
the speaker was Chief Justice Warren Burger at a lunch in Washington, DC.
He had just been appointed to lead the Bicentennial Commission celebrating
the two-hundredth anniversary of the United States Constitution, and
Senator Ted Stevens of Alaska, who was a close friend of his, had invited me
to have lunch with the two of them to discuss the plans for the celebration.

What would I propose that was worthy of celebrating religious freedom,
and what it has meant to America? I am an Englishman, and I had arrived in
the United States less than two years earlier. I had been a BBC reporter for a
documentary on the role of religion in President Reagan's election, and at the
time I was a Visiting Fellow at the Brookings Institution in Washington, DC.
While there, I had written, purely for my own eyes, a one-page memo on the
genius of the first sixteen words of the First Amendment to the Constitution.
For one thing, freedom of religion and conscience for all is history's most
profound answer to the basic human challenge of how we live with our deepest
differences. For another, this freedom comes as close to the secret of the

greatness of the American republic as any other single feature. Through an unlikely series of circumstances, the memo had fallen into the hands of the senator, who had just been appointed to the Bicentennial Commission himself.

That incident in my early days in the United States raises the challenge of the sixth question on the checklist: *How do America's current views of freedom allow Americans to handle the challenge of modern diversity, and in President Kennedy's words, "make the world safe for diversity"? In particular, how are Americans to handle disagreement and opposition from their fellow Americans?* Technically known as *pluralization,* an explosion of diversity has burst on to the world in the last generation, created by the combined effects of the media, travel, and scholarship, including the mass movement of peoples (most obviously the migrants recently flooding into Europe). Pluralization is a central fact of the modern world and modern life, and it certainly characterizes modern America as the world's lead society. As it is said, "everyone is now everywhere."

Socially and politically, pluralization raises the question of how we are to live with our deepest differences, especially when those differences are religious and ideological. The issue, needless to say, has been at the heart of America's culture wars for more than fifty years, but not just because of religious and ideological differences. There is an important additional reason why it remains highly combustible now. A key feature of Left/liberal strategy and its political correctness has been the way it silences disagreement and opposition—another resemblance to 1789. How we live with our deepest differences and how we handle disagreements and opposition are also an immense problem for the world at large.

I thought rapidly when I heard the Chief Justice's question, and suggested that Americans should celebrate the genius of the religious liberty provisions of the First Amendment in a charter that honored and reaffirmed the significance of freedom of conscience and religion for America and the world. Shortly afterward, I found myself addressing the full Bicentennial Commission in the Annapolis State House, outlining the same ideas in greater depth. Nearly two years later, the proposal had grown into the Williamsburg Charter, a celebration and reaffirmation of the genius of the first sixteen words of the First Amendment, the religious liberty provisions. The charter was published in Williamsburg at the Hall of the House of Burgesses on June 25, 1988. It was signed by a distinguished group of American leaders, led by former presidents Gerald Ford and Jimmy Carter, and the signers included both chief justices Warren Burger and William Rehnquist and leaders from a wide spectrum of American society and life.

It would be fair to say that the Williamsburg Charter was a substantive success, but fell well short of its political and educational goals. (Among other things, we had in mind no less than a restoration of civic education on freedom of religion and conscience for the public schools.) It has been described as the best statement on religious freedom in the last century, and its key notion, the "civil public square" still offers the best solution to the fruitlessness of the culture wars. But the Williamsburg Charter encountered two obstacles that proved fatal. For a start, it was attacked by key players on the religious right, who went out of their way to block President Reagan's support. ("The culture wars are in the interests of Republicans," one cabinet secretary said to me, "so you will only get to the president over my dead body.") Later, it became clear that for many of the signers it was a bicentennial statement in "red, white, and blue" rather than a serious and costly dedication to standing for a constructive political vision of freedom today.

Be that as it may, what matters is that at the time of the two hundredth anniversary of the US Constitution there was still a broad if somewhat shallow consensus on the place of religious freedom for all in American life. In spite of nearly thirty years of culture warring, ever since the early Madalyn Murray O'Hair lawsuits opposing school prayer, the consensus on the importance of freedom of religion and conscience still struck most people as highly important and deeply American. With hindsight, it is clear that the last gasp of this broad consensus was the passing of the Religious Freedom Restoration Act in 1993, which was passed by both houses of Congress with near unanimity and had the full support of President Clinton and even of the ACLU.

The Great Sea Change

By the end of the Obama administration, less than twenty years later, that consensus had collapsed, and the landscape of the discussion of freedom of religion and conscience was unrecognizable—not only for those who remember the late twentieth century but for those who have read Alexis de Tocqueville on America in the 1830s and those who appreciate the struggles and victories of such earlier heroes as Roger Williams, William Penn, Isaac Backus, James Madison, John Leland, and Thomas Jefferson. This recent sea change on religious freedom in America is stunning, and it has titanic significance for the broader issues of freedom, for religious freedom has always been a primary and critical part of America's overall freedom, and for America's significance for the wider world. This tragic degeneration deserves far more serious attention than it has received.

The results of this sea change are often surreal. As I write, for example, the Student Activities Commission at Georgetown University is examining charges that Love Saxa, a student group promoting Roman Catholic views of marriage and sexuality, is guilty of sanctioning "hatred and intolerance." In other words, in true Mad Hatter style, a Catholic group is attacked at a Catholic university for positions that lie at the heart of Catholicism.

What is behind this sea change? There were certainly weaknesses in the defense of freedom of religion and conscience before the Religious Freedom Restoration Act. It was bizarre, for example, that so many conservatives thought and acted as if religious freedom could be defended by law and litigation alone, without any attention to civic education and what Tocqueville called the "habits of the heart." That distorted emphasis on law at the expense of civic education had long been a fallacy of 1960s liberalism. But as the culture wars deepened, it became a hallmark of conservatives too, and led to the deepening bitterness of the culture wars as batteries of lawyers, each with huge defense funds, lined up on either side of every passing issue. Yet such weaknesses are nothing compared with what has happened since 1993, for America is now experiencing an open assault on freedom of religion and conscience. What was the founders' "first liberty" and the freedom that (Lord Acton wrote) "secures the rest" is in danger of being dislodged from its central and time-honored place in American life.[1] The significance of this blunder reverberates far beyond the importance of freedom of religion and conscience by itself. Five major factors have contributed to the recent sea change.

The Radical Rs

First, there are *the reducers*, those who shrink freedom of religion and conscience to a size that would be unrecognizable to America's earlier champions such as Roger Williams and James Madison. For example, leading contemporary voices, including President Obama and Secretary of State Hillary Clinton for a time, referred to freedom of religion and conscience as "freedom of worship" in a way that, wittingly or unwittingly, undermined the robustness and comprehensiveness of the right and its protection. Many other voices followed suit. As a result, many people no longer understand freedom of religion and conscience to be about "free exercise," and certainly not to do with any "free exercise that touches public life." It is now said to be a purely private affair, with no impact on speech or conduct in public life.

Whether deliberate or not, that shrinking of a foundational human right is wrong, retrograde, un-American, and disastrous. Freedom of religion and conscience, which the religious liberty clauses of the First Amendment protect as "free exercise," is far more than freedom of worship. There is hardly a dictator worthy of the name who has not allowed his people freedom of worship—in other words, the freedom for people to believe whatever they like between their two ears so long as they stay in their homes and keep their mouths tightly shut. But that is not what is meant by freedom of religion and conscience in America. In May 1776, George Mason's draft of the Virginia Declaration of Rights had proposed the word *toleration*, which was routinely used at the time. But the shy, young "Gemmy" Madison advanced the cause of freedom light years when he struck it out and replaced it with the words "free exercise," which were later enshrined in the Bill of Rights in 1791.

Far more than "freedom of worship," freedom of religion and conscience is the comprehensive right to seek, hold, exercise, share, and change one's ultimate beliefs, based solely on the dictates of conscience. Article 18 of the Universal Declaration of Human Rights is even clearer and more specific than the First Amendment, and there is no question that the free exercise of the religious liberty provisions in the First Amendment and Article 18 go far beyond freedom of worship. Only the comprehensive right of freedom of religion and conscience would have allowed Dr. Martin Luther King Jr. to speak out in American public life rather than in his Ebenezer Baptist Church alone, and only the same strong right can protect those who run the risk of death for "apostasy" when they choose to convert from one religion to another.

Second, there are the *removers*, those who have aggressively attempted to change freedom of religion and conscience from freedom *for* religion to freedom *from* religion. Some people have argued for this removal on the grounds that religious freedom was merely freedom for the religious and therefore biased and not inclusive. That is entirely wrong. Freedom of religion and conscience is *freedom for everyone*, and it has always included all ultimate beliefs, whether religious or naturalistic, transcendent or secularist—it includes atheists and agnostics no less than Jews, Christians, Muslims, Buddhists, Hindus, Mormons, and all other religions. The real problem is not that secularists have been excluded from freedom of religion and conscience, but that many secularists (though not all) have refused to acknowledge that their secularism is also an ultimate belief, with all the attendant rights and responsibilities that that means.

The more practical reason for the drive for freedom *from* religion was the terrorist attack of September 11. In the Lowell Lecture at Harvard in 1992, Gore Vidal had argued that radical monotheism of Judaism, the Christian faith, and Islam was "the great unmentionable evil" at the heart of Western civilization. In the same tenor, Christopher Hitchens flamboyantly countered President George W. Bush's claim that terrorist countries were the "axis of evil" by saying that "the real axis of evil" was the same three Abrahamic faiths that more than half the world believed. The attacks on 9/11 reinforced and accelerated this reaction against religion, which is now equated automatically with violence and extremism—though, ironically, the Obama administration consistently refused to refer to "radical Islamic terrorism."

There is no question that in most liberal circles now, religion has gained a negative reputation. Even at the more popular level, the current vogue is firmly for "spirituality, not religion." In the longer term this fashionable notion will be seen as a distinction without a difference, and it will not endure for long, but in the short term it makes it all too easy for people to move on to the notion that the solution to religious extremism is to remove religion from public life altogether—which in its strong form is a brand of secular extremism and highly illiberal as well.

Third, there are the *rebranders*, those who turn the notion of freedom of religion and conscience upside down and inside out, and then attack it as a form of power play that is dangerous and should be abolished. There are two types of rebranders speaking out at the moment. The more prominent ones are the activists on behalf of the sexual revolution who hijacked the notion of discrimination from the 1960s civil rights movement. They brandish it to attack all who disagree with them as discriminating, prejudiced, bigoted, and hateful. For example, Martin Castro, Obama's chairman of the US Commission on Civil Rights, wrote that "The phrases 'religious liberty' and 'religious freedom' will stand for nothing except hypocrisy so long as they remain code words for discrimination, intolerance, racism, sexism, homophobia, Islamophobia, Christian supremacy, or any form of intolerance. . . . Present day 'religious liberty' efforts are aimed against the LGBTQ community."[2] In a move that is either ignorant or illiberal, or both, major newspapers have even begun to put scare quotes around "religious freedom," as if it were a so-called right that is only a code word for bigotry.

This attack is born of the fear that religious freedom is being weaponized, used as a weapon against the sexual revolution and alternative relationships. To be sure, some people may see it this way and try to use it this way, but three considerations should offset an overreaction to this fear. First, freedom of religion and conscience is primarily a shield and not a sword. It stands to protect the believer's believing rather than to promote the believer's beliefs. Second, freedom of religion and conscience is not a right for some but for everybody, and its test is always the status of how it protects the smallest minority and the most unfashionable group. And third, there is as much danger in misusing nondiscrimination as a weapon as in using freedom of religion and conscience as a weapon.

Fortunately, there are distinguished supporters of LGBTQ rights who also recognize the importance of freedom of religion and conscience, and who therefore repudiate the charge that all disagreement is discrimination. The blanket charge is a blunder of historic proportions, with grave implications for freedom that are highly illiberal. It is a subversion of liberty to characterize (demonize) all disagreement and dissent as discrimination without investigation into real cases. The current targets of such attacks are mostly Christians, whether Evangelicals or Roman Catholics, but soon the victims will be Jews, for all three Abrahamic faiths in their orthodox forms stand for a different way and disagree with the policies of the sexual revolution. The blanket antidiscrimination tactic, which makes no distinction between principle and prejudice, covers many other religions too. And eventually it will boomerang back on the heads of liberals and progressives themselves.

The truth is that antidiscrimination can be made into far too sweeping a category to be just, for all thoughtful people discriminate in the original positive sense of making discerning distinctions. Making distinctions, for instance, is inescapable and at the heart of human speech, because our words are specific and refer to certain things and not others. Making distinctions is also at the heart of human logic. According to the principle of noncontradiction, A cannot simultaneously be A and non-A. The truth is that discernment comes through making distinctions between two realities. It is therefore vital to be able to distinguish between making proper distinctions and improper discrimination, and not to lump together all disagreements as discrimination, prejudice, and bigotry.

Jews, Christians, Muslims, Mormons, and many religious believers immediately fall foul of the rebranders' charge for a deeper reason. They make essential distinctions that are rooted in God's creation—the distinction between holy and unholy, sacred and secular, true and false, right and wrong, wise and foolish (and male and female, heaven and earth, and God and humans). Such distinctions are basic to their views of the world and therefore of their freedom to be faithful. They do not see such distinctions as accidental, or a matter of prejudice, because the distinctions go back to their understanding of the origins of the universe and to God himself. Creation in the biblical worldview is essentially "a process of separation" (Leo Strauss) or a "process of demarcation, distinction, separation" (Leon Kass). Distinction is the means by which chaos and disorder are brought into order.

The point is not that all distinctions are necessarily right and true. In a free society, that remains to be discussed. But there is no question that they may be sincerely held, intellectually serious, culturally consequential views of the universe. As such, they represent an alternative worldview, and they cannot be dismissed as mere prejudice without a hearing. Disagreement may or may not be prejudice. According to the biblical view, God himself is the great "separator and distinguisher."[3] Daniel Elazar states simply, "The universe rests upon making and maintaining proper distinctions whose roots go back to creation," and sin is seen as the transgression of such boundaries, whether deliberately or unintentionally.[4] Rabbi Heschel underscores the same point: "The power to make distinctions is a primary operation of intelligence. We distinguish between white and black, beautiful and ugly, pleasant and unpleasant, gain and loss, good and evil, right and wrong. The fate of mankind depends upon the realization that the distinction between good and evil, right and wrong, is superior to all other distinctions."[5]

In Rabbi Sacks's words, it is a feature of the Jewish priestly mind to see the universe in terms of "distinctions, boundaries, domains, in which each object or act has its proper place and must not be mixed with another." In short, "goodness equals order," "disorder in the moral universe is like entropy in the physical universe," and such disordering is sin as transgression of a moral boundary and the disruption of the social harmony. Thus "Jews are charged to respect and honor boundaries and differences by obeying the will of God, Creator of the world and Architect of its order."[6]

From the biblical and the classical Greek and Roman perspective, this conviction means that when the extremes of any revolution reject such distinctions altogether, they are courting either chaos or insanity. For the rebranders, however, it means that Judaism and the Christian faith, and their defense through freedom of religion and conscience, are guilty of "discrimination"—by definition. The charge is sticking for the moment because of its novelty and the hijacked prestige of the civil rights movement, though its illiberalism and confusion are bound to show through. It represents an insidious attack on freedom of religion and conscience in the form of an uncompromising scorched-earth, take-no-captives, zero-sum style of "antidiscrimination."

True liberals should think again before advancing such illiberal arguments. Such accusations entangle them in inconsistencies. Deeply held convictions over two entirely different ways of life may be a matter of honest dissent and not discrimination in the sense of prejudice. If, then, any one is accused of discrimination, why is the accuser not guilty too? Or is the only difference the degree of power and popularity of the one who makes the charge? It is vital today to see how "antidiscrimination" arguments are being erected into a damning prohibition of three foundational rights: political dissent, conscientious objection, and civil disobedience. These are essential to moral politics and the triumph of right over might, and they have long been a bulwark of freedom and justice and of genuine liberalism.

Worst of all, there is a distinct whiff of totalitarianism in the air in the manner by which "antidiscrimination" activists stifle dissent and override conscientious objection. Like Marxism and communism, some proponents of the Left/liberalism demonstrate a form of "antidiscrimination" that is hardening into a comprehensive political ideology that brooks no dissent and seeks to sweep all before it, including what is seen as "superstition" (religion) and all the forces of "reaction" (again, religion). One professor from the Harvard Law School touted the hard line without shame when he advised his fellow liberals:

> For liberals, the question now is how to deal with the losers in the culture wars.
> That's mostly a question of tactics. My own judgment is that taking a hard line
> ("You lost, live with it") is better than trying to accommodate the losers, who—
> remember—defended, and are defending, positions that liberals regard as
> having no normative pull at all. Trying to be nice to the losers didn't work well
> after the Civil War, not after *Brown*. (And taking a hard line seemed to work
> reasonably well in Germany and Japan after 1945.) I should note that LGBT
> activists in particular seem to have settled on the hard line approach.[7]

Quite apart from the professor's invidious equation of Western tradition with
Nazism, the implications for freedom of religion and conscience, and for dissent,
conscientious objection, and civil disobedience, are profoundly troubling.

Jewish thinkers have long been alert to the dangers in these illiberal arguments, and the danger goes directly back to 1789 and the French Revolution's
treatment of the Jews. Prior to the revolution, Judaism was either tolerated
or persecuted *as a whole community*, and there was little difference between
personal and public expressions of faith within Jewish communities. But in
the name of Enlightenment tolerance, the revolution set down a new principle that was an enforced schizophrenia, which struck at the heart of the
Jewish (or any other believer's) freedom to be faithful. ("To the Jews as citizens, everything; to Judaism as corporate community, nothing.") This principle, in its turn, produced a damaging outcome: a coercive privatization of
faith. (The choice as the Jews put it, "Be a Jew at home, a human being when
you go out.")[8]

The effect of this tolerant intolerance, in Jacob Neusner's words, was to
"de-Judaize the Jews, to define the terms of their existence in ways that
denied the Jews the right to be themselves."[9] His conclusion on whether
Jews should celebrate the French Revolution was blunt. "No, we Jews
gained nothing on Bastille Day, but we lost a great deal. So I don't think
we have anything to celebrate in the French revolution. It was very bad for
the Jews."[10]

Years later, in a 1962 lecture, "Why We Remain Jews," Leo Strauss added
a further warning to his fellow Jews that goes to the heart of today's
menace. If liberals tried to try to stamp out discrimination altogether, they
would spell the end of liberalism because the law would have to reach right
into the private world and destroy not only private faith but private life
itself. "The prohibition against every 'discrimination' would mean the

abolition of the private sphere, the denial of the difference between state and society, in a word, the destruction of liberal society."[11]

More than fifty years later, America has witnessed the success of Rudi Dutschke's "long march through the institutions," such as universities, the press, and the media. Strauss's prediction came closer through President Obama and his regulators. The intended targets of the Left are religious believers and conservatives, and all who differ from the sexual revolution, but true liberalism and genuine diversity are the unintended casualties. The vile medieval notion that "error has no rights" is alive and all too well in circles that once took pride in being liberal but are fast cementing their status as the radiating centers of illiberalism. When talk of *liberation* becomes a fig leaf for absolutism, and *expanding rights* becomes a stalking horse for totalitarian-style coercion and a denial of rights, it is time for true liberals to stand up and challenge the proto-totalitarian left-wing wolves now marauding in liberal sheep's clothing.

The less prominent rebranders are the postmodern thinkers who expand on the notion of power in the ideas of Friedrich Nietzsche and Michel Foucault, and therefore charge that advocacy of freedom of religion and conscience is a form of power play to oppress other peoples and nations. Again, like the "antidiscrimination" tactic, this charge will backfire on its postmodernist advocates, because once they have removed truth from the equation, all arguments become a form of power play—including their own. The accusation of powermongering is particularly galling and false when leveled against freedom of religion and conscience. The truth is quite the reverse of what the critics say. The demand for freedom of religion and conscience has always been the cry of the weak, the powerless, the marginalized, and the oppressed—those who know that it takes truth to make a stand against power.

The first two mentions of religious liberty in history are by Tertullian and Lactantius, Christian writers in the early Christian centuries who represent the young and much-persecuted church, and who long predated the hierarchical power structures that the Roman Catholic Church unfortunately borrowed from the Roman Empire.[12] Tertullian in his *Apology* was the first to use the term *religious freedom* (*libertatem religionis*) and to link it with the idea of a human and natural right. Lactantius spelled out religious freedom clearly in his own writing, but more importantly, he was tutor to Constantine's son. He was therefore behind the twin emperors Constantine and Licinius and their famous

Protocols of Milan in AD 313. This was the first official document to set out the notion of religious freedom and to distinguish it clearly from mere tolerance.[13]

Later heroes of modern religious freedom, such as Roger Williams, John Leland, and William Penn, would have been astonished to find themselves accused of being voices on the side of power, let alone the establishment. For example, Williams's 1644 classic *The Bloudy Tenent of Persecution for Cause of Conscience* is a passionate cry for justice against the oppressions of government. The fact is that today's real "paternalists" and "colonialists" are the advocates of the sexual revolution who are attempting to impose their agenda on many societies around the world, using law and economic aid to bulldoze their will on global cultures regardless of local conscience. Freedom of religion and conscience, in contrast, assumes and requires persuasion rather than coercion. It may seek to persuade anyone of anything, but it coerces and imposes on no one. This distinctive principle has long been one of the surest and most solid bedrock protections of the powerless and the oppressed. It is therefore time to say to our brave new rebranders: "Deconstructionists, deconstruct thyselves!"

Fourth, there are the *reimaginers*, those global utopians who join John Lennon in dreaming of a borderless world with no heaven, no hell, no countries, and no religion, when humankind will be at peace and "the world will live as one."[14] The dream of peace is not new. A messianic passion was first heard in the stirring voices of the Hebrew prophets, and it has been a recurring theme down the centuries. But in its aggressively antireligious form, it has been given fresh twist through globalization, connectivity, and the sexual revolution. John B. Watson, the pioneer of behaviorism, worked to create "a new individual who needed no country, no party, no God, no law, and could still be happy."[15] The jet age and the global era have done it for him. Those who now travel the world as their hometown regard themselves as "citizens of the world" and live closer to their fellow elites than to their fellow citizens. It is they who tend to view religion with disdain and have no idea of what it means to ordinary people.

From their superior viewpoint on life from penthouse suites and corporate jets at thirty thousand feet, religion is small, local, petty, and parochial, a source of conflict and war. Such global elites do not so much attack religion as rise above it altogether in their superiority and impatience. Their desired world-state is a world beyond all differences, all countries, all wars, all religions, and all moral restraints.

Such utopians and globalists are as dangerous as they are naive. They celebrate diversity in theory but hammer it flat in practice. The fact is that there is no true human life without bodies, without families, without neighborhoods, without countries, without languages, and without religions— in short, without the stubbornness of particularity and the messiness of real diversity. The world may be global, but we will never all speak Esperanto, daily life will always be local, and for better or worse there will always be religions. So long as humans believe in truth and goodness, they will always believe that some things are true and good, and some things are false and bad. And the differences will lead to divisions, and divisions to conflict. Even the cosmopolitanism of the imagined Grand World Union would create conflict, for there would be, and there are, those who disagree with it strongly.

G. K. Chesterton remarked wryly on the cosmopolitanism of George Bernard Shaw in the 1920s,

> He says in his innocent way that Utopia must be a world-state, or else people might make war on it. It does not seem to occur to him that, for a good many of us, if it were a world-state we should still make war on it to the end of the world. . . . The fact is very simple. Unless you are going deliberately to prevent a thing being good, you cannot prevent it being worth fighting for. It is impossible to prevent a possible conflict between civilizations because it is impossible to prevent a possible conflict between ideals. If there were no longer our modern strife between nations, there would only be a strife between utopias.[16]

Enough, then, of the current liberal Left hypocrisy of celebrating diversity but flattening real differences and insisting on uniformity! The human challenge is not to remove all differences but to recognize and respect genuine diversity, to give it space, and to know how we are to live with our deepest differences with the maximum freedom and justice for all. In Rabbi Sacks's happy term, there is a "dignity of difference," and that dignity should be respected.

Not surprisingly, the fifth and final factor in the sea change is *exhaustion.* After fifty years of the American culture wars, during which religion has festered as a constant source of controversy, many Americans simply wish that the whole messy business would simply go away. "A plague on both your houses," they say. "We are understandably tired of the issue."

In his "Memorial and Remonstrance" in 1785, James Madison declared that "it is proper to take alarm at the first experiment on our liberties. We hold this prudent jealousy to be the first duty of Citizens."[17] Because of this profound sea change, America today is well past the first experiments on liberties that have been central for three hundred years. All who have a "prudent jealousy" for America's "first liberty" should make it their "first duty" to examine the activists' proposals with great care, and where they are wrong to resist them with courage.

The totalitarian overtones of the scorched-earth, take-no-prisoners, no-exemptions approach of some of the activists on the Left should be troubling to freedom-loving people. In their view, all dissent is to be crushed as discrimination, all conscientious objection is to be ripped away as a fig leaf to cover bigotry, and all civil disobedience in the mode of Thoreau, Gandhi, and Martin Luther King is to be rejected as hateful. Will the legal bulldozer of the progressive Left soon be turned against religious advocacy in public life, against religious and home schooling, against religious nonprofit activity and status, against religious speech that is deemed incorrect, and even against churches, synagogues, and mosques? Any compulsion may be unfortunate, they say, but in the chilling words of a New Mexico Supreme Court ruling against religious freedom and a small business owner, compulsion is "the price of citizenship."[18]

Humanity at Stake

For anyone who surveys this massive sea change and its huge implications, it is clear that America's first liberty has been turned upside down. A false and cancerous "freedom" has started attacking healthy freedom. The United States is not only in danger of losing a critical component of its basic freedoms but of squandering part of its unique heritage that is vital to its survival. Even as a foreigner I watch with amazement, mixed with sorrow and outrage, because of the implications for the world. For what is at stake is not so much the loss of a single freedom, vital though freedom of religion and conscience is, but a vital way of protecting and negotiating all other freedoms. The reason lies in the double benefit of religious freedom. On the one hand, freedom of religion and conscience protects the foundational human search for meaning and belonging. On the other, the condition of freedom of religion determines society's capacity to promote religious freedom for everyone, and to negotiate peaceably the differences that will obviously arise through such freedom.

Why should freedom of religion and conscience be given a central place today? It can and should be argued that freedom of religion and conscience is the first liberty, though integrally related to the other core political rights; that it is a vital key to a healthy civil society; and that it is essential for harmony in societies that value both diversity and freedom. Beneath those crucial points, freedom of religion and conscience is important because it is the direct expression and the deepest protection of our freedom and responsibility to be human. *Freedom of religion and conscience affirms the dignity, worth, and agency of every human person by freeing us to align "who we understand ourselves to be" with "what we believe ultimately is," and then to think, live, speak, and act in line with those convictions.* Nothing comes closer to the heart of our humanity than the self-understanding and the self-constitution made possible through freedom of religion and conscience. As a right, it is primary, foundational, and indispensable. Freedom of speech, for instance, is simply freedom of conscience expressed in words.

There are important qualifications to this right—above all the equal rights of all others, as well as consideration for the public peace and the common good.[19] Or put differently, this freedom is absolute at the point of belief, but qualified at the point of behavior, because behavior touches other people and other things. Someone is free to believe in paganism, for example, but not to sacrifice an animal or another human being. But that said, the primary and foundational character of the right must never be lost.

What is at stake with freedom of religion and conscience is nothing less than human dignity, human self-determination, and human responsibility. In the words of Rabbi Joseph Soloveitchik, written in the scorching afterglow of the Holocaust,

> Man is born as an object, dies like an object, but possesses the ability to live like a subject, like a creator, an innovator, who can impress his own individual seal upon his life and can extricate himself from a mechanical type of existence and enter into a creative, active mode of being. Man's task in the world . . . is to transform fate into destiny, a passive existence into an active existence; an existence of compulsion, perplexity, and muteness into an existence replete with powerful will, with resourcefulness, daring, and imagination.[20]

Soul liberty was Roger Williams's stirring seventeenth-century term for the freedom of religion and conscience.[21] Williams and his fellow pioneers regarded this right as inherent not only in common law but in the nature of humanity and the human family. It was rooted in the inviolable dignity of each human person and in particular in the character of reason and conscience, the twin organs of thinking and moral intuitions. For Williams and others, such as John Milton and John Locke, these ideas in their turn were rooted in the conviction that humans possessed this dignity because they were made in the image of God. Each human has a measureless worth that goes beyond any possible descriptions of status, function, and utility. All other descriptions are vulnerable to our being reduced to our functions and utilitarian qualities—we are merely voters or viewers or buyers or consumers or passengers or statistics and so on. But made in the image of God, we each possess an equal and inalienable worth that is prior to every other category and consideration. This dignity and worth is therefore inalienable and inviolable.

What true liberal or what freedom-loving conservative can argue with each person's right to think and order their lives in accordance with what they believe to be true, based on the dictates of conscience? To be sure, it will have to be decided how the freedom this right gives to each person is to relate to the equal freedom of all others, to the public peace, and to the common good. But it anchors the principle that what needs to be negotiated is an absolute right and not merely a matter of tolerance, let alone a benefit conferred by the state. As Lord Acton declared simply, "By birth all men are free."[22] Or in the powerful words of Timothy Shah: "Anything less than full religious freedom fails to respect the dignity of persons as free truth-seekers, duty bound to respond to the truth (and only the truth) about the transcendent in accordance with their own judgments of conscience. . . . When people lose their religious freedom, they lose more than their freedom to be religious. They lose their freedom to be human."[23]

Let the truth ring out throughout the world. Freedom of religion and conscience is not a code word for bigotry or prejudice. It stands as a sure and essential protection of human dignity and freedom.

Which Model Serves Freedom Best?

That point raises the question that lies at the heart of this chapter: Which model of religion and public life serves freedom best? No one who follows the American culture wars can fail to see the two competing visions now battling for supremacy. The myriad changing issues at stake may appear to be confusingly different—prayers in public spaces and on official occasions, head scarves or turbans in places of work, crosses or crescents worn as symbols of faith, the Ten Commandments as historical memorials or a religious expression, exemptions for conscience over practices such as adoption, abortion, contraception. For fifty years, controversies such as these have made the American public square into a cultural war zone rather than a forum for public deliberation and decision, and in the election of 2016 it was tragically clear that the divisions had grown highly dangerous.

Yet closer inspection shows that all the kaleidoscopically changing controversies are an expression of the battle between two starkly different visions of public life—on one side there are the proponents of what Richard John Neuhaus called a *naked public square*, those who would exclude religions and religious expression from public life, and on the other, the proponents of a *sacred public square*, those who would give some religion or ideology a preferred, established, or monopoly position in public life at the expense of everyone else.

To be sure, there are mild and strong versions of each model of the public square elsewhere in the world, and there are many societies that range somewhere in between. Take the different varieties of the naked public square, where all religion is excluded. The exclusion of religion sought by many American secularists and separationists is a relatively mild case, though it leads decisively in the direction of French-style *laïcité* rather than the settlement constructed by their own founders. At the other extreme, the People's Republic of China practices a brutally harsh version of the naked public square that is the scourge of its people today and will be the shame of Chinese generations to come. The Beijing government is unashamed to flout human rights, persecute religious believers of many kinds, and without any qualms ruthlessly repress all signs of opposition to its totalitarian rule. Kemal Atatürk's settlement for Turkey once stood between these two extremes, owing much to the French separationist precedent, though President Erdogan now seeks to take Turkey in the direction of a more oppressive Islam that endangers the freedom and the lives of all who disagree with it.

A similar range can be seen among the varieties of the sacred public square. The Church of England stands at the mild end of the spectrum. It can truly say that it has no blood on its hands since the Glorious Revolution of 1688 and has therefore provoked no militant, French-style anticlerical hostility against itself. But today, its own government bans the wearing of the church's central symbol at places of work, and many of its friends fear that in its present institutional form it will not last another generation. Little wonder that many of its adherents are described as "belonging rather than believing," and cynics say that the established church's amiable but feeble condition is fit only for the "hatching, matching, and dispatching" (baptizing, marrying, and burying) of citizens and should soon be disestablished as the Lutheran state church was in Sweden in 2000.

At the other end of the spectrum, harsh examples of countries with a sacred public square would include Iran, Saudi Arabia, Pakistan, Afghanistan under the Taliban, and Burma under the generals. Their treatment of religions other than the established religion—Islam in the first four cases and Buddhism in the latter—is draconian, barbarous, a complete affront to human dignity, and a monumental disgrace to the faiths they claim to espouse. Their blatant denials of freedom can no more be countenanced by the world than the brutally similar repressions of the Chinese and North Koreans.

Clearly, for all the variations on either side, neither of the two models fulfills the requirements of freedom and justice for all under the conditions of the exploding diversity of the global era. In truth, both models are now exposed as finally unjust and unworkable, and those concerned for humanity would challenge both of them on behalf of the primacy of soul freedom for each of the diverse faiths within their jurisdictions. The conclusion is incontrovertible: Extreme versions of either model, China and North Korea on one side and Iran and Saudi Arabia on the other, are the world's major source of brutal governmental repression and the leading roadblock to advancing freedom and justice in the global era. Let there be no mincing of words when it comes to such roughshod flouting of human dignity. No secularist, however ardent, should defend the former, and no religious believer, however devoted, should justify the latter. The blood and tears of humanity cry out that there must be a better way.

Tweedledums and Tweedledees

A closer look reveals a further, though more controversial, fact. There is more extremism in the American culture warring than many acknowledge, and this extremism is on both sides. Extremism rarely grows by itself. It grows in reaction to something. Extremism over religious issues is no exception, though because of people's philosophical prejudices and social locations, each side tends to see only the extremism of the other side. Few admit the problem on their own side. The splinter in the other's eye looms large and dangerous, while the beam in one's own goes undetected.

In most educated circles in the West, the extremism on the religious side sits in the stocks in the full glare of the media, for all to deride and pelt. Indeed for some people, religion and extremism are synonyms. Unquestionably, few tyrants in history have matched the oppressive alliances between religion and government that end in coercing conscience and compelling belief. But little real thought seems to be needed to cook up some strong prejudices that run far beyond such facts.

Start with the single ingredient of a monopoly religion. Throw in a mention of how established religions have dealt with dissenting opinion, such as the Inquisition, the slaughter of the Albigensians, and the St. Bartholomew's Day massacre. Then season with a sprinkling of the contemporary cruelties of the Taliban or one of the idiotic acts of some purported religious leader, such as the burning of the Qur'an. Stir according to taste, and the argument can be left to marinate to perfection. Plainly, religion is evil, divisive, and violent—in fact, doubly evil for being evil in itself and evil too for the evils it rationalizes. Religion poisons everything.

Prepared according to such a recipe, the American religious Right can clearly be served up as Al Qaeda with smoother chins and slicker PR. How else could otherwise fair-minded liberals pretend with a straight face that the Moral Majority, the Christian Coalition, and Focus on the Family are "American Ayatollahs," "American theocrats," and "American fascists"? Was it the American groups themselves they did not really investigate, or was it the bogeymen they were comparing them to? Does it matter? According to the new atheists, religious moderates are no better than religious extremists. All are equally dangerous, and none are to be tolerated. Religious extremists are not to be tolerated, say Richard Dawkins and Sam Harris, but neither, they say openly, are religious moderates who tolerate extremists. By definition, religion itself is extremism.

This prejudice is not new. The philosopher Jeremy Bentham used to refer to organized religion as "Jug," which was short for juggernaut, as he charged that all religion was oppressive and rode over people like the infamous Hindu vehicle that crushed the devotees under its wheels. But in truth, he was blind to all that people of faith were doing even in his own lifetime. William Wilberforce, for example, was the greatest social reformer of all time and Bentham's contemporary, and never before had so many inspiring faith-based reforms been underway at the same time.

Christian "reconstructionists" in America are sometimes paraded as examples of dangerous Christian extremism, but they are a tiny group with no chance of wider political success, and only a paranoid should inflate their significance. Far more significant are the Islamist groups in the West that find themselves in Muslim-minority situations but still hew to the traditional Muslim-majority maxim that "Islam rules. It is never ruled." The result is a response summed up by Omar Ahmed, the cofounder of the influential Council on American Islamic Relations (CAIR): "Islam isn't in America to be equal to any other faith, but to become dominant. . . . The Koran, the Muslim book of scripture, should be the highest authority in America, and Islam the only accepted religion on Earth."[24]

But who dares speak of the extremism on the secularist side? The call for a partnership between responsible religious believers and responsible secularists is not a stalking horse for an assault on secularism, but the unashamed intolerance of the new atheists shows how there are secularist Tweedledees as well as religious Tweedledums. China's Cultural Revolution was an atheist inquisition for millions rather than thousands. The Hall of Infamy in the modern world includes Lenin, Stalin, and Mao alongside Torquemada from an earlier time. If there is little religious freedom in Saudi Arabia, there is no more in China.

"Religion poisons everything," Hitchens cried, yet "Religion is poison" was the slogan Mao used to launch his vicious assault on the people of Tibet. If Al Qaeda places bombs in the public square to kill, the ACLU puts up barriers in the public square to keep out, and the square is empty either way. For every Christian fundamentalist such as Jerry Falwell, there is a secularist fundamentalist such as Richard Dawkins. If there is the dire menace from theocrats, there is an equally dire menace from *seculocrats*, those illiberal liberals who directly oppose all religion and seek to exclude all religious voices from public life.

Centuries ago, the philosopher Leibnitz had predicted, "The last sect in Christendom and in general in the world will be atheism." Its way of propagating itself would show that "the world is already in its old age."[25] And a century after Wittgenstein, Terry Eagleton comments similarly on Richard Dawkins, "His anti-religious zeal makes the Grand Inquisitor look like a soggy liberal."[26] Lord Patten, chairman of the BBC and chancellor of Oxford University, noted dryly: "It is curious that atheists have proved to be so intolerant of those who have a faith."[27]

Again, I am not claiming moral equivalence between the two extremes. Sometimes one side is the clear leader in infamy, sometimes the other. What matters is that neither extreme holds the answer. On one side, we face the problems of a sacred public square, with its advocates seeking to favor one religion at the expense of everyone else. On the other, we face the equally real problems of a naked public square, with its advocates seeking to force all religions out of public life and thus, at least unwittingly, to favor some form of secularism, whether atheism in the West or communism in China. Dare anyone stand between the two sides when they fight in the same society? Who will step forward and declare, "A pox on both your houses"? The time has come for an honest recognition that each side can be as bad as the other, and that neither is the best model for the future. The need is for the courage to challenge both, not just the one that one side or the other happens to dislike more.

A Civil Public Square

Is there an alternative to these two extremes? The alternative is the vision and model of what is called a "civil public square." *A civil public square is a vision of public life in which citizens of all faiths and none are free to enter and engage public life on the basis of their faith, as a matter of freedom of religion and conscience, but within an agreed framework of what is understood and respected to be just and free for people of all other faiths too, and thus for the common good.*

This framework is political and not religious. In John Courtney Murray's apt description, it is a matter of "articles of peace" rather than "articles of faith." As such, it has to be agreed, affirmed, and then handed down from generation to generation until it truly becomes a "habit of the heart" for the citizenry. At its core are the three *R*s of freedom of thought and conscience: *rights*, *responsibilities*, and *respect*. A right for one person is a right for another and a responsibility for both and for everyone. Freedom of religion and conscience therefore means that there are no special rights, no favored faiths, and no especially protected beliefs. It is the conscience of believers, not the content of beliefs, that is protected.

A civil public square is the direct expression of covenantalism. It ensures a foundational respect for the reality of diversity and disagreements, but is a form of *covenantal pluralism* in that reciprocity, mutuality, and universality are the key principles of its vision. As Roger Scruton notes in his blistering critique of how both Left and Right annihilate dissent, "The question of opposition is, however, the single most important issue in politics."[28] In this sense a civil public square is the political embodiment of the Golden Rule. "Treat others with the respect you would like to be treated with yourself, and protect for others the rights you would like protected for yourself." Thus a right for a Christian is automatically a right for a Jew, an atheist, a Muslim, a Buddhist, a Mormon, a Hindu, a Scientologist, and for every believer in every faith under the sun as the earth turns. All human rights are the rights of all human beings. They are for the good of all. I write as a Christian as well as a visitor, but let no one say that I am striving for anything other than freedom of religion and conscience for everyone and for the good of all.

Many Americans today, and especially the younger generation, have become cynical about the political process. Recent elections have been too rancorous to be able to afford another passing spasm of civility talk. And there are in fact solid reasons why civility is scorned today. First, civility is confused with niceness and dismissed as a wimp word. At best it is viewed only as a matter of manners and etiquette, having a mild tone of voice, or feeling a refined distaste for the nastiness of differences. Far from it. Civility is a tough-minded classical virtue and duty that enables citizens to take their public differences seriously, debate them robustly, and negotiate and decide them peacefully rather than violently. Extremes on both sides, whether communism or fascism, the sacred public square or the naked public square, will always be inimical to those who disagree with them. But as philosopher Scruton argues, "In truth there is an opposite of all the 'isms,' and that is negotiated politics, without an 'ism' and without a goal other than the peaceful coexistence of rivals."[29]

Second, civility is too often discussed by itself and taken as a stand-alone virtue, as if it could somehow magically transform public life into sweetness and light all by itself. Again, far from it. Civility is a classical virtue and duty essential for both republics and democracies and especially for societies that need to negotiate a strong degree of diversity among the citizens. But civility is not an end in itself. It stands in the service of the higher good—soul freedom for all. Indeed, the greatest benefit of civility is that it provides the best conditions within which freedom of thought and conscience can grow strong and active.

As such, civility is only one part of the complete resources of the well-formed citizens, who together can take pride and responsibility in building and maintaining a healthy civil society and a vigorous but civil public square. An uneducated citizenry will quickly be overrun by powermongers, manipulators, cynics, and moneyed seducers. Such people are not destroying civility alone, but soul freedom itself, as well as the bonding of the republic and the duties of their own citizenship. Hand in hand with the complete responsibilities of citizenship, civility makes for a thriving republic and a truly open democracy. It speaks, after all, to our human nature as men and women who can speak, listen, weigh, decide, and live up to our human responsibility.

From Sword to Word

Needless to say, such a vision of a civil public square has numerous implications. A civil public square is absolutely essential to a free and open America, for without it there can be no open ground for discussing the common good in terms illuminated by public reason. As Cicero argued passionately before the Roman senate, if public reasoning is undermined, so also is the foundation of what constitutes a republic. All who care for free societies must therefore review their assumptions and follow the logic of these assumptions in rebuilding and maintaining the public square with care—whatever the costs of facing down the obdurate religious extremists on one side and the obdurate secularist extremists on the other. Make no mistake about the alternative: If words and persuasion fail, violence and coercion will be at the door.

Civility in public life carries many positive consequences, but there are also some notable traps it is easy to fall into. The right to free exercise in public life requires civility, and civility in public life assumes in turn that public discourse must shift from coercion to persuasion—from the *sword* to the *word*, as Roger Williams put it. Those who would prevail in public affairs have to persuade others in the public square. To make a persuasive public case under the conditions of contemporary pluralism means that advocates of any policy have to translate their case into terms that make sense to others. They have to know how to address the interests and ideals of others, and persuade believers of different faiths and worldviews.

One particular concern is common at this point. Many people fear that granting someone the right to enter and engage public life is tantamount to giving them a license to impose their views on everyone else. Needless to say, nothing in a postmodern world is held to be worse than imposing morals on anyone else (as if all law were not a moral imposition of some sort). So the obvious safeguard is to restrain free exercise in public life by coming down on the side of *no establishment*. But there are many reasons why this response is undemocratic and un-American. First, it curbs the democratic freedom of the First Amendment right to the free exercise of faith. Second, it makes the mistake of opposing the two halves of the religious liberty provisions, when both *free exercise* and *no establishment* were designed to serve the same end: freedom of religion and conscience. Third, it forgets that everyone has assumptions, so every single democratic decision, with no exceptions, will express (and therefore "impose") someone's assumptions. Fourth, it overlooks the fact that in a democracy no one can impose their views on others without persuading others that their views are right and good, and even then they have to win a sufficient majority to enact a law in their favor. Whether the prevailing majority is liberal and hopes to promote the sexual revolution or conservative and seeks to deny it, it can only prevail (impose) through democratic persuasion, and even then there should always be respect for the rights that protect the dissenting minority.

Contrary to recent demands and much misunderstanding, persuasion and its need for publicly accessible arguments does not mean that public discourse has to have a secular haircut and be shorn of all religious content when entering the public square. What it does mean is this: We need to recognize that arguing with people who do not understand us is ineffective, and citing authorities to those who do not share them is a waste of time. So the reason why we must all translate in order to persuade is not because of any phony threat that we are violating the separation of church and state but because of our desire to persuade people of different positions, different perspectives, and different policies. Persuasion, in short, is not imposition. It is a highly liberal exercise, and it follows naturally from freedom of thought and conscience and free exercise.

Differences Make a Difference

Like civility itself, the vision of a civil public square is surrounded by a thicket of misunderstandings and misgivings. One common misunderstanding is that a civil public square must be reached by a search for a lowest common denominator unity, whether a "no label" political movement or a form of interfaith dialogue and interfaith cooperation. "No label" movements are well-intentioned and understandable reactions to the gridlock of extreme partisanship. But they are utterly misguided because politics is essentially partisan, and civility stands for a protection and negotiation of differences, not their elimination.

Interfaith efforts are always welcome and often beneficial, as are the many new initiatives in citizen diplomacy. As Winston Churchill said, it is always better to "jaw jaw" than to "war war." But it also has to be said frankly that these initiatives are limited, and they will never reach the desired goal we are seeking. At the end of the day, whatever reconciliation is effected by interfaith dialogue is limited to some religions, rather than all, and the reconciliation usually does not include citizens who are secularists. Besides, the blunt fact is that the differences between core beliefs, including secularism, are irreducible, ultimate, and here to stay. As such, they will never be bridged by any lowest common denominator, however long we talk and however nice we are.

Besides, contrary to the foggy multiculturalism of the postmodern era, it is important to go beyond a celebration of diversity in the abstract. This often turns out to be one group's way of promoting its difference over others. What we really need is to examine what those differences mean in reality. Differences make a difference, both to individuals and to whole societies and even civilizations. Those differences are important, and they have to be engaged honestly and debated fearlessly.

So once again, let there be no misunderstanding: a civil public square does not require or depend on interfaith dialogue. Nor does it require any ultimate ecumenical unity. That hope, which is attractive to some and faithless to others, is utopian. Rather, a civil public square is forged through an agreed political framework of rights, responsibilities, and respect, within which each faith is free to be faithful to its own beliefs and yet responsible to know how to deal respectfully and civilly with the vital differences of other beliefs.

Here lies one of the greatest advantages of the civil public square: it protects the freedom to be faithful. *A civil public square promotes the highest freedom of religion and conscience, the strongest civility between faiths, and the greatest freedom for each faith to be true to its own truth claims—and all within a framework that respects disagreement and opposition.* Under no other model—neither the naked public square nor the sacred public square—are all citizens encouraged to be true to the faiths they live by and yet taught to be civil to others and care for the common good of the society they live in.

Dangerously Unstable?

The last widespread misgiving about civility and a civil public square is that, at best, the two ideas are inherently and dangerously unstable and therefore exceedingly foolish in today's world. The fear is that, in protecting the equal rights of all beliefs, the door will be open to dangerous beliefs that will undermine the system itself. A common current fear, for example, is that Muslim extremists may use the freedom of the civil public square to press for their own advantage in order to gain the victory and put the "enemies of God" out of the game—"one man, one vote, one time," as the Middle Eastern maxim goes—or more simply, to exploit the freedom of the host countries in order to plot their destruction.

That scenario is certainly a possibility and a serious danger. All free and open societies are inherently unstable, and in fact there are two major ways, not just one, in which an open society can always be undermined. The obvious danger is that, in their freedom, free societies may open the door to the enemies of freedom. The other is that freedom may breed such tolerance that it degenerates into anything-goes indifference, to the point where the whole system slumps into apathy. It was in fact a combination of these two follies, reinforced by an ill-considered multiculturalism, that led the British, the Dutch, the French, and Swedish to welcome radical Islamists and allow them to build their enclaves with such destructive consequences.

But neither of these potential dangers is unique to the vision of a civil public square. They are inherent in the notion of democracy itself. They can be countered only by a vigilant attention to the obvious requirements of a healthy, open society—including the vital importance of civic education and commitment to free, unfettered debate that engages with any and all ideas that are inimical to its health. Does any freedom-loving society deserve to survive if its citizens pay so little attention to freedom that they allow hostility or indifference to prevail through their own carelessness?

The Egypt of the pharaohs certainly lasted for thousands of years, whereas the democracy of Pericles and Demosthenes lasted only a few decades, but that is not an argument for giving up on democracy. It means, rather, that if we value democracy, we attend to the essentials that are necessary if free and open societies are to flourish and endure.

Some may fear that this rich, full notion of "soul freedom" for all is a mirage, or that this vision of civility and a civil public square is an impossible pipe dream. Such misgivings must be thoroughly answered if we are to progress. Only time can show how realistic freedom is for humanity, but our convictions and decisions today are what will shape the outcome of those questions tomorrow.

President Woodrow Wilson, it is often said, undermined himself through the naivety of his own progressive idealism. He entered World War I to ensure a "world safe for democracy," but the Great War, which was launched as "the war to end all wars," led to the Treaty of Versailles, which turned out to be "the peace that ended all peace." Was President John F. Kennedy's vision of "a world safe for diversity" similarly flawed by its idealism, or did his play on the words of his predecessor mask the urgency of a supremely practical problem for humanity in the global era: "How do we live with our deepest differences?" Much earlier, the German philosopher Schopenhauer had captured the problem with a graphic simplicity. The problem of freedom and diversity is the problem of porcupines in winter. If they huddle too closely, they injure each other with their quills, but if they stay too far apart, they freeze and die. All that was missing in his illustration is the fact that modern-day porcupines have automatic guns and may soon have nuclear-tipped quills. Or in Reinhold Niebuhr's words, we humans have not yet learned to live together without "covering each other 'with mud and with blood.'"[30]

Again, will it be said that freedom was a challenge too hard for Americans to overcome? Here, then, is the sixth question on the checklist that Americans must answer constructively: *How does your view of freedom allow you to handle the challenge of modern diversity?*

What do you think of the reducers, the rebranders, and the reimaginers? Which model of public life—the sacred, the naked, or the civil—best answers the requirements of freedom and justice? What would it take to resolve the conflicts of the culture wars? How do Americans live with their deepest differences, especially when those differences are grounded in different religions and ideologies? There can be no ducking this question. Today's desire for freedom has to be answered with a clear understanding of how today's level of diversity complicates the issues, and how the issues may be resolved.

HOW DO YOU JUSTIFY
YOUR VISION *of a* FREE
and OPEN SOCIETY?

*T*he US election of 2016 left the watching world alternately amused, entertained, shocked, dismayed, aghast, and smug. Was that the way for the world's lead society to conduct its affairs? Was that what freedom had come to mean to the once-proud land of the free? Was that what Americans meant by *democracy* as the self-rule of the people? The real winner, it was said, was not Donald Trump or Hillary Clinton, the Republicans or the Democrats, but China, Russia, Iran, and Saudi Arabia—countries with an open disdain for freedom and democracy. "The race to the bottom will make people rethink the value of democracy," one Chinese state-owned newspaper commented. Another stated that the presidential race had become "an unprecedented joke."[1] What President Xi Jinping calls China's "consultative democracy" was far better than American democracy, the Chinese claimed. The ugly American election of 1800, long taken as the benchmark for raucous and uncivil politics, had finally been surpassed by the angry and scandal-ridden election of 2016. The American republic no longer seemed to be working. Americans tore at each other's throats and competed with each other in seeing how far anyone could go in challenging the legitimacy of those they disagreed with.

At the end of the 2016 election, the gale-force logic of trends that had begun to course through American society for several decades did not subside. There was no question that the candidates and their surrogates were responsible in part, but beyond them a generation of developments had suddenly combined to form a perfect storm of mud-slinging invective and power politics that was destructive not only to American civility and freedom but to the republic itself. Above all, both candidates, both parties, and pundits and commentators on all sides demonstrated the dark logic of the hurricane of unbounded power that was raging through America. Friedrich Nietzsche's notions of post-truth, truth-free power, amplified powerfully by the postmodern analyses of Michel Foucault and others, and carried by the social media, swept like a hurricane through the centers of academic and political power, destroying what was in its path.

The 2016 election and its buildup was a perfect illustration of Andrew Schmookler's *Parable of the Tribes* and its portrayal of the danger of the logic of power that is uncontrolled and uncontrollable. The logic of post-truth power is inexorable. When freedom is untrammeled, as contemporary libertarian freedom is, it becomes a striving for expansion and for new spheres in which to exercise its freedom—and therefore for the power to do so. But this situation soon becomes disordered and anarchic. Freedom, when considered from the perspective of the individual, is chaos when viewed from the perspective of society as a whole. Such freedom quickly descends to a form of Thomas Hobbes's war of all against all in which "no one can choose that the struggle for power shall cease." The outcome and the overall lesson is then plain: "*No one is free to choose peace, but anyone can impose upon all the necessity for power.*"[2]

America's political activists and culture warriors must therefore stop and think. There are always a thousand reasons why the other side presents us with every excuse to answer insult with insult, accusation with accusation, and power with power. But down that scorched-earth path lies disaster for everyone, for the common good and for the American republic. Unbounded and disordered freedom that is reduced to power is an invitation to social chaos, political anarchy, and national decline. Schmookler's conclusion is sober: "Power is like a contaminant, a disease, which once introduced will gradually yet inexorably become universal in the system of competing societies. . . . *A selection for power among civilized societies is inevitable.*"[3]

Can such disordered freedom and its rampant abuse of power be corralled once it has broken loose? Without a sufficiently shared moral and political understanding, there will eventually be a collapse of the rules of the game. The most troubling aftermath of the 2016 election was the lengths to which the losers were willing to challenge the legitimacy of the result—even if it meant that they called into question the republic itself. The way that the

Democrats took to "resistance" rather than "loyal opposition" was in contrast to Al Gore's magnanimous attitude in 2000. The overall trajectory of America's descent was troubling for the future.

Needless to say, the problem of the abuse of power was what the founders' ordering of freedom was designed to answer in the first place, with its constitutional framework, its separation of powers, its checks and balances, its underlying realism about the abuse of power, and its insistence on civic education and the golden triangle of freedom. There were to be rules of the contest for all the players, rules for the contest to be fair for all the players, and rules for the contest to remain a contest and not a brawl. Which means that the rules of the contest had to be accepted and respected by all the players, with no exception. All that broke down in the 2016 election.

Far from being outmoded and irrelevant as the progressives claim, the Constitution's "rules of the game" are more relevant than ever. Indeed, today's post-truth politics and its bullying and chaos are precisely what the great experiment was set up to prevent. But such are the destructive forces at work in America today that chaos is not the end of the problem. An even deeper issue is at stake—the question of American legitimacy, the legitimacy of the American republic—and this is what the seventh question on the checklist addresses: *How are Americans to justify their vision of a free and open society?*

Is There a Final Why?

"Is it a god or some human being, strangers, who is given the credit for laying down your laws?" The famous opening words of Plato's *Laws* are a question put into the mouth of an Athenian stranger who poses it to Kleinias, a Cretan lawmaker who has been given the task of founding a Cretan colony. They raise a question that no society can duck or dismiss, and certainly not a society founded like the American republic. As we have stressed, America is a nation by intention and by ideas, and one that aspires to be free and to remain free forever. In Tocqueville's tribute, the indomitable Puritans braved the inevitable miseries of exile because they wished to ensure the victory of *an idea*. So call it philosophical and moral justification, call it legitimation, or call it a matter of roots and foundations, but there has to be a why in answer to all the founding assumptions that underlie a free society, and there has to be an ultimate why.

In George Steiner's famous comment, human beings are not so much *Homo sapiens* as *Homo quaerens*, "the animal that asks and asks." This means that for the American republic there has to be a why. Why the Constitution? Why human dignity? Why freedom and equality? Why justice? Why the rule of law? Why the "right to life, liberty, and the pursuit of happiness"? Why the separation of powers? Why respect for authority? Why freedom of religion and conscience? Why accept election results, even when your party loses? The whys go on and on, and they demand an answer in ways that are compelling generation after generation, and in ways that face the challenges raised in each new generation. The end result of having no *why* here would be a nihilism that spells the death of freedom.[4]

The present age, for example, glories in the thrill of transgression and deconstruction. Every authority, tradition, convention, boundary, taboo, and even the notion of law itself stands as an invitation to a fresh assault in the name of some daring new freedom. Again and again, what is possible is endlessly claimed and used to undermine what is permissible—for example, the impact of pop culture on language, sexual desire, and pornography. Why then respect authority, why follow tradition, why listen to your parents, and why obey the law when all laws are open to suspicion, and there is the thrill of disobeying them? Why not challenge everything and then challenge yourself? Why not follow the idols of the hour when all your peers seem to be doing so? At the same time, the advanced modern world has witnessed the countervailing trends of both decreased privacy (one nation under surveillance) and increased anonymity (through travel and technology). Why then be ethical when morality has lost its traditional link to accountability through visibility? Or in Václav Havel's illustration, why bother to buy a ticket for the tram if there is no conductor on board, and there is no one to see whether you pay or you don't?

In short, if the highest freedom is obedience to the unenforceable, why should anyone restrain themselves if truth and goodness are no longer objective, substantive, or even compelling, but merely what someone can get away with—as even the candidates for the highest office in the land demonstrate repeatedly?

Such questions are not new. They can be found in both the Bible and in the Greek and Roman classics—for example, in the stories of David and Bathsheba or Plato's shepherd Gyges, who was able to make himself invisible and therefore to commit crimes with impunity. But they are raised with a fierce intensity today. From one side, both personal anecdotes and serious research join hands to underscore the seriousness of the breakdown of standards and accountability in area after area. From another, the same two sources remind us every day of what happens when trust is no longer the coin of the realm—in family life, in the business world, in journalism, and in the rough and tumble of politics. Yet how is such trust to be grounded and justified in a post-truth secular world? To whom or what are we accountable, and why so, when "my word is my bond" has become archaic, and "So help me, God" means little or nothing. And how is the American republic itself to justify itself and its ideals, whether before others or to itself?

The Titanic Wager

Needless to say, the American republic does not look to Marduk like the Babylonians, to Ra and Amun like the Egyptians, to Athena and Apollo like the Athenians, or to Jupiter and Mars like the Romans. More importantly, the republic did not tie itself to the Roman Catholic Church as France, Spain, and Austria once did; to Anglicanism or Presbyterianism as England and Scotland have for so long; to Islam as so many modern Muslim nations still do; or to atheism as the Soviet Union once did and China and North Korea continue to do. Once again the republic was a great experiment, for in disestablishing religion it broke with centuries of the European practice of state religion, whether Catholic or Protestant.

But if the First Amendment disestablished religion at the federal level, it did not drive it out altogether. Rather, the republic can be described as a titanic wager against history. For the First Amendment represented an audacious gamble in that it established two principles that might at first sight appear contradictory. On the one hand, the republic *openly relies* on ultimate beliefs, for otherwise it would have no right to the rights by which it thrives. On the other hand, it *officially rejects* any formal, national statement of what those beliefs are to be. There is no national heresy in America because there is no national orthodoxy. Religion and ideology were disestablished from the start.

That of course is a gamble, a wager, because it assumes and requires that the best beliefs will prevail in an open debate—best in the sense that such beliefs are most conducive to the flourishing of the ideas and ideals that serve the flourishing of America itself. But there is no guarantee of this happy outcome. "Truth is great, and shall prevail," Jefferson wrote confidently, quoting the ancient Irish maxim. But truth may not prevail, and it certainly will not prevail in a brazenly post-truth culture that scorns the idea of truth. (A friend's amended version, which saw him through the rigors of the Nixon White House, is more realistic: "Truth will prevail in the end, not because people are honest but because they like to trap liars.") The openness of this wager on the need for the best beliefs serves to highlight two major ways in which the republic could be undermined. On the one hand, it would be in danger if the best beliefs were ever to lose their cogency, or some damaging beliefs were to prevail—damaging in the sense that they undermined the ideas and ideals that are necessary for the republic to flourish. On the other hand, the republic would be in trouble if its openness led to a slack-mouthed tolerance that tolerated everything indiscriminately and ended by slumping into apathy.

What this means is that the American experiment is built on a wager-like principle that requires a high degree of vigilance. Americans must always pay close attention to the state of the union and its ideas, and in particular they must watch to see whether the best beliefs, those most conducive to the flourishing of the republic, are continuing to prevail in every generation. This vigilance, in turn, requires two things: an ongoing analysis of the specific beliefs animating citizens at any time, and an assessment of how any and all beliefs are free or not free to relate to American public life at any time. Both those points merit urgent attention today, and that is the significance of the clash between 1776 and 1789. It is the second point and not the first that is the focus of this chapter—for a simple reason. Left/liberal activists who are advocates of the naked public square, the removers who desire to remove all religion from public life, are doing so in a way that undercuts the philosophical and moral justification of the American republic itself. Call it delegitimation, call it a self-induced crisis of cultural authority, or call it the cut-flower syndrome, but the crisis calls into question the health and future of the American republic.

The Republic and Its Roots

This argument for healthy roots has been made before as I and others have put it forward in earlier books, but it bears repeating once more because of its urgency.[5] The question before the American republic—and also before many other freedom-loving democratic countries—is how to build states that are modern, pluralistic, and *secular* (in the sense of this-worldly, but not in the sense of either a *secularist* state or a strictly neutral state, because no state should be neutral about its own survival). Seven considerations would encourage such a constructive vision to proceed. Again, let me stress that these points are not an argument for an improper *secularist* state, which establishes or favors believers in a secularist worldview, but for a proper *secular* (this-worldly) state, which protects the foundational freedom of all believers, whether religious or secularist, and in the process allows for the philosophical and moral justification of the state itself—without making the mistake of resorting to any official established religion or ideology.

First, the American republic, like other modern secular societies, depends on the ultimate solidarity of its citizens as a nation. The greater the liberty the republic enjoys, and the wider the diversity of citizens the republic welcomes, the more important is the question of their unity or social bond that holds them together despite their differences. If the earlier American motto *e pluribus unum* is to hold, the *unum* must always be as strong as the *pluribus*, for it will form the core of the identity and the bonds of the unity. There is no question that it is a special challenge to sustain a stable and united society under the conditions of modern liberty and diversity. To be both positive and strong, this solidarity must be built on more than simply law, technology, border control, and general prosperity. It requires thriving values and strong nurturing institutions, including robust civic education, which passes the nation's values from one generation to the next.

Unquestionably, the bonds of this solidarity are gravely weakened in America today, when the current reality is no longer *e pluribus unum* (out of many one) but *ex uno plures* (out of one many), as diversity without unity leads to ever greater division and then to factions and balkanization.

Second, the American republic, like other modern liberal secular societies, depends on ideas and ideals that the state itself cannot promote, but must protect. The fact is that reason cannot justify itself by reason alone, and in the same way a truly neutral state cannot justify itself by purely neutral values. There are no such things. Values are particular. Both reason and the modern liberal state must therefore become aware of their own limitations and realize that they have to look to sources outside themselves for the moral foundations that they need in order to survive.

Unquestionably, these ideas and ideals are not fostered or encouraged in America today, and in many cases they are actively discouraged.

Third, the American republic, like other modern liberal secular societies, has risen from and still depends on philosophical, ethical, and political traditions that come from outside the state itself. As we have seen, it is a matter of simple, historical record that most of the indispensable foundations of "life, liberty, and the pursuit of happiness," including notions such as the Constitution, the dignity of the person, the sanctity of life, freedom, justice, equality, and virtue are all prepolitical and religious in character. The secular republic therefore depends on more than the purely secular.

Unquestionably, these traditions have been systematically discouraged in America recently, producing the cut-flower syndrome.

Fourth, those citizens within the American republic who hold naturalistic or secularist worldviews are part of traditions that are limited to certain classes and social locations just as more religious worldviews are. Like all others, such secularist and naturalistic worldviews are simply one set of ultimate beliefs and worldviews among many others. They have the right to every human right and every civil right, but they have no right to be privileged above any others and no more right to be universalized today than certain religious views were in the past. In particular, liberal and secular elites have no right to privilege secularist beliefs above religious beliefs.

Unquestionably, secularist beliefs have been unfairly privileged in America recently and in ways that are highly illiberal and discriminating.

Fifth, the American republic, like other modern liberal secular societies in the West, should be viewed as pluralistic and therefore postsecularist just as much as post-Christian. To be sure, the broad Jewish and Christian consensus that characterized America right down through to the end of the 1950s has gone, but the myth of the purely and strictly secularist state has been shown up starkly too. The American republic today is a nation of many faiths, or ultimate beliefs, in the sense that the diversity of religions and ideologies is an inescapable social fact. It is therefore in the interests of the liberal state to pay due attention to the full range of the voices of its citizens and to the sources and norms of its solidarity. Religious believers of all kinds make important claims to truth as well as important contributions to civil society, so their rights should be respected and their voices heard if the nation is truly to be open, free, liberal, and democratic.

Unquestionably, religious beliefs have been unfairly sidelined in America recently, above all in the various forms of the naked public square and the proponents of freedom *from* religion.

Sixth, it is a plain fact of history that there are examples of the dark pathology of secularism as well as of religion. No one need go further than the story of the Soviet Union and China. Secularists and religious believers should each acknowledge these pathologies with candor and humility. Both secularists and religious believers have brought blessings to the world, and both have brought curses to the history of civilization and the story of freedom. The balance sheet of each should be totaled up accurately and fairly, and both sides treated with respect as they seek to pursue freedom and justice in our own time.

Unquestionably, the analysis and blame has recently been one-sided, and a balanced assessment of the costs and benefits of both secularism and religion needs to be drawn up and acknowledged.

Seventh, the relationship of religious and secularist believers is critical to the future of the American republic, as it is to other modern liberal secular societies, and this is true above all in their relationships in public life. If their present antagonism is not to prove the undoing of liberal democracy, they must come together in the common cause of freedom, justice, and humanity. Nothing is more urgent for the American republic than the forging of a civil public square that does justice to the interests of all partners in the relationship.

Unquestionably, there is no more vital partnership than that between secularists and religious believers if there is to be a solid hope of building a free and open society.

This vision of a cobelligerent partnership to reinforce the foundations of the American republic requires the participation of at least three major groups who in turn can reach out to embrace all American citizens: first, the Jewish people, whose ideas are the principal ideals underlying the American experiment; second, Christians, who down the centuries have been the main bearers of those ideas in American history and are still the majority faith in America; and third, secularists, who now occupy positions of power in the leading centers of American thought. There is no question that such a partnership between Jews, Christians, and secularists (and all others who would wish to join them, including Muslims who agree with these American first principles) is literally utopian—at the present moment it exists nowhere. But why is it impossible, and what is to stop it? Americans are sick and tired of the present state of the culture wars, and were they to reflect on the lessons of their stirring, if sometimes checkered, story of the promise of freedom of religion and conscience, they would see what should be its true fulfillment today—the vision of an expanded civil public square, open to all Americans, guarding and guaranteeing the rights of all, and enabled to flourish through the cultivation of the "three Rs of civility," the rights, responsibilities, and respect of all for all.

Such a cobelligerent partnership between Jews, Christians, and secularists on behalf of freedom may sound unlikely, but it is urgent. It is also the crucial response to the absurd and dangerous alliance between two groups that by themselves represent the two most serious threats to the American experiment: radical Left/liberalism and radical Islamism. Already, their alliance has had the effect of branding all public criticisms of Islamist extremism as "Islamophobia." Doubtless, the assumption behind the dangerous alliance of the Left and Islamism is the old notion that "My enemy's enemy is my friend." But in this case that maxim is dead wrong, and its fruits could be bizarre. The truth is that "My enemy's enemy may well be my enemy too." Just imagine the fate of atheists, gay people, and transgender people under the Islamic State or the Sharia law. Or consider the fact that many mainstream Muslim intellectuals and leaders in the Middle East shake their heads at the incredible naivety of Americans toward radical Islamist ideology, such as the Muslim Brotherhood.

Yet what matters supremely are the consequences for American freedom. In the long term, the growing cooperation between American extremists, European radicals, and Middle Eastern jihadis represents the gravest menace to both Western civilization and the American experiment. But quite apart from that, does any serious, thinking liberal secularist really believe that Islamism holds a better key to freedom for all than Judaism and the Christian faith? The roots of the problem, of course, are far older than the rise of the Islamic State and Islamism in its recent form, for the Left has a long and shameful record of romanticizing dictators such as Stalin and Mao, rationalizing evils such as the terror famines, the gulag, and the killing fields of Cambodia, and generally turning a blind eye to the illiberal legacies of the Enlightenment.

What is missing in America is constructive leadership at the highest level on the issue of religion and public life. What is plain to outsiders is that America is staggering under the weight of academic conferences, historical studies, statistical assessments, legal briefs, political tracts, and popular movements on behalf of one issue after another. But where are the positive remedies that go beyond the constant warring against the alleged violations of whoever and whatever is "the other side"? With a few distinguished exceptions, such as Charles Haynes at the Religious Freedom Center in Washington, DC, there is a conspicuous dearth of Americans setting out constructive solutions to the culture warring over religion and public life. But were there to be American leaders who offer constructive solutions that fulfill the best of American history as well as match the challenges of the present hour, the way forward should be within America's reach, even now. The Williamsburg Charter was proposed with just such a constructive vision in mind, as was the American Charter of Freedom of Religion and Conscience, published in Washington, DC, in 2018.

There can be no truce between 1776 and 1789. The clash of freedoms has to be settled in favor of one way or another, for they lead in entirely different directions. But a cobelligerent partnership between secularists and religious believers is possible within the broad framework of the American settlement of religions and public life. Indeed, such a partnership is essential if there is to be a way forward with many of the problems now dogging American public life. Some would dismiss this vision as idealistic, but that has always been an accusation leveled against freedom, for what looks like idealism becomes realism when the alternative is sufficiently dire. Make no mistake: short of such a partnership, there is only the disastrous prospect of endless culture warring and deepening divisions until one extreme or the other prevails at the expense of freedom for the good of all. Down that way lies a continuing refusal to play by the rules of the game, and in the end the destruction of the game itself—in other words, the sorry end of the American republic and of its guardianship of the deepest human hopes of human justice and freedom.

Can Americans achieve a better way at this late hour? Were such principles to be agreed between religious believers and secularists, or at least accepted as talking points on an agreed agenda, a good conversation might begin without suspicion and without rancor. Eventually a fruitful partnership might emerge. Certainly it would take leadership to achieve it, a costly leadership that would call each side to lay down its arms and join forces to forge a way forward. And it would take courage from both sides to break out of the destructive culture warring of the past fifty years.

The alternative is stark, best captured in Aesop's parable of the frog and the scorpion. Asked to ferry a scorpion across the river on its back, the frog at first refuses, but then agrees to do so as long as the scorpion promises not to sting him. Half way across, however, the frog feels the sting he had feared all along, and as he feels the death paralysis spreading over him, he simply asks, "Why?"

"Because it's my nature," the scorpion replies.

Again, will it be said that freedom was too hard a challenge for Americans to overcome? Here, then, is the seventh question on the checklist that Americans must answer constructively: *How do you justify your vision of a free and open society?*

What would happen if America were to lose one or other of its twin poles of unity and diversity (*e pluribus unum*)? Which one is in greater danger today, and what do you see as the solution? Where might different faiths and worldviews disagree over their respective views of the world but work together to make American democracy successful and the republic viable? There is too much anger and suspicion in play on both sides at the moment, but progressives and secularists must speak for themselves as to what they claim is their true nature and their real vision of freedom, just as religious believers must too. Do leading secularists, for example, agree with Jürgen Habermas, the European secularist, that to exclude religious voices from the public square is illiberal? And do Christians remember that the one they follow was (in Machiavelli's words) the "unarmed prophet," and the one who shed no blood except his own? Christians who seek to advance his kingdom as Jesus did should have no poison in their armory. Whether both sides can declare a truce in the midst of their centuries-long conflicts and work together for the good of humanity is an open question. It is also a vital key to the future of America, and even to the future of humanity.

WHERE DO YOU GROUND YOUR FAITH *in* HUMAN FREEDOM?

W hat's it all about, Alfie?" The eminent philosopher Bertrand Russell was once asked a version of that question by a London cabbie ("What's it all about, Bertie?"), and he was famously speechless because he held that only precise questions deserve precise answers. Later, the Harvard philosopher W. V. O. "Van" Quine was asked what the meaning of life was, and he replied, "Life is algid. Life is fulgid. Life is what the least of us make most of us feel the least of us make the most of. Life is a burgeoning, a quickening of the dim, primordial urge in the murky wastes of time."[1]

What on earth was the great philosopher talking about? If his listeners understood him rightly, Quine either meant that only a few make the most of life, and they make the rest of us feel that we are wasting our time. Or more simply, that the question was stupid and beneath him. In Terry Eagleton's wry words that open his attempted pocket wisdom on the subject, "The meaning of life is a subject fit for either the crazed or the comic."[2] Monty Python's *The Meaning of Life* compounded the two options: questions about the meaning of life are stupid and the answers are absurd. Life is a joke.

One of the funniest evenings of my life was when my wife and I spent time in Greece with Douglas Adams, author of *The Hitchhiker's Guide to the Galaxy*. His own answer to the big question was the story of his fictional computer Deep Thought. When asked to work out the meaning of life, it took seven and a half million years and finally came up with the answer: 42. The world then had to build another larger computer to find out what the question was. The search for the meaning of life is perhaps the only meaning there is to life.

Such attitudes are surely some of the silliest ideas in our sophisticated modern age. The simple fact is that *Homo sapiens* lives by more than animal instincts. We are meaning mongers. No one can live without meaning and belonging. We all need to make sense of life, find security in the world, and follow a story line in our lives. Without answers to such questions, meaninglessness becomes a serious problem and suicide a serious possibility. "He who has a why to live for can bear almost any how," Nietzsche wrote in *Twilight of the Idols*.[3] And in the dark, black why-less night of Auschwitz, Viktor Frankl found again and again that the search for meaning was an indispensable motivation for surviving, as death seemed to offer the only escape when life was hell. Without purpose, his fellow inmates became "blanket cases" and took to their bunks, gave up, and died. That central insight later became the dynamic core of his meaning-centered treatment, "logotherapy."[4]

Albert Camus wrote similarly in the celebrated opening words of his *Myth of Sisyphus*: "There is but one truly serious philosophical problem, and that is suicide. Judging whether life is or is not worth living amounts to answering the fundamental question of philosophy."[5] In contrast, Eagleton tells the story of the poet Gertrude Stein, who on her deathbed was rumored to have asked again and again, "What is the answer?" before finally muttering, "What is the question?" His own comment: "A question about a question posed while hovering on the brink of nothingness seems a suitable symbol of the modern condition."[6]

Yet neither ivory tower philosophers nor the cynicism of humorists should blind us to the importance of the meaning of life. How do we see reality? Why do we prize human dignity or demand equality? Where do we anchor our sense of identity and purpose, and develop our understanding of morality and love? What is a good life? And how do we pursue happiness? What is a successful human being? Why should we care for our neighbor and the other? None of these questions can be answered without an underlying sense of the overall meaning of life—and the same is true of freedom. Our understanding of freedom will be shaped by our understanding of life and reality, our view of humanity and the world. The point is not that each of us has to think through each question for ourselves and completely from scratch. That would be impossibly arduous and redundant because so many thinkers have raised and pursued the questions before us. We all, including philosophers, have to assume some answer to the question of the meaning of life if we are to live meaningfully. "The unexamined life," as Socrates said just before his execution, "is not worth living." And that is true not only for individuals but for whole societies and for nations.

What is inexcusable is to deny the questions and to remain indifferent to the answers. Yet that is what many American leaders are now doing when it comes to human dignity and freedom—two issues that are decisive for international as well as domestic affairs. It is one thing for individuals to espouse secularism as their conclusion to a genuine search for an examined life. It is another for elites to behave as if secularism were true by cultural fiat, and then to take a tin-eared stance toward other views of the world and to pretend that the differences make no difference. A crucial weakness of the foreign policy of the Obama administration was its blindness to both the religious roots of America's culture of freedom and the zealously religious motivation of America's self-professed enemies.

Looking Where It Can't Be Found

Where then is the best and surest foundation of freedom to be found? That is the vital question for Americans now and for all lovers of freedom in today's world. For while the human search for meaning is universal, there are many different answers as to what the meaning of life is, and therefore within each answer what freedom is and how best it should be understood and pursued, either by individuals or societies. In short, we are back to chutes and ladders again. There are choices and there are consequences. There are differences, and the differences make a difference.

If you shake a kaleidoscope, the colors and patterns also change. In the same way, freedom will look entirely different within the different views of the meaning of life and the different theories of what reality is. The same English word *freedom* might be used to translate different terms across all the different views, but what freedom means in each case will vary according to the kaleidoscope of perspectives that different people and different societies bring to freedom. The challenge for inquirers is to resist being paralyzed by the vertigo of relativity and instead to be clear about what sort of freedom they are looking for, and what are the personal as well as the public consequences of the different kinds of freedom that are on offer. The previous questions on the checklist should have sharpened the criteria that Americans must bring to the search. Only a robust and well-grounded notion of freedom can meet the exacting demands of the American experiment. The eighth question on the checklist therefore asks: *Where do Americans ground their belief in freedom? And which worldview best undergirds the robust and self-reliant freedom that the American republic requires?*

The great Austrian satirist Karl Kraus was famous for a sketch in which he played a drunk looking for his keys under a lamp post, even though he had lost them elsewhere—there was more light under the lamp post he said. In the same way, many people in the Western world are blithely counting on a freedom that cannot be found where they are looking. Countless others can be heard mouthing clichés about freedom as if freedom were the constant state of the world and will stay that way forever. Were such people to remember history, they would know that freedom is not the norm, it does not simply happen, and it cannot last unless it is understood and sustained with care. If Americans at large were to debate the issues, they would see that this is no time to be complacent about freedom. The cultural ground has shifted under their feet in the last generation, and claims from the past no longer have the solid footing they once had.

Two obvious truths confront the West today. First, we must face up to the fact that, over the past two hundred years, the West has chosen to cut itself off decisively from the Jewish and Christian faiths that once provided its roots and its moral and social ecosystem. By its own choice, the West has become a cut-flower civilization. It forgets that flowers in a vase may be beautiful, but they simply will not last. The flower of freedom is no exception. If the Jewish and Christian roots are severed, where does the West seek to ground its freedom now?

Second, we must clarify what we mean by freedom today because of pluralization and the explosion of diversity in our modern global world. Humans, it is said, represent the most diverse form of life on planet earth. But not all the world's worldviews undergird the worth of individual human beings, as for example Judaism does ("A single soul is like the universe"). Many in fact do the opposite (Zen Buddhism: "Man is a stone thrown in the pond who causes no ripples"). It means that those who prize freedom must choose with care between the different views of life that we are offered. For the blunt fact is that some of the views on offer today provide no basis for freedom, and others are an open contradiction of human freedom.

For all practical purposes, the overwhelming majority of people in the world take their views of the meaning of life and their views of freedom from one of the three major families of faith—the Eastern, the secularist, and the Abrahamic. When used of faiths, the word *family* refers to the fact that certain religions, worldviews, and philosophies share a common family resemblance because they stem from a similar understanding of what is behind everything or what is ultimate reality. There is no common core unity between the world's faiths and philosophies. There are differences between the different families of faiths, and the differences make a difference for whole societies as well as individuals. Remembering the checklist of questions I have raised so far, our focus is not on a general comparison of the families of faith but on the significance of their differences for our concern for freedom.

Forget It

The first major family of faiths is the Eastern family, which would include Hinduism, Buddhism, Jainism, and different varieties of the new age movement. They share a similar understanding that the ultimate reality of the universe is an impersonal ground of being, from which we have become alienated. (In the understanding of a major branch of Hinduism, each of us is a manifestation of "God's temporary self-forgetfulness.") As seen from the viewpoint of this worldview, human life is a life of bondage on the wheel of *samsara*, the cycle of affliction, suffering, aging, death— and reincarnation (determined by the balance sheet of each person's *karma* from their previous incarnations). What drives us and keeps us bound to the wheel is desire, which leads to craving, which leads in turn to attachment. The problem is not that we die but that we are reborn and bound to the wheel all over again.

The Eastern family of faiths is therefore deeply concerned with freedom. But what does *freedom* mean within this view of the world? And what does this perspective mean for personal and political freedom? The Sanskrit term for freedom is *moksha*, which means "liberation" or "release" (used of a horse released from its harness). This freedom centers on liberation from the world of *maya* or illusion. Thus freedom is highly desired in the Eastern religions, but it is quite different from the traditional Western notion. The road to freedom, represented by *moksha*, requires different paths or ways of living within this life, but its overall trajectory is essentially one of renunciation or withdrawal from the illusion of individual selfhood in this life.

Different schools of Eastern thought have differences over the *from what* and the *how* of freedom. For Hindus, such liberation can come from following many paths, including *yoga*, each one leading toward union with the divine: *Brahman*, the one supreme Self and Ground of Being. But all the paths involve renunciation of the human self, in the same way that salt loses itself as it dissolves in water and rivers end as they run into the sea. For followers of the Buddha, liberation comes along the path of "right mindfulness," rejecting the extremes of self-indulgence and asceticism, and taking the middle path that leads to Nirvana, the "great deathless lake of extinction." The differences between the Eastern religions are important, and they should never be minimized, but common to most of them is the notion that freedom is not freedom to *be* an individual, for that is to remain caught in the world of *maya* or illusion. Freedom is freedom *from* individuality, for the individual self is an illusion. "It [not I] is liberated," cried Siddhartha Gautama when he became the Buddha, the enlightened one. He had attained the not-self. At last, said his disciple Buddhaghosa after his own enlightenment, "I am nowhere a somewhatness for anyone."

What does such a view mean for either personal or political freedom? Clearly this view of freedom has much to say about personal freedom, though in a strenuously negative form. Is there freedom and the hope of fulfillment for the individual self in this world? Forget it. To pursue such a goal is to pursue an illusion and to remain caught in the world of illusion. That view in itself is strikingly different from the Jewish and Christian view that holds to the inalienable dignity of the individual person, according to which every single life matters, so that by definition there can be no outcasts and no untouchables.

At the same time, the Eastern views have little or nothing to say in addressing the political freedom that is central to Western democracy and to the arguments surrounding the American experiment. To be sure, Eastern views and the practices such as yoga are popular in the advanced modern world. But they represent a sort of escapist ideology in the world of modernity. They provide a refuge from the rush, din, and stress of the advanced modern lifestyle rather than a faith that drives and shapes the world of science, technology, and business—and the politics of freedom.

Do It Yourself

The second major family of faiths is the secularist family, which includes atheism, agnosticism, naturalism, materialism, and physicalism. What these worldviews share in common is a firm rejection of God, gods, the supernatural, and the insistence that the ultimate reality in the universe is chance. According to this view, all that exists is a product of chance plus time plus energy plus matter—Bertrand Russell's "chance collocation of atoms," Jacques Monod's "chance and necessity," Richard Dawkins's "blind watchmaker," or simply, "We won the lottery!"

Secularism, it must be said, glories in its affirmation of freedom, and for many atheists this is its first and greatest appeal. There is no God, there are no gods, and there are no supernatural beings behind the universe, atheists say. So we humans are on our own, life is all up to us, and we are each masters of our own fate and captains of our own souls. We are free to think and to live as we like, and this freedom is brandished as the trump card in many a secularist's argument. If God is dead or absent, everything *is* permitted. Free of God, the atheist is untethered from outside control and free to think freely and to live freely.

How does such a view of freedom work out? True, there is no one and nothing we are accountable to, or to interfere with what we choose to do. If everything comes from chance, there is no meaning in the universe that we need to discover. So if we want and need meaning, which of course we do, it is up to us to make it for ourselves. Russell's picture of the Greek giant Atlas carrying the world on his own shoulders is the perfect expression of the secularist worldview. Frank Sinatra's "I did it my way" is the perfect musical accompaniment to Friedrich Nietzsche's "Thus I willed it" and Ayn Rand's "And I meant it." If the essence of the Eastern attitude to the freedom of the individual self could be distilled into two words, "Forget it," the essence of the secularist attitude can be captured in three: "Do it yourself."

Again and again, atheists witness to their joy in their newfound individual freedom. Don't just read Nietzsche's *Thus Spake Zarathustra*. Sing its exhilarating song of freedom aloud to yourself! Atheism is freedom, and atheists are free thinkers. The worst thing to be said about God, they say, is that if there were such a God, he would be meddlesome, the great interferer. But there is no Father, no Big Brother, or anyone or anything behind the universe. There is no one to spoil their pleasures or cross their will. There is no all-seeing eye and no divine surveillance. There is no one to interfere. There is no one to impose. There is no one to whom any of us is accountable, and no one with the right to determine how each of us should think and live except ourselves. Rejecting any and all kinds of religion, the supernatural, and all authorities beyond the human, atheists declare that they are free and autonomous. They are independent sovereign selves.

But this ecstatic cry of individual freedom is untethered from reality. Even Nietzsche was unable to live as he wrote. There is an obvious practical problem in stating secularist freedom in terms of unrestrained individual freedom—other people are similarly free, and that creates the fundamental social and political problem of how we are to create a harmonious society out of a cacophony of competing selves all claiming freedom in a million different ways. The danger of such a view is that it quickly becomes a form of negative freedom run riot. By nature, it does not provide any counterbalancing place for the positive freedom of equally important notions such as community and commonwealth. But that said, there is a far deeper theoretical problem with the secularist view of freedom. If naturalistic science is counted on to replace religion and provide all the needed explanations for secularist knowledge and wisdom, as secularists claim, does naturalistic science provide any grounds for human freedom? The answer, which is becoming increasingly evident, is no.

B. F. Skinner, the champion of behaviorism, put all his cards on the table in the title of his bestselling book *Beyond Freedom and Dignity*. ("What is being abolished is autonomous man . . . the man defended by the literature of freedom and dignity.")[7] Skinner was following the work of John B. Watson, who in pioneering the principles of stimulus-response claimed that he had discovered the psychologist's equivalent of the atom, the basic building block humanity came from. Skinner argued that while the traditional Jewish and Christian view of humanity supported Hamlet's exclamation, "How like a god!" this new Pavlovian view supports the statement, "How like a dog!" But that should be considered an advance and not a setback, he said, for it is the truth that science tells us.

More recently, new atheist philosopher Sam Harris comes to the same conclusion. "Free will *is* an illusion. Our wills are simply not of our own making. . . . We do not have the freedom we think we have."[8] Even Albert Einstein, humanitarian and resolute antiwar pacifist though he was, disavowed freedom. "In human freedom in the philosophical sense I am definitely a disbeliever. Everybody acts not only under external compulsion but also in accordance with inner necessity." His position, he said, was that of the philosophical pessimist Schopenhauer: "A man can do as he will, but not will as he will."[9]

Yuval Harari summarizes how, according to this secularist view, science has driven nails into "freedom's coffin." "To the best of our scientific understanding, determinism and randomness have divided the entire cake between them, leaving not even a crumb for 'freedom.' The sacred word 'freedom' turns out to be, just like 'soul,' a hollow term empty of any discernible meaning. Free will exists only in the imaginary stories we humans have invented." But of course, this bleak judgment spells the end not only of freedom but of liberalism too: "However," Harari continues, "over the last few decades the life sciences have reached the conclusion that this liberal story is pure mythology. The single authentic self is as real as the eternal soul, Santa Claus, and the Easter Bunny."[10]

Ideas have consequences. What begins as an idea washes down in the rain as behavior. For if humans are not free, then life is not meaningful as they believe it to be, and they are not responsible. Societies with no place for personal responsibility can move in only two main directions: chaos or control. In *A Writer's Diary*, Fyodor Dostoevsky predicted the former. What would happen if there is no responsibility and everything could be blamed on people's environments and backgrounds, so that there was no crime and no guilt? Then everyone and everything could be explained and excused, but the result of such nonresponsibility would not be peace. Instead, he argued, the outcome would be "crime as a duty." Better barbarism than boredom, Baudelaire had argued. Better mayhem than non-entity, Dostoevsky warned. Responsibility neutered would express itself as anything but neutral. It would exert itself in violence (caused by far more than easy access to guns). "Since society is organized in such a vile fashion, one can only break out of it with a knife in hand."[11]

The way out is to remember that there is all the difference in the world between science and scientism, the belief that science knows all there is to know. The truth is that for all the importance, the brilliance, and the indispensable character of science and the scientific method, there is more to be known than science will ever know. Freedom, along with its accompanying ideas such as purpose and intention, cannot be captured by the scientific method for two reasons. First, freedom looks forward, whereas the scientific method by its nature looks backward. Scientific knowledge and scientific explanations depend on the relationship of cause and effect. And second, freedom, being free, is not caused, so it cannot be captured by the insistence on the caused and the repeatable. It is unique and unprecedented.

If a plane is flown into a skyscraper, and the skyscraper falls, the collapse is the effect and the plane and its pilot are the cause. With causal relationships the process is never the other way around, which means simply that scientific explanations are retrospective, and they have to be. Just as the processes of big data codify the past and predict the future only in terms of the evidence of the past, so scientific explanations work backward. They lack the human imagination to create the future. By their nature and their logic they cannot see ahead, let alone prove anything forward. They can only speculate on the future based on the evidence of the past. Big data loses the trees for the forest. It cannot see the individual because it sees only the group and the past, and in a similar way science as normally understood simply cannot prove freedom. Insisting on repeatability, what happens all the time, and what happens in the same way in all times and all places, science cannot—by definition—see the singular, the extraordinary, and the unprecedented that happens only one time.

To be sure, that problem is true of science as normally understood or science understood in the classic Newtonian way. But those who understand reality in light of quantum mechanics see things quite differently. Following Walter Heisenberg, they break with the strict determinism of Isaac Newton's universe. According to quantum mechanics, the mind is not simply an observer but an agent. It has an independent and decisive role in shaping reality and therefore makes the reality of human freedom possible, and makes life and moral choices meaningful. Physicist Henry Stapp points out that in the causally mindless mechanical world of the materialist, "this power of our minds is denied, and that denial eliminates any possibility of a rationally coherent conception of the meaningfulness of one's life. For how can your life be meaningful if you are naught but a mechanical puppet, every action of which was completely fixed by a purely mechanical process pre-determined already at the birth of the universe?" Instead, he argues, our mental selves are not "mere passive witnesses to an inexorable sequence of material events that lie beyond the capacity of our thoughts, ideas, and feelings to affect in any way. . . . 'Free choice' stipulates that this choice is not fully determined by the material aspects of reality alone, but is influenced by an input from the mind of the observer."[12]

This means that, like many other things in life, freedom does not have to be "scientific" in the sense of being proved by the scientific method. The truth is that science—for all its glories—is not the first, last, and only word on life. Freedom will always elude a certain type of scientific scrutiny, and the scientific method can never justify freedom. To ask science to do so is as futile as Kraus's drunk looking for his keys where he knew they weren't, even though there was better light there. We are all grateful heirs of the scientific method and its extraordinary illuminating power, and not for one moment do we repudiate science. But science and its scientific paradigm are not the sole or the final guides to truth, and they can no more prove the reality of freedom than they can verify love, describe the color of evil, or hope to capture the supernatural in a test tube. It is no criticism of science to say that it can only do what it is designed to do and does so brilliantly. But to ask it to do more is untrue to science and damaging to freedom.

Put differently, the glory of science is among the highest human achievements, but it includes a paradox. The approach that succeeds in the scientific exploration of nature may fail in the scientific exploration of human nature, for the detachment that helps scientists to see when it comes to nature may make scientists blind when it comes to humans. In G. K. Chesterton's words, "That same suppression of sympathies, that same waving away of intuitions or guesswork which makes a man preternaturally clever in dealing with the stomach of a spider, will make him preternaturally stupid in dealing with the heart of a man. He is making himself inhuman in order to understand humanity."[13]

Down the way of scientism, or dogmatic naturalistic science, lies the unfreedom of a thousand determinisms and the dismal swamp of reductionism and "nothing buttery." There is no freedom left when the present is always pronounced to be determined by the past and the highest human ideals are pulled down from their pedestals as nothing but this and nothing but that. Better far the humility that values the scientific method but acknowledges its limits, and then uses it gratefully for what it is designed for. There are important things in life that science cannot discover and cannot assess, but we should never say that they are unreal or irrelevant for that reason. Science has a hard time doing justice to love, to beauty, and to notions such as justice. Human freedom is too important to be dismissed like that, and the point is clear. Within the bounds of science, humans can never be more than objects, by definition. Sam Harris's admission about freedom and science is telling. In the light of science, freedom is only a feeling and an illusion: "We can't make sense of it in scientific terms."[14] The truth is that neither the rationalist nor the scientist can ever establish human freedom. Freedom is not the fruit of either logic or lab.

The truth is—and the third family of faiths has always insisted on this fact—nature itself cannot prove human freedom, and nature is also inadequate to provide ethical guidance for human behavior. Nature has no heart. Nature is deaf to human cries and indifferent to our concerns. Nature is morally silent. Witness the barbarism of those, like the Social Darwinians and the Nazis, who have made the mistake of grounding ethics in nature. It takes history and theology to demonstrate that humans are not only objects but subjects and agents with dignity and genuine freedom. And it takes revelation from outside nature to guide us on how we are to live in relation to our fellow human beings.

Rabbi Heschel states, "Patient, pliant, and submissive to our minds is the world of nature, but obstinately silent. We adore her wealth and tacit wisdom, we tediously decipher her signs, but she never speaks to us."[15] Or as Leon Kass observes, "The heavens may, as the Psalmist sings, declare the glory of God (Psalm 19:1), but they say not a peep about righteousness. Not only is nature silent about right and justice; absolutely no moral rules can be deduced from even the fullest understanding of nature."[16] That sort of humility is rarely part of the understanding of the second family of faiths, which of course underscores the recurring point in our discussion. Once again, there are choices and there are consequences. Philosophies and worldviews are consequential because they provide the lenses that determine what we see, but because of their limitations and inadequacies they may also be the lenses that determine what we will never be able to see—and fail to see to our loss.

Freedom as a Gift, History as a Task

The third major family of faiths is the Abrahamic family, which includes Judaism, the Christian faith, and Islam. Today more than half the world lives by one of these three faiths, and in the form of the first two—Judaism and the Christian faith—they have been the primary shapers of the Western world, along with the Greeks and the Romans. What the two directly biblical faiths share in common is their belief that behind the universe is a personal and infinite God, and that two momentous truths flow out of who God is and what God has done: *human freedom*, God's greatest gift to humankind, and *meaningful history*, the arena in which we live and act. In terms of God's character, there are three decisive occasions in the Torah when God discloses himself to his people Israel as YHWH: once to Moses alone, once to the elders of Israel, and once—the moment that Jews consider the most important in all their history—to the entire nation at Mount Sinai.

YHWH is the name of God that Jews do not pronounce, or that was pronounced only at Yom Kippur and by the high priest. It is translated from the Hebrew either as I AM WHO I AM, or more literally as I WILL BE WHO I WILL BE. In God, the past, the present, and the future are one, for he is the creator of time and is outside time. The God who spoke to Abraham, Isaac, Jacob, and then to Moses and the entire people of Israel is sovereign—and God's sovereignty spells freedom, the capacity to exert his will regardless of any restraint or interference. God determines, speaks, and acts not because he has to but because he wills to. He is sovereign and therefore free, absolutely free. In Rabbi Heschel's words, "The most commanding idea that Judaism dares to think is that freedom, not necessity, is the source of all being. Behind mind and matter, order and relations, the freedom of God obtains."[17]

This God, the Jewish and Christian Scriptures declare, created humans in his image and likeness. As such, creation was the act of God's freedom, and it created humans who are significant in their freedom and responsibility just as God is sovereign in his. Human freedom is therefore a gift from God through which we resemble our Creator, and it opens up the possibility of meaning in history. In the words of Rabbi Heschel, the second premise of Judaism is that "man is able to surpass himself. Such ability is the essence of freedom."[18]

When God rescues the Israelites from slavery in Egypt, or calls people to himself today, he does so as a free God who liberates people to become free. He calls them to worship him freely, to become a people who live and walk before him in freedom, and to demonstrate a new way of human life and a new type of society built on dignity, justice, and freedom. Rabbi Sacks writes, "It is as if God had said, 'My name is in *the future tense*.'" This means that

God cannot be predicted or controlled. He cannot be confined to categories known in advance. Being free, he will be what he chooses to be, not randomly but as an expression of his character. "I am the God of the radically unknown future, the God of surprises. You will know me when you see me, but not before."[19] This freedom is the gift of God to humans created in his image. Always influenced by a thousand causes, yes, but unlike the rest of creation, humans are capable of thinking and acting freely, not because of causes from the past but through choices to do with an imagined future. Again Rabbi Sacks: "The key word of the first chapter of Genesis is *Yehi*, 'Let there be.' Creation, human or divine, means actualizing what has not yet been."[20] "Imagine," John Lennon sang, but the world that he and Yoko Ono dreamed of and advocated for came no nearer. "Let there be," God said, and "there was." God's word expressed God's will, and the cosmos sprang into being as the effect.

Such freedom of the will "is not accidental to human existence as Judaism conceives it. It is of its very essence."[21] The same was true for the early Christians. In the second century, Irenaeus wrote famously, "The glory of God is a human being fully alive."[22] Tertullian in the same century quoted Genesis 1 many times and argued from it to ground human freedom. "Man was created by God as free, with power to choose and power to act. . . . There is no clearer indication in him of God's image and similitude than this."[23] For both Jews and Christians, freedom is precious beyond all counting because it is the gift through which we most resemble our Creator. "Without taking freedom seriously," Heschel concludes, "it is impossible to take humanity seriously."[24]

The immensity of this claim about human freedom and meaningful history is radical and awesome, and it deserves to be pondered. As Jews and Christians see it, the choice is not between being free and being determined, as if it were a matter of either-or. Rather, the challenge is to exert one's freedom and responsibility against all the surrounding forces that threaten to determine and condition, including the weight of one's own character insofar as it has been determined by sin, wrong, and error. Freedom therefore lies in the act of overcoming the necessity that is born of normal processes. In today's climate, such a view of freedom is too easily dismissed as religious mumbo jumbo. Yet in reality it is a truth mercifully different from ancient paganism (Sophocles: "Pray not at all, since there is no release for mortals from predestined calamity").[25] And it is excitingly different from the maximum-security prison cell of contemporary secular reductionism and determinism—so much so that it holds the key to a human future with genuine responsibility, growth, hope, love, and flourishing.

Humans are free and humans are responsible. But importantly, this majestic claim for freedom comes with an insistence on the need for self-limitation. In the biblical view there are two sides to both God's freedom and our freedom, and in each case the second is as important as the first, though often overlooked. God is sovereign and therefore free, but God chooses to limit his own freedom in order to respect the freedom of humans he has made in his image. God enters the human heart only when invited. In the words of Rebbe Menachem Mendel of Kotzk, God lives where we let him in. In Roger Williams's daring term, God does not "rape" the human conscience. In Holman Hunt's famous picture "The Light of the World," Jesus stands at the door and knocks, but the door has no handle on the outside. It must be opened from the inside.

There is a similar double truth in human freedom too. Created in the image of God, we humans are free and therefore significant. We can rise above determinisms, but we must remember that freedom requires self-limitation from us too. Human freedom requires self-limitation in two ways: through our own character that freedom requires, and through the consistency that respects the same freedom for others. In terms of character, personal freedom must always be exercised within the framework of the truth of who we are and how we should live, and in terms of consistency, personal freedom must always respect the equal freedom of all others, our fellow human beings. Only so can a just and free society be built and sustained for the good of all, and not just for the rich and the powerful.

This Jewish and Christian view of freedom means that on the one hand, there is no freedom like human freedom, giving humans the ability and responsibility to help determine themselves decisively and to care for creation. The call of God in a human life means that we actually become partners with God in caring for our neighbors and the world. On the other hand, it also means that there is no freedom like human freedom that is able to undo creation and create chaos and cause violence. As Mircea Eliade states, the Bible's view of human freedom means nothing less than "*absolute emancipation from any kind of natural 'law' and hence the highest freedom that man can imagine: freedom to intervene even in the ontological constitution of the universe. It is, consequently, a preeminently creative freedom.*

In other words, it constitutes a new formula for man's collaboration with the creation." All other views, whether ancient or modern, Eliade claimed, lead not only to determinism and unfreedom but to a terrifying view of history as fate and meaninglessness and, "in the end, to despair."[26]

Is it any wonder that 1776 and America's great experiment in political freedom owed everything to the Hebrew Bible and to the book of Exodus in particular? And that none of this basis for freedom can be found in 1789 and its secularist heirs? Does this not mean that America's future freedom depends on whether Americans remember and acknowledge their biblical roots? Rabbi Sacks puts the immensity of the historical significance of Exodus simply: "It poses a fundamental question: Can we make, on earth, a social order based not on transactions of power but on respect for the human person—each person—as 'the image of God'?"[27] Exodus as the grand master story of Western freedom gave rise to the United States as the world's sole modern nation dedicated to freedom at the core of its being and to the high purpose of acting into history with meaning. Rabbi Sacks concludes simply, "History does not give rise to hope; hope gives rise to history."[28]

This means that it is a serious mistake to trivialize the precedent of Exodus by leaving it at the level of ancient history or reducing it to a slogan (Let my people go!). Like Jewish freedom, early American freedom was anchored in the character of God as mediated through his nation-forming covenant with his people. Freedom was therefore covenantal (later, constitutional). It required a framework and a way of life that protected and perpetuated the freedom won by the victory over pharaoh (and over Britain). Liberty began with liberation (revolution), but it was far more than liberation. It was an ongoing mission, and not a once-and-for-all given, and it required an entire way of life, and not just a single day of release. Like a muscle, freedom is not static. Exercise it, and it grows. Neglect it, and it withers.

Amazingly, the Jews even dared to use the same word, *avodah*, for serving and worshiping God as they had used for slaving for Pharaoh, even though slaving for Pharaoh had meant cruel bondage whereas serving God was the service that was perfect freedom. The point was deliberate. As Rabbi Sacks explains, "The difference is not that one is hard and the other is easy. They are both hard work, but one breaks the spirit, the other lifts and exalts it."[29] Can there be any question that America owes it to Exodus that covenantal (constitutional) freedom is in the DNA of the American republic?

To be sure, the biblical grounding for human freedom is precious, but it can be all too easily diverted in two dangerous directions: toward a selfish individual narcissism or to an arrogant powermongering by the strong and the wealthy. To be the robust and caring human responsibility it is called to be, freedom must be balanced with ethics and directed by the accompanying truth of history charged with meaning and led with purpose. Is life only "a tale told by an idiot," as Shakespeare's Macbeth declares?[30] Is history no more than Joseph Heller's "trash bag of random coincidences blown open by the wind," as his protagonist Bruce Gold asserts?[31] Not so within the biblical perspective, where history is the arena open to the action of responsible human freedom under God. Western civilization takes purposeful history as self-evident, but once again it is the gift of the Jews passed on through Christians. Paul Johnson admits that one of the reasons he wrote his own book *A History of the Jews* was this unique sense of purpose in history. It helped him answer "the most intractable of all human questions: what are we on earth for?" "No people had ever insisted more firmly than the Jews that history has a purpose and humanity a destiny. . . . The Jews, therefore, stand at the center of the perennial attempt to give human life the dignity of a purpose."[32]

To be sure, there is a cautionary check and a certain encouragement for America in the reminder that Israel did not maintain and practice this stance on freedom consistently for long, and this relapse must also be acknowledged openly. All too soon and all too easily the book of Numbers followed the book of Exodus, and the book of Judges followed Numbers. Degeneration followed liberation, and eventually freedom was denied and then lost. The same was true of the Christian church in its turn. When the fourth-century Western church was victorious over the gods of mighty Rome, for example, and it moved into its seat of power, it took over too many of Rome's institutions uncritically. Erasmus, for one, pointed out how the papacy reflected the Caesars, so that Pope Julius, the worldly secular princeling, resembled Julius Caesar more closely than Jesus of Nazareth. In the process of improper assimilation, the church had abandoned the covenantal basis of the Old Testament's political order and had established a hierarchical order of governance that dominated Christian Europe from the fourth century until the Reformation in the sixteenth century.

Unquestionably, the deepest expression of this view of human freedom and responsibility is biblical, the clearest statements of it today are Jewish, and no one is more eloquent in expounding it than Rabbi Sacks, speaking with his distinguished background in Cambridge philosophy:

> Human freedom and the self-consciousness that accompanies it are the great unknown and unknowable within the otherwise orderly processes of nature mapped by science. There can never be a science of freedom, for the concept is a contradiction in terms. Science is about causes, freedom about purposes. Science explains phenomena in terms of other phenomena that preceded them. Free action, by contrast, can only be understood in terms of the future we intend to bring about, not any past event, historical, biochemical or neurophysiological. To be sure, there are many influences on human behavior: some genetic, others cultural and environmental. But they are *influences,* not *causes* in the sense in which the term is used in the natural sciences.[33]

A Worm in the Apple

Freedom is at the heart of the biblical view of human dignity, and at the heart of history with meaning and purpose. According to this Jewish and Christian view, humans are created to act into history while aiming for an ideal that is higher than history and reaches beyond the horizon of their individual lives. But importantly, there is another distinctive feature of the Jewish and Christian views that is critical to the biblical understanding and to its success in defending freedom. The Bible is realistic about the human capacity for evil and vigilant about the abuse of power, and therefore aware that freedom never lasts and rarely turns out as its advocates hope. The reason is sin, the natural human inclination to do wrong and to go wrong. What Immanuel Kant famously described as "the crooked timber of humanity" was long foreshadowed in Genesis, the book of beginnings and the story of prototypical humanity. As Leon Kass comments in his magisterial book *The Beginning of Wisdom*, when we investigate the meaning of stories such as the garden of Eden, the flood, and the Tower of Babel, "readers are shown the dangerous natural tendencies of humankind: on the one hand, toward order-destroying wildness and violence, on the other hand, toward order-transforming efforts at self-sufficiency and mastery of the world."[34] Our English translation of Kant's German came from philosopher R. G. Collingwood ("Out of the crooked timber of humanity, no straight thing was ever made"), but Kant himself was only quoting the Bible ("That which is crooked cannot be made straight" [Eccles 1:15 KJV]).

This Jewish and Christian realism about evil is critical for guarding freedom, because it counters the danger of utopianism that is at the heart of the Enlightenment, and it tempers the irresponsibility that might flow from an emphasis on freedom alone. In the words of Rabbi Sacks again, "Without limits, freedom for the strong means slavery for the weak. Freedom for the rich means misery for the poor. These limits have nothing to do with nature. The limits of nature are about power: they are about what we *can* do. The limits God places upon humankind are about ethics: what we *may* do."[35]

According to this biblical view, humans have an inalienable dignity and worth because they are created in the image of God. While still creatures, like the animals, they are God-like in the sense of being made in God's image. They are therefore free and responsible, and both the freedom and the responsibility must be respected, cherished, and protected—against all determinisms and all despotisms. But the same biblical view also underscores that the power that makes freedom possible can become the power that corrupts freedom fatally. With freedom, responsibility and risk go hand in hand and stand as a reminder that America may be the New World, but the American is still the Old Adam. James Madison was tutored by the redoubtable clergyman John Witherspoon at Princeton College, and his two essays, the *Federalist Papers* 10 and 51 are America's most celebrated political exposition of the biblical view of sin, the danger of the abuse of power, and the vital importance of limiting power. Creation and corruption are never far apart.

> Ambition must be made to counteract ambition. The interest of the man must be connected with the constitutional rights of the place. It may be a reflection on human nature, that such devices should be necessary to control the abuses of government. But what is government itself but the greatest of reflections on human nature? If men were angels, no government would be necessary. If angels were to govern men, neither external nor internal controls on government would be necessary. In framing a government which is to be administered by men over men, the great difficulty lies in this: you must first enable the government to control the governed; and in the next place oblige it to control itself.[36]

The last three centuries have underscored Madison's realism with red flags of their own—the nineteenth and twentieth centuries through control via social engineering, and the twenty-first century through control via big data.

Some of the fruits of the Enlightenment have turned out to be so poisonous that it must forever be "the Enlightenment" or the so-called Enlightenment. And one of its most telling lessons is that some of the vilest crimes against humanity were carried out in the name of utopianism, not malice or misogyny.

This utopianism, as we shall see, is the fatal flaw in the vision of the sexual revolution, but one that too few recognize. For the moment, think of the monstrous outcomes of Mao Zedong's pretensions to be an artist painting a new China on a blank canvas, killing tens of millions of his own people in the process. The practical expression of the contrasting biblical realism, and the surest bulwark against utopianism, is the insistence on a separation of powers, an appreciation for the necessity of checks and balances, and a respect for the role of prophets as social critics. No leader is so wise and so virtuous that they do not need to be checked and balanced, especially those who pride themselves on their intellectual brilliance or their ethical uprightness (which are rarely claimed together). Nor can there be such a paragon in the biblical view.

For the Jewish people, this separation of powers was expressed institutionally in their famous "three crowns" of authority (the king, the priest, and the prophet), each of them under God. Some absolutely vital ideas were at work in this principle: first, a *separation* of powers; second, a *suspicion* of power; and third, a *secularization* of power. This meant that the prohibition against idolatry ruled out the idolatry of politics. Politics was therefore relativized. It was never central or foremost in Israel, as it was in Aristotle's Greece and in the modern "politicization" of life and society by today's Left. The king was not the priest, the priest was not the king, and the prophet was the social critic whose responsibility was to hold the nation accountable to the standards of the covenant and thus to call the king, the priest, and the people back to their covenantal commitments.

Later in Jewish history, the lines became blurred. Kings, such as Jeroboam and Solomon, appointed their own priests, and in the time of Herod and his Hasmonean successors, the lines were effectively erased as the kings became high priests and priests became hopelessly entangled in politics. This confusion of powers contributed to the twin catastrophes of AD 70 and 133. For the American founders, the same insistence on the separation of powers led to the three branches of government: the executive, the legislature, and the judiciary. A free and independent press and charismatic leaders such as Dr. Martin Luther King Jr. later filled the roles of the recurring voices of prophetic criticism.

Needless to say, such realism about the flawed nature of humanity and the enduring necessity of a clear separation of powers is conspicuously absent in America today, especially on the Left where utopianism is never far away. It is a key reason for the persistent dangers of overreaching presidential power, an overreaching judiciary, the practice of burgeoning executive regulations, and the idolatry of politics that is represented by politicization, which leads in turn to the idolatry of the state and state control. Together these trends are changing America beyond recognition, and in the process menacing freedom. Thus a generation too sophisticated to talk of old-fashioned and politically incorrect notions such as sin and evil becomes a generation enamored and bogged down in ever-cleverer styles of corruption and overreach.

Presidents, judges, and movement activists who believe they are correct and on "the right side of history" rarely show respect for such notions as checks and balances, encroachment, and the will of the people. Arrogance replaces humility, persuasion is considered a waste of time, scalability becomes a virtue, and coercion becomes the handiest tool to reach for the domination that consistency calls for. Clearly, the American elites can project their own will onto the general will of the American people—"the expert knows best." And in the grand manner of Jean-Jacques Rousseau, all other wills, including those of the majorities who disagree with them, can be made to go along with their executive actions and legal decisions, all dressed up of course as "freedom." Rousseau wrote, "Whoever refuses to pay obedience to the general will shall be liable to be compelled to it by the force of the whole body. And this is in effect nothing more than that he may be compelled to be free."[37] Joseph de Maistre described the result: the revolutionary will of the First French Republic was "a battering ram with twenty million men behind it."[38]

"Compelled to be free"? A battering ram on behalf of liberty? And how many died in its path? Such a vile paradox and its outcome takes us back to chutes and ladders again. Are Americans content that these things should be so? That certain elites are suppressing dissent and conscientious objection in the name of a bogus charge of discrimination? Do Americans realize what they are choosing, and what their choices will mean for future generations? Are the elites to allow no alternatives to their way of thinking and living? Without a solid basis for freedom, there can be only determinism and despotism, and without a sure barrier against the abuse of freedom, there will be only exploitation and corruption. True lovers of freedom must be realists as well as idealists, and such realism is essential if freedom is to have a chance of lasting and not becoming its own worst enemy.

The central challenge of this last question to America can be put in the form of what might be called the Tocqueville reminder and the Jefferson query. Tocqueville noted, "Every religion has an affinity with some political opinion."[39] Which worldview, then, has the closest affinity with American freedom: the Hindu or Buddhist? The secularist or the Muslim? Or the Jewish and Christian? Jefferson was more pointed still: "God who gave us life gave us liberty. And can the liberties of a nation be thought secure when we have removed their only firm basis, a conviction in the minds of the people that these liberties are the Gift of God?"[40]

Was Jefferson's claim pure cant, in the same way that so many of his statements on freedom were hypocritical and never applied to his ownership of slaves? Or on this point was he realistic and right? If so, what are the grounds needed to justify American freedom? Which are the most adequate? Which best fits the American republic as it was founded and best fits its requirements nearly two and a half centuries on? But perhaps the question should be sharpened today: Why are rights such as freedom of religion and conscience and freedom of speech considered "inalienable"? If they are no longer considered God-given or rooted in the unique nature of human reason and conscience, as recent challenges have claimed, are they in fact inalienable any longer? And what does that mean for human rights? Are they simply *fiat* rights, paper rights, fictional rights?

These three families of faiths and their very different relationships to personal and political freedom today are clear. But there is little American thinking on the order of Jefferson or Publius now. Much of what is best about America is simply taken for granted. Too many Americans are repeating unexamined clichés and platitudes; too many are mouthing claims that they can no longer justify; and too many are putting their confidence in fashionable ideas whose consequences they have not examined. If a serious discussion about the foundations of freedom were to be opened, it would soon be choked off in the acrid air of the culture war hostilities on one side and the poisonous political correctness on the other.

Again, will it be said that freedom was too hard a challenge for Americans to overcome? Here, then, is the eighth question on the checklist that Americans must answer constructively: *Where do you ground your faith in freedom?*

Why do notions such as human dignity, freedom, justice, and equality need any foundation at all? Do most people that you know lead what Socrates called an "examined life," or do they just take over what their peers and the social media hand down to them? What will happen if there is a growing mismatch between the ideas and ideals that Americans believe now and those on which the republic was founded? Human dignity, freedom, and genuine liberalism itself are all under threat from various ideas and developments today. As Yuval Harari expresses the point, there are challenges that go far beyond philosophical challenges. "We are about to face a flood of extremely useful devices, tools and structures that make no allowance for the free will of individual humans. Will democracy, the free market and human rights survive this flood?"[41]

Nothing is more important than an open and continuing debate over these matters. Without solid foundations, without sure claims to truth, and without appropriate ways of living, there will be no lasting freedom, and without a free and open debate, there will be no chance to decide what is true and wise and good. Free people and genuine liberals can thrive only when everything is open to debate, though always within the rule of law, the bonds of civility, and a keen-eyed respect for the good of all. Can American freedom survive today's culture wars, today's political correctness, and today's identity politics—with all their accompanying styles of repression? Can American freedom survive conservative obscurantism and liberal illiberalism? Once again, today's choices are shaping tomorrow's consequences, and the choices need to be considered with far greater care.

ARE YOU VIGILANT ABOUT *the* INSTITUTIONS CRUCIAL *to* FREEDOM?

A Republic or a Democracy?

*O*n my first visit to the United States in 1968, I had the privilege of meeting Mario Savio. He had been the leader of the Berkeley Free Speech Movement, which in many ways had lit the fuse that set off the explosion that became the 1960s counterculture. His most famous speech was the "Operation of the Machine." He delivered it before four thousand people at Sproul Hall in December 1964. ("If this is a firm, and if the board of regents are the directors; and if President Kerr is in fact the manager; then I'll tell you something. The faculty are a bunch of employees, and we're the raw material! But we're a bunch of raw materials that don't mean to be . . . made into any product!") Savio's fierce commitment to freedom of speech was admirable and unquestionable. Like John Milton and George Orwell before him, heroes to many who are passionate about freedom of speech, he knew that post-truth politics is impossible. Freedom of speech begins, ends, and runs throughout on an unshakable commitment to truth and to addressing truth to power.

Nearly fifty years later, that meeting with Mario Savio came to mind as I watched two entirely different campus responses to President Trump's election in November 2016. On the one hand, there was the "milk and water" response. Their favorite daughter had lost. The "wrong" candidate had defied all expectations and won, and campus after campus across America was in the process of setting up safe places and therapy sessions for traumatized students—replete with puppies, coloring books, Play-Doh, and LEGOs. The University of Michigan offered "post-election self-care," Yale put on a "group-scream," and Cornell students were invited to a "cry-in."

A student in Madison, Wisconsin, put up a Post-it note on a window with the words, "Suck it up, you p____!" The trivial note was thunderously attacked by a dean in a three-page letter as a "hate crime" and an "act of political intimidation" that "violated every value for which the college stood." At George Washington University, students pressed to join the list of "sanctuary universities," while others—presumably tongue in cheek—requested sanctuary from exams, from repaying student loans, and from obeying the laws regarding the age of drinking (which they claimed were causing emotional distress). Many colleges and universities canceled classes and exams so professors could express their sympathy to fearful students who felt they had been "othered." All in all, "It's a generational/racial/gender/cultural thing. You who don't understand wouldn't understand."

On the other hand, there was the "blood and iron" response, as left-wing riots broke out at Cal Berkeley, New York University, Middlebury College, and elsewhere. Demands for free speech had degenerated into the silencing of all speech, as insults, threats, violence, and arson were used to strong-arm opponents they disagreed with. The wheel had come full circle. Just as American sex, from early feminism to the hookup culture, had gone from one objectification to a new and worse objectification, so American speech has gone from one repression to a new and worse repression as the United States has become caught in an ugly culture of "trolling," "flaming," "group-trolling," "crap-flooding," and "doing it for the lulz" (*lulz* being derived from LOL, laughing out loud). In the words of one commentator, "the more you talk online, the more likely you'll be nasty; talk long enough, and it's a certainty."[1]

The newspaper has given way to the internet, and the integrity and wisdom of the old-fashioned adult editor has been ousted by a toddler's style imperative to command attention. And what commands attention more than the shocking and the outrageous? The final commandment in the *12 Commandments of Flaming* is "When in doubt, insult."[2] In the high-decibel cacophony of American incivility, the best way to be heard is to insult and be outrageous. So who today talks with the cool reason of the Greeks or listens for the "still, small voice" of the Hebrews?

Where are the moral courage and the sense of history in the young American mind today? Where is the realism about life in generations that have experienced no depression, no world war, and take prosperity and invincible military superiority as their birthright? Both the silliness and the seriousness of the student responses were unmistakable. Campus events in 1964 triggered a passion for justice, a wave of robust dissent, and a fresh commitment to free speech that galvanized the world and even brought governments to their knees. Campus events in 2016 reduced American campuses and American students to the level of either 1920s anarchists or a kindergarten, with juvenile behavior more appropriate for toddlers in a playpen.[3]

When a sports team is defeated, it sets about making sure it never happens again, and the same is normally true of political parties in a democracy. In the next election they will work to reverse the result of the previous defeat. But not in America today. America's "sore loser culture," with its politics of blaming and victim playing has become either a cauldron of all-out political resistance, fired by a self-righteous anger that is toxic, or a hospital ward of sensitivities, suspicions, and slights, hugging to itself the consolation that there is one thing better than being right—being wronged.

Many Americans have become the great affrontables, and much of American public life has become a simmering stew of hypersensitivity, self-pity, resentment, rage, protest, and complaint. "We lost," but "life is not fair," so now is the time for a recount. There is always someone, something, somewhere, to blame—especially for a generation well trained in detecting microaggression, the art of spotting ever smaller splinters in the eyes of neighbors, and detecting the concealed weapon in every word. But the damage to democracy and the outcome of such sorry behavior are impossible to deny. If the responses of the younger generation are any indication, American freedom and responsibility are languishing. The capacity to recover from an insult or an attack is always the measure of an individual's and a nation's self-reliance and sense of responsibility, which suggests that young Americans are not taking responsibility robustly, and are not recovering well.

To be fair, there are reasons for the so-called snowflake generation (emotionally pampered children and students who melt when they hit the ground). There are many real wrongs and real victims in America, especially racial and sexual, and there should always be an important place for human compassion and for a penetrating analysis of what caused the wounds and the injustice in the first place. And to be fair too, the silliness and the illiberalism are broadly Anglo-American and not uniquely American. Earlier in England, for example, a protest against the "no-platforming" of the radical feminist Germaine Greer led to the no-platforming of the protester Peter Tatchell, and then to the no-platforming of Richard Dawkins, who had protested the previous no-platformings. Thus in quick succession, and with no sense of the comic hilarity, three grand icons of liberalism—one a pioneer feminist, one a leading homosexual advocate, and one a champion new atheist—had all been caught in the toils of political correctness and silenced for their pains.

Democratic and Republican?

What do such shenanigans have to do with freedom? Slippery-slope arguments are notoriously prone to becoming a form of scare-mongering. Yet James Madison was surely right to declare in his "Memorial and Remonstrance" in 1785, "It is proper to take alarm at the first experiment upon our liberties."[4] After all, freedom, as we have seen, is mercurial and protean, and needs to be guarded jealously if it is to thrive and endure. Change, of course, is at the heart of the modern world, and change may well be for the better and not for the worse. But that is precisely what Americans must assess, so they must constantly follow the trends, developments, and changes, and judge how they are affecting freedom in their time—to judge whether the changes are indeed for the better or for the worse. This, then, is the ninth question on the citizens' checklist: *Are Americans vigilant about the institutions that are crucial to freedom in America today?*

There are countless current issues that bear on the state of freedom today, but let me open up just two areas in two separate chapters: first, the many current challenges to American democracy, and, second, the problems posed by different sets of ideas flowing through the American republic. The latter is particularly crucial as it forms the conflict that throughout this book I have called the "tale of two revolutions," as the heirs and allies of 1776 clash with the heirs and allies of 1789. The importance of the first, the challenges to democracy, lies in the fact that most Americans have already replaced the concept of republicanism with the term *democracy* or *liberal democracy* as their term of choice to describe America. So there is an added danger if democracy is undermined in its turn.

The primacy of democracy over republicanism owes much to the impact of Alexis de Tocqueville's *Democracy in America*, to Lincoln's stirring definition at the end of the Gettysburg Address, and to the glory of America's heroic victories over despotism and totalitarianism in the world wars. The leaders of the nation had come to the field of the recent battle, Lincoln declared, to demonstrate their resolve "that this nation, under God, shall have a new birth of freedom—that government of the people, by the people, for the people shall not perish from the earth."[5]

Lincoln's definition was simple, bold, and clear-cut, and it gave democracy an air of solidity, permanence, and grandeur that is easy to state and hard to argue with. George Orwell called it the Gettysburg ideal, and always sought to steer by it. Democracy is the order of the day. Democracy is the spirit of the times. If freedom is self-determination, then self-government for a free people follows as naturally as two plus two equals four. Democracy, then, is as grand and clear-cut as the carving on the wall of Lincoln's magnificent memorial in Washington, DC. And if that is democracy, who in their right mind would choose to give up the chance of ruling themselves? Surely only a madman or a fool would hand over control of their lives to a monarch or an aristocracy.

But democracy is like freedom—far from self-evident, anything but easy, and all too often short-lived. Lincoln's words were not in fact original, as he and his contemporaries knew well. They were a quotation from John Wycliffe, the master of Balliol College, Oxford, in the late fourteenth century, and the man who was called the "Morning Star of the Reformation." They came from Wycliffe's introduction to his translation of the Bible into English in 1384, and were among the ideas for which he and his followers were severely persecuted by the medieval church—"This Bible is for the Government of the People, by the People, and for the People." In other words, religious freedom goes hand in hand with civil freedom, just as negative freedom requires the complement of positive freedom for it to be full freedom. People can be trusted (and are therefore free) to read and interpret the Bible for themselves, without the intervention of priests and scholars. And with certain assumptions in place, they can also be trusted (and should therefore be free) to have their say in ruling themselves, without the intervention of overbearing political authorities and burdensome experts. The self-rule and responsibility of the faith-based freedom of the Bible make possible the self-rule and responsibility of democracy.

Lincoln's definition is no less powerful for being a quotation, but the fuller story stands as a reminder of the rise and fall of the career of ideas over time, especially those that are controversial and changeable. There were many centuries between Wycliffe and Lincoln, centuries when democracy was as far from reality in Europe as it looks in certain countries today that use the word but make a mockery of the meaning. Words alone are never enough, however eloquent. As the Greeks and Romans knew well, the wheel is always turning. So there is always the danger that the tyranny of the minority will be replaced by the tyranny of the majority. Or in Lord Acton's words, there is the risk that just as monarchy hardens into despotism, and aristocracy contracts into oligarchy, democracy will "expand into the supremacy of numbers" and then become "mob rule and tyranny."[6] The status quo must never be taken for granted. One generation's certainty easily becomes another generation's doubts, another's question mark, and yet another's target for ridicule and rejection.

So the question for Americans is, How is liberal democracy faring in America today with the double challenge of a *large* democracy and a *lasting* democracy? And what does the answer say about the founders' republicanism? An obvious opening question is, What does the self-rule of the people mean when American democracy numbers more than three hundred million people? Even at its best, democracy is not really genuine self-rule but the rule of the majority of the people over the minority. For how else can three hundred million people express its will apart from speaking and being counted? But what then does self-rule mean for the individual citizen when it is obvious that each individual is only one in three hundred million? How does each individual feel as the smallest possible, indivisible mathematical unit of democracy, when each has to cast their vote anonymously, secretly, and with no legal responsibility for the outcome? Every vote counts, but the individual as individual is practically, though not completely, powerless. As a mathematician, Bertrand Russell put the point like this when Britain had only twenty million citizens rather than America's more than three hundred million: "You have, it is true, a twenty-millionth share in the government of others, but only a twenty-millionth share in the government of yourself. You are therefore much more conscious of being governed than of governing."[7]

This means that when the question about democracy is, Who rules? the answer seems simple and inspiring. We are free. We are sovereign, "the

Rulers R Us." We are ruling ourselves. But as soon as the question changes to, How are the rulers to rule? the problems proliferate on all sides, and the sense of genuine self-government starts to weaken appreciably.

Liberal to Left/Liberal

Some of the changes in liberal democracy since Lincoln are plain and undeniable. On the positive side of the ledger, new groups, such as women and African Americans, have been franchised and made eligible to vote, but at the same time there has been a fateful transformation of the first of the two terms. As we have seen, the term *liberal* has changed from a concern for personal freedom to a concern for progressive freedom. For Lord Acton, John Stuart Mill, and the nineteenth century at large, personal freedom was the required assumption that made someone liberal and constituted liberalism (*liber* being Latin for "free"). They therefore held that it was the duty of the government to limit itself, and to protect and promote the freedom of the individual person and of private life as the untouchable arena of freedom.

This view of freedom has been stood on its head, so that suffrage has been expanded but the understanding of *liberal* has changed. Whereas nineteenth-century liberals sought to protect personal freedom by limiting the role of government in private life, twentieth-century liberals sought to achieve each purported advance of freedom by expanding the role of government in more and more of life, including private life. Freedom as individual citizens saw it for themselves has changed into freedom as the government sees it for everyone, and thus limited government has morphed into statism, ever-expanding government, and less individual freedom—1789 once again.

The seeds of this shift can be seen in Rousseau's ideas of sovereignty and the general will of the people, and they flowered fatefully in the French Revolution. But in the English-speaking world, Christopher Dawson raised a lament for classical liberalism in the 1930s, and noted how democracy was used to justify the shift:

> Liberalism is a dying power. What the non-dictatorial States stand for today is not Liberalism but Democracy, a very different thing. . . . Liberalism stands for the rights of the individual and the freedom of private opinion and private interests, while Democracy stands for the rights of the majority and the sovereignty of public opinion and the common interest.[8]

More recently, F. A. Hayek defended personal freedom in his famous classic *The Road to Serfdom*. He commented caustically on this huge change: "It has been part of the camouflage of leftish movements in this country, helped by the muddleheadedness of many who really believe in liberty, that 'liberal' has come to mean the advocacy of almost every kind of governmental control."[9]

So how do Americans assess the result of that shift in the United States and view the status of freedom in relation to liberals and liberalism? Does this new liberalism of the Left/liberals make Americans less free, as the former liberals who are now conservatives lament? Or are Americans today freer, as twenty-first-century Left/liberals, progressives, and socialists claim? Americans must weigh the reality and decide for themselves what they want: personal freedom from government or progressive freedom under government.

In some areas the overall balance sheet is hotly disputed, and benefits such as health care are now part of the equation and a vital part of arguments about freedom. But whichever answer wins, a key part of the challenge to the original concept of freedom itself has been clear from the beginning. Before power corrupts, power expands, or in the words so favored by earlier Americans, it *encroaches* and *annexes*. Power must therefore be watched, and especially the encroaching power of the government that is called on to advance progressive freedom. Based on the human potential for the abuse of power, such warnings go all the way back to the earliest Puritan tradition. For example, John Cotton, the father of New England Congregationalism, cautioned, "Let all the world learn to give mortal men no greater power than they are content they shall use, for use it they will. . . . It is counted a matter of danger to the state to limit prerogatives; but it is further danger, not to have them limited."[10] The political problem is therefore unavoidable, Thomas Hobbes argued. All humans share "a perpetual and restless desire of power after power, that ceaseth only in death."[11]

Direct or How?

Another change to be watched and weighed concerns the second of the two terms *liberal democracy*. The founders were in favor of republicanism and notoriously wary of democracy, for what they regarded as democracy was the direct democracy of Athens. That was the system through which the free men of Athens, never more than a few thousand, could come in person to the *agora*, the civic and political center, and take part in the debates and deliberations that decided the policies of their city-state. With the free men expanded from a relative handful to more than three million citizens in 1776, with little chance of intimate relationships, and a population scattered over an area far vaster than Athens could even imagine, such a direct democracy was obviously impossible for the new American republic. It is even more impossible today.

Besides, the founders and many American thinkers since then all shared the skepticism born of history that had built up around direct democracy. Plato detested democracy because he had seen his beloved mentor Socrates condemned and executed by democrats. But the founders were equally wary of the chronic volatility of democracy and of its proneness to mob rule and the slide toward the tyranny of the strong man. Indeed, historian Martin Diamond noted that "not a single American voice was raised in unqualified doctrinaire praise of democracy." On the contrary, "All the American revolutionaries knew that democracy was a problem in need of constant solution, in constant need of moderation, in constant need of institutions and measures to mitigate its defects and guard against its dangers."[12]

In the seventeenth century, John Winthrop called democracy "the meanest and worst of all forms of government."[13] In the nineteenth, Herman Melville wrote of the "Dark Ages of Democracy." ("Better to be secure under one king, than exposed to violence from twenty million monarchs, though oneself be one of them.")[14] Immanuel Kant described direct democracy as "necessarily a despotism."[15] But John Adams was the bluntest of all in the eighteenth century. History shows beyond a shadow of doubt, he argued, "proofs irrefragable that the people, when they have been unchecked, have been as unjust, tyrannical, brutal, barbarous, and cruel, as any king or senate possessed by an uncontrollable power. The majority has eternally and without any one exception usurped over the rights of the minority."[16]

The founders' choice, like that of England, where they had come from, was for representative democracy rather than direct democracy. And around it they built an ingenious system of checks and balances to encourage the promotion of seasoned wisdom and to safeguard against the weaknesses of direct democracy—including the provision of the much-maligned electoral college to provide a balance to the more populous states. To be sure, representative democracy creates its own challenges for freedom, contained in the relationship between the representatives and those that they represent. Should the representatives speak and vote for themselves, exercising their own wisdom and judgment, or are they to be merely the chosen mouthpiece of their electors? Edmund Burke's "Speech to the Electors of Bristol" in November 1774 remains the classic expression of the first view. ("Your representative owes you, not his industry only, but his judgment; and he betrays, instead of serving you, if he sacrifices it to your opinion. . . . You choose a member indeed; but when you have chosen him, he is not a member of Bristol, but he is a member of *Parliament*.")[17]

Opinions Versus Likes

But what do such arguments mean now? American citizens now number more than three hundred million; civic education in public schools has collapsed; there is an increasing reliance on political instruments such as referendums; and the rise of the social media means that the "consent of the governed" has been transferred from *establishing* the government to *daily and hourly feelings* (Likes) about everything the government does. The numerical expansion creates problems by itself, for in Bertrand Russell's terms, every added citizen means that there are more people having a say in the government of each single citizen than the single citizen believes he has in governing himself. Further, democracy is not strictly self-government at all but government by numbers, or the decision of the majority, and government of the majority through the wisdom of the specialist/expert/lobbyist/activist/pollster, who is the advance guard of a new oligarchy.

The overall problem of size adds the challenge of a *large* republic to the challenges we saw earlier of a *lasting* republic. The problem of size was identified and addressed in the nineteenth century as suffrage expanded, and more and more Americans became eligible to vote. But the answer, they thought then, was simple. All it took was for universal education to expand and keep pace with universal suffrage. (President Garfield: "We confront the dangers of suffrage by the blessings of universal education.")[18] Democracy could steadily expand its base and still be safeguarded so long as the widening electorate was educated well and the citizens were sufficiently wise to be able to choose their representatives wisely. Hence the vital importance of education as well as civic education and the significance of the "melting pot."

Have all the requirements for such a large republic been kept fresh and updated? What happens if educational standards decline; civic education disappears; money floods the political landscape like a deluge; the mainstream press grows biased toward one side or the other; the branches of government are confused; the twenty-four-hour news cycle means the endless chewing, rechewing, and spitting out of breaking news; truth-free "fake news" sprouts like tares among the wheat; and the social media corrupt the possibility of deliberation, civility, and wisdom? When the term *opinion* was used in the Declaration of Independence, it meant considered thought, seasoned reflection, and many have argued that the idea of the US Senate was to act as the "chamber of second thoughts." Tocqueville argued in the same vein when he wrote that "Newspapers become more necessary in proportion as men become more equal."[19]

Even the best American papers have failed to strive for so responsible a role today, but recent evidence raises the question whether such considered thought is even possible now. Popular referendums, with their simplistic either-or choices, are a return to the direct democracy that the founders feared. Incessant polling and the social media reinforce feelings (Likes) at the expense of thought, information at the expense of knowledge, and knowledge at the expense of wisdom. And America's new "bubble democracy," with its echo chambers, serves to compound prejudices, exclude unwanted alternatives, block compromise, fuel anger, incite instant mob-making, and excuse evils such as cyber bullying and e-lynchings. Henry Kissinger raised a concern on behalf of statesmanship in international affairs, but his question applies far more widely: "Can democracy avoid an evolution toward a demagogic outcome based on emotional mass appeal rather than the reasoned process the Founding Fathers imagined?"[20]

Death by a Thousand Nibbles

Many other factors now bite into Lincoln's definition of democracy like an army of mice nibbling at a rope, and all the factors need to be addressed in their turn if the lifeline is not to become frayed. For a start, the founders warned against the potential dictatorship of the judiciary if it were allowed to usurp the place of the legislature, but judicial activism now overturns the voice of the people routinely. First, following Justice Oliver Wendell Holmes, the law is only what the judges say it is, regardless of the original intent of the author. And second, judges can be planted and counted on to block the initiatives of any White House or Congress they disagree with. The result is worse than mere obstruction. Jefferson wrote to William Jarvis in 1820 that if judges were to become the "ultimate arbiters of all constitutional questions," that would be "a very dangerous doctrine indeed, and one which place us under the despotism of an oligarchy."[21]

Or again, the founders built in checks and balances for power with a fierce determination to prevent the abuse of power at every level, but they did so only for political institutions. Now, however, there are powerful state and federal agencies outside the three main branches of government, such as the CIA and the FBI, and extremely powerful actors such as Google, Facebook, and Amazon, who were not elected and have no public accountability—apart from the goodwill of their executives. Google's famous founding motto is "Don't be evil," but there is mounting disquiet over its silencing of dissent. When Mark Zuckerberg was asked what were the checks and balances for Facebook now that it had become "the most influential commercial enterprise ever created, with its personal data on nearly 2 billion people, and its unparalleled power" to shape the way people see and think about the world, his answer was vague. It went little beyond the fact that he saw himself as the one-man check and balance, and that he could be so simply by "listening to what people want" and seeking to give people "the power to share" as he pursued his own mission to "connect the world."[22]

Yet, as critics noted, when it comes to the unprecedented power of the tech giants to shape American thinking and discourse, the triple problems of monopolistic power, secret algorithms, and lack of accountability have yet to be addressed satisfactorily—if they are not to make a mockery of democracy and genuine diversity, and if the social media are not to become gigantic data-harvesting "surveillance machines." In the industrial revolution, a monopoly over the means of production was seen as a leading threat to justice. In today's information revolution, a similar threat comes from any near monopoly over the means of communication.

Or yet again, the election of 2016 underscored another lesson of history. Under a constitutional monarchy, when a king or queen succeeds another ("The King is dead! Long live the King!"), the succession typically reinforces the sense of unity in the nation. As Thomas Aquinas taught, and Queen Elizabeth II has shown with such distinction, a key role of a monarch is to be a uniting force for the people. In American democracy, by contrast, an election now signals a decisive division, and the greater the differences between the parties, the greater the divisions in the handover from one party to another. Hence today's concerns about the "deep state," the administrative, bureaucratic state. For entirely different reasons, both Abraham Lincoln and Donald Trump shared the same bitter legacy of their respective victories. Their opponents were not only opposed, in the style of a loyal opposition, but spoke and acted as if they were out to prevent their governing at all (#notmypresident). European-style shadow government has degenerated into open resistance and a shady new form of continuing Washington bureaucracy, in which holdovers from the previous administration spy, leak, block, and obstruct the new administration as much as they can.

One final consideration, and another distinctive lesson of history, is that democracy and freedom are not the Siamese twins they are often taken to be. As the story of democracy shows, 51 percent of the people can violate freedom, oppress minorities, and legitimately still call itself democratic. Adolf Hitler, for example, was voted in by a majority of the German people in 1933, just as the terrorist group Hamas was in Palestine in 2006. Supporters of both aristocracy and anarchism, though poles apart in their conclusions, like to point out that an old-fashioned dictator may guarantee peace, stability, and freedom—especially freedom in the private sphere—far better than a freedom-loving democracy that regulates and snoops on its citizens at every turn, as the intelligence services are now capable of doing. Americans today, it is said, are far less free under modern presidents than the American colonists under King George. The point is not to assert equivalency or to defend other forms of government, but to be vigilant about the relationship of freedom and democracy, and to ensure that democracy does not degenerate into the tyranny of the majority led by an elite minority in the name of the majority.

At the end of the day, the questions now asked of democracy in America are mounting. Is representative democracy still possible under modern conditions? Is modernity mocking us, one moment bringing self-rule closer as an aspiration and the next pushing it away as a reality beyond our grasp? Will the constant calls for fully participatory democracy (a.k.a. direct democracy) cause anything but gridlock and chaos? Why is America so often accused of hypocrisy around the world as American intelligence routinely interferes in elections in other countries, while—thanks, for example, to WikiLeaks exposure of political campaigns—Americans can be seen doing their utmost to contradict genuine democracy at home? China's current term of choice to describe its politics is *consultative democracy*, a fancy rhetorical fig leaf to cover for Chinese authoritarianism. But is the day coming when calling American democracy the "government of the people, by the people, for the people" strains credulity too?

What would happen if a sufficient number of Americans no longer believed that anything close to Lincoln's definition of democracy still operated? And if the country remains as deeply divided then as it is today, might more and more Americans become too frustrated, cynical, or angry to want to be part of the process at all, let alone to play by the rules? Or at a deeper, though quieter level, what would happen if a sufficient number of Americans reached the point at which they said they wanted *strong government* rather than *self-government*, and saw the two as mutually exclusive—and then reached out for a strong man to carry out their will and put things right?

Plainly, American democracy is now sailing in troubled waters, and Americans should reflect on John Wycliffe and Abraham Lincoln with greater care. For example, consider Yuval Harari's blithe and breezy argument that politics is now one with all modern life in being ordered by humanist maxims and ruled only by our feelings—with no need for divine authority or cosmic meaning. Do we need to listen to God any longer? No, he declares. "Listen to yourself, be true to yourself, trust yourself, follow your heart, do what feels good."[23] Freedom of choice, or the freedom to follow feelings, is the "authentic inner voice" that has become "the ultimate political authority."[24] It tells modern citizens how to vote just as it tells them how to run their lives without divine authority or cosmic meaning in a thousand areas. "Likes" have simplified and replaced true, false, right, wrong, wise, foolish, and all previous intellectual and moral categories. This advance from the will of God to the will of the people, Harari claims, is what has made modern democracy and what drives our modern world.

Harari is doubly wrong. Inner feelings and freedom of choice did not make democracy and it will not sustain democracy. It will in fact bring down democracy. What in fact made democracy possible in Western history was not humanism, let alone the primacy of feelings, but the Reformation and its rediscoveries of the Bible. As Wycliffe argued rightly, though long before his time, it was the Bible and its teaching about covenant, human dignity, human freedom, and human responsibility that made it possible to achieve "government of the people, by the people, for the people." It is questionable whether democracy will survive the primacy of inner feelings, and it is a certainty that it will not if the wider truths of the Bible continue to be repudiated decisively.

Harari is correct about one thing. Where did the authority of inner feelings come from? The tale of two revolutions enters again. The source of the primacy of inner feelings is emphatically not 1776. No such idea could be further from John Adams, George Washington, James Madison, and Andrew Hamilton. It comes directly from 1789, and in this case from Jean-Jacques Rousseau's novel *Emile*. If anyone wishes to look for life's rules of conduct, Rousseau wrote, they can be found "in the depths of my heart, traced by nature in characters which nothing can efface. I need only consult myself with regard to what I wish to do; what I feel to be good is good, and what I feel to be bad is bad."[25] What Harari calls Rousseau's "bible of feelings" has become the bible of modern feelings, and democracy—not to speak of Rousseau's wife and children, and countless broken modern families after them—is the loser.

Again, will it be said that freedom was too hard a challenge for Americans to overcome? Here, then, is the ninth question on the checklist that Americans must answer constructively: *Are you vigilant about the institutional challenges that are crucial to freedom?*

What must also never be forgotten is the relationship between democracy and republican liberty. For the founders and for all who love freedom, republican liberty is the goal, and democracy is only the means. To mistake the means for the goal is to put the cart before the horse, and to keep on doing it stubbornly is to pronounce a death sentence on freedom and the republic—"Likes" or no likes.

ARE YOU VIGILANT
ABOUT *the* IDEAS
CRUCIAL *to* FREEDOM?

Which Revolution Do They Serve?

*I*f one grand cluster of questions now surrounds American institutions, another grand cluster surrounds America's ideas. The latter grows out of the way a succession of ideas, theories, and ideologies passes through America, capturing the national imagination for a time and stamping its imprint on freedom. I have argued that America's fractious and rancorous politics is the outward symptom of the conflict of ideas at the heart of American culture—the tale of two revolutions, 1776 and 1789.

That claim about the power of ideas needs qualifying, because the power of the systems and structures of modernity has an enormous impact on thinking and is sometimes as great as the power of any ideas. American consumerism is an obvious example, as "having it all" and the "life with goods" has completely eclipsed any notion of the good life. *Connectivity* is another example. Farsighted thinkers such as Jacques Ellul have long argued that technology and technique are the most important philosophy of our times. High-tech connectivity is only one small part of technique, but it is as influential in the current global world as any modern faith or philosophy. It means, for instance, that the city of London and its elites are far closer to Wall Street and its elites than London is to Birmingham or Wall Street is to Harlem and the Bronx, not only professionally but philosophically—a powerful reinforcement of modern elitism. Yet that is nothing compared with the future potential of the connectivity of the grand "Internet of All Things," which is predicted to connect not only all humans but all animals and all nature. "Eventually," one writer muses, "we may reach a point where it will be impossible to disconnect from this all-knowing network even for a moment. Disconnection will mean death."[1]

But only a fool would go to the other extreme and underestimate the power of ideas and their impact on freedom for good or ill. "Ideas have consequences,"[2] as Richard Weaver wrote, and that is especially the case when those ideas become dominant in elite institutions such as the universities, the press and media, and the world of entertainment. For then they become the ruling philosophy of the educators of the coming generations. And all the more so when in their extreme form they are funded by multibillionaires on the left or the right, and promoted through radical tactics, such as those of Saul Alinsky. It is at that point that today's clash between the heirs and allies of 1776 and the heirs and allies of 1789 becomes clearest and most consequential.

It is naive to think that bad ideas die when the movements that carry them are defeated. Nazi Germany and the Soviet Union may each have bit the dust after World War II and the Cold War, but the seeds of their bad ideas live on, and they may sprout again at any time—as we are seeing with Nazism, communism, and the evil of anti-Semitism today. It also goes without saying that there is a vital difference between disagreeing with ideas and public policies and disrespecting the people who hold those ideas or find themselves caught in them.

My concern here is American freedom, and for the sake of freedom, we must be prepared to identify and challenge many questionable ideas. But at the same time we must always respect the human dignity of those who hold the ideas and have sympathy when the ideas harm their lives. There may be people who are caught up in the movements surrounding them, often despite themselves, and we must have nothing but the utmost respect and compassion in engaging with them—for example, immigrants and refugees caught in the toils of controversies over multiculturalism, or the victims of the gender revolution who are faced with mounting temptations to loneliness and suicide. Challenging an idea does not mean disrespect for the person who holds the idea. Respect for the person, always. Acceptance of bad ideas, never.

After 1776, when the genius of the Sinai covenant had blended with the "ancient liberties of the English," the first new philosophy to come forward as a suitor to American freedom was indeed 1789, the French Revolution and a broad constellation of its Enlightenment ideas. For a while, Paris and its thinkers captured the heart and mind of Thomas Jefferson, but fortunately Edmund Burke in England and the majority of the American founders did not follow the Sage of Monticello. And as we saw earlier, their judgment proved wiser than his. The character and consequences of America's freedom were quite different from those of France, the French Revolution, and the Continental Enlightenment.

One lesson from those early days still applies now: Contrast is the mother of clarity. As free thinking people, Americans should always be open-minded, but for those who understand the uniqueness of their own revolution (never forgetting its blind spots), there is no natural affinity with philosophies that may look appealing but in the end lead to the poisoning of republican freedom.

Over the course of the last century, a number of such philosophies have come forward to present their credentials and offer themselves as indispensable to the American experiment. Many of them contributed some good points, and they were often a needed correction to the status quo of the day. But most of them were eventually seen to be rooted in the tradition of 1789, and while attractive for a time, their shortcomings became apparent in the end. (With the more recent debates, that grand assessment is still underway.) The challenge is therefore the same today as in the past. For all the promise each philosophy offers, Americans always have to ask whether the philosophies in question truly respect and augment America's distinctive freedom, or whether their promise is deceptive and the existing resources of the republic are more than adequate to face the challenges raised. Here, then, is the tenth and final question on the checklist: *Are Americans vigilant about guarding the ideas that are crucial to freedom?* Every generation of citizens must ask and keep answering such questions if the American experiment is to continue and continue well.

Beyond the major philosophies shaping America today are two sets of philosophies that should be identified for discussion, but for the moment have less impact. On one side are the *superprimitivists* (or self-professed anarchoprimitivists), such as John Zerzan and his allies, those who hope to dismantle civilization and return to the harmony of the hunter-gatherer world before the rise of agriculture and technology. These ideas are prominent in the movements protesting globalization. On the other side are the *superprogressives*, such as Ray Kurzweil, who eagerly press in the entirely opposite direction, toward the world of superintelligence, singularity, and transhumanism. The former can be seen and heard in the antiglobalism protests. They represent the brakes on civilization. The latter, by contrast, are the accelerator. But they both agree in openly rejecting the philosophy and attitudes of 1776. In a forward-thrusting country such as the United States, the superprogressives are obviously more in tune with the times than the superprimitivists, and will appeal more widely, though for the moment neither is a major shaper of current American thinking. My focus will be on four philosophies that are currently more influential.

You Can't Change Your Grandfather

The first such philosophy in the last century was *multiculturalism*, with its three later variants, *identity politics*, *victim politics*, and *tribalism*. Beginning with Horace Kallen and his 1905 article "Democracy Versus the Melting Pot," the then-new philosophy of cultural pluralism was an important reaction to the hyperindividualism of the late nineteenth century and the tacit coercions of the melting pot as they were argued by Israel Zangwill and demonstrated in melting pot pageants in the early twentieth century. Kallen charged that a key part of the idea of the melting pot was simply wrong. Ethnicity was indelible and unmeltable. No one can change their ethnicity. ("Men may change their clothes, their politics, their wives, their religions, their philosophies, to a greater or lesser extent; they cannot change their grandfathers."[3]) The United States should be seen as a union of nationalities, cultures, and groups working together through common institutions.

Leading liberal voices, such as John Dewey and Walter Lippmann, opposed this new idea at the outset, and it was hardly congenial in the xenophobic climate after World War I. Later, it was equally contradictory to the core tenet of Martin Luther King Jr. and the early civil rights movement: People should be judged by the content of their character, and not by the color of their skin. So the idea languished until the 1970s when a new wave of immigration hit much of the Western world, and multiculturalism was hailed as the new, best way of negotiating the exploding diversity of the modern world. Indeed, multiculturalism was seen as the old ideal of seventeenth-century tolerance now dressed in more fashionable seventies language.

The results of multiculturalism have been disastrous for the West and for the American republic. We humans are social, so there is always a collective dimension to our lives. It is essential to us that we are members of families and many other groups and associations. But the overall impact of multiculturalism has been blunt, lopsided, and damaging in two ways. First, the stress on group identity has meant a diminished respect for the dignity and worth of the individual person, regardless of the group they belong to, and therefore a diminishing of the importance of individual human rights. Needless to say, other modern factors compound this problem—supremely the impact of big data. In a digital economy, we are all crunched into numbers and put into groups, analyzed by data scientists, passed around by data brokers, and microtargeted by businesses and political campaigns. As the mathematical modelers see us, we are only numbers, not individuals. We are "batched, bucketed, and bundled," defined by our zip codes, our e-scores and credit ratings, and all the other externals of the "birds of a feather" flock the computers find that we fly with. In short, we are subjected to algorithmic profiling and assigned to new behavioral tribes. With big data, of course, the dehumanization is unwitting and often hidden, but with multiculturalism it is deliberate.

In addition, multiculturalism has upset any pretense at balancing three foundational tensions that are critical to the American experiment and to any free society. First, there must be a balance between unity and diversity, universality and particularity, commonality and differences. Second, there must be a balance between *kinship* and *consent*, the former being citizenship that comes through birth and descent, and the latter being citizenship that comes through belief and assent, as with an immigrant to the United States. And third, there must be a balance between the American *unum* and the American *pluribus*. In a free society there should of course be an emphasis on universality, commonality, the good of all, and the reciprocal responsibility of all for all—simply because of our common humanity and the solidarity of the American Constitution. All humans are free, in contrast to all animals and all machines. At the same time, there should be an equal emphasis on individuality and diversity, because our differences make us individuals, our differences give us our identity, and our differences make our societies diverse. Multiculturalism as a social policy betrays these needed balances, and particularly the dignity of difference. For all its vaunted claims about diversity, it quickly degenerates into an imposed uniformity that is the enemy of genuine diversity as well as true individuality.

These two initial outcomes are pernicious to freedom, even before the rise of identity politics, and the poison spreads from there. All citizens are now viewed, polled, analyzed, and treated as members of groups rather than as individuals. All Americans are tribal now. But then, the postmodern assumption of relativism is added to the mix of groups, giving rise to the notion of different truths for different tribes—feminist truths, black truths, homosexual truths, Hispanic truths, millennial truths, Left and Right truths, Fox truths, CNN and MSNBC truths, and the like. Each group sees the world its own way, lives in its own world and wants its own perspectives confirmed, so each is automatically suspicious of the perspectives of others. Next, the original notion of ethnic groups has been further subdivided, and the tribes now include age cohorts (boomers and millennials) and people of different sexual orientation (gays and straights). Then crucially, with both persuasion and civility discarded as unrealistic, *identity* becomes its own reason and its own justification. And last, the experience and legacies of victimhood have also been stirred in, and the result is today's American variation on Orwell's *Animal Farm*. All tribes are equal, but formerly oppressed tribes are more equal than others.

The outcome of all these trends is disastrous for America's identity and unity as a nation. Throughout Western history, it is plain that that factionalism, tribalism, and sectarianism are common responses to the perceived failure of politics and public life. That is certainly true of America after the Watergate crisis, though other factors have been added to the multicultural mix. The old notions of melting and assimilation have been thrown out as coercive, and there is no longer any national, core, or mainstream identity for anyone to be assimilated into. In the jargon of today, talk of the melting pot is aggression against immigrants. But along with the melting pot, out went any recognition of the need for American identity and American unity, and therefore for proper integration and Americanization. Instead, people from different cultures were encouraged to go their own way, with little or no understanding of how they should relate to their host country or to each other, and with no necessary loyalty to anyone apart from themselves and their group. The result became the fever of identity politics, then victim politics, and most recently open door immigration politics (which in the present situation is tantamount to forced multiculturalism).

There are three distinct but closely related *P*s at work in these trends. If pluralization was the underlying *process*, and relativism was its accompanying *philosophy*, then multiculturalism has been the political and social *policy* of choice in response. The outcome has been not so much Samuel Huntington's macroproblem of "civilizations in conflict" (the West versus the rest) as the microproblem of "cultures in conflict" (the West versus itself). For the Dutch, the English, the French, and the Swedish, the results of multiculturalism and identity politics were quickly disastrous and led to tension, conflict, and open violence. Multiculturalism and its follies were behind the *banlieues* and terrorist attacks in Paris, the no-go zones in the north of England, the murder of Pim Fortuyn and Theo van Gogh in Amsterdam, the 7/7 bombers on the London Underground, and the crime and riots in "dish cities" (with their sprouting satellite antennae keeping them in touch with propaganda from their countries of origin), such as Rinkeby and Rosengard in Sweden.

For a long time, the result of such cultures in conflict was less dramatic for America. But the earlier contrast with Europe disguised the fact that multiculturalism was deadly for the United States in terms of national character, democratic institutions, social stability, and sovereignty—and deadly for the character of American liberalism. This last point is often overlooked, because liberals presently tend to espouse multiculturalism without a thought, when in fact its implications can be highly illiberal.

Standing Martin Luther King Jr. on his head, multiculturalism and identity politics see everyone as a members of groups and classify them according to their age, the color of their skin, or the choice of their lifestyles— whites, blacks, Asians, Hispanics, straights, gays, lesbians, boomers, millennials, and so on. There lies the fatal flaw of multiculturalism for a true liberal. It fails to do justice to the dignity of the individual person and the dignity of difference that makes up the diversity of society.

At the heart of true liberalism there is an eye for the identity and freedom of each individual person and the content of their character, regardless of their membership of any group or tribe. For the true liberal, each individual person is absolutely unique, and each has their own special worth. The individual may be only one member of a far larger group or tribe. Such a person may be replaceable in a task force and can be substituted in a sports team, but each person is irreplaceable and unsubstitutable in their individuality. That is the heart of genuine liberalism and of its concern for individual freedom. The Jewish sages expressed this truth in an unforgettable way: "When a human being makes many coins in the same mint, they all come out alike. God makes every human being in the same image, His image, and they are all different."

The damaging impact of multiculturalism on American identity and unity is more obvious. The fatal blend of multiculturalism, identity politics, victim politics, tribalism, and open door immigration has led to a brazen contradiction of America's original motto and enduring challenge. Under the influence of multiculturalism and identity politics, America has become all *pluribus* with little or no *unum*, and a hurt and angry *pluribus* at that. The outcome is that America's sense of shared identity started to fray in the sixties, and has been fraying ever since. With the notion of the melting pot scorned, with civic education abandoned, and with a de facto open border policy in place, there was no unity and no clear national identity to balance the diversity. Indeed, notions such as sovereignty, unity, and identity were themselves viewed as coercive or white colonialism, and therefore to be rejected. Newcomers no longer needed to adapt to their new country or even to gain a legal standing if it was difficult. The country needed to adapt to them, and sanctuary cities were opened.

In sum, with the American founding already under a cloud, the result has been fateful: Immigration is now more decisive for America than the Revolution, and the republic of the founders is assaulted from yet another side. Lenin's "Who? Whom?" applies to immigration too. Without civic education to balance immigration, America faces the question: Who is assimilating whom?

Multiculturalism advances hand in hand with identity politics and victim politics. With America's growing inequalities addressed clumsily, grievances have festered, factionalism has deepened, and group after group now claims its place in the sun as *more victimized than thou*, citing ancient injustices to justify present conflicts. Not surprisingly, the uniting symbols of the country came under suspicion. The result was that what the British could not do at Fort McHenry in 1812, multiculturalism, identity politics, victim politics, and certain political activists have succeeded in doing. And this time, the Stars and Stripes has not emerged from the night of battle unscathed. As the "kneeing crisis" in the National Football League showed, Old Glory no longer speaks for all Americans as a uniting symbol and a "promissory note" that waves above the fray and beckons across the chasms.

Woe betide the day if the Stars and Stripes descends further still and is viewed in the same way as the Confederate flag. There is no question that identity politics from one side and globalism from another side have together begun to erode American identity and unity. Certain politicians and journalists dismiss talk of sovereignty and identity as "dog whistles" for racism, and those who object find themselves attacked as racists, bigots, misogynists, xenophobes, and white supremacists. Yet with no Abraham Lincoln to speak for the better angels of the American experiment, all the talk of the *wall* on one side and *sanctuary cities* on the other side simply avoids the core question of American identity, unity, and the vital issue of transmitting American ideals and principles to future generations.

In short, multiculturalism, identity politics, victim politics, and tribalism are relentlessly driving nails into the coffin of the founders' republic, and there are fewer and fewer Americans who seem to know how things have gone so wrong and what to do about it. Neither a border wall nor sanctuary cities touch on the core of the real problem. Once there was an American *unum* to balance the American *pluribus*. Once there was a prizing of the individual that counterbalanced the significance of the group. No more. But the fact is that a passion for American unity and identity must always partner with a passion for true individuality and genuine diversity if 1776 is not to give way to 1789 with disastrous consequences for freedom.

When PC Is Not Personal Computer

A second philosophy to beguile Americans is *political correctness*. "Fake news" is the current concern, though the shift in reporting news is far from new. R. G. Collingwood, the Oxford philosopher, complained that the *Daily Mail* had led the way in shifting from "news that responsible readers ought to know" to "news that might amuse its readers to know."[4] But political correctness is far deadlier than that. The term can be traced back to 1930s communism, but its roots go back to the French Revolution and the notion that controlling language is the way to control people. More recently, it owes much to Antonio Gramsci, the Italian Marxist, and his use of Niccolò Machiavelli and the power politics of *The Prince*. Thus the term *political correctness* is the natural expression of post-truth politics, where everything is reduced to power, and controlling language is made the key to mastery or cultural hegemony. The term *PC* describes the way a ruling elite, "the modern Prince," attempts to exert its power and advance its cause by using language to prioritize the interests of the movement over reality itself. As it develops, political correctness becomes party-line thinking that both closes down other ways of thinking and dictates how people should think and express themselves.

George Orwell recognized that all revolutions start with control of language, and he introduced the term *Newspeak* as part of his attack on totalitarianism in *1984* (tellingly barred in China). Reality is "regime-defined reality," and it may change from day to day. But for all these radical roots, PC also entered recent Western conversation in a far less threatening way. When the Jewish and Christian consensus held sway in the English-speaking world, there was an unspoken etiquette, a courtesy, and a civility that characterized the general way of speaking, at least for most people and in public. Not only did this consensus erode and collapse in the 1950s and 1960s, it was assaulted and overthrown as being the dead hand of tradition and yet another instrument of repression.

On the one hand, the collapse of the old consensus led to an eruption of the "rude, the crude, and the lewd" as natural and necessary expressions of freedom. Locker-room language became living-room language, the F-word became commonplace, tedious, and meaningless, and slogans arose, such as "Violence is the voice of the voiceless, and the cry of the silenced."

On the other hand, the collapse of the traditional consensus led to a counterbalancing sensitivity movement that insisted there should still be certain ways of speaking with respect for people's dignity, and certain ways that were wrong and insensitive. *Sin* was out, and *evil* was dismissed as judgmental. But categories such as racism, sexism, and ageism were used to replace sin as the egregious evils of the day that still needed confronting. The trouble was that this laudable attempt to create sensitive public speech was hijacked politically, not by communists but by liberals, progressives, and activists on the left. First, they used their ideological assumptions to define the only acceptable way of seeing things. Then they wielded their political interests in language that defied reality itself, with the result that the Left/ liberals pulled off their own version of the earlier communist fallacy ("Comrade, your statement is factually incorrect." "Yes, comrade, it is. But is it politically correct?").[5]

The results have been disastrous. Words intended to describe reality have been subverted in order to express power and to cast their spell over independent thinking. Political correctness has become a deranged dictator as language has been mustered and manipulated to devalue, marginalize, and silence opposing views of truth and reality. The rich dimensions of disagreement have been reduced to a single approach—full-throated, implacable hostility. America and the Western world are still living with the consequences—speech codes, censorship, charges of microaggression, silencing, no-platforming, thought police, shaming, cyberbullying, and division after embittered division. Hate-speech laws are nothing less than a posthumous triumph for the censorship of Joseph Stalin and a slavish mimicry of the unfreedom of Islamist blasphemy laws. For the architects and enforcers of the hate-speech laws have caved in to the very menaces to freedom so magnificently resisted by Eleanor Roosevelt at the drafting of the Universal Declaration of Human Rights and then at the later International Covenant on Civil and Political Rights. Nothing demonstrates more clearly how classical liberalism morphed into Left/liberal ideologies, and in the process has decisively abandoned 1776 for 1789.

Anyone disputing this claim has only to read Herbert Marcuse's influential 1965 essay "Repressive Tolerance" and his footnote in 1968, the year that was America's *annus calamitosus*. Critiquing the Western liberal idea of tolerance as oppressive, he openly argued for a "discriminating tolerance in an inverse direction." That meant simply "intolerance toward prevailing policies, attitudes and opinions and the extension of tolerance to policies, attitudes, and opinions which are outlawed or suppressed." Or, as he spelled it out, he favored tolerance toward minorities that are "intolerant, militantly intolerant and disobedient to the rules of behavior." Fifty years later, Marcuse's wish has been fulfilled and his selective intolerance has gone mainstream in the worlds of higher education, the press, and entertainment. His "inversion" is complete. The "intolerance of the tolerant" is the new orthodoxy, and his baldly stated goal has succeeded faster than he could have imagined. "Liberating tolerance, then," he stated with a shameless candor, "would mean intolerance against movements from the Right and toleration of movements from the Left."[6]

The day-to-day problems of PC at the ordinary level could be listed interminably. But the overall damage to American freedom, American education, and the Western mind is incalculable—the body blow to truth, civility, and persuasion; the muting of free speech; the stifling of dissent and alternative opinion; the muzzling of conscientious objection; the discouragement of civil disobedience; the hypocritical turning against the faiths of the West while turning a blind eye to itself; and the general poisoning of liberal democracy and free and open education at all levels. Imposing their own definitions, often through the diktats of courts and university administrations, and rarely allowing any opposing argument, progressives and the Left have used political correctness to enforce their ideas and to create whole categories of people that Hillary Clinton disdained as "deplorables," the so-called clueless 95 percent who are therefore ruled out of the discussion by definition. The fact is that many of these dissenting voices are highly educated, respectful, well-reasoned, articulate, and strongly ethical. No matter. By definition, they are instantly and automatically excluded from the conversation and branded as racist, sexist, homophobic, or victims of false consciousness simply because they disagree with what some elite has decided is the politically correct position.

So much for Thomas Jefferson's "Truth is great and shall prevail." And so much for the time-honored Jewish and Christian understanding that lies behind Mr. Jefferson—that both truth and justice, and therefore debates, education, and law courts, require a proper hearing and due process. A hearing means that there are at least two sides to every issue, and one or other should prevail only after both have been heard and heard fairly. That is what political correctness denies, and that is why political correctness is so dangerous and so illiberal for the American republic and for the American universities. If it triumphs finally, it will mean the complete closing of the American mind. Already, far too many diverse voices have been silenced this way, their participation in debates conspicuous by their absence, their books never reviewed, and their ideas shouted down. The immediate loser is American political discourse. But when power replaces truth and a sneer replaces the seminar, the worst and most lasting damage is the catastrophic impact on American higher education, on American thinking at large, and above all on American freedom.

John Etchemendy, the former provost of Stanford University, is among the courageous voices warning of the dangers of politically correct intellectual blindness in the university. In a speech to his board of trustees, he said he was more worried by threats from within the universities than without.

Over the years, I have watched a growing intolerance at universities in this country . . . a kind of intellectual intolerance, a political one-sidedness, that is the antithesis of what universities should stand for. It manifests itself in many ways: in the intellectual monocultures that have taken over certain disciplines; in the demands to disinvite speakers and outlaw groups whose views we find offensive; in constant calls for the university itself to take political stands. We decry certain news outlets as echo chambers, while we fail to notice the echo chamber we have built around ourselves.[7]

"Political correctness is neither," it is said, and the reach of PC goes well beyond the purely political. In the Anglo-American-university world, political correctness represents a quadruple triumph—the triumph of identity politics ("I am in pain. Pay attention and validate me, or face the consequences of my justified rage"), the triumph of the therapeutic (to safeguard the purportedly vulnerable and assuage the injuries of cultural trauma), the triumph of the litigious (and aversion to risk), and the triumph of emotionalism (Rousseau's feelings and the world of "Likes" again).

Specific results are often absurd and even comic—the banning of the word *brainwashing*, for example, because it might offend those who suffer from epilepsy. The charge of microaggression indicts people not for what they have actually said or done, but for what they are thought to have intended in what they said or did. In other words, the indictment is in the eyes of the beholder, and the accused are presumed guilty and cannot be proved innocent. Yet what matters are the overall results that are disastrous for freedom and academic freedom: the rise of a new paternalism, the deification of safety, the infantilization of students who cannot be trusted with daring ideas and tough-minded debate, the new intolerance, the recycling of victimization, and the ironic rise of a new form of censorship, self-imposed and from below.[8]

Colleges and universities have been rightly described as the finishing schools of the modern world, but in its PC form American higher education no longer represents a schooling in freedom or even aims to be the vital seedbed for the American republic. An article in the *Harvard Crimson* set out its position brazenly in its title: "The Doctrine of Academic Freedom: Let's Give Up on Academic Freedom in Favor of Justice."[9] Devotees of political correctness often deny the PC label and claim they are merely being sensitive, aware, responsible, and morally attuned—for example, in their defense of the demand for trigger warnings. But social psychologist Jonathan Haidt aptly points up the dilemma that the PC movement raises for the universities: Is their mission to be a "Truth University" or a "Social Justice University"?[10]

There is a major but often unnoticed effect of such political correctness. It is doubly illiberal not only in silencing free speech but in undermining personal dignity. Human dignity is devalued when attackers use theoretical categories to reduce individuals to isms and then wipe them out with a single charge. This happens when people resort to the well-stocked armory of today's ready-made labels. Their opponents are racists, sexists, or homophobes, often simply by definition because they disagree with them. Such attacks encourage laziness, because the attacker need think no more and need waste no more time on argument. But they are also a violation of human dignity, because the person is eliminated even before given the chance of a hearing.

To argue is to give voice and to reason, and to reason is to negotiate, but labeling obliterates the individual through the power of the ism. Such is the agenda and thought style of PC Newspeak that there must be no compromise and no concession. The accused so labeled is automatically beyond the pale, because the label has built the pale. Whether the person is now a deplorable, a reactionary, or an unfortunate victim of false consciousness because of race, gender, or age, they are simply not worth the effort of conversation. Thus the people who claim to give "a voice to the voiceless" end in reducing individuals to isms and silencing all voices not their own.

The truth is that political correctness and the truly liberal American republic cannot coexist for much longer. The illiberal liberalism of the Left has been so extreme that the American mind is gasping for air. A generation of political correctness has choked its free inquiry, its freedom of expression, and even its ability to think freely. For the purposes of discussing freedom, the conclusion is inescapable: Political correctness is a blot on the record on the liberal Left and a calamity for the American republic. But make no mistake: It must be said plainly that the Jacobin and brown-shirted tactics of political correctness are the child of 1789 and not of 1776. To paraphrase both Lincoln and Wycliffe, political correctness has become the governing style of the elites, by the elites, for the elites. Nothing could be further from Mount Sinai, 1776, John Milton, Thomas Jefferson, John Stuart Mill, and America's noble experiment in freedom and free thinking.

No Givens, No Rules, No Limits

A third philosophy with potentially dire implications for freedom is *social constructionism*, a set of ideas that is the natural extension of secularism and postmodernism, with their bald insistence that God is dead, truth is dead, and knowledge is power. Social constructionism as a theory is rarely encountered at the popular level, though its consequences are strongly felt there too. Once again its origins are commendable, for it is vital to be able to understand how our ideas and the way we think are shaped by our social context—by the worlds in which we live, and not only by other thinkers. Such an understanding is essential to living an "examined life" and a "good life." But there is a fully responsible version of the theory, led by Peter Berger and Thomas Luckmann's *The Social Construction of Reality*, and there is a far more radical version. The former analyzes "what passes for knowledge" in a social setting and then hands over that analysis to the discipline of philosophy. It is the task of philosophy to decide whether or not what *passes for* knowledge is in fact *true*.

The more radical and dangerous version claims that there is no objective reality or external truth *at all*. In their view, everything without any exception is socially constructed and can therefore be constructed, deconstructed, and reconstructed at will. The web of meaning may be compelling for a while—"We hold these truths to be self-evident," for example—but the meaning exists solely in the common imagination. In a word, it is a fiction, and when it unravels, later generations are amazed that anyone could have believed it. According to this view, the world may be divided between different religions and different ideologies, but Islam and Buddhism, capitalism and communism, all share the same hollow status: they are "shared fictions" and nothing more.

This radical form of constructionism is unmistakable in the "battle of the binaries." "Male" and "female" are seen as entirely social constructions, mere conventions and not biological realities, so they are there to be reengineered at will. Plainly, the sexual revolution thrives on this, especially as it flowers in the limitless freedom of the internet underworld. (Rule 38 of the *47 Rules of the Internet*: "No real limits of any kind apply here—not even the sky"; Rule 42: "Nothing is sacred.")[11] Fueled by this spirit, each wave of activists vies not only with the status quo but with their own fellows in their rush to abolish all conventions in pursuit of ever greater and greater freedom. Others are caught up in the utopian drive to conquer death itself and therefore to challenge the greatest boundary of all that has defined us as mortals—the distinction between life and death, and heaven and earth.

Yet for all the thrusting drive of the new Prometheans, their self-interest is striking, for the one binary distinction that they never attack is the difference between the rulers and the ruled, between themselves and the rest, the enlightened experts and elites and the great unwashed. And if their day comes, even that yawning gap will be swallowed up in the coming inequality between the so-called "ens" and "uns," the biologically and technologically enhanced and the unenhanced. Talk of the future is where their radical claims can be heard most clearly. There, like the builders of Babel but using biological engineering and cyborg engineering rather than astrology and glazed bricks, social constructionists are setting out to break down the distinction between life and death, heaven and earth, and even God and humanity.[12] Zoltan Istvan, a leader in the transhumanist movement, is candid about his ambition: "to live forever, or as long as possible—10,000 years or so."[13]

The title of Yuval Harari's bestselling *Homo Deus* says it all, and his later descriptions of the coming "Gods of Planet Earth" and the "new godlings" are merely commentary.[14] For thousands of years of history, humanity has been a constant, but the grand project of the twenty-first century will be "attaining divinity"—to "acquire for us divine powers of creation and destruction, and upgrade *Homo sapiens* into *Homo deus*."[15] Man can now be God, Harari says, for everything is socially constructed, and humanity can therefore deconstruct and reconstruct itself at will. There are "no givens," "no rules," and "no limits." "Scientists today," Harari writes strikingly as a Jew, and from Jerusalem, "can do much better than the Old Testament God."[16] Anders Sandberg, a Swedish transhumanist, argues that since there is no natural state of humanity (no givens), freedom is the capacity to go as far as our imaginations can take us. "I believe that humans are acorns that are unafraid of destroying themselves in order to become oak trees."[17]

Boosted by notions such as big data, superintelligence, and transhumanism, social constructionism now makes a promise to humanity that is unprecedented in history and represents the epitome of 1789 at its highest reach: *Humans have the total freedom to become whatever they want to be and do whatever they want to do. Nothing imaginable is impossible.* It may take time, but if anything still holds humanity back from the complete and natural freedom that is its birthright, it must be what still remains of Monsieur Rousseau's chains. All that humans need to do to throw off these last chains is to summon up their courage and imagination, recast Pico's *On the Dignity of Man* in a secularist framework, march out with comrades who also have Saul Alinsky's *Rules for Radicals* in their pockets, and trust that one of them has the cool resources of a Larry Ellison, an Elon Musk, or a Mark Zuckerberg.

Once again the differences between 1776 and 1789 could hardly be wider and more decisive. Rabbi Heschel pointed out that definitions of humanity are always expressions of human self-understanding—"man's way of identifying himself, holding up a mirror in which to scan his own face."[18] Is there any question that constructionism speaks of human invention and human self-sufficiency taken to the highest level? According to the Jewish and Christian view, which inspired 1776 and gave it its cautions about the abuse of power, the grand pretensions of social constructionism are sheer hubris. They are a repeat of the ancient folly of the Tower of Babel and will invite a similar confounding. In particular, the deliberate obliteration of boundaries and distinctions, male and female, heaven and earth, is a final rejection of what the rabbis call "the Author of all being" and therefore of the final authority behind all morality and the notion of just society.[19]

Yet when that day comes, where will the checks and balances be that once grew from the realism that knew how such a power could be abused? It is always the greatest utopians who produce the vilest hells, and the wildest dreams of reason that create the worst monsters. Today, we are forbidden to discriminate and judge. We are trained to get used to everything and shocked by nothing. Soon the day will come when evil itself is cool and all the barriers to evil will once again be gone. To wake up then will be too late, so now is the time to sound the alarm. As many have noted, there was less than a century between the soaring aspirations of Nietzsche's Zarathustra, dreamed up in Swiss Alpine air, and Hitler's subhuman applications that constructed the horrors of Belsen, Dachau, and Auschwitz-Treblinka. Those who set out to flout all boundaries eventually crash against the final boundary of reality, and the lesson for these brave new transgressors will be plain. In Rabbi Sacks's words, "the ontological divide is fundamental. God is God; humanity is humanity. There can be no blurring of the boundaries."[20] The best and brightest of Silicon Valley will no more breach heaven and become gods tomorrow than the best and brightest of Mesopotamia managed to do in their day.

It is noteworthy that the builders of Babel had premonitions of their coming confusion before they built the tower. Just so, today's constructionists sometimes drop dark hints about the end of *Homo sapiens* and sometimes forecast it blithely as if it will be no big deal. (Harari: "Yet the rise of humanism also contains the seeds of its own downfall. While the attempt to upgrade humans into gods takes humanism to its logical conclusion, it simultaneously exposes humanism's inherent flaws . . . attempting to fulfill the humanist dream is likely to cause its disintegration.")[21] But more often their dominant note is a soaring superconfident insouciance, especially when their pretensions are no more modest than their vision of upgrading humanity. If everything, absolutely everything, has been socially constructed, then there is no truth, no bedrock reality, no natural or created order, no man or superman, and certainly no male or female. What we call reality is only "reality" as socially accepted, and if it was socially constructed in the first place, then it can be socially deconstructed now—and reconstructed as we wish, whenever we wish, and as many times as we wish. We are free, totally free, to be whatever we want to be.

The constructionist philosophy is an open invitation to storm the ramparts of the status quo and attack any aspect that anyone does not like as repressive to the way that they feel or see themselves. *This means that in today's America social constructionism is an invitation to total revolution in the name of total freedom, but with no standard of objective truth to cramp the creator or to judge the results.* According to this view, the will to live is the will to power, *truth* is only power, *freedom* is the powerful player's capacity to move and exert their will against all other wills, and *justice* whatever serves the interests of the powerful.

Social constructionism is most attractive and most accessible at the point of individual identity. No longer fixed, a matter of fate, or tethered to science, personal identity is now seen as self-chosen, subjective, and shifting, so Americans are endlessly promised that they can be whomever they want to be regardless even of biology. But as Camille Paglia notes, there is an absurdity to the basis of this claim:

> Liberals who posture as defenders of science when it comes to global warming (a sentimental myth unsupported by evidence) flee all reference to biology when it comes to gender. Biology has been programmatically excluded from women's studies and gender studies programs for almost 50 years now. *The cold biological truth is that sex changes are impossible. Every single cell of the human body remains coded with one's birth gender for life.*[22]

Stated in its full-blown form, the promise of social constructionism is simply false. No one is ever completely free. For though there is a sense in which we can choose our identity, it is always within limits, and there has to be a counter-reminder. Freedom means freedom of identity, but it is not arbitrary. There is an important sense in which our true identity chooses us and challenges us to live in a certain way if we are to be true to ourselves. The same is true of American citizens collectively. Americans are free, "autonomous individuals," whose self-creation is crucial to their freedom. But Americans are also citizens of a free republic. As such, American citizens are carriers of freedom in the world, so they are as free as any people in history. But that very identity also determines Americans. It lays on them the responsibility not to live as they please but to respect what it takes for their freedom to stay true to itself and to last. Once again, 1776 is more realistic than 1789, 1917, and 1949. Freedom is not the permission to do what you want, but the power to do what you ought. And the quickest way to find this maxim to be true is to flout it and face the consequences.

One of the more pernicious effects of postmodernism, constructionism, and identity politics is rampant today but often missed. If truth is dead and everything is socially constructed, nothing need be discussed in terms of true or false, right or wrong, wise or foolish, rational or irrational. Instead, everything is a matter of "where you come from." It is all about the unconscious baggage formed by the motives of your class, your race, your politics, your religion, or your generation. (One young American woman said to a friend of mine recently, "Every time I hear an older white male speaking to us, I bristle.") Needless to say, this is merely another form of cultural profiling, and clearly the playing field is no more level now than it was before. Certain classes (the middle class), certain races (white), certain political affiliations (conservative), certain faiths (Christian, especially Evangelical and Catholic), and certain generations (the middle aged and older) have replaced the old categories as automatically reactionary, and prime suspects for the crimes of racism and sexism, unless proved innocent. Such attitudes are the intellectual equivalent of New York's infamous stop-and-frisk policy for young blacks. They are a form of cultural profiling that is highly illiberal in that they silence whole groups by definition. But that tactic is not only wrong, it is irrational and antidemocratic because it silences the real debate that Americans need to conduct if republican freedom is to remain healthy.

Social constructionism is especially appealing because of its promise to the sexual revolution: be whoever you wish to be—he, she, zhe, or several other possible pronouns for starters. But when the same ideas are applied politically, their poisonous effect becomes deadly at once. They eviscerate the Declaration of Independence and hand down a death sentence for the American experiment. Jefferson and the Declaration of Independence were wrong, they say. There are no self-evident truths. No one has inalienable rights, dignity, or equality. Such claims only worked for a while because a sufficient number of Americans "colluded" in believing them. But we now know better, they say. All that counts is power. *Right* is another word for might. In sum, under the conditions of social constructionism, America's republican freedom would be turned inside out and upside down, and summarily ended forever. Social constructionism may sound abstract and theoretical, but its consequences are concrete and catastrophic. Once again, the influence of 1789 is unmistakable and its harm to 1776 irreparable.

There Is More to It Than Playboy

A fourth, and somewhat overlapping philosophy is the *liberationism* of the sexual revolution, and here again the links to 1789 are plain and undeniable. This revolution has immense implications for American freedom, and though seemingly unstoppable in its present momentum and appeal, it will surely prove destructive for the republic. The appeal lies in the word *liberation*, as it does with all revolutions, for the call for freedom triggers an insatiable desire and carries an argument that sounds unanswerable. There is no one who does not at some point desire freedom. This means simply that, however spurious the claims and however disastrous the results, there will always be more freedom to be claimed and always more people to respond.

As we saw in discussing question two, there was all the difference in the world between 1776 and the American Revolution, whose understanding was essentially biblical and classical, and 1789 and the French, Russian, and

Chinese revolutions, whose understanding was essentially secular and anti-religious. The former believed in incremental change and worked from the inside out, taking seriously the potential for sin and the abuse of power, and achieved a substantial, if incomplete, measure of freedom. The latter, in contrast, believed in instant, total, political transformation, working from the outside in and from the state down, and believing in the adequacy of reason and the essential perfectibility of humanity, but routinely ended in the mass slaughter of millions of people.

The sexual revolution now sweeping America and the West is a direct child of 1789, and one of its central ideas is that freedom is won by removing everything considered repressive. (Again, Rousseau's famous opening words of *The Social Contract*: "Man is born free, but everywhere he is in chains.") It is a multigenerational project that from the beginning was a close twin to Enlightenment ideas of political revolution. Both revolutions trace their roots to the ideas and theories behind the French Revolution and carry much of the same baggage. Yet most Americans ignore the roots of the sexual revolution and view it as more recent and more benign than political revolution. They see it either as a genuine advance in freedom or as the slow and steady release from the uptightness of previous generations, or at least as the somewhat wayward child of the sexual big bang of the 1960s: the pill, *Playboy*, and permissiveness. They therefore view its impact as merely the bumpy and uneven process of liberalization that any society is bound to undergo as part and parcel of its becoming modern.

That sunny and myopic view is naive. The sexual revolution started as the twin to the French Revolution, and it remains the most calculated, deliberate, radical subversion of the American republic and Western civilization since the French and Russian revolutions. It had its clear designs and its fundamental animosity to religion from the beginning. Its origins must be remembered even though the most comprehensive manifesto of the sexual revolution came years later in Wilhelm Reich's *The Sexual Revolution* in 1930. This book was described as "the *Mein Kampf* of permissiveness" in that it was published in the same era as Hitler's manifesto in 1924. Like *Mein Kampf*, it promised nothing less than a new cultural order and set out to deliver what it promised, and at the present moment is carrying all before it.

The architects of the sexual revolution were unambiguous about their goals. They hailed it as "an authentic revolutionary upheaval of our cultural existence . . . awakening from the sleep of millennia."[23] True to its origins, it goes back to eighteenth-century Europe, it comes from the militantly secularist tradition set off by the French Revolution, and it fiercely opposes the Jewish and Christian faiths and all the tenets of the biblical tradition that have been the primary shaper of American freedom and of Western civilization.

There is a sense in which the sexual revolution is neo-Marxist, in that its present form is an odd combination of Karl Marx and Sigmund Freud. It owes its success to its own Rudi Dutschke–style "long march through the institutions" and its scaling of the power centers of American culture. But its roots are earlier than Marx, Freud, or Gramsci, and it has important differences from the purely political versions of Marxist and communist revolutions, as well as from Freud. There is a simple reason why it has a better chance of succeeding in America than Marxism, communism, and fascism ever had—its obvious appeal to sex and to the popular culture.

It is important to recognize the distinctiveness of the sexual revolution. For a start, the sexual revolution has different prophets from the political revolution. Rousseau stands behind it, but its other leading proponents are not Hegel and Marx so much as the Marquis de Sade, "the apostle of eroticism"; André Breton, "the pope of surrealism" and author of *The Surrealist Manifesto* (1924); and Wilhelm Reich, the man who coined the term *sexual revolution* in his book by the same title. Many other radical thinkers have taken the movement forward in different ways, including William Godwin, Mary Wollstonecraft, Percy Bysshe Shelley, Alexandra Kollontai, Magnus Hirschfeld, Alfred Kinsey, Simone de Beauvoir, Herbert Marcuse, Betty Friedan, Germaine Greer, Judith Butler (the architect of the current gender revolution), and of course Hugh Heffner.

Importantly too, the ideals of the revolution were to be sexual freedom, which is much more appealing and much less demanding than economic justice and political revolution. (Reich: "Today, the principal social question no longer is: 'Are you rich or are you poor?' but 'Do you endorse and do you fight for the greatest possible freedom for human life?'")[24] And the revolution's new terms, *progressive* and *reactionary*, were chosen to replace the old terms that were clumsy and foreign-sounding, *proletarian* and *bourgeois*. Most important of all, the chosen agents of the revolution were to be neither the working class nor the vanguard of the intellectual elite, but Mr. and Mrs. Average Consumer and their children in the affluent society. For surely, the allure of sexual freedom, unlike the cost of mounting the barricades and risking your life, would be a temptation impossible for the average consumer to refuse. (Reich believed that to be healthy, people needed at least three orgasms a week, because "The core of happiness in life is sexual happiness.")[25]

The day-to-day results of the sexual revolution have been spectacularly effective in America—a three-hundred-year-old revolution from France that has led to a titanic fifty-year revolution in America over sexual ideas, morality, behavior, language, publishing, dress, music, modesty, and social conventions. Through an energetic network of richly funded American elites, organizations, and international conferences, the revolution that was sparked by France and England spread to the United States, and then to the United Nations and back to the European Union. It now quite literally seeks to impose its gender agenda on the entire world, colonial style. Anyone wishing to understand its goals in its own terms has only to read *An Activist's Guide to the Yogyakarta Principles*, the manifesto of the gender revolution that was set out in Yogyakarta, Indonesia, in November 2006 as a toolkit for activists. The principles were then to be translated into policies around the world—so that, for example, when Hillary Clinton was US Secretary of State, she planned to advance the gender revolution by replacing "Mother" and "Father" on the US Customs forms with the more gender-neutral terms "Parent 1" and "Parent 2." ("Passport Change Will Be Inclusive," the *Washington Post* declared.)[26]

In *Civilization and Its Discontents*, Sigmund Freud argued strongly (and somewhat hypocritically) that civilization depended on the restraint of instincts and in particular on the "sublimation of the sex drive." Later anthropological research, for example, by J. D. Unwin in 1934, confirmed his thesis. The stronger the sexual restraints in a society, the higher the level of culture it achieved and vice versa. But the sexual revolution has fought to stand this claim on its head. Critics rightly point to its fundamental relativism with regard to truth, and its permissiveness with regard to moral restraints, and the chaos that results. They then argue the obvious point that in loosening restraints the permissiveness is ripening a harvest of personal and social ills, from broken families, identity confusion, loneliness, pornography addiction, mounting suicides, the sexual abuse of children, and endless rationalizations. (When Margaret Sanger's husband, Bill, found out all that she was up to, he described it as a "hell-hole of free love, promiscuity, and prostitution masquerading under the mantle of revolution.")[27] It was an earlier form of such social chaos, and the massive backlash that sexual liberation produced in the Soviet Union after the revolution, which Lenin and Stalin stamped out ruthlessly in their purge in the mid-1920s.

This point about the link between unbridled passions, unfettered freedom, sexual anarchy and social chaos is cogent, but a different and deeper critique has also been raised since the French Revolution. Sexual liberation attacks all moral and cultural restraints on passions in the name of increased freedom, but often its unintended or ironic effect has been to introduce new controls and new forms of bondage. As we saw with the paradox of freedom, "liberation" can often lead to bondage, not freedom. Sometimes the bondage is the result of increased freedom for the passions that, when unbridled, lead to deeper enslavement and addiction, as with alcohol, drugs, and pornography. Sometimes the bondage is the result of political passivity, as the government's indulgence of the passions keeps citizens happily diverted and submissive, allowing the elites to continue undisturbed in ruling as they wish ("bread and circuses" in a suburban form).

Sometimes the bondage is deliberate as the consumer's sexual desires are used to sell a product. (In the early Lucky Strikes commercial, the subliminal appeal was intentional, as Edward Bernays, Freud's nephew, acknowledged: "The cigarette is a phallic symbol, to be offered by a man to a woman. Every normal man or woman can identify with such a message." Encouraging women to smoke cigarettes, another colleague said, would be "like opening a new gold mine right in our front yard."[28]) Sometimes the bondage is the result of tacit or overt forms of social and political control, because "someone somewhere" knows too much about the behavior of everyone else for anyone to have the freedom to stand against them. (Such tacit blackmail moves upward in the case of intelligence and downward in the case of the tabloids.) As ever, giving the public what it wants is a sure way to control what it wants. Control the stimuli, and you control the stimulated. Or in the words of an eighteenth-century architect of revolution, "Study the peculiar habits of each, for men may be turned to anything by him who knows how to take advantage of their ruling passion."[29]

The third criticism is more personal and concerns the understanding and experience of love and human personhood. As we saw earlier, covenant love is reciprocal and mutual, the I-Thou relationship in its highest form. Each person speaks and acts with a love that carries unspoken respect for the dignity of the other person, including the heart, the mind, the body, the aspirations, and the frailties of the other. Thus the institution of marriage harmonizes the foundational relationships between men and women throughout society as a whole. But when the sexual revolution destroys the notion of one man–one woman marriage, strips away all barriers to sexual relationships, and cancels all binding ties and responsibilities, as in the hookup culture, the uncommitted sex that follows is only about the subjective self that seeks partners for its own satisfaction. The other, whether the sexual partners are few or many, is simply there for the sexual satisfaction of the self. All others are only instrumental and temporary. With no ties to bind and no responsibilities that are mutual, the "other" becomes merely an aid to sexual satisfaction for the self—in effect, a toy. Lenin's words about sex fit the hookup culture perfectly: "So we simply take advantage of the few short hours of release that are granted to us—there is nothing binding, no responsibility."[30]

To put the point bluntly, sex within the terms of the full-blown freedom of the sexual revolution is reduced to a form of masturbation—as its architects asserted from the beginning. It is Keith Richards's "making love to your best friend," even if countless others also happen to have taken part. "The philosopher," the Marquis de Sade wrote of the freethinkers of his day but anticipating the cheap sex of the hookup culture of our own, "sates his appetites without inquiring to know what his enjoyment may cost others, and without remorse."[31] In a world dominated by the ethos of Darwin, Nietzsche, and Ayn Rand, the self, not the "other," is the prime consideration.

Yet this point is the reason why, in rejecting the integrity of both love and personhood, the hookup culture so often ends in one of two outcomes— either the boredom, disappointment, guilt, and restlessness of cheap sex, or the abuse and sexual aggression of powerful males. In the end the myriad relationships lauded by the sexual revolution spell out the logic of the culture of death, for without procreation, which is the natural logic of love, there is no perpetuation. The same is true, needless to say, of the American republic itself. Without transmission, as a generation lives thoughtlessly only for itself, there is no enduring freedom passed on.

Nothing is more damning to the sexual revolution than the personal stories of the sexual revolutionaries and their unsatisfactory experiences of

free love. Again and again they swung restlessly between an extreme rejection of convention in the name of freedom (throwing off Rousseau's
"chains" of marriage, fidelity, and respectability) and an equally extreme dis-
satisfaction with free love (sometimes leading to unacknowledged guilt,
sometimes to resentment when others treat them as they treated others, and
sometimes to despair and suicide—as with Mary Wollstonecraft and others).

The fourth and final line of criticism is more publicly significant, and
again concerns the perpetuation of the American republic. Great nations
need great citizens to become great leaders, but if the nation's greatness is not
to be fleeting, the nation needs to hand on the secrets of its greatness from
generation to generation. And that, it should go without saying, requires not
only civic education but parents, and especially mothers. As history has underscored with countless variations, from the Bible to the Greek and Roman
classics to the comments of Alexis de Tocqueville on American women and
democracy, it takes women to bear children and to bring up children if every
new generation is to have the same dedication to the ideas and ideals that
made the nation great. In other words, mothers (and families) are uniquely
indispensable for both their generative power and their educational role. Yet
in America today, these essential tasks have been decimated by the lifestyles
and the confusions of the sexual revolution. For both nations and religions,
as demographers note, there will always be a link between faith and fertility.
The sexual revolution and its multiple confusions are quite simply sapping
the ongoing vitality of 1776 and the American republic.

These four arguments are powerful, but the fact is that no mere argument will settle the issue. The wrangling over the stories and results of
the sexual revolution will continue angrily until the evidence becomes
incontrovertible, either to the individuals involved or to American society
as a whole as it picks up the pieces or is itself broken in pieces. But many
people forget that the course of the sexual revolution has been stopped in
its tracks twice before, and it can be reversed again if Americans recognize
the dark and loveless future that the hook-up culture represents. For all
the talk of "the right side of history" (and often from those who have no
basis for either right or meaningful history), history is shaped by freedom,
not fate. The first reversal of the sexual revolution took place in England
and came as a result of principle and persuasion, when the spiritual revival
of 1739 under John Wesley and the "reformation of manners" under

William Wilberforce led the nation to a decisive turnabout that turned its back on the mores of 1789 and grew into the Victorian Age.

The second and different kind of reversal took place under the Soviets, a savage and draconian purge in the mid-1920s that was purely pragmatic and coerced. Such was the social chaos triggered by Alexandra Kollontai and her fellow sexual liberationists that Lenin and Stalin put a halt to the spread of free love. ("To be truly free," Kollontai had announced, "woman must throw off the contemporary, obsolete, coercive form of the family that is burdening her way.")[32] In particular, Lenin put an end to their "glass of water" theory that free sex should be as easy and casual as satisfying your thirst. (Lenin: "This glass-of-water theory has made our young people mad, quite mad. It has proved fatal to many young boys and girls.")[33]

We Are Not What We Think We Are, But What We Think, We Are

Anarchy and madness lurk in the extremes of the sexual revolution in America, but its outcome is not inevitable. The free-love culture depends on the free choice of its citizens to say yes or no. *In a democracy, the sexual revolution depends on collective cultural consent just as sexual intercourse depends on an individual's personal consent, and being forced is rape in either case.* To consent or to refuse to consent culturally means making that choice wisely, which requires assessing the "freedom" the sexual revolution offers the American republic. It is therefore important to stand back and consider many aspects of the sexual revolution that have been prominent features of 1789 since the beginning.

First (echoes of 1789 and in complete contradiction of 1776), the sexual revolution is built on the utopian assumption that complete and absolute freedom is possible, that humans are essentially good and need only to be freed from sexual and cultural repressions to be happy, peaceful, and fulfilled. This notion was once understood as human perfectibility. (The only perversion left is the use of the word *perversion*. "There is no pornographer except in the eyes of a puritan.")[34] This point is important for three reasons: Utopianism directly contradicts the realism of the American experiment and the concern for the abuse of power, it is a leap of faith that far outstrips any religious belief, and there is always a straight line between utopianism and violence for a simple reason: when the gap between the ideal and the real cannot be bridged by persuasion, it will be bridged by force.

Second (echoes of 1789), the sexual revolution goes on to offer the utopian promise that sexual permissiveness will produce the greatest human freedom. ("Class will be no more," the Marxists promised; "Jews will be no more," the Nazis promised themselves; and "Repression will be no more," the sexual revolutionaries promise us all.) After all, the Marquis de Sade argued, "No passion has the need of the widest horizon of liberty than sexual license."[35] By themselves alone, these first two utopian features of the sexual revolution are likely to prove as harmful to "liberated" society as the purported male chauvinism, paternalism, and misogyny that represent the other extreme that the revolution set out to combat.

Third (shades of 1789 yet again), the sexual revolution advances the claim that gender identity should be decided by subjective feelings rather than objective science and biology; that all other judgments, such as true and false, good and bad, are a matter of discrimination; and that any other human rights should be subordinate to the rights of gender orientation. In the battle of the binaries, it has been said, there are no longer two genders, male and female, but as many possible genders as there are days in the year and feelings in the day. As with Rousseau in *Emile*, what matters is how you feel. (What I feel to be good is good, what I feel to be bad is bad.)

Fourth, and in open contradiction to the previous point, the sexual revolution argues that naturalistic science is adequate to answer all the questions of life, and all other sources of knowledge, especially those that are transcendent, are redundant. (Reich: "Natural science confronts its greatest task: to assume the responsibility for the future destiny of a tortured humanity.")[36] Science is therefore called on to trump religion, though if necessary, feelings alone can still trump science, as is happening now with transgenderism.

Fifth (echoes of 1789), the sexual revolution claims that the two decisive sources of repression are the monogamous family (because of its role in generation, education, and tradition) and religion, the Jewish and Christian faiths being considered the most repressive of all ("disgraceful medieval sexual legislation," and "medieval irrationalism").[37] The two institutions should therefore be attacked together. (Marx had argued earlier that the secret to the Holy Family is the earthly family. To make the former disappear, the latter must be destroyed, in theory and in practice. Breton later:

"Everything remains to be done, every means must be worth trying, in order to lay waste the ideas of family, country, religion.")[38] Breton therefore urged surrealists to "laugh like savages at the French flag, to vomit their disgust in the face of every priest, and to level at the breed of 'basic duties' the long range weapon of sexual cynicism."[39]

Sixth (echoes of 1789, the Marquis de Sade, and Wilhelm Reich), the sexual revolution holds that, contrary to Freud's understanding of civilization, all sexual repression should be removed completely, starting at the youngest age. This means that parents must be replaced decisively as the primary shapers of their children, assisted by comprehensive sex education for all school children (compounded by the reinforcing influences of advertising, the internet, the media, music, and film). It appears that even the once-trusted and sophisticated Conde Nast now subscribes to this doctrine. In 2017, its *Teen Vogue* published "anal 101 for teens, beginners, and all inquisitive folk," complete with diagrams and counsel. (Such sex is hailed as "the great equalizer" in the sexual revolution.) In response to the outrage that followed, the magazine's digital editor, Phillip Picardi, tweeted his response: "Here's my only reply I'll be giving to any of the messages," his tweet accompanied by a photo of Picardi kissing another man while holding up his middle finger to the camera.[40] Clearly the sexual revolution regards parents as a nuisance and considers itself beyond the need for approval or subtlety.

Seventh (echoes of the Marquis de Sade), the sexual revolution teaches that no forms of sexual relations of any kind should be prohibited, lest the machinery of discrimination and repression (Rousseau's "chains") would come back in action again, and that sexual freedom should be entirely divorced from procreation. (Yet those in favor of sex without children become more and more concerned about those who are not—and they are therefore committed to control them in the name of a greater reproductive freedom, also known as nonreproductive sex.)

Eighth (echoes of the French Enlightenment), the sexual revolution represents an aggressive, systematic, and uncompromising assault on all surviving sources of transcendent faith. (Voltaire's famous *"Écrasez l'infâme!"* was seconded by Shelley's "Oh! I burn with impatience for the moment of Xtianity's dissolution, it has injured me.")[41] The belief is that if freedom is to succeed at all, nothing, absolutely nothing must be allowed to stand in the way of the freedom of the sexual revolution. There must therefore be severe social, political, and even legal penalties for those who oppose the gender revolution ("the price of citizenship"). Worst of all, all other human and civil rights must be subordinated to the fundamental right of sexual orientation— sexual freedom over freedom of conscience.

Such features of the sexual revolution are obvious to anyone with their eyes open, but too often the significance of the revolution is only considered anecdotally. (Who am I to judge my son/grandson/friend/sister-in-law/ neighbor/colleague?) And of course, not everyone following these ideas goes to every possible extreme. (We all know magnificent exceptions.) But a moment's thought and a look at its three-hundred-year history, as well as the full-blown range of its philosophies and policies, would show the extent of its radical vision. The sexual revolution is truly a complete subversion of the old order and its replacement by a different world and a different way of life—Nietzsche's "transvaluation of all values" in a sexual and cultural form. Three thousand years of Western history and its accepted consensus about reality, humanity, marriage, the family, and freedom are being obliterated, and not as a matter of democratic decision and consent but as an imposition by an elite that is often unelected and unaccountable—the government's "rape" of the people once again. In short, the will of a minority is being imposed on the majority through coercion, not persuasion. In the grand manner of Rousseau, the elites know best, and the majority is "forced to be free"—a grotesque contradiction of true freedom if there ever was one.[42]

The last point requires underscoring in light of the different "whiffs of totalitarianism" in certain Left-wing statements today and the violence in their actions. For one thing, it has been argued that the decadence of the sexual revolution in the Soviet Union and then in Weimar Germany helped to create the revulsion that brought Stalin and Hitler to power. For another thing, the progressive philosophy echoes Rousseau's ideas of the battering ram of the "General Will" of the people through which citizens can be "forced to be free." For yet another thing, the same dire animosity to transcendence was at the heart of the earlier, secular, and political paths to revolution, and in each case it led to tragic consequences. In 1789, for instance, the "bloodless terror" waged in the republic of letters preceded and led to the "bloody terror" of Robespierre and the guillotine.

I am not predicting that tumbrils will roll down New York's Fifth Avenue or Washington's Pennsylvania Avenue. But long before that prospect, the danger is that the militancy of the antireligious animosity will spell the end of genuine Western liberalism and robust American freedom, including freedom of religion and conscience, and the fundamental right to political dissent, conscientious objection, and civil disobedience. Hence, as highlighted earlier under questions eight and nine, there is a vital importance to the cobelligerence between secularists, Jews, and Christians who genuinely love freedom and who see the foundational importance of freedom of religion and conscience for all, for the good of all.

To be sure, the sexual revolution claims to be all about love and freedom, but what kind of love and what kind of freedom? Does anyone really think that liberating sexual vitality, animal impulses, and physical urges will provide the key to full human freedom, including political freedom? Where has such pagan vitalism led before? What of all the missing themes, even in the area of love, such as romantic love, lasting love, or the sacrificial love of covenantal love loyalty? And have today's devotees of their love and revolutionary freedom considered the actual lives of their high priests and priestesses—Jean-Jacques Rousseau, Mary Wollstonecraft, Alexandra Kollontai, and Wilhelm Reich, for example?

Reich was passionate about the claim that his vision was all about freedom. He called for "Revolution, Now and Forever," and originally announced its launch as "the European freedom movement."[43] But he deliberately flouted Freud's warning that civilization can be built only on the restraint of instincts. And if the radical form of social constructionism calls into question the character of the American republic, the radical form of the sexual revolution poses an even greater challenge to the West and its Jewish and Christian roots. (Breton, his fellow surrealists, and his *Surrealist Manifesto* made no bones about the showdown. "*The decisive battle against Christianity could be fought only at the level of the sexual revolution.* And therefore the problem of sexuality and eroticism is today the fundamental problem from the moral point of view.")[44]

Many who read the wilder claims of the sexual revolution wonder how anyone could believe such ideas that are variously radical, irresponsible, unrealistic, and directly opposed to the freedom on which America was founded. "Complete and absolute" freedom? The words of Jesus of Nazareth form the motto of more universities and colleges around the world than any other, and express the heart of the classical Western understanding of freedom: "You will know the truth, and the truth will set you free" (Jn 8:32 NIV). Freedom assumes and requires both truth and ethics. Prime Minister José Luis Rodriguez of Spain (2004–2011), a socialist and radical proponent of the gender revolution, was candid about his entirely different objectives and understanding of freedom: "We stand before a global project of social transformation with the goal of destroying the old order and building a new order. We have never passed so many laws in such a short time that change the lives of the individual." He therefore proposed his own countermotto to replace that of Jesus: "It is freedom that makes us true. Not the truth that makes us free."[45]

The mind boggles at such reasoning. What comes to mind is Hans Christian Andersen's fairy tale for children, "The Emperor has no clothes!" But the emperor's naked vanity hurt only himself, whereas from 1789 on, failed revolutions have consistently crushed millions in their wake and guillotined the genuine impulses toward freedom. Will 1789 and the neo-Marxist, neo-Freudian sexual revolution prove to be any different?

For Jews, Christians, and all who take the Bible seriously, there is an additional reflection that the sexual revolution prompts. There are two stark and enduring contrasts in the Bible. The first is the contrast between monotheism and paganism, and their attendant views of life, history, and human worth. The second is the culture of covenantal love, ethics, and responsible interpersonal relationships in contrast to the culture of sexual anomie that destroys covenantal relationships and leads to powermongering and chaos-producing violence—including men dominating women. The sexual revolution is pagan in its espousal of rampant sexuality. The main difference is that the extravagance was once justified in the name of ensuring fertility, and now it is promoted in the name of reducing fertility.

There is no question on which side the American republic was born, and no question which of the two sides America is now openly choosing to live in. Nor is there any question what the consequences were for those earlier cultures and what the outcome will be for the Americans and for the American republic if the present generation does not call a halt to the madness of sexual lawlessness. Under the banner of First Amendment rights and spurious claims for natural instincts ("born to porn"), unbounded sex will continue to be shamelessly commercialized, men will be left as dissatisfied as they are desensitized, and women and children will be degraded and trafficked.

That last point and the logic behind it must not be minimized. A potent blend of permissiveness, promiscuity, profit, and pornography has created the so-called American "pornado" and transformed America from Puritan to "pornified."[46] But as the furor over sexual aggression shows, that is not the end of the problem. Vile as male aggression is, there is an element of hypocrisy in the recent shock over its prevalence. As with the post-truth power worlds of politics and economics, dominance in the post-truth, porn-saturated world of sex goes to the strong (or the older, the richer, and the more famous), while the weak (or the young, the inexperienced, and those starting out) find themselves on the receiving end of unwanted aggression.

The Hebrew prophet Amos attacked the powerful men who ground the faces of the poor in the dust, and feminists are absolutely and unequivocally right to attack the powerful men who assault the women within their reach. Outrage over sexual harassment is long overdue. But to anyone who recognizes the crooked timber of our humanity, that is what the powerful always do, and will always do—unless their power is restrained by truth, their might is curbed by right, and their temptations are tamed by character and moral behavior. "Consent" as the sole remaining justification for anything and everything sexual is ethically deficient, because there are too many reasons why "consent" can be coerced.

The danger as well as the hypocrisy of the present situation is becoming apparent. Hugh Hefner had just been lionized after his death for his role as a sexual revolutionary, but Harvey Weinstein was roundly castigated for excusing his behavior by blaming it on the sixties ("I came of age in the '60s and '70s when all the rules about behavior and workplaces were different"). The *New York Times* was justified in calling it his "get-out-of-jail-free card" and a "poor excuse," but the links between the earlier ideas and the later consequences were undeniable and have still not been faced.[47]

Out of words come worlds and ways of life. Out of the philosophy came the culture, and out of the culture came the behavior. To men who saw themselves as an end to themselves, all women are purely a means to their end. The Holocaust did not begin with the building of the crematoria; the sexual abuse did not begin with the founding of Miramax. In the name of the sexual revolution, permissiveness was widely lionized, moral restraints were thrown off as reactionary, male entitlement was empowered and popularized, and the only people to be challenged were those who challenged the consequences.

But then in a sudden about-turn, as if to camouflage the earlier direction, the unfreedom of the permissive-born abuse was roundly outed. One generation had flouted the moral standards of its forebears, but the next still had the moral capacity to be horrified by the consequences of that flouting. But without the restoration of the ethics of their forebears, new problems have been stirred. Sex has now been weaponized, as race was earlier, and the result is making sex as controversial, divisive, and incurable as race has long been in America. Among various disastrous consequences, the completely innocent and the slightly guilty have found themselves as vulnerable to suspicion, accusation, and instant ruin as the egregiously guilty—with little or no evidence required, and with no due process allowed. Careers of a lifetime can be vaporized in a second, and all on the basis of unproven accusations from unknown accusers.

Where is Nathaniel Hawthorne when we need him now?

Half a century of the sexual revolution has achieved the reverse of expanding freedom. Freedom as "obedience to the unenforceable" has been systematically assailed and broken down. But instead of rebuilding the restraints of dignity and respect, character and ethics in order to restore the freedom of the unenforceable, Left/liberalism has gone in the opposite direction. Sex has become fraught, relationships have been poisoned, yet another intractable division has opened in American society, and intrusive new rules and regulations are being trundled out to solve the problems—all of which only plays into the hands of greater social control and less real freedom.

Every man in America is now every woman's potential aggressor, and every woman in America is every man's potential accuser. Fortunately, as with the dark excesses of anticommunism earlier, history will prove more truthful than propaganda and the excesses of the new sexual McCarthyism will be seen for what they are. But innocent men and women will suffer along with the guilty, just as the innocent suffered earlier under the aggression that followed from the loosened moral restraints on the sexually powerful.

America's brave new pornucopia has been pouring out the blessings of its purported liberation since the 1960s. God was declared dead, and everything was declared permitted. Yet permissiveness for all turned out to be a permit for the promiscuous and the powerful to play the predator. Thus the different precedents set by Hugh Hefner, Ted Kennedy, Larry Flynt, Bill Clinton, Bill Cosby, Harvey Weinstein, Kevin Spacey, Matt Lauer, and others are not an aberration. Unfettered sexual desire blended with post-truth power without principle means that the powerful alpha male will always treat less powerful women as the means to their ends and the objects for their lust—and then use the same power to silence would-be whistleblowers who might challenge their unbridled conquests.

Certain behaviors have now been highlighted and outlawed as currently unacceptable, but the post-truth philosophy is far from dead. Post-truth power may be rooted in race, money, athletic prowess, political power, or gender, but whoever and whatever it meets, power exploits and manipulates. To the powerful, people and objects are valued not for themselves, only for their usefulness. They have instrumental worth, not intrinsic dignity. Thus in the post-truth power world, reality means availability, and manipulation leads to consumption, whether plundering nature or women. Post-truth ideas have consequences. As a friend has remarked pointedly: *ideas have consequences, but bad ideas have victims.*

Make no mistake. The sexual revolution has run true to form in degrading, objectifying, and abusing American women. The logic should surprise no one who knows its eighteenth-century roots. The "divine marquis" blazed that trail long ago, as any reader of *Justine* will know. Since then whole industries have been built on the exploitation of women, but what is not logical is that so many women have been cheerleaders for the very culture that has done it to them. As Caitlin Flanagan argued in *The Atlantic*, Bill Clinton was championed by feminist icons such as Gloria Steinem (shielding him from rape charges) and "rescued by a surprising force: machine feminism. The movement had by then ossified into a partisan operation, and it was willing—eager to let this friend of the sisterhood enjoy a little *droit de seigneur*."[48]

The plain truth is that permissive, pornified, and commercialized sexual freedom will never be freedom for women, and it will certainly not be love. The present war between the sexes therefore spells disaster for America. A free and open society requires trust, and especially trust between men and women. The harvest of the sexual revolution is ripening, "diversity" as virtue signaling is not the answer, and America needs far more than new "rules, regulations, and codes" to right the current wrongs. (A current headline and sign of the times: "U.S. Congress Requires Anti-Harassment Training.") What America really requires is a national about-turn over the sexual revolution itself. It needs a genuine change of mind and heart (a.k.a. the Hebrew *teshuva* or "repentance") and the restoration of solid foundations for respectful and trusting relationships, and for love and loyalty, none of which is possible within the stated terms of the sexual revolution and the logic of 1789.

England in the eighteenth century turned back from the logic of 1789 and the sexual revolution in a peaceful way. The Soviet Union turned back in the twentieth century, though in a hypocritical, violent, and authoritarian way. Will Americans be so infatuated by false freedom that they press on blindly to the point of disaster, or will they return to their right mind and call a halt to the lemming-like rush to the precipice?

Which leads back to the point stressed at the beginning of this look at the sexual revolution. There is a world of difference between the villains of these ideas and the victims of their thinking. There is also a practical difference between "hating the sin and loving the sinner." For those who follow the way of 1789, there is no such distinction. The exposure or even the accusation of sin leads at once to the short and logical step from greatness to guillotine for the "sinner"—all with a merciless suddenness and no hope of reprieve, as the French aristocrats discovered in their time. For those who follow the way of 1776 and the very different truths of grace and forgiveness that lie behind it, genuine wrongs can lead to genuine repentance, and then to genuine forgiveness and the possibility of a genuine second chance in life and restoration in the community.

That said, there must be no reprieve for either the core principles or the extreme policies and practices of the sexual revolution itself. There is little disagreement that the sexual revolution is the spawn of 1770's Paris, 1910's Greenwich Village, 1920's Vienna, and 1930's Weimar and Berlin. It goes far beyond Hugh Hefner and carries grave implications for America and for its republican form of freedom. (A New York editor announced that March 15, 1913, the year of the Armory Show, was "sex o'clock in America.")[49] By their choices and in their lifestyles, Americans today are casting their vote in an election even more important and decisive than any single presidential election. At the least there should be no question that there must be an open debate on the issues, and a debate that is worthy of the gravity and immensity of the stakes. Freedom itself is staked on the outcome.

Once again, will it be said that freedom was too hard a challenge for Americans to overcome? Here, then, is the tenth and final question on the checklist that Americans must answer constructively: *Are you vigilant about the current ideas that are crucial to freedom today?*

Why has there been such a decline in trust and in mutual respect in so many American institutions and so many ideas and ideals? How would you draw up your own balance sheet of the impact of such forces as multiculturalism, identity politics, political correctness, postmodernism, and the sexual revolution? Which beliefs and customs best serve the interests of human flourishing, and which ideas and ideals do you believe are most needed for the perpetuation of the American republic? Which of the two revolutions do they serve?

The overall lesson from this last question is impossible to ignore. Advanced modernity is throwing up an unprecedented series of challenges to the American republic and to American freedom, and they must each be weighed and assessed. Powerful trends and developments are swirling through the social and political terrain, and the differences between 1776 and 1789 are vast and consequential. All these issues need to be monitored with care and decisions made as to their significance. Quite simply, the decisions Americans make in the next generation will shape the course of American freedom and decide the fate of the American republic.

CONCLUSION

AMERICA'S CHOICE

Covenant, Chaos, or Control?

*W*riting only a few months before the Declaration of Independence in July 1776, John Adams engaged in a perceptive and charming correspondence with his wife, Abigail. He was in Philadelphia drafting a new code of laws, and she had urged him to "remember the ladies and be more generous and favorable to them than your ancestors." After all, Abigail reminded him tartly, "Remember, all men would be tyrants if they could. If particular care and attention is not paid to the ladies, we are determined to foment a rebellion, and will not hold ourselves bound by any laws in which we have no voice or representation."

Abigail was deftly pressing her husband to practice his own revolutionary principles and apply them more widely. In this case he did not follow her counsel. Nor, sadly, were other founders any more consistent when it came to their African slaves and to Native Americans. The consequences of such blind spots stain their record still and raise an insurmountable barrier against uncritical adulation of 1776. Adams was more consistent than most, but he was not so intoxicated with freedom as to be unaware that revolutions represent a decisive break with tradition and authority, create their own momentum, and are therefore an open invitation to follow the lure of freedom wherever it leads.

"We have been told," he replied to Abigail, "that our struggle has loosened the bonds of government everywhere: that children and apprentices are disobedient; that schools and colleges were grown turbulent." But her letter, he continued, "was the first intimation that another tribe, more numerous and powerful than all the rest, were grown discontented."[1]

The revolution was "loosening the bonds of government everywhere"? "Another tribe, more numerous and powerful than all the rest" was now discontented and pressing to be free? Seen that way, the history of freedom in America can be viewed as the shining story of one tribe after another loosening its bonds, staking its claim to its place in the sun, and cashing in on the Declaration's "promissory note" of freedom and equality. But as we have also seen, many of history's dreams of freedom have run to excess and courted disaster. They had roots that were a far cry from the founders, and many of them assaulted a boundary too far, while some pursuits of freedom proved to be only a mirage, and others turned into nightmares.

Doubtless if the founders could return to the republic they strove so hard to create, Adams and the great majority would surely welcome how Lincoln followed their better angels, reversed their Faustian bargain, and led their descendants to give freedom to the slaves that they themselves did not free. But what would Martin Luther King Jr. think of the way his declaration that the content of character mattered more than the color of one's skin has been transformed into reverse racism and attacks on white privilege? How would Mario Savio, the fiery and passionate leader of Berkeley's Free Speech Movement in 1964, respond to the state of free speech on American universities a generation after his struggle? The muzzling of the messiness of dissent, the provision of safe places as a coddled protection against the risk of offense, the practice of trigger warnings, the disinviting and no-platforming of speakers considered too provocative for fashionable opinion, and the arson and violence? The recruitment of masked and hooded thugs to beat up opponents in the name of "social justice warriors"? This is not exactly the freedom that Savio and his generation protested for in the universities—let alone the freedom of speech that John Milton and John Stuart Mill had fought for in their time.

And what would Roger Williams, William Penn, James Madison, and Thomas Jefferson think if they were to hear elite opinion reducing their First Amendment's free exercise of religion to "freedom of worship" between the ears and dismissing their first freedom as "partisan," a "code word for bigotry," a right that it is right to overrule, and merely a power play? Freedom, in those and other ways, can become its own worst enemy, and those who love freedom must never be blind to its ironies and never disown the children that it breeds in its profligacy.

Political revolutions explode into history packed with intended and unintended consequences like the long-running aftershocks of a powerful earthquake. Not even the most farsighted statesmen are able to see all that they have achieved, and much of the best or worst of the outcomes may have been brought about despite them. There is no question that John Adams could see far farther than most people, but even he could see only so far.

Yet as we have seen, there is more to America's story today than ironies, unintended consequences, and unknown aftermaths. The seismic shifts accompanying the 1960s counterculture, and in particular the shift from the older classical liberalism to the new Left/liberalism, were deliberate. They represented a powerful counterrevolution that at numerous points has shown itself the true heir of 1789 (and 1917 and 1949) rather than 1776. The shift is closer to describing where the liberal Left appears bent on taking America. In his minor classic, *Weimar Culture: The Outsider as Insider*, historian Peter Gay recounts a bitter joke that Arthur Koestler, the Hungarian writer, used to hear when he was working in Berlin in 1932 in the last days of the Weimar Republic. It was doing the rounds of Ullstein, the Jewish publishing house where he worked. It captured the mood of the times perfectly and hinted at what was to come as the Weimar freedoms sputtered out and Hitler and the National Socialists plotted their path to power.

> There was once, so the story runs, a Chinese executioner named Wang Lun, who lived in the reign of the second emperor of the Ming Dynasty. He was famous for his skill and speed in beheading his victims, but all his life he had harbored a secret aspiration, never yet realized: to behead a person so rapidly that the victim's head would remain poised on his neck after he had died. He practiced and practiced, and finally, in his seventy-sixth year, he realized his ambition. It was on a busy day of executions, and he dispatched each man with graceful speed, heads rolling in the dust. Then came the twelfth man; he began to mount the scaffold, and Wang Lun, with a whisk of his sword, beheaded his victim so quickly that he continued to walk up the steps. When the man reached the top, he spoke angrily to the executioner,
>
> "Why do you prolong my agony?" he asked. "You were mercifully quick with the others!"
>
> It was Wang Lun's moment. He had now crowned his life's work. A serene smile spread over his face. He turned to his victim, and said, "Please would you just nod!"[2]

Such was the skill and precision of the executioner's coup de grâce that his victim was dead before he knew it. So too, and soon, were the freedoms of democratic Weimar's naive citizens and of all the unsuspecting victims of the National Socialist coup that led to the rise of Hitler. Milton Mayer's celebrated study of the early 1930s captured the naivety perfectly: "They thought they were free."[3] The sorry end of the short-lived liberal republic of Weimar was said to be part murder, part wasting sickness, and part suicide. Could American freedoms be facing a similar fate if certain antidemocratic trends are allowed to run their course? Today's choices must be made with eyes wide open. Once when Henry Kissinger was secretary of state, he explained his legendary realism to a colleague, "My father was a good man in a world in which goodness had no meaning, and I will never make the same mistake."

The Great Showdown

Where is America now? Has America reached the stage where wider and wider freedoms are all the fulfillment of the founders' "promissory note"? Or have unforeseen and ill-considered consequences taken the founders' republic off course? Or could it be that America is nearing the end of 1776 and republican freedom, in a fate long envisioned by some Americans and worked on with an executioner's precision that needs only its victim's nod to show that the head has already been severed? America today is torn between its competing views of freedom, and the two main competitors are approaching their high-noon showdown. They cannot both be right, for 1776 and 1789 are profoundly contradictory and are on a collision course with each other over issues that are decisive for the American future— including the character of freedom itself.

After going through a checklist such as the one set out here, the question Americans must decide is, Which view of freedom answers the foundational questions in ways that are best and true and essential? Which one most suits the American republic as it was set up by the founders, and which one serves the different requirements of American freedom today, whether freedom for individuals, freedom for groups, or freedom for the republic itself? Conversely, which of the competing views of freedom is most likely to betray the trust and hope of those who champion it? Just as Lincoln in his "house divided" speech in 1858 warned that the United States would not stay "half slave and half free" but would become "all one thing, or all the other," so the open tensions over freedom by the forces of 1776 and 1789 are bound to come down on one side or the other, but which is it to be?[4]

Such is the chaos and poisonous confusion of the current culture warring, through the airwaves and the social media, that any description of the competing forces would instantly become part of the raging disagreements itself. But as I have argued throughout, the deepest issue is not just between Democrats and Republicans, liberals and conservatives, Left and Right, rural and urban, red states and blue states, religious believers and secularists, heartlanders and coastals, or between the globalists and the nationalists—the "Davos men" who favor the perspectives and benefits of globalization and the "Main Street guys" who champion local and national priorities. The conflicts at their core swirl around two principal sets of forces, which I have described as the spirit, the heirs, and the allies of 1776, and the spirit, the heirs, and the allies of 1789.

Both sides are fighting for freedom, but with different views of what freedom is and how it may be attained. On one side, there is the classical liberal understanding of freedom championed by the Jewish and Christian faiths and by many believers in other world religions. On the other side, there is the Left/liberal understanding of freedom, championed by the forces of progressive and postmodern secularism, challenging all customs, conventions, and tradition, and transgressing all unwanted boundaries and taboos.

To describe the showdown in terms that seventeenth- and eighteenth-century Americans would have understood, the contest is between the forces of *federal* liberty (*foedus* being the Latin for "covenant"), the freedom to act freely but within the terms of traditional moral life and the American Constitution and its ways, and the forces of *natural* liberty, the freedom for Americans to act as they please so long as they do no harm to others and they can survive the consequences. Or to describe the showdown in the terms argued by sociologist Philip Rieff, the dispute is between those whose views of freedom stem from *faith* and those whose views of freedom stem from *fiction*, in the sense that the latter reject any view of objective truth or a given moral order and openly acknowledge that their views are self-devised and self-constructed. Or again, in the terms put forward by Rabbi Sacks, the clash is between the forces of the *will to life* ("Choose life" being the greatest biblical command) and the forces of the *will to power* (relativism and a rejection of objective moral standards being the foundational assumption of postmodernism and social constructionism).[5]

Whichever terms are used, the contest is far deeper than other levels of the culture wars, and the result will not be a clear and reasoned debate between two opposing sets of pure ideas. Indeed, the battles will not be fought on even ground. There are numerous reasons why the contest is confused and skewed: These range from the distorting impact of whichever worldview has the better voices in universities, the press, media, the law, and the social media; to the breakdown of the rules of the contest; to the mounting fear that the world beyond America's borders will not wait for America to finish its debate; and to the intensification of all such issues during election campaigns. There is also a titanic difference between the two sides: the voices in support of 1789 are in full cry, but there is a striking absence of any twenty-first-century equivalent of Abraham Lincoln speaking on behalf of "the better angels" of the American experiment.

Whose View Serves Freedom Best?

Now is the time when American citizens should pause, step back from their immediate quarrels, and review their answers to the foundational questions in the checklist and make their judgments as to which view of freedom offers the best responses.

First, which view does justice to the way America was set up to be?

Second, do Americans care enough to examine the issues and offer adequate answers?

Third, which view defines freedom best, doing justice to all the different aspects of freedom that are essential?

Fourth, which view does justice to answering the central paradox of freedom, that freedom is the greatest enemy of freedom?

Fifth, which view is the most realistic in facing the difficult task of sustaining freedom?

Sixth, which view best guarantees freedom while doing justice to today's increasing diversity?

Seventh, which view offers the best philosophical and moral case for justifying the vision of a free, open, and stable society? And which can achieve the necessary alliances for accomplishing this goal?

Eighth, which view provides the most solid grounds for undergirding and expounding human freedom itself?

Ninth, which view is most vigilant in terms of the *institutions* that are crucial to freedom today?

Tenth, which view is the most vigilant in terms of the *ideas* that are crucial to freedom today?

The battle between the competing views is close to the decisive stage when the consequences will become clear and irreversible. To be sure, the American experiment was never a covenant *with God*, as the Jewish covenant at Mount Sinai was, but it is no longer what it has long been: a covenant or constitution *under God*. Today, following the rapid post-1960s secularization of public life and the determined efforts of organization such as the ACLU and individual activists such as Michael Newdow, the American experiment has increasingly become a constitution *without God*.

This move away from "under God" sounds purely verbal and therefore trivial, but it has two major consequences. First, without a standard higher than the human, the search is on for an ultimate human power for citizens to look to and reach for—the state, the market, science, technology, or—of course—a human leader with self-deifying pretensions. The result is a ceaseless competition for control of this power, a competition in which the strong prevail, the weak fall behind, and economic and social inequalities are widened. Second, without "under God" and its standard that is higher than the human, social criticism will never amount to more than an expression of the competing power plays in society—criticism in the interests of the dominant power or those who wish to dethrone the dominant power and put themselves in its place.

When "under God" is respected as the standard of final accountability, the moral commitment that forms the covenantal or constitutional pledge automatically becomes the standard by which citizens can assess and correct the condition of the country. In that sense, prophets, whether Amos, Isaiah, and Jeremiah to the Jewish people or Frederick Douglass and Martin Luther King Jr. to Americans, are the social critics who hold the country accountable to the covenant or constitution that the citizens and their ancestors have made. When that covenant or constitution is rejected, so also is the shared standard of critique. The result can be a cacophony of public accusations that is anything but constructive, an expression of social and political power plays rather than standards of truth and justice.

Beyond that, the most important question after the collapse of the covenant is: Will the center hold, and in America's case, will the US Constitution do what it was designed to do? Will the covenant remain the unbreakable framework that protects and perpetuates American freedom? Can American freedom survive and thrive independently of the faiths that were decisive at its birth, as the progressive, liberal, secularist, and constructionist side insists? Or will the center fail to hold, and an increasingly elastic Constitution finally withers into insignificance, so that American freedom and the republic itself inevitably decline, as supporters of the Jewish, Christian, and classical tradition have warned?

What the Issue Is Not

The core issue must not be confused, as it is in several common confusions that swim like red herrings through many current debates. First, the question is not whether America was once a Christian nation, but no longer is. The United States was never a Christian nation in any official, formal, or established sense, as Catholic Spain and France, Anglican England, and Presbyterian Scotland were. The First Amendment firmly and decisively disestablished religion at the federal level in New York in 1791, and slowly the states followed until there were no established churches left at the state level either. From then on, much of America's uniqueness and vitality have flowed from that momentous act of disestablishment. It is true that most of the early Americans were Christians, and most of the ideas that shaped early America were distinctively Jewish and Christian. But the relationship was indirect, creative, and consciously contained an element of a wager. In the words of the Williamsburg Charter, which celebrated the two hundredth anniversary of the Constitution and the First Amendment,

> The founders knew well that the republic they established represented an audacious gamble against long historical odds. This form of government depends upon ultimate beliefs, for otherwise we have no right to the rights by which it thrives, yet rejects any official formulation of them. The republic will therefore always remain an "undecided experiment" that stands or falls by the dynamism of its non-established faiths.

The question, then, is not whether America was or is Christian, but whether the nonestablished faiths current at any moment in America's history are strong enough to support the ideas and ideals that are required for America's flourishing.

Second, the question is not whether people can be good (and in this case, remain free) without God. Of course they can. Jews and Christians have always held that because humans are made in the image of God, they are capable of countless expressions of truth, beauty, justice, goodness, compassion, and altruism, whether they believe in God or not. The question is whether entire societies can be just and free without faith in God, whether societies can stay that way without a shared moral framework, or whether they must increasingly rely on coercion to compensate for the lack of faith and virtue.

It is beyond question that in recent history societies that have been officially or predominantly secularist, such as the Soviet Union, the People's Republic of China, and North Korea, have been totalitarian and notoriously oppressive—and it is also an undeniable fact that almost all the greatest mass murderers in modern history, such as Stalin, Mao, and Pol Pot, have been atheists and saw their atheism as central to their political vision. But we are talking of secularist societies that claim to be democratic, and there is always a crucial difference between individuals and the societies they live in, as Reinhold Niebuhr argued famously in his classic book *Moral Man and Immoral Society*. Many consequences flow from Niebuhr's important distinction. A key one is that while individual people commonly act better than the philosophies they believe, societies commonly act worse.

The question then is whether the American republic can remain just and free without a definite, though unofficial, commitment to the importance of faith and the importance of freedom of conscience as citizens engage in public life.

Third, the question is not whether the founders of the American republic were right on every issue or not. As we have seen, their Faustian bargain over slavery and their glaring hypocrisies clearly show that they were seriously wrong in places, supremely over slavery, women, and Native Americans. But that does not mean the founders' work should be thrown out, baby, bathwater, and all. On certain issues, such as freedom of religion and conscience, they got things almost nearly perfectly right from the beginning, and on these issues they did a far better job than Americans have done in the last half century. The truth is that no generation in history has attempted such a daring, brilliant, and ingenious project to create and sustain a free society that can reasonably hope to remain free. At the very least, to reject this attempt because of certain of the founders' flaws would mean starting again from scratch. And it would court the mediocrity and fate of history's series of failed exercises on behalf of freedom.

As we saw earlier, there are four main ways Americans dismiss their founders today—rejecting them for their evils and hypocrisies, accusing them of a hidden agenda, charging that history and events have rendered their ideas outmoded, or simply forgetting them altogether. These dismissals are all very different, but their combined effect has been to cut the American republic from its roots, so that like Western civilization in general, America has become a cut-flower society and political culture.

The question, then, is whether Americans today have the understanding, the respect, and the will to repair and continue their founders' great experiment. It bears saying again: *All these ideas are thinkable and debatable, and ideas that are debatable must be debated. But not all ideas are livable, either for individuals or for nations.* Thus, it will not do for people to consign to the dustbin of history what they consider unwelcome ideas and then dismiss them as indefensible and a waste of time to debate. The first part of that attitude is often born of chronological snobbery, the second of arrogance, and both are recklessly foolish for a free society.

Fourth, there is no proposed way forward that would provide a silver bullet solution to the present crises. A good proposal could be a vital and necessary part of the answer, but no single solution would be the sole or sufficient answer. As many have noted, the challenges facing the American republic today are infinitely complicated, like a gigantic Rubik's Cube. One problem leads to another problem, and to another and another. To remedy one thing you have to solve something else, and to solve that, something else in turn, which leads to yet another problem demanding yet another solution. Just so crime, murders, broken families, mediocre schools, blinkered universities, alienation, epidemic addictions, porous borders, disrespect for the flag, an angry Main Street, a greedy Wall Street, an out-of-touch Hollywood, and a thousand other issues are all inextricably related so that none can finally be fixed apart from the others. But certain things at least are clear. Politics alone can never solve the problems, as politics is downstream from the major sources of the problems. The deepest remedies require a reordering of American society and a restoration of its wellsprings. No solution to America's crises is likely to succeed if it does not take seriously the code of America's constitutional (and covenantal) DNA.

The Decider

I write as a resident alien and a longtime, though deeply concerned, admirer of the American republic. For me, at least two conclusions are almost beyond dispute.

First, there is little question that it is the assumptions and ideas of 1776—the American revolution, with its essentially Jewish and Christian views, and not the assumptions and ideas of 1789, the French revolution with its essentially progressive and secularist views—which fits the founders' understanding of freedom and the requirements of a free republic as the founders established it. That by itself is unsurprising, because the American Revolution was not the French Revolution, and almost all the founders and their generation subscribed to the Jewish and Christian understanding of freedom. But it is a significant conclusion, for if there is such a close fit between the biblical view and the American founding, then the outright rejection of the biblical view will lead to an equally emphatic rejection of the American founding as it was.

Second, and more importantly, there is little question that it is the assumptions and ideas of 1776 that answers the checklist of questions comprehensively, adequately, realistically, and constructively.

It is the biblical view, and not the progressive secularist view, which puts freedom and responsibility squarely at the heart of its view of humanness, politics, and a free society. While America has increasingly become a cut-flower culture, there is no question that it was 1776 and not 1789 that provided and nourished the roots of the American understanding of human dignity, freedom, equality, constitutionalism, separation of powers, and a score of other foundational elements of the republic.

It is the biblical view that insists on the essential place of truth, rejecting the dangers of the post-truth, power-driven world, and therefore provides a secure basis for freedom and for trust in society as well as a standing critique of the constant danger of the abuse of power.

It is the biblical view that sets out a way of life in which true freedom can flourish and there can be both liberation as an event and ordered liberty as a way of life.

It is the biblical view that provides for the freedom of conscience for all, without exception, including all those who differ and dissent from the biblical view.

And it is the biblical view that is fully realistic about the crooked timber of humanity that provides the ultimate check and balance on human power, the abuse of power, and utopianism.

Seen in that light, we may say that 1776 answers freedom's questions better than 1789, and that 1789 and its way of thinking represent a disordered view of freedom that spells political suicide for the American republic—exactly as Lincoln warned. But to stop there is too casual, though I tremble before the momentous stakes at a deeper level. Freedom and the American future may be the immediate issue, but the ultimate decision lies even deeper than the difference between 1776 and 1789. It raises the grand question for the human future and for such notions as singularity and transhumanism. Is faith in God the highest form of life affirmation, and does humanity have a better future "under God," as 1776 and the West have long believed? Or is faith in God the worst form of life negation, and does humanity have a better future "as God," as 1789, 1917, and 1949 and their heirs and progressive allies now assert? (Nietzsche: "Life is at an end where the kingdom of God begins.")[6]

One Nation Without God

Needless to say, these conclusions are arguable and this grand question is debatable. In the consumerist world, such issues seem a heady irrelevance, and in the fractious political climate of today many people will reject them without a moment's thought. But my own conviction after several decades of observing American public life is plain: *The key to the remedy of the American crisis of freedom lies in a fresh exploration of the Hebrew notions of creation and covenant that lie behind both American freedom and the US Constitution.* It is arguable, theoretically, though unlikely to the point of unthinkable, that the progressive secularist account of freedom could create an even more just and free society than America has known so far. In two and a half centuries, it has failed to do so anywhere—not France, not Russia, not China, and not anywhere else. But the outcome will not be decided on paper or through words alone. It will be decided in the crucible of life and history, and that crucible is relentless in its demonstration that choices have both costs and consequences.

In terms of consequences, one foreseeable result is obvious. The open rejection of the Jewish and Christian roots of the American Revolution will mean that all the flowers that grew directly from those roots will someday die. Notions such as human dignity, freedom, justice, equality, Constitution, the separation of powers, and forgiveness have been cut off from their roots. Sooner or later they will become unrecognizable and die. But there is an even deeper consequence for America, as the precedent of Jewish history shows. For as with the story of the exodus from Egypt, the liberation of the American Revolution highlights three possible responses to the original role of faith in achieving freedom.

One response is to appreciate and celebrate the role of faith in freedom, and so to remember it and to hand it on from generation to generation. Such a living memory leads in turn to gratitude that keeps faith and freedom fresh, and an ongoing commitment to strive for the justice and freedom of other peoples who are oppressed now as Israel was in Egypt and the American colonies were under the British. If America responds in this first way, America would remain a powerful and appealing force for freedom down through history and throughout the world.

A second possible response would be for America to turn a blind eye to the original role of faith in freedom, or to turn against faith in moderate ways, and so to distort a living faith into a conventional religion that is used as justification for the status quo. Religion then becomes what Karl Marx criticized rightly as the "opium of the people." This abuse has been the constant temptation of American civil religion when faith was publicly praised but smoothly domesticated in the decades after the Second World War. By idolizing the role of religion in binding America together, civil religion is essentially a form of American self-worship, which in the end brings on its own self-destruction.

A third possible response would be destructively radical if it rejects the role of faith in freedom altogether, both in terms of its place in the exodus and the American Revolution, and its importance for today. By default such a rejection of the role of faith in freedom would create an antireligion that denies freedom and grows authoritarian in its place. Karl Marx, along with Spinoza and Freud, was one of the three great Jewish titans who rejected their own Jewish faith and created an idol out of antireligion. The irony is inescapable. As the eminent sociologist David Martin often expressed it, Marx argued that the beginning of all criticism was the criticism of religion, only to create a political pseudoreligion that ended all criticism and made a god of the state. The warning is clear.

Final Accountability?

At the present moment, it is plain that America's Left/liberal advocates appear intent on greasing the skids for a repeat of that third option. In the great crucible of life and history, one last great contrast between 1776 and 1789 is likely to prove telling. The Achilles' heel of the progressive secularist view of freedom, as with numerous failed views of freedom before it, is its lack of final accountability.

Again and again, as the question about the paradox of freedom demonstrated, freedom has proved to be its own greatest enemy because it is unable to restrain itself. Freedom is never a greater enemy to freedom than when it becomes *freedom as power* or *freedom without principle*. Look at faith one way and you highlight trust and reliance. Look at it another way and you highlight the fear of God that is a standard for moral integrity, civil respect, and accountability. Both faith and the fear of God have been vital for freedom, but the latter especially so, for without accountability freedom corrupts itself and degenerates into mere power, as we have shown in the postmodern thinking and politics of Nietzsche, Foucault, and today's left-wing activists.

Such a collision of claims about accountability is unavoidable, and no one can have it both ways. In *Twilight of the Idols*, Nietzsche stated flatly that the rejection of accountability is the heart of atheism. "We deny God. In denying God, we deny accountability: only by doing *that* do we redeem the world."[7] The challenge to accountability in that statement is clear. From the three branches of government to the golden triangle of freedom, to the Electoral College, the founders tried to devise history's most ingenious system of checks and balances in order to prevent the abuse of power and hold leaders accountable. But "under God" in the national motto and "so help me God" in numerous oaths were always freedom's final, if unofficial, check and balance. The most common expression of accountability is the citizen's Pledge of Allegiance, the highest is the presidential Oath of Allegiance to the Constitution, but there are numerous others in between, all once powerful with meaning. Not only are these words the highest true standard for the oath taker, they are also the standard for the ongoing prophetic critique that covenantal freedom always required.

All freedom requires restraint, and the greater the freedom the greater the restraint and the stronger the accountability it requires. So what is adequate to restrain freedom at its most powerful and prosperous? What could possibly be adequate when progressive intellectuals put their faith in the utopian fallacy that technological progress also means moral progress? Or that improved management can devise systems so brilliant and smooth running that no one needs to be good? Edmund Burke highlighted this problem in the eighteenth century when he wrote to a member of the French National Assembly in 1791. The essential qualification if civil liberty was to flourish and endure in any society was the people's capacity to put "moral chains" on their own appetites. "Society cannot exist unless a controlling power upon the will and appetite be placed somewhere; and the less of it there is within, the more there must be without. It is ordained in the eternal constitution of things, that men of intemperate minds cannot be free. Their passions forge their fetters."[8]

Lord Acton underscored the same point in the nineteenth century in his famous judgment that Athenian democracy foundered for lack of such accountability. The Athenians, he wrote, were the only people of antiquity who grew great through democratic institutions. But they were never able to overcome the tyranny of the majority when the majority became unaccountable.

> But the possession of unlimited power, which corrodes the conscience, hardens the heart, and confounds the understanding of monarchs, exercised its demoralizing influence on the illustrious democracy of Athens. It is bad to be oppressed by a minority, but it is worse to be oppressed by a majority. For there is a reserve of latent power in the masses which, if it is called into play, the minority can seldom resist. But from the absolute will of an entire people there is no appeal, no redemption, no refuge but treason. . . .
>
> It follows that the sovereign people had a right to do whatever was within its power, and was bound by no rule of right or wrong but its own judgment of expediency. On a memorable occasion the assembled Athenians declared that it was monstrous that they should be prevented from doing whatever they chose. No force that existed could restrain them; and they resolved that no duty should restrain them, and they would be bound by no laws that were not of their own making. In this way the emancipated people of Athens became a tyrant; and their Government, the pioneer of European freedom, stands condemned with a terrible unanimity by all the wisest of the ancients.[9]

Americans should ponder Nietzsche's assertion, Burke's comment, and Lord Acton's summary of the conclusion of the ancients: "They understood that for liberty, justice, and equal laws, it is as necessary that Democracy should restrain itself as it had been that it should restrain the Oligarchy."[10] This point cannot be stressed too strongly, yet it is blithely ignored in much of America today when accountability is slighted or has collapsed. As Harari admits, "Yes, we moderns have promised to renounce meaning in exchange for power; but there is nobody out there to hold us to our promise."[11] If faith, character, and personal integrity are vital for sustaining freedom, they are equally, if not more, vital as the moral limit to power. It is easy and all too fashionable to dismiss ethics when we are talking of virtue and freedom, as with the golden triangle of freedom. But it is dangerous in the extreme to dismiss ethics when we are talking of the moral limits to power.

Only right can counter might. Only truth can prevail over lies. Only integrity can counter America's spreading corruption. Only a conviction of justice, compassion, and humanity, grounded in the fear of God, can prompt a civil disobedience prepared to stand against Leviathan. Science progresses inevitably, but morality can go backward as easily as forward. Tyranny is wrong and always wrong, but its wrong is compounded explosively when it is not accountable. Both the best and the worst chapters of the long struggle for freedom agree: From the conscientious objection of Pharaoh's midwives who rejected his command to kill Jewish babies, to Martin Luther King's "Letter from Birmingham Jail" and his stands at Selma and Montgomery, the accountability of right, of truth, of the fear of God, and of the moral limits to power is precious and indispensable for freedom, and to reject it spells a death sentence for the American republic.

Reaping the Whirlwind

If that is so, the fate that befell Athens is likely to be the fate of the heirs and allies of 1789, and the reason why their "victory" would be pyrrhic. Progressive secularist elites have grown accountable to no one. They have thrown off restraint for themselves and respect for others. They have decided they are the rulers, and all others are the ruled. They have rejected the role of faith in the American founding, repudiated the place of faith in public life today, and are now intent on stifling the free exercise of faith wherever they can. But in doing so, progressive elites will find that they are fostering a loss of accountability that will be their undoing. They are no longer accountable to God, they are not accountable to others, and they are not accountable to the future—they are accountable only to themselves.

If progressive secularism were to triumph completely, America's cut-flower ideals would reach the limit of their lives and wither rapidly. The American falcon would lose contact with the falconer altogether, and the center would not hold. Losing its grand conductor, the orchestra playing the great American symphony would grind toward a raucous halt. Intellectuals who all their lives have been living off the whiff of an empty bottle would suddenly realize the bottle was empty. The founders' great experiment would come to an inglorious end. And in the meantime, certain clear and unavoidable prospects would have become plain.

First, with the death of God and the postmodern dismissal of truth in private and public life, there will be no true freedom. Freedom requires truth and a solid grasp of reality, beginning with the freedom to speak the truth, to challenge political correctness, and to dismiss the fog of gossip, rumors, and lies—and then to provide the grounds for positive freedom. If Americans continue to deny truth, then the crisis of the post-truth world will accelerate the diminishing trust in American institutions. Eventually, social capital will be impoverished, and all relationships, and politics in particular, will be about power and only power. Truth-free power plays and manipulation without end will characterize all relationships. What will still be called freedom will be merely the lifestyle perks of the rich, the famous, and the powerful. Justice will be whatever legal outcome serves the party or people in power. And more American leaders will prostitute the access that their public service provides for fame, money, and power, whether during or after their term in public office.

Second, unchecked truth-free power politics in America will lead to ever greater inequalities between the powerful and their victims, with victory going to the strong and the weak going to the wall. Without a positive nonutopian vision of the desired alternative society, all efforts to bring it in will prove negative and destructive, leaving a wasteland of deconstructed ideals and institutions, such as the family and voluntary associations considered to be in the way. Such a wasteland will do great harm not only to the poor, the sick, the elderly, and the left behind, but to countless ordinary citizens across American society.

Third, an American generation, long made soft by the unrestrained freedom of feelings and boosted by the politics of self-esteem, entitlement, and identity, will experience these inequalities as insufferable abandonment, until its wounded grievances are stoked into an even angrier politics of resentment that will fuel the flames of social conflict, violence, and a mounting refusal to play the American game. The narcissism of identity politics and the victim culture has already become a politics of hypersensitivity, suspicion, offense, insult, resentment, hate, and vengeance, all fanned by activists and a partisan media. It eschews all compromise and reasoning together, and ensures that politics will be as feverish as the image that Americans carried of themselves was inflated. To this contemporary stoking of factions and frustrations will be added countless grievances from the past, as generations with no personal experience of the injuries and injustice suffered by their ancestors seek to settle the score for them and fight their battles all over again in our time. Ruinous divisiveness and vengeful demands for reparation and redress will become destructive and insatiable. As the *annus calamitosus* of 1968 warns, envy-fueled politics is likely to rise to a climax of violence, scapegoating—and assassination.

Fourth, the philosophy of constructionism will betray its promise of freedom and objectify human beings and turn them into objects of usefulness and expediency. Humans themselves have always been the subjects and not the objects. But now when humans routinely "construct" themselves too, they will become objects to themselves. So they will even judge themselves as products by their usefulness. Women have rightly protested how they are objectified in pornography and in advertising, but in the brave new world of radical constructionism and the sexual revolution, everyone so constructed will be objectified. And those so constructed will be their own products, objects of their own chosen constructions, and therefore assessed according to their usefulness rather than their intrinsic dignity—death by a thousand objectifications and dehumanization in another form.

Fifth, the basic rejection of truth and the commitment to ever more linguistic and socially constructed realities will lead to a greater estrangement and alienation from reality, the very definition of madness. If the Jewish, Christian, and classical views of reality are correct, there *is* a natural and created order, so the greater the attempt at pure social construction, the greater the estrangement and alienation from reality. Just as the impossible pretentions of Babel ended in confusion, and just as Icarus flew too close to the sun for the wax in his wings, so there are aspirations to self-creation and to transformations in the name of expanded freedom that will flout reality for a while but then crash and burn in eventual despair and self-destruction—first in the case of individuals, then with entire movements and philosophies, and finally with the once-great American experiment itself. This kind of self-made individual, as it used to be said, has relieved God of the responsibility. They alone are responsible for their fate.

Culturally and linguistically constructed *worlds within the world* are a feature of our creative capacity as human beings. Even the most far-fetched of them may make a world of difference for a time, but they cannot defy reality forever. There is reality. Every thought is thinkable, but not every thought is livable. Not even the greatest heroes and supermen, from Hercules to Nietzsche's dream superman, could leap the chasm between the earth and heaven and attain a new form of immortality.

Truth is in fact the lifesaver, for without truth there can be neither freedom nor sanity. George Orwell wrote in *1984*, as his protagonist Winston fought for his sanity against the politically correct doublethink of the ancestors of today's Left, "*Freedom is the freedom to say that two plus two makes four. If that is granted, all else follows.*"[12] Or as philosopher A. C. Grayling warns bluntly about the spin masters of the post-truth world, "You don't need facts, you just lie."[13] At a certain point, there can be only one result when Americans close their eyes to facts, shut off their minds from admitting the consequences of what they are doing, and mistake their fantasies for freedom: the madness that comes from being at war with reality.

Sixth, there will be such personal and psychological confusions bred by the radical constructionist views of freedom that the outcome will deepen America's psychological confusion, social lawlessness, political chaos, and economic debt, all serving to reinforce the decadence and decline of the American republic. "Be careful what you wish for" has always been sage advice. King Midas was given the golden touch he longed for, and Achilles gained the glory in battle he hoped for, but neither achieved what they really desired. Just so, many of today's Americans, and America itself, may well accomplish the novel, nature-defying freedoms they aspire to, but then wake up to rue the results.

Seventh, the rejection of the Jewish and Christian faiths does not mean the end of religion, as the radicals hope, but the resurgence of not one but two ancient religions in their place. From one side, we are seeing a return to paganism, and from the other, social constructionism and the technological revolution fosters the rise of a new gnosticism. Wilhelm Reich's revolution gained its energy through its vaunted "liberation" from all repressions, whether moral, social, or religious, and its glorying in the "vitality" of the life force. But the result is neither novel nor revolutionary. It is merely a return to nature and the worship of the sum of the forces of nature that was at the heart of the pagan world and is now reemerging with the idolizing of naturalistic science. The Greeks, the Canaanites, and many ancient societies would have recognized this religion at once.

At the same time, there is a growing chasm between the subjective *I*, which decides what identity it will create for itself, and the objective body that is worked on as the product to achieve these ends. The unwitting outcome is the renewal of the religion of gnosticism, with its own special elite of priest/experts, today's technocrats and scientist kings. These are the people that philosopher José Ortega y Gasset described as "totalitarian scientists" because they expand the prestige of their real knowledge to pretend that it covers the whole of life. From the creation of the pill to the latest advances of the scalpel, cosmetic surgery, and radical enhancement, to the near- and far-term dreams of biogenetic engineering, artificial intelligence, and cyborgs, technology has long aided and abetted the promise of infinite and endless possibility. But now the *I* and its feelings are hailed as sovereign, and the biological body we were born with loses its integrity and becomes mere spare parts for its starry-eyed constructor man-gods. At best, bodies will be "disposable escape pods that will have done their job if they keep us alive just long enough to achieve electronic immortality."[14]

Body bad—mind good. Biological body unwanted—newly minted identity desirable and possible. Body limited—digitally enhanced mind infinite, soaring, and unstoppable. Together, hi-tech innovation, social constructionism, the gender revolution, bioengineering, the internet, and the feelings culture are collaborating to build a shining launch pad for the new gnosticism. Already they are advertising their free ride to immortality and the stars. Little wonder that its devotees call such heady optimism the "new religion" of Silicon Valley, the "religion of humanism" or "the religion of dataism."[15] "Eventually," Harari writes, "the Internet-of-All-Things may become sacred in its own right"—the Tower of Babel in its advanced modern form.[16]

Early aspects of these seven trends and developments are already coursing through American society, and the leading progressives who pursue these goals need to be reminded how the naivety of such utopian revolutionaries usually ends in the revolution devouring its own children. The world too should be put on notice as to where they are leading "the land of the free," for the first words of the writing on the wall are already visible. If the drive for so-called natural freedom proceeds unchecked, America will be rushing lemming-like to a state of nature somewhere between Thomas Hobbes, Jean-Jacques Rousseau, Weimar Germany, and the Israel of the book of Judges when "there was no king in Israel; everyone did what was right in his own eyes" (Judg 21:25).

Under that scenario, the prospects for the once-great American republic and for the world are grave. The degeneration of America and American leadership over the last few decades is all too evident, leaving a yawning vacuum for the strong man or the powerful elite. What matters is who or what takes over from 1776. Berthold Brecht wrote prophetically in 1941 in *The Resistible Rise of Arturo Ui*, "Do not rejoice in his defeat, you men. For though the word has stood up and stopped the bastard, the bitch that bore him is in heat again." All who love and admire America should ponder the ancient maxim: *The worst is the corruption of the best.*

The Earth, a Footnote to History?

Visitors to the National Museum of Natural History in Washington, DC, often tread on one of the most interesting exhibits without ever noticing it. It is embedded in the floor of the Hall of Biodiversity. The exhibit is arranged around a plaque that notes that there have been five major extinction events on the earth since complex animals emerged, each extinction surrounded with the remains of the victims. It then announces, "Right now we are in the midst of the Sixth Extinction, this time caused solely by humanity's trans-formation of the ecological landscape." Among supporting quotations is a statement of Paul Ehrlich, the ecologist from Stanford University, "In pushing other species to extinction, humanity is busy sawing off the limb on which it perches." What *Homo sapiens* did to other animals and to the rest of nature, our own advances and developments are threatening to do to us. "Looking back, humanity will turn out to have been just a ripple within the cosmic data flow."[17]

In her Pulitzer Prize–winning book *The Sixth Extinction*, Elizabeth Kolbert reflects on the fact that if a visitor stands at the edge of the exhibit, the only place from which to see it well, "you are positioned right where the victims of the Sixth Extinction should go."[18] The point is as plain as it is poignant. We humans are both the dangerous species and the endangered species. We may deny that we humans are made in the image of God or have any special status as anything more than another animal species, but in doing so we have achieved our own dark special status as the one species that can threaten all other species—though the victims will also be us. People may argue over how *Homo sapiens* arrived at this point and what we should do to avoid mutually assured destruction, but the point is becoming unassailable. With the grand issues of the global era converging to create an enormous crunch of questions and problems, the coming generation is the crunch generation whose choices will be critical to the future of humanity and to the earth that is our home.

It is a paradox that the same people who take this issue seriously when the focus is the future of the earth often appear astonishingly careless when the focus is the future of freedom—though a similar warning resonates through the Bible, the classics, and down the centuries of history. Freedom has always been the greatest enemy of freedom. Powerful free people are brought down by no one but themselves. America still stands before the inescapable truth of Lincoln's prophetic comment: "As a nation of free men, either we shall live free for all time, or die by suicide."[19] Americans must therefore ask themselves, What have we done that makes the danger so possible, and what can we do in our time to make the danger impossible?

The Recovenanting of America

There is of course a more hopeful possibility: the recovenanting of America, or the renewal of the American covenant of freedom, which could lead to a genuine new birth of freedom and justice. Without a renewal of the American ideas and ideals, America will never become great again, however prodigious the effort. *As with other covenantal societies, the truth is that the United States goes forward best by going back first. It must return to its roots in constitutional or covenantal freedom, renewing the ideals that made it possible, and righting the wrongs where America has betrayed its founding promise. By recovenanting and going back first, the United States is in fact able to go forward.*

Properly understood, recovenanting is progressive. Covenantalism and constitutionalism acknowledge the past with gratitude, but they do not remain in the past. There is no golden age they wish to return to. Renewed by the wellsprings of the past, they are partly conservative, but as they strive for a future that includes the best of the past that is still to be achieved, they are partly progressive, in the best sense of the word. Never simply people of the past, they are not yet fully people of the future, so there is always more to do, always more to strive for.

Humans do not keep promises well, so covenants can be broken and betrayed, and constitutions can be destroyed. But both covenants and constitutions can be restored and renewed, and mistakes and evils acknowledged, confessed, and put right. Over against the unquestionable reality of today's spiraling cycle of racial injustice, grievance, and resentment, for example, there can be national repentance, forgiveness, and rededication to freedom and equality for all. America can return to its right mind. America's abiding curse of racism can finally be resolved and not perpetuated forever. Hard though it may be for the proud to swallow, there are times when a covenantal nation requires penitential citizens, and without it there is no way forward.

Strong renewal is always possible, and repentance and forgiveness are realistic and can lead to a genuine return and true homecoming. No one who knows the history of the Jews can be anything other than awed by the near-miraculous way their covenant kept them intact down the centuries, across the continents, and in spite of the most the most extreme scattering and the most vicious persecution. In the words of Rabbi Sacks, "*Covenant renewal defeats national entropy. A people that never forgets its purpose and its past, that reenacts its story in every family every year, a nation that attributes its success to God and its failures to itself, cannot die.*"[20]

For those Americans who agree with Rabbi Sacks, the words "God keeps faith" contain a double truth. God keeps his word, yes, absolutely. Behind the universe itself, behind all that is, all that has ever been, and all that ever could and will be, there is one whose word truly is his bond, a promise maker who is the ultimate promise keeper. Life itself, the existence of the universe, and science all depend on that covenant. That is the immediate truth in the words, but there is an ultimate truth too. *God keeps faith with his people and with humanity. So we have faith in God. But God also has faith in us and, despite us, keeps faith with us.*

God keeps faith with humanity? There is an immensity of hope in that second covenantal truth. Contemporary descriptions of post-Auschwitz, post-Hiroshima, pre-singularity humanity tend to be dark and fearful, and the present state of the global affairs offers meager grounds for revising the estimate. "Man has very few friends in the world," Rabbi Heschel remarked dryly. "The Lord in heaven may prove to be his last friend on earth."[21] Or, as he put it in an unforgettable image, humanity is "the knot in which heaven and earth are interlaced."[22] Many Americans have no concern for God, but the good news is that God still has a concern for Americans and America.

History shows beyond a shadow of doubt that it is utopians such as Jean-Jacques Rousseau, Karl Marx, Wilhelm Reich, and Mao Zedong who cause the greatest havoc. They start out seeing no problem in humanity, only certain chains restraining natural human goodness and freedom. But in trying to remove the chains, they end in producing history's most egregious evils, most dismal failures, and most murderous regimes. They attempt to storm the stubborn gap between the real and the utopian dream, and end in violence. By contrast, it is the one who knows the worst about us from the start, who understands the radical inclinations of the human heart, who takes into account the crooked timber of our humanity, who still keeps faith with us despite everything. In spite of all that we humans have done to each other, have done to our fellow creatures, and have done to the earth that is our planet home, God still keeps faith with humanity. That is the covenant that the original rainbow affirms. That is the truth that ensures that no situation is beyond hope and no crisis should ever be written off as hopeless— even America's today.

Will a covenantal and constitutional renewal take place in America as the century unfolds? Is there an American leader with the vision, the courage, and the knowledge of history to be the covenant restorer in the land? Is there a statesman who understands the genius of the American republic, and knows the challenges and failures of the American experiment, who can appeal to the better angels of the American character, righting what was wrong at the start and rebuilding what has been lost or destroyed in its recent history? Is there a champion who has the courage to alert the country to the siren seductions of false freedoms and call America to a "new, new birth" of freedom? And if such a leader were to issue such a call, would it still have the resonance to rouse the American people from their anxiety, apathy, and anger even now? Could there be an American renaissance on the horizon? Could America rise to be a partnership-for-freedom nation again?

Both commentators and gamblers would agree. The present odds of American leaders leading and American followers following, so that there is a successful restoration of the ideals of the American republic, are long—very long. The repudiation of the past is too hardened, the present wounds are too deep and raw, the alternative options are too entrenched, and many Americans simply prefer to keep their heads down and muddle through as best they can. But freedom is never a matter of the odds. If it were, Lexington, Concord, Yorktown, and the "miracle at Philadelphia" would never have happened in the first place. Freedom is a matter of leadership, choice, and courage, whatever the odds, and also a matter of faith, for the last freedom is always the freedom to pit personal determination against circumstances, however dire they seem. As we have seen with Abraham Lincoln and Winston Churchill, genuine leadership could change the landscape almost overnight.

Daniel Elazar did more than anyone to rediscover the influence of the covenantal tradition that is the missing key to American freedom. He liked to remind his readers that covenants originated in a culture of oases. What characterizes an oasis is that it is centered in a spring that is the source of its water and its life. No oasis is ever larger, more luxuriant, and longer lasting then the strength of the wellspring at its center—and neither is the nation whose form of government is a covenant or a constitution. If America is to be made great again, it will only be through remembering what made America great in the first place and renewing both the covenant and the relationship to the faith that was and is its wellspring.

The challenge of the present moment therefore confronts Americans with a titanic choice: covenant, chaos, or control? Renewal or decline? Wellspring or social and cultural desert? The coming generation will be the crunch generation for freedom, just as they will also be part of the crunch generation for the future of the world. Will Americans return to their right minds, remember what freedom is, and rededicate themselves to shoulder the responsibility that freedom requires of every citizen?

It is therefore time for Americans to pause and to think. The gravity of the present *kairos* moment lies not just in its stakes but in its singular uniqueness as a moment. The freedom of the American experiment hangs by a thread. The present moment is singular as well as momentous in its significance. There is a decisive parting of the ways over freedom, and the present generation has to make its choice. Freedom is never a fait accompli or a "mission accomplished." "If not for this very moment" (and the choices Americans make now), future generations will say, the story of freedom would be different.

All who came before you in your history, all who will come after you, including your children and your children's children, and all across the world who long to live in freedom as you have, call on you to consider things well and to rise to the challenge of this hour. America, your striking genius for freedom has become your Achilles' heel and now threatens your premature and quite unnecessary decline. Ponder the choice between 1776 and 1789 with care. Think again and look to what needs to be restored before the darkness falls on your great experiment in republican freedom. This is your hour, the American hour, and a moment on which everything turns. There is a way before you that can lead to renewal and restoration, or one that leads to decadence and decline. The choice that you must make is yours and yours alone. So also will be the consequences.

Choose, then, America, whether you wish to stay true to the better angels of your founding promise and shoulder the burden of being the world's beacon of responsible and enduring freedom. Choose whether you desire life or death, blessings or curses, freedom and flourishing or chaos and decline. Choose as the Jews chose before you and your early American ancestors chose in their turn whether you will again be "a city on a hill" or become "a story and byword throughout the world."

America, America. Do you know what time it is? Do you understand the meaning of this moment? Freedom is at stake. Act worthy of yourselves, your great experiment in freedom, your unfinished story, and the challenge of the hour and of humanity. God, history, and the watching world await your answer. In the words of your greatest president, will you as a free people do what it takes to live free forever, or will you die by your own hand? Will you listen, reflect, and turn around, or will you continue to rush headlong toward, like Rome, a fall beyond belief? The hour for your decision is now.

ACKNOWLEDGMENTS

*I*t doesn't take a village to write a book, but it certainly helps to live as part of a rich community of thinking friends whose presence has been a constant spur to thoughtfulness and discernment over many years. Among those I am especially aware of in writing this book are the following: John and Julia Anderson, Will and Debs Andrews, John and Donna Bechtel, Barry Black, Don and Carolyn Bonker, John and Nancy Brandon, Barbara Bryant, Nick and Annie Chance, Shelby and Mary Lee Coffey, Jenny Cromartie, Sarah Davis, Danielle DuRant, Bill and Barbara Edgar, Harry and Minerva Edwards, Caroline Firestone, Steve and Polly Friess, Troy and Angelique Griepp, Nabil and Peggy Haddad, Jamie and Andy Haith, Charles Haynes, Ann Holladay, Madeline Jackson, Peb and Sharon Jackson, Greg Jesson, Tim Keller, Dick and Mardi Keyes, Hooman Khalili, John and Sarah Kim, Bob and Diane Kramer, Phil and Moyne Lawson-Johnston, John and Sally Lennox, Joe Loconte, Stuart and Celia McAlpine, Jack and Kathy Macdonough, Dick and Mary Ohman, Frog and Amy Orr-Ewing, Dean and Linda Overman, Ryon and Jan Paton, Rich and Christine Park, Michael and Anne Ramsden, Erik and Kristen Rannala, Malcolm and Karis Riley, Mark and Leanne Rodgers, Skip and Barbara Ryan, Birgitte Santaella, David and Tina Segel, Tim and Rebecca Shah, Jim Sire, Tom and Lyn Shields, Bud and Jane Smith, Fred Smith, Ian and Rosemary Smith, Suzelle Smith, Tom Tarrants, Prue and Edwina Thompson, Caroline Trevor, Ralph and Lynne Veerman, David and Mary Virtue, Rick Warren, David and Jane Wells, Woody White, Bill and Dana Wichterman, Don and Patty Wolf, Frank and Carolyn Wolf, John and Susan Yates, Daniel Young, David and Suzy Young, Davy and Ashley Young, Glenn and Suzanne Youngkin, and Ravi and Margie Zacharias. A long list admittedly, but friendship owes its debts.

There are some people, however, without whom this book would never have come to life in the form it has, and I am especially grateful to the following: Mary Lee Coffey, Bill Edgar, Kurt Jaros, and Dick Ohman, whose initial reading and candid reviews of the book saved me from many blunders and strengthened my hand at the hardest stage of the writing, and Bud and Jane Smith, whose magnificent Dallas library was the inspiring setting for writing a key part of this book.

As always, I am deeply indebted to my friendly and tireless literary agent, Erik Wolgemuth, and to Jeff Crosby, Al Hsu, Drew Blankman, Alisse Wissman, Ellen Hsu, Elissa Schauer, and the incomparable team at InterVarsity Press.

And always and supremely, my beloved family, Jenny and CJ, and special thanks to Jenny, who in this case was brilliant in editing as well as unfailing in love.

NOTES

Introduction

[1] Thomas Sowell, *The Quest for Cosmic Justice* (New York: Simon & Schuster, 1999), 189.

[2] John Emerich Edward Dalberg-Acton, *Essays in the History of Liberty*, ed. J. Rufus Fears (Indianapolis: Liberty Fund, 1985), 1:xix.

[3] For example, Jonathan Sacks, *The Home We Build Together: Recreating Society* (London: Continuum, 2007), 37; and Gabrielle Kuby, *The Global Sexual Revolution: Destruction of Freedom in the Name of Freedom* (Kettering, OH: LifeSite, 2012).

[4] Personal conversation with a European ambassador at the United Nations, September 2014.

[5] Abraham Lincoln, in his Address at a Sanitary Fair, Baltimore, April 18, 1864.

[6] Abraham Lincoln, "Address to the Young Men's Lyceum of Springfield, Illinois," in *The American Republic: Primary Sources*, ed. Bruce Frohnen (Indianapolis: Liberty Fund, 2002), 518-22.

[7] See, for example, James Davison Hunter and Carl Desportes Bowman, *The Vanishing Center of American Democracy: 2016 Survey of American Political Culture* (Charlottesville, VA: Institute of Advanced Studies in Culture, 2017).

[8] Daniel J. Elazar, *Covenant and Commonwealth: From Christian Separation Through the Protestant Reformation* (New Brunswick, NJ: Transaction Publishers, 1996), 137.

[9] Abraham Lincoln, Letter to H. L. Pierce, April 1859, in *Collected Works of Abraham Lincoln*, ed. Roy P. Basler, The Abraham Lincoln Association, 2006.

[10] See Joseph J. Ellis, *The Quartet: Orchestrating the Second American Revolution* (New York: Vintage Books, 2016), 13; Ernest Lee Tuveson, *Redeemer Nation* (Chicago: University of Chicago Press, 1968), 156; Thomas Jefferson, *The Papers of Thomas Jefferson*, 4:237; Abraham Lincoln, "Gettysburg Address," 1863; Herman Melville, *White-Jacket* (Oxford: Oxford University Press, 1967), 153; and John Fitzgerald Kennedy, address to be delivered at the Trade Mart in Dallas on November 22, 1963, "Full Text: JFK's Never-Delivered Speech from Dallas," *Pittsburgh Post-Gazette*, November 21, 2013—he was assassinated before he reached his destination.

[11] Henry Kissinger, *World Order* (New York: Penguin, 2014), 373.

[12] Shelby Steele, *Shame: How America's Past Sins Have Polarized Our Country* (New York: Basic Books, 2015), 198.

Question One: Do You Know Where Your Freedom Came From?

[1]Winston Churchill, quoted in James C. Humes, *The Wit and Wisdom of Winston Churchill* (New York: HarperCollins, 1994), 183.

[2]See Daniel Hannan, *Inventing Freedom: How the English-Speaking Peoples Made the Modern World* (New York: HarperCollins, 2013).

[3]John Adams, *The Political Writings of John Adams* (New York: Liberal Arts Press, 1954), 68.

[4]J. R. Tanner, *English Constitutional Conflicts of the Seventeenth Century* (Cambridge: Cambridge University Press, 1962), 63.

[5]William Penn, quoted in Hannan, *Inventing Freedom*, 127.

[6]Susan Sontag, quoted in Jonah Goldberg, *Liberal Fascism: The Secret History of the American Left from Mussolini to the Politics of Meaning* (New York: Doubleday, 2007), 369.

[7]Ibid., 368.

[8]Abiel Abbot, quoted in Jonathan Sacks, *The Jonathan Sacks Haggadah* (New Milford, CT: Maggid, 2003), 77.

[9]Heinrich Heine, quoted in ibid., 76.

[10]Friedrich Nietzsche, *On the Genealogy of Morals*, trans. Douglas Smith (Oxford: Oxford University Press, 1996), 20.

[11]Sacks, *Jonathan Sacks Haggadah*, 9.

[12]Daniel J. Elazar, *Covenant and Polity in Biblical Israel* (New Brunswick, NJ: Transaction Publishers, 1995), xiii; and Daniel J. Elazar, *Covenant and Constitutionalism: The Great Frontier and the Matrix of Federal Democracy* (New Brunswick, NJ: Transaction Publishers, 1998), xi.

[13]Elazar, *Covenant and Constitutionalism*, 15; and Michael Walzer, *In God's Shadow: Politics in the Hebrew Bible* (New Haven, CT: Yale University Press, 2012), cited in ibid., 200.

[14]Elazar, *Covenant and Commonwealth*, 22.

[15]Walzer, *In God's Shadow*, 5.

[16]Plato, *The Republic*, 3:415, trans. G. M. A. Grube, revised by C. D. C. Reeve (Indianapolis: Hackett, 1992), 91.

[17]Abraham Joshua Heschel, *God in Search of Man: A Philosophy of Judaism* (New York: Farrar, Strauss & Giroux, 1955), 423.

[18]Jonathan Sacks, *To Heal a Fractured World: The Ethics of Responsibility* (New York: Schocken, 2005), 154.

[19]Michael Walzer, *Exodus and Revolution* (New York: Basic Books, 1985), 97.

[20]Walzer, *In God's Shadow*, 210.

[21]Ibid., 4.

[22]Jonathan Sacks, *Covenant and Conversation: Exodus, the Book of Redemption* (New Milford, CT: Maggid, 2010), 14.

[23]Jonathan Sacks, *Essays on Ethics: A Weekly Reading of the Jewish Bible* (New Milford, CT: Maggid, 2016), 133.

[24]Elazar, *Covenant and Polity*, 24.

[25]Oswald Spengler, *The Decline of the West*, trans. Charles Atkinson (New York: Alfred Knopf, 1928), 3:105; emphasis added.

[26]Jonathan Sacks, *Ceremony and Celebration: Introduction to the Holidays* (New York: Maggid, 2017), 56.

[27]William Perkins, quoted in Elazar, *Covenant and Commonwealth*, 239.

[28]John Leland, "The Rights of Conscience Inalienable," in *The American Republic: Primary Sources*, ed. Bruce Frohnen (Indianapolis: Liberty Fund, 2002), 85.

[29]Alexis de Tocqueville, *Democracy in America*, trans. Arthur Goldhammer (Boone, IA: Library of America, 2014), 2:343.

[30]Adams, *Political Writings of John Adams*, 95.

[31]John Adams, quoted in Jonathan Sacks, *Radical Then, Radical Now: On Being Jewish* (London: Bloomsbury, 2000), 3.

[32]Roland Hill, *Lord Acton* (New Haven, CT: Yale University Press, 2000), 65.

[33]Sacks, *Ceremony and Celebration*, 66.

[34]Elazar, *Covenant and Commonwealth*, 150-51.

[35]Tocqueville, *Democracy in America*, 1:13.

[36]Ibid., 338.

[37]Ibid., 341.

[38]Ibid., 30.

[39]Sacks, *Jonathan Sacks Haggadah*, 16-17.

[40]Sacks, *Ceremony and Celebration*, 169.

[41]Niccolò Machiavelli, *The Prince*, bk. 18, trans. George Bull (London: Penguin, 1999), 73-77.

[42]David Hume, *Treatise on Human Nature*, bk. 3, section 4.

[43]Thomas Hobbes, *Leviathan* (Harmondsworth, UK: Penguin, 1986), 132.

[44]G. W. F. Hegel, quoted in Benjamin Wiker, *Worshipping the State: How Liberalism Became Our State Religion* (Washington, DC: Regnery, 2013), 212.

[45]Ernst Arndt, quoted in ibid., 212.

[46]G. K. Chesterton, quoted ibid., 327.

[47]Christopher Dawson, *Beyond Politics* (New York: Sheed & Ward, 1939), 18.

[48]Abraham Lincoln, *Collected Works*, ed. Roy P. Basler (New Brunswick, NJ: Rutgers University Press, 1953), 4:239.

[49]Samuel Johnson, quoted in Anne Midgley, "How Is It That We Hear the Loudest Yelps for Liberty Among the Drivers of Negroes?," *Saber and Scroll* 5, no. 3 (2016), article 10, https://digitalcommons.apus.edu/saberandscroll/vol5/iss3/10.

[50]Frederick Douglass, "What to the Slave Is the Fourth of July? (1852)," in *The*

Portable Frederick Douglass, ed. John Stauffer and Henry Louis Gates Jr. (New York: Penguin Random House, 2016), 195.

[51]Joseph J. Ellis, *The Quartet: Orchestrating the Second American Revolution* (New York: Vintage Books, 2016), 141.

[52]Martin Diamond, *As Far as Republican Principles Will Admit*, ed. William A. Schambra (Washington, DC: AEI Press, 1992), 71.

[53]G. K. Chesterton, *Heretics* (Mineola, NY: Dover, 2006), 14.

[54]T. S. Eliot, *The Rock* (London: Faber & Faber, 1934), 51.

[55]Martin Luther King Jr., sermon at Temple Israel of Hollywood, February 26, 1965.

[56]Dean Acheson, quoted in Erik von Kuehnelt-Leddihn, *The Intelligent American's Guide to Europe* (New Rochelle, NY: Arlington House, 1979), 407.

[57]John Winthrop, "A Modell of Christian Charity," in *The American Puritans*, ed. Perry Miller (Garden City, NY: Doubleday, 1956), 82.

[58]Lyndon B. Johnson, "The President's Inaugural Address," January 20, 1965, online by Gerhard Peters and John T. Woolley, The American Presidency Project, www .presidency.ucsb.edu/ws/index.php?pid=26985.

[59]Roger Scruton, *Fools, Frauds and Firebrand: Thinkers of the New Left* (London: Bloomsbury, 2015), 1.

[60]H. Richard Niebuhr, "The Idea of Covenant and American Democracy," *Church History* 23 (June 1954): 133.

Question Two: Are There Enough Americans Who Care About Freedom?

[1]Saul D. Alinsky, *Rules for Radicals* (New York: Vintage Books, 1989), xiii.

[2]Abraham Joshua Heschel, *God in Search of Man: A Philosophy of Judaism* (New York: Farrar, Strauss & Giroux, 1955), 389.

[3]Ibid.

[4]Ibid.

[5]Michael Walzer, *In God's Shadow: Politics in the Hebrew Bible* (New Haven, CT: Yale University Press, 2012), 62.

[6]John Winthrop, "City upon on a Hill," sermon delivered July 2, 1630, www .greatamericandocuments.com/speeches/winthrop-city-upon-hill/.

[7]Sherry Turkle, *Alone Together* (New York: Basic Books, 2011), 278.

[8]James Madison, quoted in Forrest McDonald, *Novus Ordo Seclorum: The Intellectual Origins of the Constitution* (Lawrence: University Press of Kansas, 1985), 6.

[9]Benjamin Franklin, quoted in ibid., 6.

[10]George Washington, *Documents of American History*, ed. Henry Steele Commager (New York: Prentice-Hall, 1963), 152.

[11]Walt Whitman, quoted in Robert N. Bellah, *The Broken Covenant: American Civil Religion in Time of Trial* (Chicago: University of Chicago Press, 1975), 139.

[12]Roger Scruton, *England: An Elegy* (London: Bloomsbury Academic, 2006), 16.

[13]G. K. Chesterton, *Heretics* (Mineola, NY: Dover, 2006), 21.

[14]Alexander Hamilton, *The Federalist Papers*, in *The American Republic: Primary Sources*, ed. Bruce Frohnen (Indianapolis: Liberty Fund, 2002), 241-42.

[15]McDonald, *Novus Ordo Seclorum*, 10.

Question Three: What Do You Mean by Freedom?

[1]John Emerich Edward Dalberg-Acton, *Essays in the History of Liberty*, ed. Rufus Fears (Indianapolis: Liberty Fund, 1985), 7.

[2]Friedrich Hayek, *The Constitution of Liberty* (Chicago: University of Chicago Press, 1960), 18-19.

[3]Jonathan Sacks, *Ceremony and Celebration: Introduction to the Holidays* (New York: Maggid, 2017), 35.

[4]Friedrich Nietzsche, *On the Genealogy of Morals: A Polemic*, trans. Douglas Smith (Oxford: Oxford University Press, 1996), 39-40.

[5]Ibid.

[6]Ibid., 67.

[7]Saul D. Alinsky, *Rules for Radicals* (New York: Vintage Books, 1989), 49-50.

[8]Augustine, *City of God* (New York: Doubleday, 1958), 40.

[9]Alinsky, *Rules for Radicals*, xxi.

[10]*Elane Photography, LLC v. Vanessa Willock*, Supreme Court of the State of New Mexico, August 22, 2013, 30.

[11]Thucydides, "Pericles' Funeral Oration" from "The History of the Peloponnesian War," 431 BC.

[12]Thucydides, "The Melian Conference" from "The History of the Peloponnesian War," 431 BC.

[13]Ibid.

[14]George Orwell, quoted in Thomas E. Ricks, *Churchill and Orwell: The Fight for Freedom* (New York: Penguin, 2017), 50.

[15]Lord Acton, quoted in Roland Hill, *Lord Acton* (New Haven, CT: Yale University Press, 2000), 300.

[16]Andrew Bard Schmookler, *The Parable of the Tribes: The Problem of Power in Social Evolution* (Berkeley: University of California Press, 1984), 22.

[17]Ibid., 22.

[18]Abraham Joshua Heschel, *God in Search of Man: A Philosophy of Judaism* (New York: Farrar, Strauss & Giroux, 1955), 364.

[19]Jonathan Sacks, *Essays on Ethics: A Weekly Reading of the Jewish Bible* (New Milford, CT: Maggid, 2016), xxiv.

[20]Jonathan Sacks, *Covenant and Conversation: Exodus, the Book of Redemption* (New Milford, CT: Maggid, 2010), 49.

[21]Booker T. Washington, *Up from Slavery* (Tampa, FL: Millennium Publications, 2015), 70.

[22]Ibid.

[23]Abraham Joshua Heschel, *The Insecurity of Freedom: Essays on Human Existence* (New York: Farrar, Strauss & Giroux, 1967), 14.

[24]G. K. Chesterton, *Orthodoxy* (New York: John Lane, 1921), 86.

[25]Henry David Thoreau, February 15, 1851 entry, in *The Journal of Henry David Thoreau*, ed. Bradford Torrey and Francis H. Allen (Boston: Houghton Mifflin, 1949), 2:162.

[26]Henry David Thoreau, *Walden and On the Duty of Civil Disobedience*, ed. Charles R. Anderson (New York: Signet Classics, 2012), 51.

[27]John Gray, quoted in Richard Lofthouse, "Forget Your Delusions and Be Happy, Advises John Gray," *Oxford Today*, December 21, 2015, www.oxfordtoday.ox.ac.uk /opinion/forget-your-delusions-and-be-happy-advises-john-gray#.

[28]Jean-Jacques Rousseau, *The Social Contract*, trans. Maurice Cranston (Harmondsworth, UK: Penguin, 1968), 49.

[29]Jonathan Sacks, *Covenant and Conversation: Genesis, the Book of Beginnings* (New Milford, CT: Maggid, 2009), 71.

[30]Heschel, *Insecurity of Freedom*, 15.

[31]John Adams, "The Real American Revolution," in *The Works of John Adams: Second President of the United States* (Boston: Little, 1856).

[32]"California: Designing Freedom," Museum of Design, London, June 2017.

[33]Roger Scruton, *Fools, Frauds and Firebrands* (London: Bloomsbury, 2017), 106.

[34]Jonathan Sacks, *Essays on Ethics*, 49.

[35]Augustine, *The Confessions*, bk. 8, 5.

[36]Walter Scott, *Marmion* (New York: Houghton Mifflin, 1896), 205.

Question Four: Have You Faced Up to the Central Paradox of Freedom?

[1]See Abraham Lincoln's "Gettysburg Address," 1863.

[2]William Wordsworth, "The Prelude," bk. 10.

[3]Charles James Fox, quoted in L. G. Mitchell, "Fox, Charles James (1749–1806)," in *Oxford Dictionary of National Biography* (Oxford: Oxford University Press, 2004).

[4]Paul Rahe Soft, *Despotism, Democracy's Drift: Montesquieu, Rousseau, Tocqueville and the Modern Prospect* (New Haven, CT: Yale University Press, 2009), 38.

[5]Ibid.

[6]Plato, *The Republic*, Book 8.561-64, trans. G. M. A. Grube, revised by C. D. C. Reeve (Indianapolis: Hackett, 1992).

[7]Michael Walzer, *Exodus and Revolution* (New York: Basic Books, 1985), 52-53.

[8]Christopher Dawson, *Beyond Politics* (New York: Sheed & Ward, 1939), 3.

[9]Ibid., 40.

[10]Erich H. Fromm, *Escape from Freedom* (New York: Henry Holt, 1969), x.

[11]Ibid., 4.

[12]Ibid., 3.

[13]Erik von Kuehnelt-Leddihn, *Liberty or Equality: The Challenge of Our Time* (Auburn, AL: Ludwig von Mises Institute, 2007), 24.

[14]Robespierre, quoted in Erik von Kuehnelt-Leddihn, *Leftism Revisited* (Washington, DC: Regnery Gateway, 1990), 71.

[15]Klemens von Metternich, quoted in ibid., 75.

[16]Ali Ahmad Said Esber (Adonis), quoted in David P. Goldman, *Why Civilizations Die (and Why Islam Is Dying Too)* (Washington, DC: Regnery, 2011), 148-49.

[17]Alexis de Tocqueville, *Democracy in America*, vol. 2.

Question Five: How Do You Plan to Sustain Freedom?

[1]Simon Bolivar, quoted in Erik von Kuehnelt-Leddihn, *Leftism Revisited* (Washington, DC: Regnery Gateway, 1990), 324.

[2]Some content in this chapter first appeared in Os Guinness, *A Free People's Suicide: Sustainable Freedom and the American Future* (Downers Grove, IL: InterVarsity Press, 2012). Used with permission.

[3]Charles Louis de Secondat, Baron de Montesqieu, *Complete Works*, vol. 1, *The Spirit of Laws*, 6.28.41, 1748.

[4]Thomas Jefferson, letter to George Washington, April 16, 1784, in *The Papers of Thomas Jefferson*, ed. Julian P. Boyd, vol. 18.4 (Princeton, NJ: Princeton University Press, 1971), 397.

[5]Abraham Lincoln, quoted in *And I Quote*, ed. Ashton White et al. (New York: Thomas Dunne Books, 2003), 268.

[6]George III, quoted in Gore Vidal, *Inventing a Nation: Washington, Adams, and Jefferson* (New Haven, CT: Yale University Press, 2003), 3.

[7]Henry Lee, "Speech Delivered to the U.S. Congress on George Washington's Death," December 14, 1799, in Frank E. Grizzard Jr., *George! A Guide to All Things Washington* (Charlottesville, VA: Mariner, 2005), 110.

[8]John Adams, "Reply to Congress After Washington's Death," December 23, 1799, in *The Wisdom of John Adams*, ed. Kees de Mooy (New York: Citadel, 2003), 254.

[9]Alexander Hamilton, *The Works of Alexander Hamilton*, ed. Henry Cabot Lodge (New York: G. P. Putnam, 1904), 2:444.

[10]Joseph de Maistre, quoted in John Gray, *Heresies: Against Progress and Other Illusions* (London: Granta Books, 2005), 145.

[11]Thomas Jefferson, "Letter to James Madison," September 6, 1789, in *Our Sacred Honor*, ed. William J. Bennett (New York: Simon & Schuster, 1997), 342.

[12]Learned Hand, "The Spirit of Liberty," in *Learned Hand, The Spirit of Liberty: Papers and Addresses*, ed. Irving Dilliard (New York: Random House, 1962), 189-92.

[13]Montesquieu, quoted in Paul A. Rahe, *Republics Ancient and Modern: Classical Republicanism and the American Revolution* (Chapel Hill: University of North Carolina Press, 1992), 17.

[14]Alexander Hamilton, *The Papers of Alexander Hamilton*, vol. 3.103, *The Continentalist* no. 6 (July 4, 1782).

[15]T. S. Eliot, *The Rock* (London: Faber & Faber, 1934), 42.

[16]Montesquieu, *Spirit of Laws*, 1.3.6.

[17]Bernard Mandeville, *The Fable of the Bees* (London: Penguin Books, 1989), 47, 51.

[18]Bernard Bailyn, *To Begin the World Anew: The Genius and Ambiguities of the American Framers* (New York: Alfred A. Knopf, 2003), 34.

[19]Edmund Burke, "First Letter on Regicidal Peace," in The *Wisdom of Edmund Burke: Extracts from His Speeches and Writings,* ed. Edward Pankhurst (London: John Murray, 1886), 171.

[20]Jean-Jacques Rousseau, *The Social Contract*, trans. Maurice Cranston (Harmondsworth, UK: Penguin, 1968), 2.12.

[21]Alexis de Tocqueville, quoted in Hugh Brogan, *Alexis de Tocqueville: A Life* (New Haven, CT: Yale University Press, 2007), 272.

[22]John Quincy Adams, *The Memoirs of John Quincy Adams,* ed. Charles Francis Adams (Philadelphia: 1874–1876).

[23]James Madison, debate in the Federal Convention, June 4, 1787, in *The Papers of James Madison,* ed. Henry D. Gilpin (Washington, DC: Langtree & Sullivan, 1840), 2:805.

[24]Benjamin Franklin, letter dated April 17, 1787, in *The Works of Benjamin Franklin,* ed. Jared Sparks (Chicago: Townsend Mac County, 1882), 287.

[25]Benjamin Franklin, quoted in David Hackett Fischer, *Liberty and Freedom* (New York: Oxford University Press, 2005), 185.

[26]John Adams, "Letter to Zabdiel Adams," June 21, 1776, in *Letters of Delegates to Congress, 1774–1789,* ed. Paul H. Smith (Washington, DC: Library of Congress, 1976).

[27]John Adams, letter to Mercy Otis Warren, April 16, 1776, *Papers of John Adams,* ed. Robert J. Taylor (Cambridge, MA: Harvard University Press, 1977), 4:124-25.

[28]Virginia Declaration of Rights, West's Encyclopedia of American Law (The Gale Group, Inc., 2005), www.encyclopedia.com/history/united-states-and-canada/us -history/virginia-declaration-rights-1776; and New Hampshire Bill of Rights, www.nh.gov/constitution/billofrights.html.

[29]Edwin Gaustad, *Faith of the Founders* (Waco, TX: Baylor University Press, 2004); and James Hutson, *The Founders on Religion* (Princeton, NJ: Princeton University Press, 2005).

[30]Edmund Burke, letter to Claude Francois de Rivarol, June 1, 1791, in *The Correspondence of Edmund Burke,* ed. Thomas W. Copeland (Chicago: University of Chicago Press, 1967), 6:265-70.

[31]George Washington, "First Inaugural Address," April 30, 1789, in David Ramsay, *The Life of George Washington* (Baltimore: Joseph Jewett & Cushing, 1832), 177.

[32]John Adams, *Diary and Autobiography of John Adams,* ed. L. H. Butterfield and Leonard C. Faber (Cambridge, MA: Belknap Press, 1961), entry from June 2, 1778.

[33]John Adams, "A Dissertation on the Canon and Feudal Law," in *The Political Writings of John Adams*, ed. George W. Carey (Washington, DC: Regnery, 2000), 13.

[34]Montesquieu, quoted in Paul A. Rahe, *Montesquieu and the Logic of Liberty* (New Haven, CT: Yale University Press, 2009), 36.

[35]Solon, quoted in Paul Woodruff, *First Democracy: The Challenge of an Ancient Idea* (Oxford: Oxford University Press, 2005), 69.

[36]Albert Camus, *The Myth of Sisyphus and Other Essays* (New York: Alfred A. Knopf, 1967), 66.

[37]George Reedy, *The Twilight of the Presidency* (New York: Word Publishing, 1970), 20.

[38]Len Colodny and Tom Shachtman, *The Forty Years War: The Rise and Fall of the Neocons, from Nixon to Obama* (New York: HarperCollins, 2009), 158.

[39]James Q. Wilson, *On Character* (Washington, DC: AEI Press, 1995), 23.

[40]Adams, "Letter to Zabdiel Adams."

[41]John Witherspoon, "The Dominion of Providence over the Passions of Men," in *Political Sermons of the American Founding Era: 1730-1805*, ed. Ellis Sandoz (Indianapolis: Liberty Fund, 1991), 549.

[42]Ibid.

[43]George Washington, "Farewell Address," in *A More Perfect Union: Documents in U.S. History*, ed. Paul Boller Jr. and Ronald Story (Boston: Houghton Mifflin, 1984).

[44]Ibid.

[45]Alexis de Tocqueville, quoted in Brogan, *Alexis de Tocqueville*, 320.

[46]Alexis de Tocqueville, *Democracy in America*, trans. Arthur Goldhammer (Boone, IA: Library of America, 2014), 2.1.3.

[47]Benjamin Rush, "Letter to John Adams," in Bennett, *Our Sacred Honor*, 88.

[48]William Cobbett, quoted in David A. Wilson, *Paine and Cobbett: The Transatlantic Connection* (Montreal: McGill-Queen's University Press, 1988), 178.

[49]Benjamin Franklin, "Letter to Unknown," July 3, 1786, in *The Writings of Benjamin Franklin*, ed. Albert Henry Smyth (New York: MacMillan, 1906), 9:522.

[50]George Washington, *Maxims of George Washington* (New York: Appleton, 1894), 341.

[51]John Adams, "Address to the Military," October 11, 1798, in William J. Federer, *America's God and Country: Encyclopedia of Quotations* (Coppell, TX: Fame Publishing, 1994), 10.

[52]John Jay, "Address to the American Bible Society," May 9, 1822, *The Correspondence and Public Paper of John Jay* (New York: G. P. Putnam and Sons, 1974), 484.

[53]Abigail Adams, quoted in O. E. Fuller, *Brave Men and Women: Their Struggles, Failures, and Triumphs*, 1884, 42-43.

[54]Thomas Jefferson, *Notes on the State of Virginia*, ed. David Waldstreicher (New York: Palgrave, 2002), 195.

[55]James Madison, "Speech in the Virginia Ratifying Convention," June 20, 1788, in *Advice to My Country* (Charlottesville, VA: University of Virginia Press, 1997), 24.

[56]Alexander Hamilton, *The Works of Alexander Hamilton*, ed. Henry Cabot Lodge (New York: G. P. Putnam, 1904), 277.

[57]Benjamin Franklin, "Letter to Ezra Stiles," March 1, 1790, *Autobiography and Other Writings*, ed. Ormond Seavey (New York: Oxford University Press, 1993), 353.

[58]Joel Barlow, quoted in Rahe, *Republics Ancient and Modern*, 753.

[59]Washington, "Farewell Address."

[60]Thomas Jefferson, letters to James Smith, December 8, 1822, *Memoir, Correspondence, and Miscellanies from the Papers of Thomas Jefferson* (Charlottesville, VA: F. Carr, 1829), 360.

[61]Roger Williams, "The Bloudy Tenent of Persecution," in Romeo Elton, *The Life of Roger Williams* (New York: G. Putnam, 1852), 67.

[62]James Madison, "Memorial and Remonstrance," in *The Mind of the Founder: Sources of the Political Thought of James Madison*, ed. Marvin Meyers (Waltham, MA: Brandeis University Press, 1981).

[63]John Adams, "Letter to John Quincy Adams," June 16, 1816, in Hutson, *Founders on Religion*, 20.

[64]Ibid.

[65]Alexander Hamilton, "The Stand III," April 7, 1798, in *The Papers of Alexander Hamilton*, ed. Harold C. Syrett (New York: Columbia University Press, 1974), 21:402.

[66]Voltaire, quoted in Gertrude Himmelfarb, *The Roads to Modernity: The British, French, and American Enlightenments* (New York: Alfred A. Knopf, 2004), 155.

[67]Ethan Allen, quoted in James Hutson, *Founders on Religion*, 96.

[68]Thomas Jefferson, quoted in Bernard Bailyn, *To Begin the World Anew*, 49.

[69]Dalberg-Acton, *Essays in the History of Liberty*, 1:30.

[70]Ibid., 93.

[71]See James Hutson, *Founders on Religion*, 165.

[72]Williams, "Bloudy Tenent of Persecution."

[73]James Madison, quoted in William Lee Miller, *First Liberty: Religion and the American Republic* (New York: Alfred A. Knopf, 1986), 143.

[74]Jonathan Sacks, *The Jonathan Sacks Haggadah* (New Milford, CT: Maggid, 2003), 15-17.

Question Six: How Will You Make the World Safe for Diversity?

[1]Roland Hill, *Lord Acton* (New Haven, CT: Yale University Press, 2000), 377.

[2]Joe Davidson, "Civil Rights or Religious Liberty—What's on Top?," *Washington Post*, September 9, 2016.

[3]Leon R. Kass, *The Beginning of Wisdom: Reading Genesis* (New York: Free Press, 2003), 28.

[4]Daniel J. Elazar, *Covenant and Polity in Biblical Israel* (New Brunswick, NJ: Transaction Publishers, 1995), 98.

[5]Abraham Joshua Heschel, *God in Search of Man: A Philosophy of Judaism* (New York: Farrar, Strauss & Giroux, 1955), 372.

[6]Jonathan Sacks, *Ceremony and Celebration: Introduction to the Holidays* (New York: Maggid, 2017), 51.

[7]Mark Tushnet, "Abandoning Defensive Crouch Liberal Constitutionalism," *Balkinization*, May 6, 2016, https://balkin.blogspot.com/2016/05/abandoning-defensive-crouch-liberal.html.

[8]Jacob Neusner, *Conservative, American, and Jewish: I Wouldn't Have It Any Other Way* (Lafayette, LA: Huntington House, 1993), 196.

[9]Ibid., 200.

[10]Ibid., 195.

[11]Richard Samuelson, "Who's Afraid of Religious Liberty?," *Mosaic*, August 1, 2016.

[12]See *Christianity and Freedom*, ed. Timothy Samuel Shah and Allen D. Hertzske (Cambridge: Cambridge University Press, 2016), 52-54, 62-66.

[13]Ibid., 63-64.

[14]John Lennon, "Imagine," *Imagine*, Apple, 1971.

[15]David Cohen, *J. B. Watson: The Founder of Behaviorism* (London: Routledge & Kegan Paul, 1979), 258.

[16]G. K. Chesterton, *Heretics* (Mineola, NY: Dover, 2006), 39-40.

[17]James Madison, quoted in *The American Republic: Primary Sources*, ed. Bruce Frohnen (Indianapolis: Liberty Fund, 2002), 328.

[18]*Elaine Photography v. Willock*, New Mexico Supreme Court, August 22, 2013.

[19]Some content in this chapter first appeared in Os Guinness, *The Global Public Square: Religious Freedom and the Making of a World Safe for Diversity* (Downers Grove, IL: InterVarsity Press, 2013). Used with permission.

[20]Joseph B. Soloveitchik, quoted in *Theological and Halakhic Reflections on the Holocaust*, ed. Bernard Rosenberg and Fred Heuman (New York: Ktav, 1992), 54.

[21]John N. Barry, *Roger Williams and the Creation of the American Soul* (New York: Viking, 2012).

[22]John Emerich Edward Dalberg-Acton, *The History of Freedom* (Fairford, UK: Echo Library, 2010), 41.

[23]The Task Force on International Religious Freedom of the Witherspoon Institute, *Religious Freedom: Why Now? Defending an Embattled Human Right* (Princeton, NJ: 2012), 28.

[24]Omar Ahmed, quoted in Art Moore, "Did CAIR Founder Say Islam to Rule America? Muslims Confront Ohmar Ahmad as Newspaper Stands by Story," WorldNetDaily.com, December 11, 2006, www.wnd.com/?page Id=39229.

[25]G. W. Leibnitz, quoted in Emil Brunner, *Christianity and Civilization* (London: Nisbet, 1947), 163.

[26]Terry Eagleton, *The Meaning of Life: A Very Short Introduction* (Oxford: Oxford University Press, 2007), 110.

[27]Christopher Francis Patten, quoted in Jonathan Wynne-Jones, "Lord Patten Attacks 'Intolerant' Secularists," *Daily Telegraph*, April 24, 2011.

[28]Roger Scruton, *Fools, Frauds and Firebrands: Thinkers of the New Left* (London: Bloomsbury, 2015), 204.

[29]Ibid., 200.

[30]Reinhold Niebuhr, *Moral Man and Immoral Society* (Louisville, KY: Westminster John Knox Press, 2013), 1.

Question Seven: How Do You Justify Your Vision of a Free and Open Society?

[1]Carrie Gracie, "Ugly US Election Race a Poor Ad for Democracy in China," BBC, October 24, 2016.

[2]Andrew Bard Schmookler, *The Parable of the Tribes: The Problem of Power in Social Evolution* (Berkeley: University of California Press, 1984), 21, emphasis added.

[3]Ibid., emphasis added.

[4]In Primo Levi's account of Auschwitz, the guard's statement of "here there is no why" represents the malignant evil of irrational and brutal authoritarianism; Primo Levi, *Survival in Auschwitz* (New York: Touchstone, 1958).

[5]Os Guinness, *The Global Public Square: Religious Freedom and the Making of a World Safe for Diversity* (Downers Grove, IL: InterVarsity Press, 2013).

Question Eight: Where Do You Ground Your Faith in Human Freedom?

[1]W. V. O. Quine, quoted in Reuben Hersh, *What Is Mathematics, Really?* (Oxford: Oxford University Press, 1997), 170.

[2]Terry Eagleton, *The Meaning of Life: A Very Short Introduction* (Oxford: Oxford University Press, 2007), 1.

[3]Friedrich Nietzsche, *Twilight of the Idols*, trans. R. J. Hollingdale (Harmondsworth, UK: Penguin, 1969), 3.

[4]Viktor Frankl, *Man's Search for Meaning* (Boston: Beacon, 2006), 98-99.

[5]Albert Camus, *The Myth of Sisyphus*, trans. Justin O'Brien (New York: Vintage Books, 1991), 3.

[6]Eagleton, *Meaning of Life*, 42.

[7]B. F. Skinner, *Beyond Freedom and Dignity* (New York: Penguin/Pelican, 1973), 196.

[8]Sam Harris, *Free Will* (New York: Free Press, 2012), 5.

[9]Albert Einstein, *The World as I See It* (New York: Citadel Books, 2006), 3, 4.

[10]Yuval Noah Harari, *Homo Deus: A Brief History of Tomorrow* (New York: Harper, 2017), 285, 293.

[11]Fyodor Dostoevsky, *A Writer's Diary*, trans. Kenneth Lantz (Evanston, IL: Northwestern University Press, 2009), 13.

[12]Henry P. Stapp, *Quantum Theory and Free Will* (Cham, Switzerland: Springer, 2017), xi, 79.

[13]G. K. Chesterton, *Heretics* (Mineola, NY: Dover, 2006), 75.

[14]Harris, *Free Will*, 64.

[15]Abraham Joshua Heschel, *God in Search of Man: A Philosophy of Judaism* (New York: Farrar, Strauss & Giroux, 1955), 172.

[16]Leon R. Kass, *The Beginning of Wisdom: Reading Genesis* (New York: Free Press, 2003), 44.

[17]Abraham Joshua Heschel, *The Insecurity of Freedom: Essays on Human Existence* (New York: Farrar, Strauss & Giroux, 1967), 13.

[18]Heschel, *God in Search of Man*, 409.

[19]Jonathan Sacks, *Future Tense: Jews, Judaism and Israel in the Twenty-First Century* (New York: Schocken, 2009), 233.

[20]Ibid., 243.

[21]Jonathan Sacks, *Covenant and Conversation: Exodus, the Book of Redemption* (New Milford, CT: Maggid, 2010), 99.

[22]Irenaeus, *Against Heresies*, bk. 4.

[23]Tertullian, quoted in *Christianity and Freedom*, ed. Timothy Samuel Shah and Allen D. Hertzske (Cambridge: Cambridge University Press, 2016), 65.

[24]Heschel, *God in Search of Man*, 410.

[25]Sophocles, *Antigone*, 1308.

[26]Mircea Eliade, *Cosmos and History* (New York: Harper, 1959), 162-63, emphasis added.

[27]Jonathan Sacks, *The Jonathan Sacks Haggadah* (New Milford, CT: Maggid, 2013), 6.

[28]Ibid., 152.

[29]Jonathan Sacks, *Covenant and Conversation: Numbers, the Wilderness Years* (New York: Maggid, 2017), 12.

[30]William Shakespeare, *The Tragedy of Macbeth*, act 5, scene 5.

[31]Joseph Heller, *Good as Gold* (New York: Simon & Schuster, 1999), 72.

[32]Paul Johnson, *A History of the Jews* (New York: Harper Perennial, 1988), 2.

[33]Jonathan Sacks, *To Heal a Fractured World* (New York: Schocken, 2015), 194.

[34]Kass, *Beginning of Wisdom*, 12.

[35]Sacks, *To Heal a Fractured World*, 137.

[36]James Madison, *Federalist Papers*, 51.

[37]Jean-Jacques Rousseau, *The Social Contract*, bk. 1, chap. 7.

[38]Christopher Dawson, *Beyond Politics* (New York: Sheed & Ward, 1939), 10.

[39]Alexis de Tocqueville, *Democracy in America*, trans. Arthur Goldhammer (Boone, IA: Library of America, 2014), 332.

[40]Thomas Jefferson, *Notes on the State of Virginia*, ed. David Waldstreicher (New York: Palgrave, 2002), query 18.

[41]Harari, *Homo Deus*, 307.

Question Nine: Are You Vigilant About the Institutions Crucial to Freedom

[1]Jamie Bartlett, *The Dark Net: Inside the Digital Underworld* (London: Melville House, 2014), 42.

[2]Ibid., 26.

[3]See, for example, Glenn Harlan Reynolds, "'Tolerant' Educators Exile Trump Voters from Campus," *USA Today*, November 14, 2016.

[4]James Madison, "Memorial and Remonstrance Against Religious Assessments," in *The American Republic: Primary Sources*, ed. Bruce Frohnen (Indianapolis: Liberty Fund, 2002), 327-30.

[5]See Abraham Lincoln's "Gettysburg Address," 1863.

[6]John Emerich Dalberg-Acton, *Essays in the History of Liberty*, vol. 1, ed. J. Rufus Fears (Indianapolis: Liberty Fund, 1985), 20.

[7]Bertrand Russell, *The First Reith Lectures* (London: Routledge Classics, 1949), 65.

[8]Christopher Dawson, *Beyond Politics* (New York: Sheed & Ward, 1939), 102, 103.

[9]F. A. Hayek, *The Road to Serfdom*, in *The Collected Works of F. A. Hayek* (Chicago: University of Chicago Press, 2007), 2:45.

[10]John Cotton, quoted in *The Puritans*, ed. Perry Miller and Thomas Johnson (New York: Harper, 1963), 212, 213.

[11]Thomas Hobbes, *Leviathan*, pt. 1, chap. 11.

[12]Martin Diamond, *As Far as Republican Principles Will Admit*, ed. William A. Schambra (Washington, DC: AEI Press, 1992), 220.

[13]John Winthrop, quoted in *Lincoln's Enduring Legacy*, ed. Robert P. Watson, William D. Pederson, and Frank J. Williams (Lanham, MD: Lexington Books, 2011), 209.

[14]Herman Melville, *Mardi—And a Voyage Thither* (Boston: Small, Maynard, 1922), 183.

[15]Immanuel Kant, *Perpetual Peace: A Philosophical Sketch*, 1795.

[16]John Adams, *A Defense of the Constitution of the United States*, new ed. (London: 1794), 3.

[17]Edmund Burke, *The Works of the Right Honourable Edmund Burke* (London: Henry G. Bohn, 1854), 446.

[18]James A. Garfield, quoted in Erik von Kuehnelt-Leddihn, *Liberty or Equality: The Challenge of Our Time* (Auburn, AL: Ludwig von Mises Institute, 2007), 117.

[19]Alexis de Tocqueville, quoted in Francis Williams, *Dangerous Estate: The Anatomy of Newspapers* (London: n.p., 1957), 111.

[20]Henry Kissinger, *World Order* (New York: Penguin, 2014), 353.

[21]Thomas Jefferson, *The Works of Thomas Jefferson: Published by Order of Congress*, ed. H. A. Washington (New York: Townsend, 1884), 178.

[22]Dave Lee, "Facebook News Row: Mark Zuckerberg Is a Politician Now," BBC, November 19, 2016.

[23]Yuval Noah Harari, *Homo Deus: A Brief History of Tomorrow* (New York: Harper, 2017), 225.

[24]Ibid., 228, 229.

[25]Jean-Jacques Rousseau, quoted in ibid., 225.

Question Ten: Are You Vigilant About the Ideas Crucial to Freedom

[1]Yuval Noah Harari, *Homo Deus: A Brief History of Tomorrow* (New York: Harper, 2017), 349.

[2]Richard M. Weaver, *Ideas Have Consequences* (Chicago: University of Chicago Press, 1948).

[3]Jonathan Sacks, *The Home We Build Together: Recreating Society* (London: Continuum, 2007), 31.

[4]Niall Ferguson, *Civilization: The West and the Rest* (New York: Penguin, 2011), xxii.

[5]Angelo M. Codevilla, "The Rise of Political Correctness," *Claremont Review of Books*, November 8, 2016.

[6]Herbert Marcuse, "Repressive Tolerance," 1965, available at www.marcuse.org /herbert/pubs/60spubs/65repressivetolerance.htm.

[7]John Etchemendy, "The Threat from Within," *Stanford News*, February 21, 2017.

[8]Frank Furedi, *What's Happened to the University? A Sociological Explanation of Its Infantilization* (London: Routledge, 2017).

[9]Ibid., 2.

[10]Jonathan Haidt, "Why Universities Must Choose One Telos: Truth or Social Justice," *Heterodox Academy*, October 21, 2016.

[11]Jamie Bartlett, *The Dark Net: Inside the Digital Underworld* (London: Melville House, 2014), 15.

[12]Jeff Bercovici, "Peter Thiel Is Very, Very Interested in Young People's Blood," *Inc.*, August 1, 2016.

[13]Bartlett, *Dark Net*, 228.

[14]Harari, *Homo Deus*, 43, 44.

[15]Ibid., 47.

[16]Ibid., 48.

[17]Anders Sandberg, quoted in Bartlett, *Dark Net*, 236.

[18]Abraham Joshua Heschel, *Who Is Man?* (Stanford, CA: Stanford University Press, 1965), 23.

[19]Jonathan Sacks, *Covenant and Conversation: Genesis, the Book of Beginnings* (New Milford, CT: Maggid, 2009), 64.

[20]Ibid., 53.

[21]Harari, *Homo Deus*, 66.

[22]Camille Paglia, quoted in "Camille Paglia: On Trump, Democrats, Transgenderism, and Islamist Terror," interview by Jonathan V. Last, *Weekly Standard*, June 15, 2017, emphasis added.

[23]Wilhelm Reich, *The Sexual Revolution*, trans. Therese Pol (New York: Farrar, Strauss & Giroux, 1986), xvii.

[24]Ibid.

[25]Ibid., xxvi.

[26]Matthew Lee, "Passport Change Will Be Inclusive," *Washington Post*, January 9, 2011.

[27]William Sanger, quoted in E. Michael Jones, *Libido Dominandi: Sexual Liberation and Political Control* (South Bend, IN: St. Augustine's Press, 2000), 141.

[28]Ibid., 257, 255.

[29]Ibid., 88.

[30]Vladimir Lenin, quoted in ibid., 238.

[31]Marquis de Sade, quoted in Maurice Lever, *Sade: A Biography* (New York: Farrar, Strauss & Giroux, 1993), 608.

[32]Alexandra Kollantai, quoted in Jones, *Libido Dominandi*, 157.

[33]Lenin, quoted in ibid., 237-38.

[34]Augusto del Noce, *The Crisis of Modernity*, ed. and trans. Carlo Lancelotti (Montreal: McGill-Queens University Press, 2014), 159.

[35]Marquis de Sade, quoted in Lever, *Sade*, 317.

[36]Reich, *Sexual Revolution*, xix.

[37]Ibid., xxvii.

[38]André Breton, "The Second Surrealist Manifesto," 1930, in Roger Scruton, *Fools, Frauds and Firebrands: Thinkers of the New Left* (London: Bloomsbury, 2015), 20.

[39]Ibid.

[40]Gigi Engle, "Anal Sex: What You Need to Know / How to Do It the Right Way," *Teen Vogue*, July 7, 2017.

[41]Jones, *Libido Dominandi*, 75.

[42]Jean-Jacques Rousseau, *The Social Contract*, trans. Maurice Cranston (Harmondsworth, UK: Penguin, 1968), 64.

[43]Reich, *Sexual Revolution*, xvi.

[44]André Breton, quoted in del Noce, *Crisis of Modernity*, 173.

[45]Jose Luis Rodriguez, quoted in Gabrielle Kuby, *The Global Sexual Revolution: Destruction of Freedom in the Name of Freedom* (Kettering, OH: LifeSite, 2012), 260, 259.

[46]Pamela Paul, *Pornified: How Pornography Is Damaging Our Lives, Our Relationships and Our Families* (New York: Henry Holt, 2005).

[47]Wesley Morris, "Weinstein, Hefner and the Poor Excuse That Explains a Lot," *New York Times*, October 27, 2017.

[48]Caitlyn Flanagan, "Bill Clinton: A Reckoning," *Atlantic*, November 13, 2017.

[49]Jones, *Libido Dominandi*, 133.

Conclusion

[1]Abigail Adams and John Adams, quoted in *The Book of Abigail and John: Selected Letters of the Adams Family 1772–1784*, ed. L. H. Butterfield et al. (Cambridge: MA: Harvard University Press, 1975), 122-23.

[2]Peter Gay, *Weimar Culture: The Outsider as Insider* (New York: W. W. Norton, 2001), 144.

[3]Milton Mayer, *They Thought They Were Free: Germans 1933–45* (Chicago: University of Chicago Press, 1966).

[4]In Roy Basler, ed, *The Collected Works of Abraham Lincoln* (New Brunswick, NJ: Rutgers University Press, 1953), 2:239.

[5]Jonathan Sacks, *Future Tense: Jews, Judaism and Israel in the Twenty-First Century* (New York: Schocken, 2009), 22.

[6]Friedrich Nietzsche, *Twilight of the Idols*, trans. R. J. Hollingdale (Harmondsworth, UK: Penguin, 1969), 138.

[7]Ibid., 54.

[8]Edmund Burke, *Reflections on the French Revolution in France* (Oxford: Oxford University Press, 1993), 289.

[9]John Emerich Edward Dalberg-Acton, *Essays in the History of Liberty*, ed. Rufus Fears (Indianapolis: Liberty Fund, 1985), 1:14.

[10]Ibid., 14.

[11]Yuval Noah Harari, *Homo Deus: A Brief History of Tomorrow* (New York: Harper, 2017), 202.

[12]George Orwell, *1984* (New York: Harcourt, 1949), 210.

[13]A. C. Grayling, quoted in Sean Coughlan, "What Does Post-Truth Mean for a Philosopher?," *BBC News*, January 12, 2017.

[14]Nicholas Agar, *Humanity's End: Why We Should Reject Radical Enhancement* (Cambridge, MA: MIT Press, 2010), 84.

[15]Harari, *Homo Deus*, 223, 372.

[16]Ibid., 395.

[17]Ibid., 401.

[18]Elizabeth Kolbert, *The Sixth Extinction: An Unnatural History* (New York: Henry Holt, 2014), 267.

[19]Abraham Lincoln, quoted in *The American Republic: Primary Sources*, ed. Bruce Frohnen (Indianapolis: Liberty Fund, 2002), 518-22.

[20]Jonathan Sacks, *Ceremony and Celebration: Introduction to the Holidays* (New York: Maggid, 2017), 246.

[21]Abraham Joshua Heschel, *Who Is Man?* (Stanford, CA: Stanford University Press, 1965), 27.

[22]Ibid., 103.

NAME INDEX

SUBJECT INDEX

ALSO BY OS GUINNESS

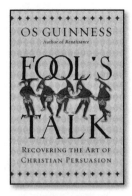

Fool's Talk
978-0-8308-3699-4

A Free People's Suicide
978-0-8308-3465-5

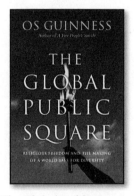

The Global Public Square
978-0-8308-3767-0

Renaissance
978-0-8308-3671-0

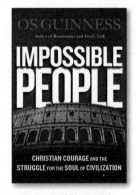

Impossible People
978-0-8308-4465-4